WOMEN IN ACADEME

PROGRESS AND PROSPECTS

WOMEN IN ACADEME

PROGRESS AND PROSPECTS

edited by Mariam K. Chamberlain

Project Director and Chair,
Task Force on Women
in Higher Education

RUSSELL SAGE FOUNDATION   NEW YORK

The Russell Sage Foundation

The Russell Sage Foundation, one of the oldest of America's general purpose foundations, was established in 1907 by Mrs. Margaret Olivia Sage for "the improvement of social and living conditions in the United States." The Foundation seeks to fulfill this mandate by fostering the development and dissemination of knowledge about the political, social, and economic problems of America. It conducts research in the social sciences and public policy and publishes books and pamphlets that derive from this research.

The Board of Trustees is responsible for oversight and the general policies of the Foundation, while administrative direction of the program and staff is vested in the President, assisted by the officers and staff. The President bears final responsibility for the decision to publish a manuscript as a Russell Sage Foundation book. In reaching a judgment on the competence, accuracy, and objectivity of each study, the President is advised by the staff and selected expert readers. The conclusions and interpretations in Russell Sage Foundation publications are those of the authors and not of the Foundation, its Trustees, or its staff. Publication by the Foundation, therefore, does not imply endorsement of the contents of the study.

Library of Congress Cataloging-in-Publication Data

Women in academe : progress and prospects / edited by Mariam K.
  Chamberlain.
    p.   cm.
  Bibliography: p.
  Includes index.
  ISBN 0-87154-204-8
    1. Women—Education (Higher)—United States.   2. Women college
  teachers—United States.   3. Women college administrators—United
  States.   I. Chamberlain, Mariam.   II. Russell Sage Foundation.
  LC1756.W659   1988
  376'.973—dc19   88-37217
                                                                             CIP

The paper used in this publication meets the minimum requirements of American National Standard for Information Sciences—Permanence of Paper for Printed Library Materials, ANSI Z39.48-1984. ∞

10 9 8 7 6 5 4 3 2 1

Preface

During the last 15 years significant, and in some cases dramatic, changes have taken place in the status of women in higher education. Under the pressure of the women's movement the complex issue of equal educational opportunity was brought under growing scrutiny by academic women and civil rights groups during the 1970s. The widespread practices of sex discrimination, both overt and subtle, moved on to the research agenda of scholars and became subjects for legal redress.

Two landmark volumes, published in 1973, documented the situation of women in higher education as it then existed. One was a volume of essays entitled *Academic Women on the Move*, edited by Alice Rossi and Ann Calderwood and published by the Russell Sage Foundation. The other was a report of the Carnegie Commission entitled *Opportunities for Women in Higher Education*. Both dealt with problems and issues relating to women as students, as faculty members, and as administrators. The reports presented research findings on topics ranging from sex differences in student enrollment patterns, degree attainment, and financial support to the underrepresentation of women in senior faculty and administrative positions. They also identified and chronicled the early history of forces for change that were then newly emerging, most notably the mobilization of academic women's groups to press for reforms, the use of affirmative action as a remedy for employment discrimination in higher education, and the development of women's studies as a means of dealing with bias against women in curriculum content.

The decade following the publication of these studies was a period of continued efforts by women's rights groups, by government agencies, and by foundations to improve educational opportunities for women.

The purpose of this volume is to examine the progress women have made during the period and to provide a comprehensive overview of the status and prospects of academic women in the mid 1980s. A further objective is to analyze the impact of women's changing roles on institutions of higher education.

The volume is based on a three-year study, undertaken in 1982 and supported jointly by the Ford Foundation, the Carnegie Endowment, and the Russell Sage Foundation. The project was carried out under my direction, as a resident scholar at the Russell Sage Foundation, with a task force of 15 members selected for their knowledge, expertise, and research interests in the various aspects of the study. Four of the task force members were among those who had contributed to the Rossi volume. Staff assistance was provided by Mary Rubin, then a research associate at Russell Sage. The project also had the benefit of an external advisory committee of leading scholars and university administrators for consultation and review of the conclusions and recommendations. The members of the advisory committee are Gwendolyn Calvert Baker, former vice president and dean of the Graduate School, Bank Street College of Education (now executive director, YWCA of the U.S.A.); David W. Breneman, president, Kalamazoo College; Cecelia P. Burciaga, associate dean of graduate studies, Stanford University; Earl F. Cheit, professor of business and public policy, University of California, Berkeley; Patricia Albjerg Graham, dean of the Harvard Graduate School of Education; Alice S. Rossi, professor of sociology, University of Massachusetts at Amherst; and Virginia B. Smith, former president, Vassar College.

Each task force member was asked to prepare a paper in her particular area as the basis for a chapter in the final report. An initial meeting of the task force was held early in 1983 to discuss tentative chapter outlines and their relationship to the overall report. During the summer of 1983, a subgroup of the task force, consisting of those compiling basic statistical data for the study, met to coordinate its efforts. In the fall of 1983 the task force met again, this time jointly with the advisory committee, to review the progress of the work and to have the benefit of comments and suggestions by advisory committee members on the scope and structure of the study. In a series of subsequent meetings, draft chapters were presented for discussion by the task force. A final meeting together with members of the advisory committee was held in December 1986 to discuss the draft of the book manuscript and to review the conclusions and recommendations.

It was my function as a director of the project to put the manuscript together, filling in gaps, eliminating duplication, and resolving any inconsistencies. The project was aided immensely by the comprehensive and analytical reports of the task force meetings and by additional background papers that were prepared by Mary Rubin. In addition to her work as a member of the task force, Maren Carden provided invaluable assistance in the editorial phase of the work.

My purpose in describing in some detail the process by which this book was written is to make clear that it represents a collaborative effort of the group as a whole. It is not a series of essays by individual authors, although each chapter is based on a paper originally prepared by a designated member of the task force. To varying degrees the chapters were influenced by the views of the group, and the entire volume reflects the collective views of its members. Of course, all members do not necessarily agree with all parts of the book. A consensus was not required. The responsibility for what eventually survived the discussion, modification, and editing is mine. There are variations in tone and style from chapter to chapter as I have tried as fully as possible to retain the tone of the papers, some of which eloquently convey the passion of the author.

I am grateful to the Ford Foundation, the Carnegie Endowment, and the Russell Sage Foundation for their support of this project. My thanks go in particular to Harold Howe II, who first suggested the idea of such a study in 1981 when he was vice president for education at the Ford Foundation; to Gladys Chang Hardy, officer in charge of the Ford Foundation's Education and Culture Program in 1982, whose advice and encouragement had much to with the ultimate form of the project; to Sara Engelhardt, secretary of the Carnegie Corporation, for her continued interest as well as financial support; to Marshall Robinson, president of the Russell Sage Foundation during the project period, for his advice in establishing the collective deliberative process, for providing a supportive and stimulating working environment, and for his confidence in the outcome of the project; and to Peter de Janosi, vice president of the Russell Sage Foundation, for his guidance and wise counsel throughout. My fellow task force members and I are indebted also to the advisory committee for their advice and suggestions at the start of the study and their helpful comments at the conclusion.

In the editorial phase of the work, I had occasion to call on a number of people and organizations for information to round out or update the manuscript and their assistance is gratefully acknowledged here. They include Phyllis Franklin, executive director, Modern Language Association; Vance Grant, specialist in education statistics, U.S. Department of Education; Sarah Pritchard, reference specialist, women's studies, Library of Congress; Carol Burroughs, governance affairs officer, American Psychological Association; Noralee Frankel, special assistant on women and minorities, American Historical Association; Bettina Huber, assistant executive officer, American Sociological Association; Sheilah Mann, director, American Political Science Association; Elaine Spaulding, senior staff associate, Council on Social Work Education; Helen Wright, yearbook staff, and Margaret Myers, director, Office for Library Personnel Resources, American Library Association; and Karla Cowell, coordinator of communication/data services, American Association of Colleges of Nursing. Barbara Lewis, formerly a member of the staff of the National Council for Research on Women, applied her computer knowledge to provide strategic assistance in the preparation of the manuscript.

Special thanks are due to Alice Rossi for her inspiration and encouragement at the start of the project, for sharing her experience and insights along the way, and for her thorough and constructive comments on the manuscript. I hope the book is a worthy sequel to *Academic Women on the Move*.

Mariam K. Chamberlain

Notes on the Task Force on Women in Higher Education

Helen S. Astin is professor of higher education and associate director of the Higher Education Research Institute at the University of California, Los Angeles. Her primary research interests are in the fields of education and career development, with special emphasis on women, adults, and disadvantaged students, and in the study and practice of leadership. Among her books are *The Woman Doctorate in America* (Russell Sage Foundation, 1970); *Sex Roles: An Annotated Research Bibliography* (U.S. Government Printing Office, 1975); *Some Action of Her Own: The Adult Woman and Higher Education* (Heath, 1976); and *The Higher Education of Women: Essays in Honor of Rosemary Park* (Praeger, 1978).

Jean W. Campbell was the director of the University of Michigan Center for Continuing Education of Women from 1964 to 1985. In earlier career phases she was a teacher and counselor, a reading specialist, an administrator in the U.S. Office of Scientific Research and Development, and a community leader and volunteer. She is the author of numerous articles, papers, and book chapters relating to re-entry women and institutional change.

Mary Ellen S. Capek is executive secretary of the National Council for Research on Women. She was formerly director of continuing education at Princeton University and coordinator of the American Council on Education's National Identification Program in New Jersey. Her research and publications have focused on women in higher education administration and governance, linguistics, technology, and writing. She is the editor of *A Woman's Thesaurus: An Index of Language Used to Describe and Locate Information By and About Women* (Harper & Row, 1987).

Maren Lockwood Carden is professor of sociology at Long Island University, Brooklyn Campus. She is the author of *Oneida: Utopian Community to Modern Corporation* (Johns Hopkins Press, 1969); and *The New Feminist Movement* (Russell Sage Foundation, 1974). She is also the author of several articles in the field of social movements.

Mariam K. Chamberlain is president of the National Council for Research on Women. During the 1970s she was a program officer in Education and Research at the Ford Foundation, later moving to the Russell Sage Foundation as a resident scholar. In prior years, she was a research associate and executive secretary of the Economic Growth Center at Yale University. She has also taught at various times—at Connecticut College, the Columbia University School of General Studies, and Hunter College. Her research interests include women in the economy as well as women in higher education, and she is the author of several articles in the field of women's studies.

Carol Frances is head of Carol Frances Plus Associates, where she specializes in economic and financial studies relating to higher education. She conducts public policy analysis and strategic planning for colleges and universities, educational associations, government agencies, and industry.

Jane Gould has spent her professional life working with women, first in the pioneer movement of helping adult women prepare to return to school and work in the late 1950s and early 1960s, and then as director of Placement and Career Planning at Barnard College from 1965 to 1972. She was a founder and the first permanent director of the Barnard College Women's Center, a position she held from 1972 until she retired in 1983. She is a member of the board of the Center for Constitutional Rights and is currently working on their women's rights program.

Lilli S. Hornig is senior consultant to Higher Education Resource Services (HERS) for New England and was its founder and executive director from 1972 to 1984. She has a doctorate in chemistry from Harvard University and has held faculty positions in that field at Brown University and at Trinity College (DC), where she was department head. Dr. Hornig has served widely on national research and policy panels, including the Commission on Human Resources of the National Academy of Sciences, where she chaired the Committee on the Education and Employment of Women in Science and Engineering from 1974 to 1983. Her active involvement with issues of women's higher education and employment dates from the mid 1960s. She has written extensively on these topics and has recently completed a major study on women in humanities fields for the National Endowment for the Humanities.

Florence Howe is director of the Feminist Press at the City University of New York and professor of English at City College of the City University. From 1969 to 1971 she served as chairperson of the Commission on the Status of Women of the Modern Language Association. In 1973 she was president of the Association. She is a founder and leader of women's studies and has written and lectured extensively on the subject since 1970, both in the United States and abroad. Her publications include *Women and the Power to Change* (McGraw-Hill, 1975) and *Myths of Coeducation* (Indiana University Press, 1985). She is the recipient of several honorary degrees for her work in women's studies.

Marjorie Lightman is executive director of the Institute for Research in History and a founding member of the National Council for Research on Women. She is co-editor of *Outside Academe: New Ways of Working in the Humanities* (Institute for Research in History and Haworth Press, 1981) and *Without Precedent: The Life and Career of Eleanor Roosevelt* (Indiana University Press, 1984).

Virginia Davis Nordin is an attorney and consultant in higher education. She is a graduate of Harvard Law School and has variously served as affirmative action officer at Dartmouth College, a faculty member in the Graduate School of Education at the University of Wisconsin—Madison, and instructor at the University of Michigan Law School. She is co-author of the textbook, *Higher Education and the Law* (Institute for Educational Management, 1979) and of numerous articles on academic and education law.

Patricia Ann Palmieri is an assistant professor of education at Dartmouth College. She received her doctorate from the Harvard Graduate School of Education and specializes in the history of education. Her first book, *'In Adamless Eden': A Social Portrait of the Academic Women of Wellesley College, 1875–1920,* is scheduled for publication by the Yale University Press. She is now working on a biography of Emily Greene Balch, professor of economics at Wellesley College and World War I pacifist.

Bernice R. Sandler has been director of the Project on the Status and Education of Women of the Association of American Colleges since its inception in 1971. The Project is the country's foremost source of information on sex discrimination in higher education. Dr. Sandler previously worked for the U.S. House of Representatives on the first comprehensive hearings about discrimination against women in education and in employment. She played a major role in the passage of Title IX, and she also conceived and spearheaded the successful efforts of the Women's Equity Action League to spur the enforcement of existing Executive Orders regarding sex discrimination in universities and colleges. She serves on numerous boards and advisory committees and has been awarded several honorary degrees.

Cynthia Secor is director of Higher Education Resource Services (HERS)/ mid-America. She is also director of the Summer Institute for Women in Higher Education Administration, held at Bryn Mawr College, and the Management Institute for Women in Higher Education at Wellesley College.

Donna Shavlik is director of the Office of Women in Higher Education of the American Council on Education. She is a founder of the council's National Identification Program for the Advancement of Women in Higher Education.

Margaret C. Simms is deputy director of research at the Joint Center for Political Studies in Washington, DC. Prior to joining the staff of the center, Dr. Simms worked at the Urban Institute, first as a senior research associate in the Women and Family Policy Program and then as director of the Minorities and Social Policy Program. She has been active in research on education and training issues as they relate to women and minorities and has served on advisory committees for the College Board and Educational Testing Service. Dr. Simms taught at Atlanta University for seven years, and she is co-editor of *Slipping Through the Cracks: The Status of Black Women* (Transaction, 1986).

Staff
Mary E. Rubin is project manager in the Office of Policy and Economic Research at New York City's Human Resources Administration. She holds a master's degree in public policy from the John F. Kennedy School of Government at Harvard University, where she was a Kennedy Fellow. She was research associate at the Russell Sage Foundation from 1982 to 1985. In prior years she was an educational policy intern at the Women's Equity Action League, and research associate at the Business and Professional Women's Foundation. She is the author of *How to Get Money for Research* (Feminist Press, 1983).

Contents

WOMEN IN ACADEME

PROGRESS AND PROSPECTS

Introduction

1

Historical Background and Overview

Nineteenth-Century Beginnings

Women first gained entry to institutions of higher education in the United States when Oberlin College admitted female students in 1837—more than 200 years after Harvard College was founded for the education of young men. In colonial America there was no precedent for higher education for women. European universities, some of which were established as early as the eleventh and twelfth centuries, were open only to men. From the perspective of the 1980s it is easy to forget that the history of women in higher education is so much shorter than that of men.

It is now 150 years since college education became a reality for women. The pressure for change from the beginning, as now, came from the broader women's movement which raised women's aspirations for a college education. Nevertheless, opportunities for women in higher education remained quite limited until after the Civil War. Up to that time three private colleges in Ohio and two state universities—Utah and Iowa—admitted women. Faced with declining enrollments, several more state universities opened their doors to women during or immediately following the Civil War. The same period saw the emergence of colleges for women offering curricula comparable to that of men. Vassar College, established in 1865, was among the earliest. Smith and Wellesley followed in 1875 and Bryn Mawr and Mount Holyoke in the 1880s.

During the latter part of the nineteenth century, the enrollment of women in higher education accelerated rapidly, and more and more universities and colleges began to admit women as well as men. In 1870 only 30 percent of colleges were coeducational. By the turn of the century the figure was 70 percent.[1] In 1900 women constituted 30 percent of the student body in higher education. They attended a diversity of institutions, including liberal arts colleges, many of them affiliated with Protestant denominations or Catholic religious orders, institutions founded after the Civil War for southern black youth, and public and private research universities. Also included among them were institutions that called themselves colleges but were really normal schools or seminaries.[2]

The foremost reason for attending colleges and universities during this period was to train for the ministry, the law, medicine, and teaching. Consequently, in 1900 less than 4 percent of the college-age population were enrolled in higher education.[3] Women moved into this educational environment to enter the teaching profession. The public school system, which since the middle of the nineteenth century had been growing rapidly throughout the country, produced a demand for teachers and for educated women who could fill this demand. Formerly, women had taught only at the most elementary levels in the private dame schools. Now they began to teach at higher levels and, although college training was not required in all circumstances, a degree meant better job opportunities. School superintendents, faced with increasing demands for teachers, hired women because they could "afford to teach for one-half, or even less, the salary which men would ask."[4] Moreover, teaching was seen as an appropriate occupation for women, seeming, as it were, a natural extension of the mothering role. In 1880, 57 percent of teachers in the United States were women; by 1918 the figure had grown to 84 percent.[5]

While the rise of women's aspirations and the need for low-paid teachers led to increased college attendance by women, financial exigencies within the colleges contributed to the trend toward coeducation. The private colleges in particular frequently found themselves in a precarious financial situation,[6] and women students represented additional revenues. Even Oberlin, so often lauded for being the first institution to award a bachelor's degree to women, had economic as well as ethical reasons for admitting women students. As a manual labor school founded in 1833, its male students worked on the college farm to help pay for their education. But there was no one to perform domestic chores. When women students were enrolled in the late 1830s, they did the laundry, the cooking, and the waiting on tables that otherwise would have to be paid for as part of board and room.[7] Most of the elite men's colleges, however, were prosperous enough to hold out against admission of women. Coeducation was further advanced by the establishment of state universities and land grant colleges under the Morrill Act of 1862. Created to promote practical as well as liberal education, these institutions introduced home economics as a course of study in higher education. In the late nineteenth century some prestigious institutions such as Harvard, Columbia, and Brown permitted the formation of independently funded coordinate women's colleges as a compromise between admitting women and maintaining their male preserves.

The entry of women into higher education in growing numbers during the late nineteenth century was not without opposition. It was widely believed that intellectual activity was contrary to feminine nature and harmful to women's health and reproductive capacity. Moreover, it was assumed that women did not have the same capacity as men for advanced education and, moreover, that they would distract males and lower standards in coeducational institutions.[8] Events proved otherwise. Indeed, their rising numbers and successful performance on campus raised new fears at the turn of the century that women would overrun higher education. At the University of Chicago the percentage of women students increased from 24 to 52 percent between 1892 and 1902.[9] During the same period women received over 56 percent of the Phi Beta Kappa awards. Concerned about the feminization of the institution, the administration established segregated classes for freshmen and sophomores, in effect establishing a separate junior college for women. The policy was abandoned after five years when the arrangement proved to be costly and bureaucratically cumbersome. There were similar concerns at Stanford University, where 102 men and 98 women graduated in 1901 and women received a higher number of awards and honors. In 1904 Stanford adopted a policy restricting the enrollment of women to a ratio of three male students to one female student, a policy that remained in effect until 1933.

Although nineteenth-century ideas about the biological and psychological differences between women and men became outmoded, cultural perceptions of appropriate roles and behaviors for women were slower to change. These perceptions, updated but still traditional, continued to influence higher education for women throughout much of the present century. Nevertheless, women continued to enter higher education in ever-increasing numbers.

From 1900 to 1930 the proportion of women receiving a bachelor's or first professional degree increased from 19 to 40 percent.[10] The proportion remained steady during the 1930s, although the actual number of degrees awarded to both men and women increased. The increase in college attendance during the Depression may seem surprising, but apparently widespread unemployment made college a better option for young men and women, even though most families had less income to spend on college education. In addition, the Depression demonstrated the advantage of having a degree as college graduates in white-collar positions fared better than other kinds of workers.[11]

World War II and Its Aftermath

During World War II, with many college-age men in the services and some college-age women engaged in war work, the number of male students declined sharply and the number of women students remained at about prewar levels. After 1945 and after the end of the Korean war in 1953, returning veterans supported by the G.I. Bill resulted in a dramatic rise in male enrollments. The huge influx of veterans restricted the number of women who could be accommodated, and men dominated the campus from the late 1940s through the 1950s. Although the enrollment of women and number of degrees earned increased somewhat during this period, women lost ground in relative terms. In 1950 women represented 24 percent of those receiving the bachelor's degree and first professional degree compared with 41 percent in 1940. By 1960 the proportion had increased to 35 percent, but the prewar rate was not regained until 1970.[12] The pattern of early marriage and childbearing that characterized the 1950s kept many qualified young women out of college.[13]

The postwar generation of women students faced many other obstacles as well. As priority was given to veterans, graduate women found that they had to be far better qualified than men to be admitted, and married women who wished to enroll part time found the doors closed. Access to assistantships and other training opportunities were severely limited. In short, women students were being treated openly as second-class citizens.[14] But change was in the offing, and the 1960s saw the start of a new era.

Social pressure toward early marriage and family formation waned and the women's movement followed in its wake, creating a climate of rising aspirations for women. At the same time, the influx of veterans into higher education institutions began to taper off and colleges and universities, with their expanded facilities, became more receptive to other constituencies of students. These conditions brought women into higher education in unprecedented numbers and with them a drive for equal educational opportunity. The time had come for an all-out attack against long-standing inequities, both overt and subtle.

The Drive for Equity

The first task for the 1970s was to identify and document these inequities. The inequities involved not only women students but women faculty members and administrators as well.[15] During this period scholars and activists alike turned their attention to discriminatory procedures and practices in higher education, their sources and their remedies. Responding to pressures from women's groups, both on and off campus, the federal government passed a series of laws prohibiting discrimination on the basis of sex in educational institutions.

Discriminatory practices in college admissions have already been noted. By 1970 the situation had begun to improve, but nevertheless the general pattern was one of lower enrollment rates for women than for men of comparable ability, especially for those from families of lower socioeconomic status.[16] Patterns of financial support, which in the past had heavily favored men, changed markedly during the 1960s when the federal government, following the launching of Sputnik in 1957, established massive programs of grants and loans for higher education without distinction by gender. Nevertheless, a study of sources of support for college freshmen in 1971, conducted by the American Council on Education, showed significant differences between men and women. Women received a much higher share of college costs than men from parents (61.2 percent compared with 48.9 percent), whereas men to a much greater extent than women relied on their own earnings or savings from employment. Women relied to a slightly greater extent on scholarships and loans than men, although this difference was offset by educational benefits for military service that some men were still receiving.[17] At the graduate level, both men and women received more university and government support, but again women were somewhat more dependent on aid from families, whereas men had more resources based on their own employment and savings. This pattern of financial support helps to explain the difference in enrollment rates between men and women from low-income families. Because women earn less, they are more dependent on family support for higher education and are affected to a greater extent than men by size of family income.

In terms of degree attainment, women have earned a steadily increasing number and proportion of bachelor's degrees since 1900. By 1920 the proportion of bachelor's degrees earned by women was 34.2 percent and by 1970 the proportion had increased to 41.5 percent. Prior to 1920, the number of advanced degrees achieved by either men or women was quite small. Since then the number has increased rapidly. In 1920 the proportion of master's degrees earned by women was 30.2 percent and in 1970, 39.7 percent. The proportion of doctorates awarded to women was 15.1 percent in 1920 and declined somewhat during the Depression to 13.0 percent in 1940. In the aftermath of World War II this figure sank below 10 percent and did not regain the 1920 level until 1972.[18] There was a similar but less dramatic decline in the proportion of bachelor's and master's degrees awarded to women in the 1950s. The actual numbers of degrees increased throughout, however. The further progress of women in degree attainment during the 1970s and beyond is discussed in chapters 9 and 10.

The fields that women have traditionally chosen as majors in college differ substantially from those of men. They are, of course, closely related to career opportunities open to women. Women have been considerably more likely than men to major in the humanities and arts and less likely to major in the sciences. In the social sciences they have been relatively well represented in some fields, such as psychology and sociology, and less well represented in other fields, such as economics and political science. In professional fields, women have primarily entered education, home economics, library science, social work, and teaching. In the past, they have not been well represented in business administration, medicine, or law. These patterns were accentuated during the 1950s and 1960s, but the wide disparities in the degree distribution between men and women narrowed dramatically during the 1970s. Chapter 9 highlights the substantial increase in the representation of women in the sciences, engineering, and other traditionally male-dominated professions during the last 15 years, while chapter 10 describes recent trends in the social sciences, the humanities, and the conventional women's professions.

Historically, women's colleges have played a critical role in higher education for women, but this role has changed with the passage of time. Originally, they were established to provide access to higher education when admission to colleges and universities was not open to women on the same terms as men. In the 1870s, when many of the women's colleges were established, they represented 60 percent of the total enrollment of women undergraduates in the country.[19] Since that time, the percentage has dropped steadily decade by decade. In the 1950s the percentage dropped below 10 percent, and the decline has continued since then as more and more formerly all male institutions, including Yale and Princeton in the Ivy League, became coeducational. The case for women's colleges today is based on other considerations than access. It is argued that they are necessary to represent the interests of women in higher education, that they provide a more supportive environment for women students, that they produce a higher proportion of women achievers than comparable coeducational institutions, and that they provide greater opportunities for women faculty and administrators. These issues are discussed at length in chapter 6 on the role of women's colleges. Other aspects of the college environment for women are discussed in chapter 2, which is primarily concerned with the college experience in coeducational institutions; chapter 4, which focuses on the educational needs and aspirations of re-entry women as nontraditional students; and chapter 5, which describes the rise of campus-based women's centers as a new kind of supportive service for women students in the 1970s.

Prior to World War II, little was known about minorities in higher education beyond their enrollment and attendance in predominantly black colleges. Minorities in higher education generally became a matter of public and scholarly concern with the civil rights movement of the 1950s and 1960s. Attention was focused at first on blacks, but was later extended to include Puerto Ricans, Chicanos, Native Americans, and, increasingly, Asians as well. For the most part, the systematic collection of data on minorities did not begin until the early 1970s. Chapter 3 brings together and analyzes the existing data on minority women, as students, faculty, and administrators. Minority viewpoints are also included elsewhere in the volume to the extent that relevant information is available.

The curriculum of higher education for women has been the subject of debate since at least the late nineteenth century. When women's colleges were formed, they consciously adopted the same curriculum as that offered by men's colleges. This was a liberal arts curriculum consisting of Greek, Latin, mathematics, science, philosophy, and literature. The primary purpose was to produce men of mental discipline and culture. It was also designed to provide the background for subsequent professional, business, or public life. For women the focus on cultural subjects was seen as preparation for teaching or for family and community roles. In contrast to women's colleges, coeducational land grant universities put more emphasis on practical subjects and vocational preparation. For men this meant agriculture and the mechanical arts, and for women, home economics. Home economics as a specialized field in higher education was introduced in land grant universities in the 1870s. By 1910 over 100 colleges and universities offered instruction in that field.[20]

During the early decades of the twentieth century, women students turned increasingly to job-related fields of study. They concentrated particularly in teaching, social work, library science, and nursing. These became known as "female-dominated professions," and they have remained so to the present day. However, they are female-dominated only in terms of the numbers of women employed, not in terms of control of the profession. The situation of women in these fields is described in chapter 10.

The 1970s brought a new and more far-reaching kind of curriculum innovation for women in higher education—the introduction of women's studies. As the scholarly arm of the women's movement, women's studies re-examines women's lives and their role in society from a historical, contemporary, and cross-cultural perspective. In the process, women's studies scholars have introduced new course content and challenged traditional assumptions about women across a broad spectrum of disciplines. The process of integration of the new knowledge into the liberal arts curriculum is still ongoing. The origins, functions, and achievements of women's studies are the subject of chapter 7.

The growth of women's studies teaching and research during the 1970s and 1980s spawned the formation of organized research centers. There are over 50 such centers in existence today, most of them campus-based but some autonomous or affiliated with other nonprofit organizations. They provide institutional resources for the work of individual scholars and create an environment for mutual support and interdisciplinary efforts. Their origins, characteristics, and activities are described in chapter 13.

In the aftermath of World War II, women lost ground not only in their participation as students but also in their representation as faculty members. At the start of the century the proportion of women on college faculties was 20 percent. In the decades that followed, there was a gradual increase to 25 percent in 1940. During the postwar period, the representation of women on college faculties declined to 23 percent in the 1950s and to 22 percent in the 1960s.[21] The prewar high of 25 percent was not regained until the 1970s.[22] The actual number of women faculty members increased steadily throughout the period, but not by enough to keep up with the overall expansion of the faculty and the growth in the number of men. Moreover, women faculty members have always been concentrated in the lower ranks and in the less prestigious institutions. They have also been concentrated in particular fields such as education, social work, home economics, and nursing.

In women's colleges the faculty situation is, of course, somewhat different. In 1940, 72 percent of the faculty of the 22 largest private women's colleges were women. Even there, however, there was a decline after World War II to about 50 percent in 1955.[23] In 1978, according to a recent report of the Women's College Coalition, the figure was 55 percent. Only Catholic women's colleges operated by religious orders are staffed and administered primarily by women.[24]

Chapter 11 provides a picture of trends in faculty representation during and since the 1970s and assesses the current position of faculty women. While some gains have been made, particularly in entry-level positions, overall progress has been slow, in spite of intensive efforts by academic women's groups and the supportive activities of women's rights organizations. Affirmative action and legal remedies have played a critical role in these efforts, and that role is the subject of chapter 8. Chapter 12 describes the strategic role of women in professional associations not only in advancing women scholars, but also in advancing women's studies in their respective disciplines.

Prior to the 1970s, women rarely held positions of influence in the administration of higher education institutions, except for women's colleges. In coeducational colleges and universities only a quarter of the administrators were women, and the positions they most commonly held were dean of women, director of library services, director of food services, and dean of home economics or nursing. Somewhat less commonly they held the positions of registrar, director of student guidance, director of student activities, or director of alumni affairs. In 1970 three quarters of the women administrators at Ivy League universities worked in student services. In chapter 14 we examine the efforts that have been made to change this picture and show what progress has been made to date. Chapter 15 focuses on the role of boards of trustees in the governance of institutions of higher education and the nature and extent of women's participation in board functions.

This brief overview of the historical evolution of women in higher education prior to the 1970s is intended to provide perspective and background for the story that follows. It shows how educational opportunities open to women in the past have been limited by the narrow definition of their social role and the restricted career opportunities available. It also reveals the extent to which the post–World War II period was a setback to the advancement of women in academic life. At the undergraduate and graduate levels, in faculty positions and in administration, women lost many of the gains they had achieved in the preceding decades. The 1960s were years for catching up. Only in the 1970s did women begin the rapid strides forward that mark the real progress from the prewar period, progress that is documented in this book.

Notes

1. Joyce Antler, "Culture, Service and Work: Changing Ideals of Higher Education for Women," in Pamela J. Perun, ed., *The Undergraduate Woman: Issues in Educational Equity* (Lexington, MA: Lexington Books, 1982), p. 19.

2. Christopher Jencks and David Riesman, *The Academic Revolution*, rev. ed. (Chicago: University of Chicago Press, 1977).

3. Patricia Albjerg Graham, "Expansion and Exclusion: A History of Women in American Higher Education," *Signs* 3 (1978):766.

4. Quoted in Thomas Woody, *A History of Women's Education in the United States*, vol. 1 (New York: Octagon Books, 1966; orig. ed., 1929), p. 481.

5. Woody, *History of Women's Education*, p. 499.

6. Jencks and Riesman, *Academic Revolution*, pp. 7–8.

7. Jill K. Conway, "Perspective on the History of Women's Education in the United States," *History of Education Quarterly* 14 (1974):6.

8. Antler, "Culture, Service and Work," pp. 17–18.

9. Barbara Miller Solomon, *In the Company of Educated Women: A History of Women in Higher Education in America* (New Haven: Yale University Press, 1985), pp. 58–59.

10. U.S. Bureau of the Census, *Historical Statistics of the United States: Colonial Times to 1970*, Bicentennial Edition, pt. 2, Series H751-765 (Washington, DC: U.S. Government Printing Office, 1975), p. 386.

11. Jencks and Riesman, *Academic Revolution*, p. 108.

12. W. Vance Grant and Thomas D. Snyder, *Digest of Education Statistics, 1983–84* (Washington, DC: National Center for Education Statistics, 1983), p. 101.

13. Solomon, *In the Company of Educated Women*, pp. 116–123, 187–195.

14. Carnegie Commission on Higher Education, *Opportunities for Women in Higher Education* (New York: McGraw-Hill, 1973), pp. 35–36.

15. For a good summary statement of the position of women in faculty and administrative positions at this time, see Patricia Albjerg Graham, "Women in Academe," *Science*, September 25, 1970.

16. Carnegie Commission on Higher Education, *Opportunities for Women in Higher Education*, pp. 38–40.

17. Pamela Roby, "Institutional Barriers to Women Students in Higher Education," in Alice Rossi and Ann Calderwood, eds., *Academic Women on the Move* (New York: Russell Sage Foundation, 1973), p. 45.

18. Betty M. Vetter and Eleanor L. Babco, *Professional Women and Minorities*, 6th ed. (Washington, DC: Commission on Professionals in Science and Technology, 1986), p. 35.

19. Mabel Newcomer, *A Century of Higher Education for American Women* (New York: Harper & Brothers, 1959), p. 49.

20. Antler, "Culture, Service and Work," pp. 25–26.

21. U.S. Bureau of the Census, *Historical Statistics*, pp. 382–383.

22. Grant and Snyder, *Digest of Education Statistics, 1983–84*, p. 101.

23. Jessie Bernard, *Academic Women* (University Park: Pennsylvania State University, 1964), p. 55; Newcomer, *A Century of Higher Education*, p. 165.

24. Women's College Coalition, *Profile II: A Second Profile of Women's Colleges* (Washington, DC: WCC, 1981), p. 83.

PART **II**

Women as Students

2

The College Experience

Toward Equity

When the decade of the 1970s began, there were no laws prohibiting sex discrimination in higher education. A little-noticed Executive Order (11246) prohibited employment discrimination by federal contractors, but no one had realized that it covered sex discrimination by universities and colleges. That situation was suddenly and dramatically changed in January 1970 when Bernice R. Sandler of the Women's Equity Action League (WEAL) filed the first charges of sex discrimination in academe, initiating WEAL's campaign to spur the federal government to enforce the Executive Order against colleges and universities. Several hundred charges were subsequently filed against academic institutions by WEAL and other women's organizations. These charges made sex discrimination in education a legitimate issue, and, in response, the Congress began to shape a new national policy to prohibit sex discrimination in educational institutions.

In the summer of 1970 congressional hearings on discrimination against women were held before the Special Subcommittee on Education of the House Committee on Education and Labor. Those hearings, chaired by Representative Edith Green, laid the groundwork for the passage of laws prohibiting sex discrimination in education.[1] Title VII of the Civil Rights Act of 1964 was amended to cover employment in educational institutions. The Equal Pay Act was amended to cover executives, administrators, and professionals, which included faculty women.

15

The Public Health Service Act was amended to prohibit discrimination in admission to programs training health professionals, including schools of medicine. And, finally, Title IX of the Education Amendments of 1972 was enacted to cover students as well as employees in all federally assisted programs. Title IX, which has been the key instrument for improving the situation of women students, states: "No person . . . shall, on the basis of sex, be excluded from participation in, be denied the benefit of, or be subjected to discrimination under any education program or activity receiving Federal financial assistance. . . ." These laws constitute what may well have been the most comprehensive national policy in the world regarding discrimination against women and girls in education. Having laws in place (even though they may not always be well enforced), coupled with strong pressures from women both on and off campus, has made a major difference in the position of women in higher education.

Many changes have occurred since the early 1970s, although obviously many problems still are unresolved. These changes may be summarized in five broad categories. (1) Most of the overt discrimination in education—that which was formalized by official policies and practices—has largely disappeared. Official policies now prohibit sex discrimination in almost all areas of campus activities and exist at virtually all campuses. (2) There is now a general awareness of sex discrimination as an issue in education—an awareness that did not exist previously. In 1970 when a major educational association was asked to testify on the bill which eventually became Title IX, it refused, commenting that there was no sex discrimination on campus. Although some people may still deny the existence of sex discrimination on *their* campus, there is nevertheless an acknowledgment that it exists somewhere and is a legitimate issue for education to address. (3) Women are energized and have organized to work on sex discrimination issues. There are over 100 caucuses and committees within the professional associations dealing with sex discrimination,[2] as well as innumerable newsletters and conferences. Additionally, there are several statewide and campus organizations of women faculty and women students across the country. Women are now a campus constituency—a constituency that did not exist until the early 1970s and a constituency that embraces minority women. These individuals and organizations represent a critical mass which can make the difference in holding on to what has been achieved and in pressing forward for change. (4) Women's issues have become institutionalized. In 1970 a campus committee on the status of women was not only a rarity, but a rather radical idea. Today, many campuses have an official committee dealing with women's issues, as well as a person who is in charge of Title IX and/or affirmative action. Furthermore, there are about 600 campus centers for women, numerous research centers and networks dealing with women, and a large number of special programs for returning women students. (5) Increasingly, the study of women is being included in the curriculum and in research. (See chapter 7.) There are now thousands of courses offered in women's studies, including black women's studies, compared with only a handful in 1969. Nearly 500 institutions have programs providing majors and minors in women's studies. The incorporation of the new scholarship on women into the mainstream curriculum has also been receiving a growing amount of attention, with about 80 specific programs to do so inaugurated on various campuses. There is no way of knowing how many faculty have, on their own, included material about women in their courses. However, although both research and teaching about women have increased in acceptance, there is still a tendency in many quarters to ascribe low status to the new scholarship. Women doctoral candidates continue to report that their thesis advisers (usually male) try to discourage them from choosing a topic in this area.

The legislation prohibiting sex discrimination and the changes that have taken place since 1970 are major accomplishments. Despite a certain amount of backlash and an unsympathetic administration in Washington in the 1980s, it is not likely that the clock could ever be turned back completely. The outcome of the 1984 Supreme Court decision in *Grove City College* v. *Bell* provides a dramatic illustration. The Court ruling in that case narrowed the scope of Title IX to specific programs receiving federal funds rather than to the institution as a whole. Following the decision a coalition of women's groups pressured Congress to enact legislation to restore the coverage of Title IX to its previous scope. The Civil Rights Restoration Act was introduced in 1984 and in succeeding sessions of Congress until it was finally passed in 1988. When President Reagan vetoed the new law, Congress voted by a wide margin to override the veto. But, even if the Supreme Court's weakening of Title IX had not been overturned by legislative action, it would still be very difficult for institutions to reinstate most of the overt discriminatory policies which were practiced in the past. The climate for women on campus as students, staff, and faculty has changed irrevocably.

The changes have been widespread, covering many areas of campus life. Specifically they include the following:

ADMISSIONS Quota systems for the admission of women in graduate and public undergraduate schools have largely vanished.[3] For example, in 1970 the University of North Carolina openly stated: "Admission of women on the freshman level will be restricted to those who are especially well-qualified." The freshman class for that year included 1,893 men and only 426 women.[4] The abolition of quotas has resulted in a marked increase in the enrollment of women in undergraduate and graduate schools, and especially in professional schools such as medicine and law. Institutions can no longer segregate applications by sex, ask different questions of each sex (such as asking women but not men about their marriage and family plans), nor evaluate each sex differently.[5] Many private undergraduate institutions, although allowed by Title IX to restrict admissions by sex if they wish to do so,[6] have nevertheless abolished quotas. Harvard, for example, no longer limits the number of women in its undergraduate classes. Thus, women no longer need higher grades than men to be admitted to most colleges and universities.

RECRUITMENT   Institutions recruit more fairly, no longer excluding women from recruiting activities. In many instances, recruiting materials have been evaluated and redesigned to appeal to women as well as men. Some schools and departments, especially those in traditionally male fields, have developed special materials to encourage women to apply.[7] There is some evidence to indicate that the existence of federal regulations prohibiting sex discrimination was a significant factor in the elimination of sexist language in college and university documents.[8]

The rapid increase in admission of women, particularly in graduate and professional schools, is itself evidence that women suffer far less discrimination than they did in the past. Many vestiges of discrimination persist, however. Discussion still continues about less blatant forms of discrimination such as bias in the Scholastic Aptitude Tests (see chapter 9). It has also been found that in medical school admissions, interview scores count more heavily for women than for men, while at the same time women in general are rated lower than men in the interview evaluations.[9] On the other hand, in the case of letters of recommendation written for students applying to graduate school, replication of older experiments that had documented discrimination showed that by the 1980s the sex of the applicant had no significant effect.[10]

Despite some increased recruiting for minority men in the early 1970s, minority women were not actively recruited and were generally not viewed as being a campus group separate from minorities and women. Since then the number of minority women on campus, including black, Hispanic, American Indian, and Asian/Pacific women, has increased substantially although not yet in proportion to the eligible population. Also, they are clustered primarily in community colleges and low-prestige institutions. To represent their interests on campus new organizations have been formed such as the Association of Black Women in Higher Education, the National Network of Minority Women in Science, and the New England Minority Women Administrators.

Access to higher education has also improved for re-entry women and for part-time students, men as well as women. Indeed, these groups have been the fastest-growing segment of the student body since 1970.[11] Many colleges and universities have been more receptive to them in part for reasons of equity, but also because of the shortage of students during this period. Institutions were concerned with the need to maintain enrollments as the population of potential students in the traditional college-going age groups declined. Older and part-time students, however, still face specific difficulties. For example, financial aid for part-time students is quite limited. Moreover, in graduate and professional schools, part-time study for the most part is still difficult and in some instances prohibited. Although some institutions have counseling services or other programs to ease the transition of adult women returning to higher education, at the more prestigious institutions such programs are conspicuously absent.[12] In the past, these programs were directed initially toward middle-class, middle-aged women whose children were grown. Today they serve the needs of a wide range of returning women including younger women, displaced homemakers, poor women, and minority women.

FINANCIAL AID   Overall, financial aid has become more nearly equitable although some disparities still exist. At the undergraduate level men and women receive approximately the same number of federal awards in the form of grants, loans, and work study opportunities, but not the same amounts. In 1981–1982 women received only 72 cents in grant money for every dollar men received; they also borrowed 84 cents for every dollar men borrowed.[13] However, over 90 percent of federal support goes to full-time students. For the most part, federal financial aid has not been available to part-time students, the majority of whom are women. Legislation passed by Congress in 1986 seeks to redress this imbalance. Under the Higher Education Amendments of 1986, colleges that count part-time students in the financial aid funds they receive must distribute a "reasonable proportion" of the money to such students.[14]

In the private sector, many single-sex awards programs for men have been opened to women; and where they have not, institutions have been required by Title IX to follow a complex pooling procedure to ensure that women are not disadvantaged by these restricting scholarships and have equivalent opportunities for receiving financial aid.

Other restrictive practices have also been eliminated. For example, marriage can no longer be used to deny women financial aid. Moreover, the need for childcare is increasingly being included in assessing the need for financial aid. Nevertheless, women are twice as likely to be classified as independent students (66 percent compared with 34 percent) and continue to have greater unmet needs.[15]

THE COLLEGE ENVIRONMENT   A host of parietal and other policies restricting women have been eliminated. Discriminatory parietal rules such as those prohibiting women but not men from staying out late are an example. In most instances, honorary and professional societies with student chapters no longer exclude women.

Sexual harassment, long a hidden issue on campus, is now explicitly forbidden on many campuses. Beginning in the late 1970s, a number of institutions conducted campus surveys to determine the extent of the problem. They include institutions as diverse as Arizona State University; the University of California at Berkeley, Santa Barbara, and Davis; the University of Cincinnati; the University of East Carolina; the University of Florida; Harvard University; Iowa State University; Pennsylvania State University; and the University of Rhode Island. The results suggest that between 20 and 30 percent of campus women have received unwelcome sexual attentions of one kind or another; between 5 and 10 percent of women students have been physically harassed or have received requests or demands for sex.[16] Although there are differences in the definition of what constitutes sexual harassment, women in general are much more likely than men to perceive the less extreme forms of behavior as harassment.

Many campuses have established specific procedures for dealing with complaints of sexual harassment, and faculty or staff found guilty of such conduct have sometimes been punished. While some feel that in the more extreme cases where physical advances have been made, punishments are not severe enough because they rarely involve dismissal, others believe that the publicity given the offender is an effective deterrent to other men. A few institutions, such as Hampshire College, Harvard University, the University of Minnesota, the University of Pennsylvania, and the University of Iowa, have issued policy statements condemning consensual relations between students and faculty.

Most institutions now have grievance procedures to handle complaints of sex discrimination, as required by Title IX. The procedures may not always be effective, but they nevertheless represent an advance from the time when sex discrimination was not "grievable" under most institutional grievance procedures. There are now at least formal channels through which this issue can be addressed.

Campus authorities have given more attention to campus lighting, building security, and other safety features. Numerous institutions have developed programs dealing with rape prevention, including activities directed toward male students as well as female students.

STUDENT SERVICES   Career counseling has improved significantly since the 1960s and is more likely to take into account the fact that most women will work for much of their adult lives. To an increasing extent women are being encouraged to expand their aspirations and to make long-term career plans. Counseling materials are no longer overtly sex stereotyped and vocational tests are no longer scored differently for males and females. Nevertheless, recent studies continue to show some bias on the part of counselors against nontraditional careers for women.[17] On the more positive side, it has been found that career classes for undecided majors, which have become increasingly popular in recent years, have a greater impact on women than on men.[18]

ATHLETICS AND PHYSICAL EDUCATION   Discrimination in athletics and physical education has been mitigated, but by no means eliminated. Prior to the enactment of Title IX, women's sports received little funding. At many campuses women's athletic teams received no funding whatsoever; women students and coaches had to raise their own money through bake sales and the like to pay for uniforms, travel, and, in some instances, equipment. At the University of Michigan, for example, where the men's athletic budget was over $2.5 million, the budget for women was zero. With the exception of a few traditionally black institutions, there were no athletic scholarships for women. At some schools training equipment as well as team doctors and health insurance were available for men only. Sometimes women could practice only when men's teams were not using the sports facilities, such as after dinner or very early in the morning.

With the advent of Title IX, budgets for women's athletics increased enormously. Increasing numbers of women are being awarded athletic scholarships, and more sports are available for women's participation. In the mid-1960s about 16,000 women compared with 154,000 men participated in intercollegiate activities. Ten years later the number of women participants was four times the previous figure, whereas the participation of men increased by only 10 percent. There are now about four women intercollegiate athletes to every ten men.[19]

Offsetting this dramatic gain, however, is the decline in influence of women coaches and athletic directors. As women's athletic departments were merged with those of men in many institutions, women administrators were placed in subordinate positions or displaced by men's athletic directors. The Association for Intercollegiate Athletics for Women, which was founded in 1971 and spearheaded the growth of women's sports under Title IX, closed its doors in 1982. Its functions were absorbed by the more powerful National Collegiate Athletic Association, which is dominated by big-time football and basketball interests. In 1973 more than 90 percent of the coaches and administrators of women's programs were women. By 1984 this figure was reduced to 54 percent.[20]

OTHER SERVICES   Health services for women have been generally improved, and gynecological care is being given increasing attention. In other student services, such as placement activities and campus employment, sex bias has been greatly reduced if not yet entirely eliminated.

With the growing diversity in the age distribution and marital status of the student population, childcare has surfaced as an important need on campus and, of course, it is one that particularly affects women students. Campus childcare programs were almost unknown in the 1960s except for demonstration programs associated with schools of education or departments of psychology. A survey conducted in 1970 by the American Association of University Women found that only 5 percent of a representative group of about 450 institutions provided some form of day care.[21] In its 1976 survey covering approximately 600 institutions, AAUW found that the proportion of institutions offering day care had increased to more than 30 percent. The U.S. Census Bureau estimates that 40 percent of U.S. colleges offer some form of childcare for children 6 weeks to 6 years of age.[22] Some are for day care only, others are for evening students, and some are drop-off baby sitting services. The majority of institutions, however, still do not offer such services.

Another kind of campus resource for women which made its appearance in the 1970s is the multi-purpose women's center. As we have already noted, there are some 600 such centers in existence today. They have varying degrees of institutional support, and many are student operated. They provide a supportive atmosphere for women and a place for meetings, lectures, film presentations, and other activities of particular concern to women. These centers are further described in chapter 5.

On the academic side, there are in addition to women's studies programs a growing number of centers or institutes for research on women. There are now approximately 50 such centers. They are described in chapter 13.

The Forces for Change

How did so many changes occur in so short a time? What forces led to such major changes?

In the first instance, there is the women's movement itself, which increased awareness of sex discrimination generally and served to legitimize sex discrimination in colleges and universities as a problem. Public policy also increased awareness of sex discrimination, and at the same time gave hope to those who were ready to press for change; it made responsible advocacy possible.

National women's organizations and projects such as WEAL and the Project on the Status and Education of Women of the Association of American Colleges played a major role in identifying sex discrimination and disseminating information about public policy to women and campus administrators. Knowledge about Title IX and other laws energized those on campus to deal with sex discrimination issues. Moreover, during the 1970s the federal government took an active role in notifying administrators about Title IX and its prohibitions. This barrage of knowledge from various sources helped to redefine campus policies and establish new norms of behavior. Title IX required an institutional self-evaluation, a general provision under which every educational institution receiving federal funds had to evaluate its policies and practices for compliance with the Title IX regulation and to modify these policies and practices where necessary to eliminate discrimination. Institutions were not required to turn in self-evaluation reports to the Department of Education but simply to keep them on file; nevertheless, many institutions took the requirement seriously, appointing committees to examine an array of policies and practices and making the necessary changes.

The vast majority of changes took place quietly. Despite much hue and cry about athletics or protests about challenges to father-son dinners, the changes in virtually all colleges and universities occurred with little fanfare, few court cases, and little actual government intervention. Less than 1 percent of the nation's schools and colleges have had a federal investigator on campus to inquire about sex discrimination. In most instances, unfair practices were identified by organized groups of women, ad hoc committees, or individual students or faculty. Institutions made changes to avoid violations of Title IX.

At the same time various women's organizations in Washington, working together in what eventually became the National Coalition for Women and Girls in Education, monitored the activity of the federal government concerning sex discrimination. The coalition also worked closely with the National Advisory Council on Women's Educational Programs, a presidentially appointed group, established under the Women's Educational Equity Act in 1974, to advise federal officials regarding the improvement of educational equity for women. The Office of Women in Higher Education of the American Council on Education (ACE) prepared materials to help institutions conduct their Title IX self-evaluation and played an important role in shaping ACE's official policy on issues affecting campus women. The Project on the Status and Education of Women of the Association of American Colleges kept many administrators and women faculty informed on the latest developments in federal policy, legislation, and litigation through its newsletter, *On Campus with Women*, and with its topical papers, which often analyzed new issues and provided institutions with ways to deal with these issues.

An important factor in the efforts of campus groups and national women's organizations to achieve educational equity was the financial support provided by grants from private foundations and government agencies. Among the major foundation funding sources were the Ford Foundation and the Carnegie Corporation of New York. The main government granting agencies included the Women's Educational Equity Act Program and the Fund for the Improvement of Postsecondary Education.[23]

The impetus to change given by the federal anti-discrimination laws and programs has slowed down markedly during the 1980s. Under the Reagan administration, enforcement efforts have declined and the impact of Title IX has been severely weakened. The Office for Civil Rights, the enforcement arm of the Department of Education, received cuts in both budget and staff, and the number of compliance reviews has dropped precipitously.[24] The Grove City College decision also served for a time to put a damper on Title IX enforcement efforts. The impact was felt particularly in athletic programs, one of the areas in which Title IX has had the greatest effect. The Civil Rights Restoration Act cannot ensure rigorous enforcement, but it should at least forestall further erosion.

The Task Ahead

In a sense, the first great wave of change is over. Overt policies of discrimination have faded and opportunities for women students have expanded. Nevertheless, full equity for women has not yet been achieved; subtle discrimination still remains and will be difficult to overcome. Although men and women may attend the same institution and sit alongside each other in the classroom, their experiences are likely to be very different.

Women have entered traditionally male-dominated fields in increasing numbers over the last 15 years, but there are persistent differences in patterns of career choice and field of college major. In high school preparation for college, girls on average have significantly more years of study than boys in foreign languages and slightly more in English and biological sciences; boys have significantly more years of study in mathematics and physical sciences and slightly more study in the social sciences. The gender gap in mathematics and science at college entrance narrowed somewhat between 1971 and 1983, but it has not been eliminated.[25] In view of the growth of computer science as a field of major in recent years and the growing use of computers in professional and managerial work, it is important to note also that women students enter college with less exposure to computers than men do.

For college men and women degree goals and choice of fields of study have converged substantially since 1971. As shown in Table 2.1, the gap has narrowed in nearly all fields, and four are virtually at parity: biological sciences, business, mathematics, and premedical studies. Both men and women have shifted away from the humanities, education, and the social sciences—the traditional areas for women. Women students still enter these fields at a proportionately higher rate than men, but the difference in 1986 was much smaller than in 1971. Both men and women have selected business as a major in increasing numbers, and the proportion of women in this field now exceeds that of men. The largest differential in favor of men is in engineering, despite the high rate of increase of women in that field.[26] This distribution of fields channels women more than men into the lower-paying occupations, with the result that women do not receive the same return on their education that men do.[27]

Aside from the choice of major, some studies indicate that women students have lower career aspirations and personal ambition than men and that the differences, although declining, have not yet disappeared. The studies were conducted by Alexander Astin and his associates at the Higher Education Research Institute at the University of California at Los Angeles. They are based on annual surveys of some 180,000 college freshmen at about 300 institutions to measure changes in the "national norms" of successive student generations. In response to the question of whether they considered it essential or important to "become an authority in my field," women students in 1966 were 10 points behind men. In

Table 2.1 Distribution of Freshmen by Probable Field of Study in All Institutions of Higher Education: Selected Years, 1971–1986

Probable Major Field of Study	1971 Men	1971 Women	1975 Men	1975 Women	1980 Men	1980 Women	1986 Men	1986 Women
Agriculture/Forestry	5.4%	0.7%	5.7%	1.9%	4.1%	1.8%	2.8%	0.9%
Arts and Humanities*	16.8	20.5	12.7	12.8	6.4	10.1	7.4	10.0
Biological Sciences	4.4	2.7	7.1	5.5	3.7	3.8	4.0	3.8
Business	18.3	14.2	20.1	17.5	22.9	24.5	26.6	27.0
Education	4.6	15.9	4.6	15.5	3.3	11.6	3.8	12.1
Engineering	13.2	0.3	14.0	1.3	21.0	3.2	19.7	2.9
Health Professions (non-MD)	2.6	16.1	1.8	13.2	1.9	13.3	2.0	9.9
Mathematics/Statistics	2.6	2.9	1.1	1.1	0.7	0.6	0.9	0.7
Computer Science					2.7	2.4	2.6	1.3
Physical Sciences	3.1	0.8	4.0	1.3	3.6	1.6	2.2	1.0
Premedical, Predental, Preveterinary					3.6	3.2	2.9	2.9
Social Sciences*	5.6	12.2	3.7	8.9	4.5	8.6	5.3	10.2
Other Fields (Technical)	7.3	2.6	10.3	6.7	8.5	2.9	6.4	1.9
Other Fields (Nontechnical)	1.4	5.0	10.2	8.8	9.3	6.9	8.0	7.9
Undecided	2.3	2.3	4.6	5.5	3.8	5.5	5.4	7.5

Source: Alexander Astin et al., *The American Freshman: National Norms,* annual series (Los Angeles: Higher Education Research Institute, Graduate School of Education, University of California, 1971–1988).

*Political Science is included in Arts and Humanities through 1975 and in Social Sciences after 1975.

1975 they were 7 points behind and in 1986 only 1 point behind. Women freshmen made comparable gains in the desire to "gain recognition from my colleagues," "to have administrative responsibility," "to be well off financially," and "to be successful in my own business."[28] A follow-up survey in 1982 of 2,500 freshmen who had answered the original questionnaire four years earlier found that the answers were essentially the same as those of the incoming freshmen.[29] These results suggest that the aspirations of women students, like those of men, are shaped to a large extent by their perception of the career possibilities open to them, and it is clear that these possibilities have improved over the last two decades. College may or may not change these aspirations, but it does influence the extent to which students are able to realize them. In this respect, there is more than a little evidence that the campus environment is less supportive of women than of men. For example, women students report that they are treated coolly in departments that have long been male preserves.[30] Women are discouraged from entering departments in nontraditional areas that are seen as unsupportive. There are numerous other ways in which the campus environment may be less supportive for women than for men. In 1982 the Project on the Status and Education of Women of the Association of American Colleges published a comprehensive report which analyzed classroom behaviors and identified subtle ways in which men and women students were treated differently.[31] These behaviors are often inadvertent and unintentional, but nevertheless they convey a negative view of women's abilities. Examples of these behaviors include the following:

- Men students are more likely to be called upon, thus communicating more interest in what they have to say and increasing their visibility in the classroom.
- Faculty interrupt women students more than male students, displaying a lack of interest in what women have to say.
- Male students tend to be "coached" more than women by professors who probe for a more elaborate answer, with questions such as "Tell me more about that" or "Can you explain that more fully?" This not only gives men students more encouragement and opportunity to develop their ideas, but also implies the expectation that they know the answer and just need to work at it a little harder. Similarly, faculty may wait longer for men than for women to answer a question before going on to another student. Giving women less time may subtly communicate that women are not expected to know the answer.
- What men say carries more weight. A suggestion or point made by a

man is more likely to be listened to, credited to him ("as Jim said"), developed in further discussion, and adopted by a group than when the same suggestion is made by a woman.

Outside the classroom there are other subtle and sometimes more overt behaviors that disparage women or otherwise favor men.[32] For example, faculty members may give more time and attention to supporting male students than female students.

In general, the achievements of women in academe are devalued, as they are in other settings, by men and to a lesser extent also by women. Numerous studies demonstrate how the gender of an individual influences the perception and evaluation of his or her achievements and behavior. The studies include experiments in which, for example, men and women are asked to rate the same items, such as résumés, professional articles, or works of art. The name of the person attached to the item is changed for each group. Those items ascribed to women for the first group are ascribed to men in the second group, and those items ascribed to men in the first group are ascribed to women in the second group. The results of these experiments are singularly consistent: If people believe a woman was the creator, they ranked it lower than when they believe a man was the creator. Both men and women do this; they devalue those items ascribed to females.[33] Under similar experimental conditions, real-life employers (primarily male) ranging from supervisors and employment recruiters to department chairpersons were more likely to evaluate female job applicants less favorably than males with the same qualifications.[34]

Not only are the accomplishments of men and women evaluated differently, but the ascribed reasons for their successes are also viewed differently. Men's success is typically seen as resulting from internal factors such as ability and competence, while women's success is often attributed to external circumstance and unpredictable and uncontrollable factors such as luck. Women themselves may internalize this pattern and attribute their own accomplishments to outside factors such as "being in the right place at the right time." Consequently, women's achievements are frequently discounted by men and women alike as reliable predictors of future success.[35]

Another source of difficulty that students face is that many men experience discomfort with women as potential colleagues and as intellectual rather than sexual beings. This discomfort may make it difficult for men to mentor or sponsor women students. Male professors are more comfortable talking with male students, sharing information, and giving advice. As a result, women students may get less feedback about their work than their male peers, whether positive or negative. The effects of these subtle forms of discrimination are not always recognized and not easily measured, but they cannot be dismissed as negligible.[36]

The campus climate for women is not, of course, the same in all institutions or even within all parts of the same institution. It may vary with the type of institution and the character of the administration. The atmosphere will depend in part on whether the institution is a major research university, an institution that emphasizes big-time sports, a liberal arts college, a women's college, a community college, or a black or other minority college. It will also depend on the attitude of the chief executive officer and the number of women in the upper levels of administration. Women's colleges are a special case, and their overall role in higher education for women is discussed in chapter 6. Of necessity, they offer a campus environment that is more supportive of women than other types of institutions, just as a study of college environments for black students found that both female and male black students do better at predominantly black institutions.[37] Women have entered community colleges in large numbers since the 1970s and now represent over 56 percent of the student body of two-year institutions, but little is known about the treatment they receive relative to their male counterparts and relative to women students in other types of institutions.

Conclusions

In the years since 1970 substantial progress has been made in equity for women in higher education. With the aid of government regulations, overt discrimination has been all but eliminated in the areas of recruitment, admissions, financial aid, and membership in honor societies. Reentry women are being admitted in larger numbers, although they do not always get the financial aid and support services they need; the childcare situation has improved; more campus jobs are being opened to women; athletic programs are expanding and are better funded; problems of sexual harassment are being recognized and confronted; and women's studies courses are being included in the curriculum.

More subtle forms of discrimination remain, however, and these will be more difficult to remedy. They lie in attitudes and behaviors that devalue women's achievements and dampen their self-confidence and aspirations. The task will be easier when there are more women on the faculty and in administrative positions and when the curriculum reflects and incorporates the new scholarship about women. In the meantime we need to know more about the effects of different environments on the college experience of women and how to help institutions make their campuses a more supportive place for women students.

Notes

1. U.S. Congress, House of Representatives, *Discrimination Against Women,* hearings before the Special Subcommittee on Education of the Committee on Education and Labor, 91st Cong., 2nd sess., Section 805 of H.R. 16098, June and July 1970.

2. See, for example, American Association of University Women, *Professional Women's Groups Providing Employment Assistance to Women* (Washington, DC: AAUW, May 1983).

3. Private undergraduate institutions are permitted under Title IX to restrict admissions on the basis of sex. Following admission, however, discrimination against students of either sex is prohibited.

4. U.S. Congress, House of Representatives, *Discrimination Against Women,* p. 300.

5. Unfortunately there are schools that do not always comply with Title IX. Some students still report instances where they are asked such questions or are otherwise treated differently.

6. See note 3.

7. See, for example, Association of American Colleges, Project on the Status and Education of Women, *Nontraditional Careers* (selected articles from *On Campus with Women,* 1981–1983).

8. Judith Markowitz, "The Impact of the Sexist Language Controversy and Regulation on Language in University Documents," *Psychology of Women Quarterly* 8 (1984):337–347.

9. Obie Clayton, Jr., et al., "Subjective Decision Making in Medical School Admissions: Potentials for Discrimination," *Sex Roles* 10 (1984):527–532.

10. Jayne E. Stalke, Elaine F. Walker, and Mary V. Speno, "The Relationship of Sex and Academic Performance to Quality of Recommendation for Graduate School," *Psychology of Women Quarterly* 5 (1981):512–522.

11. See chapter 4.

12. According to a survey conducted for the American Association of University Women in 1976, one third of the institutions sampled offered continuing education programs for women. Other institutions offered minimal services such as off-campus classes or refresher courses. See Suzanne Howard, *But We Will Persist: A Comparative Research Report on the Status of Women in Academe* (Washington, DC: American Association of University Women, 1978); and Carol Eliason, *Women in Community and Junior Colleges: Report of a Study in Access to Occupational Education* (Washington, DC: American Association of Community and Junior Colleges, 1977).

13. American Council on Education, *Report of the National Commission on Student Financial Assistance* (Washington, DC: Division of Policy Analysis and Research, ACE, 1984). For a policy analysis of how the different educational and life patterns of women affect their financial requirements for school, and how apparently equitable policies for awarding student aid can disproportionately limit a woman's opportunity to pursue a college education, see American Association of University Women, *Women and Student Financial Aid: A Policy Brief* (Washington, DC: AAUW, 1985).

14. *Chronicle of Higher Education*, October 8, 1986, p. 28.

15. *On Campus with Women*, Spring 1984, p. 6.

16. Committee on Women, Iowa State University, *Sexual Harassment of Students at Iowa State University, Subcommittee Report Approved by the University Committee on Women* (Ames: Committee on Women, 1982); Billie Wright Dziech and Linda Weiner, *The Lecherous Professor: Harassment on Campus* (Boston: Beacon Press, 1984), pp. 13–14; Michael P. Johnson and Suzan Shuman, *Sexual Harassment of Students at the Pennsylvania State University* (University Park: Pennsylvania State University, 1983); Robert L. Whitmore, *Sexual Harassment at UC Davis* (Davis: University of California, 1983).

17. Marilyn Haring et al., "Sex Biased Attitudes of Counselors: The Special Case of Non-Traditional Careers," *Counseling and Values* 27 (1983):242–247.

18. William Dale Goodson, "A Career Class Does Have an Impact: A Ten Year Follow-up," paper presented at the Convention of the American Personnel and Guidance Association, Detroit, March 17–20, 1982.

19. R. Vivian Acosta and Linda Jean Carpenter, "Women in Athletics—A Status Report," *Journal of Physical Education, Recreation and Dance*, no. 6 (August 1985):30–34.

20. *New York Times*, December 15, 1985.

21. Ruth M. Oltman, *Campus 1970: Where Do Women Stand?* (Washington, DC: American Association of University Women, 1970).

22. "What's Happening with Child Care on Campus," *On Campus with Women*, Summer 1986, p. 2.

23. *Financial Support of Women's Programs in the 1970's*, a report to the Ford Foundation (New York: Ford Foundation, 1976), pp. 18–19.

24. *Chronicle of Higher Education*, July 31, 1985.

25. Based on information provided by the College Entrance Examination Board.

26. Further discussion of this subject may be found in chapter 9.

27. J. L. Crane, *Salary Comparisons of 1979–80 College Graduates by Sex in 1981: Analytic Report* (Washington, DC: U.S. Government Printing Office, 1984).

28. Alexander W. Astin, Robert J. Panos, and John A. Creager, *National Norms for Entering College Freshmen: Fall 1966* (Washington, DC: American Council on Education, 1967); Alexander W. Astin, Margo R. King, and Gerald T. Richardson, *The American Freshman: National Norms for Fall 1975* (Los Angeles: Higher Education Research Institute, Graduate School of Educa-

tion, University of California, 1975); Alexander W. Astin et al., *The American Freshman: Norms for Fall 1984* (Los Angeles: Higher Education Research Institute, Graduate School of Education, University of California, 1984).

29. Kenneth C. Green et al., *The American College Student, 1982: National Norms for the 1978 and 1980 College Freshmen Two and Four Years After Entering College* (Washington, DC: American Council on Education, 1983).

30. Carole Kovalic Holahan, "Stress Experienced by Women Doctoral Students, Need for Support and Occupational Sex Typing: An Interactional View," *Sex Roles* 5 (1979):425–436; and James C. Hearn and Susan Olzak, "The Role of College Major Departments in the Reproduction of Sexual Inequality," *Sociology of Education* 54 (1981):195–205.

31. Roberta M. Hall and Bernice R. Sandler, *The Classroom Climate: A Chilly One for Women?* (Washington, DC: Project on the Status and Education of Women, Association of American Colleges, 1982).

32. Roberta M. Hall and Bernice R. Sandler, *Out of the Classroom: A Chilly Campus Climate for Women* (Washington, DC: Project on the Status and Education of Women, Association of American Colleges, 1984).

33. See Phillip Goldberg, "Are Women Prejudiced Against Women?" *Trans-Action* 5 (1968):28–30. Several more recent studies have confirmed Goldberg's findings, such as Michele A. Paludi and Lisa A. Strayer, "What's in an Author's Name? Differential Evaluations of Performance as a Function of Author's Name," *Sex Roles* 12, nos. 3–4 (1985):353–361; and Michele A. Paludi and William D. Bauer, "Goldberg Revisited: What's in an Author's Name?" *Sex Roles* 9, no. 3 (1983):387–390.

34. For an overview of research in this area, see Veronica F. Nieva and Barbara Gutek, "Sex Effects of Evaluation," *Academy of Management Review* 5, no. 2 (1980):267–276; F. L. Geis, M. R. Carter, and D. J. Butler, *Research on Seeing and Evaluating People* (Newark: Office of Women's Affairs, University of Delaware, 1982); and Bernice Lott, "The Devaluation of Women's Competence," *Journal of Social Issues* 4 (1985):43–60.

35. Constantina Safilios-Rothschild, *Sex Role Socialization and Sex Discrimination: A Synthesis and Overview of the Literature* (Washington, DC: National Institute of Education, 1979), pp. 38–41; Irene H. Frieze, "Women's Attributions for and Casual Attributions of Success and Failure," in Martha T. Mednick, Sandra S. Tangri, and Lois W. Hoffman, eds., *Women and Achievement: Social and Motivational Analyses* (Washington, DC: Hemisphere, 1975), pp. 158–171; Patricia Hayes Andrews, "Upward Directed Persuasive Communication—Attribution of Success and Failure Toward an Understanding of the Role of Gender," paper presented at the Communication, Language and Gender Conference, Oxford, Ohio, October 14–16, 1985; Susan Powers-Alexander et al., "Attribution of Success in College to Women: Effort or Luck?" paper presented at the annual meeting of the American Educational Research Association, Montreal, April 11–15, 1983; Elizabeth P. Smith et al., "Role Appropriateness of Educational Fields: Bias in Selection," paper pre-

sented at the annual meeting of the American Educational Research Association, Montreal, April 11–15, 1983.

36. For an opposing view, see Jack F. Heller, C. Richard Puff, and Carol Mills, "Assessment of the Chilly Climate for Women," *Journal of Higher Education* 56 (1985):446–461.

37. Jacqueline Fleming, "Sex Differences in the Impact of the College Environment on Black Students," in Pamela J. Perun, ed., *The Undergraduate Woman: Issues in Educational Equity* (Lexington, MA: Lexington Books, 1982), pp. 229–250.

3

Minority Women

It is difficult to write about minority women in higher education for two reasons. First, the group includes a diverse set of people with different cultural, language, and experiential background. While that may be true for any group whose major bond (at least on the surface) is gender, it is especially true of this particular group. Black women, for the most part, have grown up in families whose ancestors have been here for several generations but have until recently been in segregated communities and segregated institutions. Likewise, American Indian women are from families that have been in this country but not of this country for over 200 years.

Asian and Hispanic women differ not only from other minority groups, but have enormous differences among themselves. Both Asian and Hispanic groups include individuals who are recent immigrants and those from families that have been in the United States for generations.[1] Among Hispanics, for example, there are Puerto Ricans, Cubans, Mexican Americans, and immigrants from Central and South America. Some definitions also include Europeans from Spain. About the only thing these people have in common is language. Other aspects of their culture may differ and their economic circumstances are quite varied. The same variety exists among Asians and Pacific Islanders. Some women of Japanese and Chinese ancestry have grown up in middle-class America while other Asians are of Vietnamese and Laotian extraction whose families entered this country in the past decade as political refugees.

There are even differences within each minority group in terms of their relationship to and with males. Among some of the groups, sexism is very strong, often based on a rigid patriarchal society. Within other racial or ethnic groups, sexism is not as significant (though in no group is it nonexistent). Yet, minority women do have one thing in common: They all fall way behind white males in terms of educational and economic achievement, and they have not, for the most part, achieved parity with white women.[2]

Another reason it is difficult to write about minority women is that they are rarely recognized as having unique needs. Consequently, separate studies and separate data are seldom available on minority women, especially by racial or ethnic group. To some extent this is a product of their small representation in higher education. Since the data available are mostly based on samples, data on a small group within a small group are seldom reported because they are considered statistically unreliable. The data most frequently reported are for black women who are the largest separate group. To some extent, then, this chapter will include more information on black women than on other groups for this reason.

A Decade of Change

When *Academic Women on the Move* was published over a decade ago, change was in the air.[3] New educational opportunities had opened up and employment and economic gains seemed to be just around the corner. By the end of the 1970s, the impact on women and particularly on minority women was noted by many. Typical of the work in this area was Richard Freeman's *The Overeducated American*.[4] While noting a decline in college enrollment rates among white males that was (apparently) related to the decreased rate of return to higher education, Freeman remarked on the increased enrollment rates among women and minorities. These increases were attributed to the fact that equal employment and affirmative action regulations had increased the economic return to a college education for these groups. He made particular note of gains made by black women, since at that time the incomes of black women who worked full time, year round were 95 percent of the incomes of white women similarly employed.

Some have attributed gains made by minority women to their status as a "two-fer." Because they fill two slots at once, both the goal for women and the goal for minorities can be advanced by just one appointment, or so the argument goes. Others, including some minority males, have argued that minority women also benefit from the fact that they are viewed by white males as being less threatening and therefore a better or safer choice for appointment. Yet, how well can one fit in, if one has neither gender nor race in common with the ruling elite?

This sense of isolation, which is discussed by Constance Carroll in *Academic Women on the Move*, has not disappeared.[5] Carroll recalls a meeting in which a black woman raises an objection to a remark that is made. Her objection is followed by a deafening silence "and then the discussion simply proceeds as before."[6] The feeling of being ignored or unsupported, whether by the "old boys" network or the "old gals" network, is one that has been noted by others. Paula Hall pointed it out in her 1981 review of the problems of minority women in science.[7] The same feeling was manifested outside academe during the recent formation of the National Black Women's Political Caucus.

The isolation increases as one moves up the educational ladder from undergraduate to graduate student and from graduate student to faculty member, as minority women become a smaller and smaller part of the group.

Minority Women as Students

Education has been viewed by minorities and other disadvantaged groups as an important means toward upward mobility—so much so that, holding socioeconomic status constant, the educational aspirations of minority youth are higher than those of whites.[8] However, economic and other barriers such as racial discrimination and legal segregation have stood in the way of minorities seeking to obtain a quality education. Yet where opportunities were available or could be made available, members of minority groups have taken advantage of them. Consequently, the educational attainment of minorities, like that of whites, has increased with each succeeding cohort. However, since whites have continued to increase their educational attainment, minorities for the most part continue to lag behind the majority population.

Table 3.1 shows the educational attainment of the U.S. population in 1980. For each of the racial and ethnic groups shown, younger cohorts are more educated than older cohorts. Larger percentages of them have graduated from high school and from college. More of them have had some postsecondary education and some postgraduate education. What is of particular interest is the gender differences within each ethnic group (holding cohort constant) and the differences by gender across ethnic and racial groups. Within each ethnic group there are few gender

Table 3.1 Educational Attainment of the U.S. Population Aged 18 and Over, by Sex, Race, and Ethnicity: 1980

Age	High School Graduate		1–3 Years College		4 or More Years College		5 or More Years College	
	Male	Female	Male	Female	Male	Female	Male	Female
White								
18–24 Years	76.6%	80.7%	24.9%	26.9%	6.8%	7.2%	1.6%	1.2%
25–34 Years	87.0	86.6	24.0	22.2	28.5	21.7	13.4	8.5
35–44 Years	79.9	79.4	17.7	17.5	25.9	15.6	14.7	6.9
45–54 Years	68.7	70.1	14.0	14.2	21.1	10.9	11.0	4.7
55–64 Years	59.2	60.9	12.1	12.3	15.2	8.4	7.6	3.5
65 Years and Over	39.5	42.2	8.8	10.3	10.5	7.6	5.2	2.8
Black								
18–24 Years	61.8	70.9	18.3	24.4	2.5	3.9	0.5	0.7
25–34 Years	73.2	75.1	22.5	21.6	11.5	11.8	4.7	4.6
35–44 Years	60.5	62.1	15.4	15.2	10.1	9.1	5.5	4.7
45–54 Years	42.9	45.9	10.7	10.4	7.6	7.6	4.4	4.1
55–64 Years	28.6	31.2	6.5	6.4	5.1	5.4	2.9	2.8
65 Years and Over	15.4	18.6	3.5	4.0	3.2	4.0	0.9	1.8
Hispanic								
18–24 Years	52.8	57.6	16.2	18.3	2.4	2.7	0.8	0.7

25–34 Years	57.5	57.0	18.9	15.7	10.8	7.9	5.5	3.6
35–44 Years	47.4	45.6	13.6	10.9	10.4	6.2	6.2	3.2
45–54 Years	38.4	35.5	10.0	7.9	8.7	5.1	5.4	2.7
55–64 Years	30.3	26.5	6.9	5.3	7.0	4.1	4.2	2.1
65 Years and Over	19.1	18.0	3.7	3.2	4.7	3.0	2.8	1.5
Asian								
18–24 Years	80.0	80.9	36.6	35.9	10.0	11.6	3.4	3.3
25–34 Years	89.6	83.4	24.5	22.2	45.8	37.2	27.4	17.0
35–44 Years	88.0	78.6	16.4	17.1	52.9	33.9	34.7	16.6
45–54 Years	77.8	69.7	15.2	14.6	37.0	17.0	21.5	7.8
55–64 Years	62.2	53.2	11.4	10.3	20.0	10.5	10.7	4.5
65 Years and Over	37.2	32.7	7.2	6.8	11.9	7.0	5.1	2.5
American Indian and Alaskan Native								
18–24 Years	57.9	62.5	14.6	17.2	1.7	1.9	0.6	0.4
25–34 Years	73.2	71.0	24.4	22.0	10.1	8.1	4.9	3.3
35–44 Years	62.3	58.1	18.7	16.1	10.7	6.6	5.8	3.2
45–54 Years	47.1	45.8	13.4	12.1	8.9	5.5	5.2	2.7
55–64 Years	39.3	39.1	9.8	9.8	8.0	4.5	4.2	2.3
65 Years and Over	21.7	23.6	5.8	5.9	4.1	3.5	2.0	1.7

Source: U.S. Bureau of the Census, 1980 Census of Population, Detailed Characteristics of the Population, pt. I, sect. A (Washington, DC: U.S. Government Printing Office, 1984), table 296.

differences in high school completion, indicating that the pool of people available to go to college is quite similar for males and females, holding race or ethnicity constant.[9]

College attendance shows a pattern similar to that for high school completion—that is, with the exception of Hispanics, little gender difference for having some college (1–3 years) and whites being more likely to attend college than minorities, except for Asians whose attendance rates are quite similar to those of whites. For black women under age 44, the proportion having some college is also quite similar to that for white women.

The large gaps began to appear in the proportion among those having completed college and among those with some graduate education. Except for the 18-to-24-year-old cohort, males in every ethnic group, except one, are more likely to have a college degree and are more likely to have some postgraduate training. Only among blacks is the proportion of women having four or more years of college similar to that of men. Comparing completion rates across ethnic groups, it can be seen that, with the exception of Asians, minority women are less likely than white women to have received four years of college training.

During the first part of the 1970s college enrollment rates for both males and females of each major racial group increased (Table 3.2). Among whites, rates for women increased more rapidly than those of men so that the gap between white men and white women started to close.[10] By 1981 the gap was virtually eliminated because of a slight decline in enrollment rates of white males. Among blacks, enrollment rates for both men and women (fairly equal in 1970) rose in parallel fashion until mid-decade; then, as rates leveled off for black males, black females began to surpass them. Less information is available for Hispanics so trends are hard to assess. In 1981 enrollment rates for Hispanic males and Hispanic females were identical. For black women the decade was clearly one of progress in terms of college enrollment. Their enrollment rates rose from 66 to 82 percent of those for white women and from 42 to 82 percent of those for white men.

The effect of the changing enrollment rates on the racial and ethnic composition of the freshman class can be seen in Table 3.3. Among males, whites dropped from 92 to 87 percent of freshmen enrollment between 1971 and 1986, a gain of 5 percentage points for minority males. Among females, whites declined from 91 to 85 percent of enrollment between 1971 and 1986, a gain of 6 percentage points for minority women. These gains appear to be holding even though there have been some fluctuations during the 1980s. These relative gains are quite impressive, given the rapid rise in enrollment rates among white women. However, a closer look at Tables 3.3 and 3.4 reveals that many of the

Table 3.2 College Enrollment Rates for the U.S. Population Aged 16–34, by Sex, Race, and Ethnicity: 1970, 1975, and 1981

Age	Whites		Blacks		Spanish Origin	
	Male	Female	Male	Female	Male	Female
1970						
16–17 Years	3.5%	3.4%	2.0%	2.3%		
18–19 Years	43.1	35.7	17.6	25.4		
20–21 Years	43.4	23.0	24.4	16.3		
22–24 Years	22.0	9.2	8.0	6.2		
25–29 Years	10.8	3.8	4.9	2.8		
30–34 Years	4.8	2.8	3.6	1.7		
All Ages	9.0	5.8	3.9	3.8		
Number of Persons (thousands)	4,066	2,693	253	269		
1975						
16–17 Years	3.0%	4.1%	2.6%	3.2%	1.2%	4.1%
18–19 Years	38.4	37.9	23.2	27.0	23.4	24.8
20–21 Years	35.4	26.8	24.5	24.5	27.7	22.2
22–24 Years	20.2	11.6	14.1	13.6	15.3	12.5
25–29 Years	12.7	6.7	10.6	7.2	11.1	4.6
30–34 Years	7.3	5.1	8.3	5.4	6.7	2.2
All Ages	9.9	7.7	6.4	6.7	6.5	5.5
Number of Persons (thousands)	4,774	3,743	442	506	219	192
1981						
16–17 Years	2.4%	3.4%	1.2%	3.9%	1.7%	3.2%
18–19 Years	37.5	40.1	24.8	29.2	19.8	22.5
20–21 Years	31.9	31.4	18.6	23.2	21.2	16.8
22–24 Years	18.7	12.9	14.4	13.1	10.2	12.1
25–29 Years	8.9	7.6	10.8	8.0	7.5	7.1
30–34 Years	5.8	7.3	6.5	6.8	5.8	2.8
All Ages	9.2	9.1	6.7	7.5	5.5	5.5
Number of Persons (thousands)						
Old*	4,514	4,469	474	606	243	243
New*	4,620	4,543	505	628	258	252

Source: U.S. Bureau of the Census, *School Enrollment—Social and Economic Characteristics of Students*, P-20, nos. 222, 303, and 373 (Washington, DC: U.S. Government Printing Office, various years).

*Old estimates based on 1970 census and new estimates based on 1980 census.

Table 3.3 Racial and Ethnic Background of College Freshmen, by Sex: 1971–1986

	1971		1975		1980		1986	
	Male	Female	Male	Female	Male	Female	Male	Female
White	92.1%	90.6%	87.2%	85.6%	87.0%	85.1%	86.9%	84.8%
Black	5.5	7.2	8.0	10.1	8.0	10.3	7.3	9.6
American Indian	1.0	0.9	0.9	0.8	0.8	0.7	0.9	0.8
Asian	0.5	0.4	1.6	1.3	1.6	1.2	2.8	2.3
Mexican American	1.1	1.1	1.8	1.6	2.1	2.0	1.2	1.3
Puerto Rican	0.2	0.2	0.7	0.6	0.8	0.9	0.8	0.9
Other	1.2	1.1	2.1	1.7	1.8	1.6	1.9	2.0

Sources: Betty M. Vetter and Eleanor L. Babco, *Professional Women and Minorities* (Washington, DC: Commission on Professionals in Science and Technology, 1987); and Alexander W. Astin et al., *The American Freshman: National Norms,* annual series (Los Angeles: Higher Education Research Institute, Graduate School of Education, University of California, 1971–1986).

Table 3.4 Total Fall Enrollment in Institutions of Higher Education, by Racial/Ethnic Category and Sex: 1976–1984 (in thousands)

	1976	1978	1980	1982	1984	Percentage Change 1976–1982	Percentage Change 1982–1984
Total	10,985	11,230	12,088	12,388	12,162	+12.32	−1.82
Men	5,794	5,621	5,869	5,999	5,824	+3.54	−2.92
Women	5,191	5,609	6,219	6,389	6,337	+23.08	−.81
White	9,076	9,194	9,831	9,997	9,767	+10.15	−2.30
Men	4,814	4,613	4,772	4,830	4,667	+.33	−3.37
Women	4,262	4,581	5,059	5,167	5,099	+21.23	−1.32
Black	1,033	1,054	1,106	1,101	1,070	+7.07	−2.82
Men	470	453	463	458	435	−2.55	−5.02
Women	563	601	643	644	635	+14.39	−1.40
Hispanic	384	417	472	519	529	+35.16	+1.93
Men	210	212	232	252	251	+20.00	−.40
Women	174	205	240	267	278	+53.45	+4.12
Asian	197	235	286	351	382	+78.17	+8.83
Men	108	126	151	189	206	+75.00	+8.99
Women	89	109	135	162	176	+82.02	+8.64
American Indian	76	78	86	88	83	+15.79	−5.68
Men	38	37	39	40	37	+5.26	−7.50
Women	38	41	47	48	46	+26.32	−4.17
Nonresident Alien	219	253	306	331	332	+51.14	+.30
Men	154	180	211	230	229	+49.35	−.43
Women	65	73	94	101	103	+55.38	+1.98

Sources: Betty M. Vetter and Eleanor L. Babco, *Professional Women and Minorities* (Washington, DC: Commission on Professionals in Science and Technology, 1986); and National Center for Education Statistics, *Digest of Education Statistics, 1987* (Washington, DC: NCES, 1987).

relative gains for minorities came early in the decade. Between 1975 and 1986 the ethnic composition of the freshman class has been relatively constant.

Total fall enrollments of racial and ethnic groups for the 1976–1984 period are shown in Table 3.4. Overall enrollment increased from 1976 to 1982 and began to taper off during the 1982–1984 period. In the 1976–1982 period the enrollment of all ethnic groups, male and female, increased except for black men. The largest increases were gained by Hispanics and Asians, exceeding those of whites, both for men and women. In 1982–1984, the enrollment of Hispanics and Asians continued to grow, while other groups, including whites, declined. Black enrollment fell at a more rapid rate than that of whites, for both men and women. For American Indians, the percentage increase in enrollment from 1976 to 1982 more or less kept pace with that of whites, but the percentage decline in 1982–1984 was higher than that of whites.

The leveling off of enrollment among blacks was noted by Lorenzo Morris in his analysis of data from the 1976–1978 period.[11] He found this to be especially true at the graduate level, which constitutes the pool from which faculty will be drawn. Figures for 1984 show further deterioration in graduate enrollment. (See Table 3.5.) Morris noted that this

Table 3.5   Racial and Ethnic Background of Enrollees in Graduate and Professional Schools: 1976, 1978, and 1984

	1976	1978	1984
Graduate			
White	83.8%	82.8%	80.2%
Black	6.0	5.8	4.8
All Minorities*	11.2	10.4	9.9
Nonresident Aliens	5.9	6.8	9.9
Professional			
White	89.5	89.4	87.4
Black	4.5	4.5	4.8
All Minorities*	9.2	9.5	11.4
Nonresident Aliens	1.2	1.2	1.2

Sources: Lorenzo Morris et al., *Equal Educational Opportunity Scoreboard: The Status of Black Americans in Higher Education, 1970–79* (Washington, DC: Institute for the Study of Educational Policy, 1981); and National Center for Education Statistics, *Digest of Education Statistics, 1987* (Washington, DC: NCES, 1987).

*Includes blacks.

leveling off in enrollment was particularly distressing since it occurred at a time of high financial aid and relatively vigorous use of affirmative action.[12] The problem can only be exacerbated in an era of declining financial aid and more cautious pursuit of affirmative action after *Bakke.* Table 3.5 also shows that while minority enrollments in graduate schools declined after 1976, their enrollment in professional schools continued to increase. This trend may also reflect reduced financial aid and limited career opportunities in academic life.

In addition to whether or not minorities go to college, we are interested in *where* they go to college. We focus here on the proportions in two-year colleges as opposed to four-year colleges and, for blacks, enrollment in traditionally black colleges versus predominantly white colleges. Students enrolled in a four-year institution are more likely to obtain the bachelor's degree; those enrolled in two-year institutions must be accepted as transfer students by four-year schools in order to move toward the bachelor's degree. Failure to do so, of course, precludes them from degrees beyond the bachelor's. As Table 3.6 shows, minorities are more likely to be in two-year institutions than are whites. Hispanics and American Indians are among the groups most likely to be in two-year schools. However, the proportion of all students, including all minority groups, enrolled in two-year institutions has declined since 1976. Among whites, women are more likely to be in two-year institutions than are men, but for most minorities there are few or no gender differences.

One of the most striking changes over the past two decades has been the declining proportion of blacks enrolled in traditionally black institutions (TBIs). In 1964, 50 percent of blacks enrolled in college were in TBIs. By 1980 this proportion had dropped to under 20 percent. Black women are slightly less likely than black men to be in TBIs, but the difference is fairly small. Even though TBIs enroll a small proportion of black students, they are still a significant source of college degrees for blacks. While TBIs enrolled only 19 percent of all blacks in college in 1980, they awarded 37.6 percent of bachelor's degrees received by blacks, 26.8 percent of all master's degrees, and 30.1 percent of all first professional degrees conferred on blacks (Table 3.7). The fact that the TBIs award such a large proportion of degrees going to blacks is related to two things—the large proportion of blacks in white institutions who are in two-year institutions and the high attrition rates among blacks in white four-year institutions.[13]

Looking at degree conferrals among women by ethnic group, it is fairly clear that minority women are underrepresented in relation to

Table 3.6   Students Enrolled in Two-Year Institutions, by Race and
Ethnicity: 1976–1984; and by Sex, Race, and Ethnicity: 1978

	1976	1978	1980	1982	1984
All	42.5%	35.8%	37.4%	38.3%	37.1%
White	44.7	34.5	36.2	36.9	35.7
Men		32.0			
Women		37.0			
Black	49.7	42.0	42.6	44.4	42.7
Men		42.6			
Women		41.4			
Hispanic	59.0	48.4	54.0	56.0	54.4
Men		48.4			
Women		48.4			
Asian	51.6	41.2	43.4	45.0	43.2
Men		39.8			
Women		42.3			
American Indian	67.2	55.1	56.0	56.0	54.9
Men		54.1			
Women		56.1			
Nonresident Alien	*	20.6	21.0	18.6	15.8
Men					
Women					

Sources: Lorenzo Morris et al., *Equal Employment Opportunity Scoreboard: The Status of Black Americans in Higher Education, 1970–79* (Washington, DC: Institute for the Study of Educational Policy, 1981); Betty M. Vetter and Eleanor L. Babco, *Professional Women and Minorities* (Washington, DC: Commission on Professionals in Science and Technology, 1986); and National Center for Education Statistics, *Digest of Education Statistics, 1987* (Washington, DC: NCES, 1987).
*Not available.

their representation in the population (Table 3.8). In 1976 the proportion of degrees awarded to women was less than 50 percent, except for black women at the bachelor's and master's level. By 1984–1985 women gained relative to men within each racial and ethnic group, and the proportion of degrees earned by women exceeded that earned by men at the bachelor's and master's level among most groups, including white, black, Hispanic, and American Indian. Only Asian women remained

**Table 3.7   Earned Degrees Conferred on Blacks, by Type of Institution:
1980–1981**

	Total Number Conferred	Conferred by Traditionally Black Institutions	
		Number	Percentage
Bachelor's Degree	60,533	22,732	37.6%
Men		10,103	
Women		12,629	
Master's Degree	17,133	4,598	26.8
Men		1,860	
Women		2,738	
Doctorate	1,265	102	8.1
Men		65	
Women		37	
First Professional Degree	2,929	883	30.1
Men		620	
Women		263	

Source: National Center for Education Statistics, *Digest of Education Statistics, 1987* (Washington, DC: NCES, 1987).

below their male counterparts in degrees awarded. Black women continue to fare better compared with black men than do other women with respect to their male counterparts. At the doctoral level only black women and American Indian women earned more degrees than their male counterparts.

Between 1976 and 1985 the proportion of all degrees going to women increased by 16 percentage points at the bachelor's level, approximately 3 percentage points at the master's level, and nearly 10 percentage points at the doctoral level. While minority women shared some of the gains at the bachelor's degree level, they made little or no progress at the graduate level. The fact that they are collecting a larger share of the graduate degrees going to minorities merely indicates that the share going to minority males must be declining.

Enrollment and degree conferral for minority women in professional schools presents a more positive picture. Between 1976 and 1983 the

Table 3.8 Percentage of Degrees Awarded to Women, by Race and Ethnicity: 1976–1977, 1980–1981, and 1984–1985

	1976–1977		1980–1981		1984–1985	
	Percentage of Racial Total	Percentage of All Degrees	Percentage of Racial Total	Percentage of All Degrees	Percentage of Racial Total	Percentage of All Degrees
Bachelor's Degree						
All Women		46.4%		49.8%		55.9%
White	45.9%	40.4	49.7%	42.9	51.1%	47.9
Black	57.2	3.7	59.6	3.9	60.0	3.9
Hispanic	45.1	0.9	50.5	1.2	53.1	1.6
American Indian	45.9	0.2	52.7	0.2	52.5	0.2
Asian	44.8	0.7	46.2	0.9	46.6	1.3
Nonresident Alien	27.8	0.5	27.7	0.7	30.9	1.0
Master's Degree						
All Women		47.2		50.5		50.0

White	47.8	40.2	52.1	42.7	53.0	42.2
Black	63.0	4.2	64.1	3.7	63.4	2.9
Hispanic	46.2	0.9	52.3	1.1	56.4	1.3
American Indian	46.1	0.1	51.5	0.2	52.9	0.2
Asian	39.1	0.6	40.0	0.9	37.9	1.0
Nonresident Alien	22.2	1.2	24.8	1.9	27.1	2.4
Doctorate						
All Women	25.4	25.0	33.2	31.1	37.4	34.1
White	38.9	20.6	45.1	26.2	51.9	28.3
Black	26.6	1.5	39.3	1.7	36.4	1.7
Hispanic	29.5	0.4	26.9	0.5	51.8	0.7
American Indian	17.9	0.1	25.3	0.1	27.0	0.1
Asian	13.3	0.9	15.2	0.7	16.6	0.8
Nonresident Alien		1.5		1.9		2.5

Source: Betty M. Vetter and Eleanor L. Babco, *Professional Women and Minorities* (Washington, DC: Commission on Professionals in Science and Technology, 1981, 1986, and 1987).

percentage of degrees going to minority women in dentistry doubled and the percentage of medicine and law degrees awarded to minority women increased by more than 50 percent. (See Table 3.9.) Since 1983 overall enrollments in these fields have declined somewhat, but the proportion of minority women has increased. During the 1986–1987 school year minority women were 5 percent of first-year enrollments in medical schools, 10 percent in dental schools, and 12 percent in law schools.[14] These figures suggest that minority students seeking post-graduate training are more likely to enter professional schools than to pursue degrees in other graduate fields. This deceleration in graduate enrollment has serious implications for the composition of present and future college faculties.

Minority Women as Faculty Members and Administrators

The search for minority faculty members during the early days of affirmative action sometimes led to cynical manipulations, even on the part of institutions sincerely interested in increasing minority representation on their faculties. One minority scholar reports that when she was interviewed for her first faculty position, faculty members who found that she could fill both a "minority slot" and a "female slot" looked at their array of goals to meet and asked (only partially facetiously), "You don't happen to speak Spanish, do you?" Such opportunities for filling quotas by use of "two-fers" and "three-fers" led to the belief that minority women were favored in the increasingly tight academic labor markets of the 1970s. Yet, the evidence does not support this assumption. Neither information on the pool of eligibles nor data on faculty composition indicate disproportionate gains by minority women.

It is difficult to establish trends in the conferral of doctorates and therefore the growth in the stock of minority women PhDs because very little good data are available. The National Research Council conducts the most exhaustive survey of doctoral recipients in the United States. However, by their own admission, the data they collect have limited value in establishing trends for minority doctorates because of large nonresponse rates in early years and three revisions in the item on racial/ethnic group in the survey questionnaire between 1974 and 1986.[15] Moreover, as is almost always the case, separate data on minority women are not available at the same level of detail as they are for women as a group or for all minorities.

In 1973, the first year for which information is available, 3,971 of the 33,727 (11.8 percent) doctoral degrees conferred were awarded to

Table 3.9 First Professional Degrees Awarded to Women, by Race and Ethnicity: 1976–1977 and 1982–1983

	Dentistry		Medicine		Law		Theology	
	Percentage of Racial Total	Percentage of All Degrees	Percentage of Racial Total	Percentage of All Degrees	Percentage of Racial Total	Percentage of All Degrees	Percentage of Racial Total	Percentage of All Degrees
1976–1977								
All Women	6.5%	7.2%	18.3%	18.8%	26.0%	22.5%	10.0%	9.9%
White	21.6	5.9	33.9	16.4	32.9	20.2	12.5	9.1
Black	8.6	0.9	19.0	1.8	18.2	1.3	8.2	0.5
Hispanic	12.5	0.1	16.7	0.0[a]	22.1	0.4		0.1
American Indian		0.0[a]		0.0[a]		0.1	0.0	0.0
Asian	9.3	0.2	18.5	0.4	32.9	0.4	14.6	0.1
Nonresident Alien	8.3	0.1	18.0	0.2	17.1	0.1	4.1	0.1
1982–1983								
All Women		16.7		24.9		36.1[b]		16.9[b]
White	16.1	14.1	23.8	21.1	34.9	26.8	18.8	13.6
Black	35.4	1.2	42.1	2.1	50.2	1.9	18.3	0.8
Hispanic	19.8	0.3	22.8	0.6	32.5	0.7	16.7	0.2
American Indian	10.0	0.0[a]	23.5	0.1	35.4	0.1	30.8	0.1
Asian	22.1	0.8	26.2	0.8	40.0	0.5	18.4	0.1
Nonresident Alien	24.6	0.3	22.3	0.2	33.6	0.6	5.2	0.2

Source: Betty M. Vetter and Eleanor L. Babco, *Professional Women and Minorities* (Washington, DC: Commission on Professionals in Science and Technology, 1981 and 1987).

[a] Less than 0.09 percent.

[b] Numbers do not add because of nonreporting.

known members of minority groups. However, only 37 percent of these degree recipients were U.S. citizens. In 1986 the proportion of doctoral degrees going to minorities was 19.9 percent, of which only 32 percent were U.S. citizens. However, the number of degrees awarded to known minority citizens increased by 37 percent, while the overall total awarded to U.S. citizens dropped by 17 percent. Consequently, the proportion of minority degree recipients among U.S. citizens increased from 5.3 percent in 1973 to 8.8 percent in 1986. In 1986 minority women received about 49 percent of the degrees awarded to minority citizens, or 3.1 percent of the total.[16] In general, black and Hispanic doctoral recipients are older than Asian or white doctoral recipients. They take somewhat longer to complete their degrees and they are more likely to opt for teaching.

These increases in degree conferrals are changing the composition of the eligible pool for faculty in some areas, but not necessarily in all areas. The best information on the stock of minority doctoral recipients is for those in the sciences and engineering. In 1973 minorities constituted about 6 percent of the pool of doctoral scientists and engineers (Table 3.10). Asians were 75 percent of the minority PhD scientists (4.5 percent of all degree holders), and blacks were the next largest group. Among doctoral scientists, blacks were more likely to be in mathematics, social science, and chemistry while Asians were more likely to be in engineering and physics.[17]

By 1981 minority representation in the pool of doctoral scientists and engineers had increased to 10.9 percent. Asians had decreased to 71 percent of the minority total (7.7 percent of all doctorates), and the number of black scientists increased but remained a fairly constant percentage of the pool of minority scientists. Further advances were made in the following years, with minorities increasing slightly to 10.6 percent of degree holders in 1985. Blacks were still more likely to be in social science and Asians were still highly concentrated in engineering. There were 7,340 minority women among the doctoral scientists and engineers in 1985, up from 4,809 in 1981—1.72 percent of the total pool and 11.5 percent of all women doctoral scientists. Over 60 percent of the minority women were Asians, 24 percent were black, 14 percent were Hispanic, and the remainder were American Indians. Among new doctoral recipients, minority women were overrepresented in engineering, social science, and psychology and underrepresented in the physical and biological sciences and in computer science.[18] Minorities were actually a smaller percentage of the pool of those with humanities doctorates, constituting only 6.2 percent of all PhDs in these fields in 1983. A subsequent study of humanities doctorates in the United States showed an

Table 3.10 Characteristics of Doctoral Scientists and Engineers, by Race and Ethnicity: 1973; and by Race, Ethnicity, and Sex: 1981 and 1985

	1973	1981		1985	
		Minority Group as Percentage of Total	Minority Women as Percentage of Total	Minority Group as Percentage of Total	Minority Women as Percentage of Total
Total Population	244,829	358,600	4,809	424,616	7,340
All Minorities	6.0%	10.9%	1.34%	11.3%	1.72%
Black	0.8	1.2	0.30	1.4	0.42
Hispanic	0.6	1.4	0.15	1.5	0.24
Asian	4.5	7.7	0.81	8.4	1.04
American Indian, Alaskan Native, and Other	0.2	0.6	0.09	0.1	0.01

Sources: National Research Council, *Minority Groups Among United States Doctorate Level Scientists, Engineers and Scholars, 1973* (Washington, DC: National Academy of Sciences, 1974); National Research Council, *Science, Engineering and Humanities Doctorates in the United States* (Washington, DC: National Academy Press, 1982); Paula Quick Hall, "Minority Women in Science: A Statistical View," *Newsletter of the National Network of Minority Women in Science* (undated); Betty M. Vetter and Eleanor L. Babco, *Professional Women and Minorities* (Washington, DC: Commission on Professionals in Science and Technology, 1987).

increase to 6.6 percent in 1985.[19] Among those with humanities doctorates, Hispanics are the largest group, followed by blacks.

While the pool of minority women PhDs has been growing steadily and their share of all PhDs awarded is growing, they have not made much progress in terms of faculty appointments and tenure. In 1983 minority women were 11.5 percent of all women faculty members, up from 11.0 percent in 1975. Their gains were much smaller than those of minority males, who increased their representation among male faculty from 6.8 to 8.8 percent. All of the gains among minority women were made by nonblack minorities (Table 3.11).

In 1983, when minority women were 11.5 percent of women faculty, they were 2.8 percent of all full-time instructional faculty. As might be expected, they were more heavily concentrated in the lower ranks, being only 1.1 percent of all full professors (Table 3.12). While some progress was made during the 1975–1983 period, the relatively static size of the college workforce limited upward mobility for those at the bottom. This problem was probably exacerbated for blacks and American Indians who were more likely to be in education, one of the fields that has been declining over the past decade. Among minority scientists, tenure rates were similar to those for whites, except among blacks. While 61 percent of the whites on science faculties had tenure and 57 percent of all minority scientists were tenured, only 45 percent of all black scientists had tenure. (Separate rates are not available for minority women.)[20]

If minority women are a small proportion of the faculties in higher education, they are a microscopic proportion of the administrative structure. Data from 1978 indicate that minority women were only 0.9 percent of higher education administrators. They are most likely to be in student affairs positions and least likely to be in chief executive positions (Table 3.13). At mid-decade (1975) minority women administrators were practically nonexistent in white, single-sex institutions and were more likely to be in two-year institutions than in four-year institutions. For black women, the greatest opportunities existed at minority (primarily black) institutions, although the pattern was similar to that for women in general—least likely to be in chief executive positions and most likely to be in student affairs positions.

One might expect a higher incidence of black women in administrative positions at black women's colleges, yet more black women have served as presidents of black coeducational institutions (three) and white community colleges. As of the early 1980s only one black woman had headed a black women's four-year institution, and when she retired she was replaced by a man. While black women have also served on the trustee boards of black institutions, few have chaired the boards.[21]

Table 3.11 Distribution of Male and Female Full-Time Faculty at Institutions of Higher Education, by Race and Ethnicity: 1975, 1977, 1979, and 1983

	1975		1977		1979		1983	
	Men	Women	Men	Women	Men	Women	Men	Women
Total	100%	100%	100%	100%	100%	100%	100%	100%
White	93.2	88.9	92.4	88.4	92.1	88.4	91.2	88.5
Minority	6.8	11.0	7.6	11.6	7.9	11.6	8.8	11.5
Black	3.2	7.9	3.3	8.2	3.3	7.9	3.1	7.0
Hispanic	1.3	1.5	1.4	1.7	1.5	1.8	1.5	1.7
Asian American	2.0	1.4	2.5	1.5	2.8	1.6	4.0	2.5
American Indian	0.2	0.2	0.2	0.2	0.3	0.2	0.3	0.3

Sources: Equal Employment Opportunity Commission, *Higher Education Staff Information Report* (EEO-6), 1975, 1977, 1979; and National Center for Education Statistics, *Digest of Education Statistics, 1987* (Washington, DC: NCES, 1987).

Note: Total percentages may not add up because of rounding.

Table 3.12 Full-Time Instructional Faculty, by Rank, Sex, Race, and Ethnicity: 1983

	Total	Professors	Associate Professors	Assistant Professors
Total Number	470,673	128,142	111,887	113,330
Male	73.0%	89.0%	77.9%	65.4%
Female	27.0	11.0	22.1	34.6
White				
Male	66.6	83.2	71.6	66.1
Female	23.9	9.9	19.9	30.4
Black				
Male	2.2	1.6	2.2	2.6
Female	1.9	0.6	1.4	2.5
Asian				
Male	2.9	3.2	2.8	3.4
Female	0.7	0.3	0.5	1.0
Hispanic				
Male	1.1	0.9	1.1	1.2
Female	0.5	0.2	0.4	0.6
American Indian				
Male	0.2	0.2	0.2	0.2
Female	0.1	0.0	0.0	0.1

Source: National Center for Education Statistics, *Digest of Education Statistics, 1987* (Washington, DC: NCES, 1987).

Table 3.13 Minorities in Higher Education Administration: 1978

	Total	White Men	Minority Men	White Women	Minority Women
Chief Executive Officer	1,127	95.6%	2.3%	2.0%	0.1%
Administrative Affairs Office	4,945	83.7	3.4	12.0	0.9
Academic Affairs	4,478	81.6	2.5	15.3	0.7
Student Affairs	4,631	79.0	4.1	15.7	1.2
External Affairs	1,434	81.9	2.3	15.1	0.7
Total	16,615	83.1	3.2	13.5	0.9

Source: Betty M. Vetter and Eleanor L. Babco, *Professional Women and Minorities* (Washington, DC: Commission on Professionals in Science and Technology, 1981).

Conclusions

While minority women have made progress during the past decade, they have certainly not achieved equality. They continue to be less likely than white men to go to college and, except for black women, are less likely than men of their own ethnic group to complete four or more years of college. The educational gains made by minorities were heavily concentrated in the early part of the decade, for by the end of the 1970s minority enrollment in both undergraduate and graduate schools began to level off. While the slowdown was greater for minority males (blacks in particular), it also affected minority women. Only in Asians and Hispanics were increases in enrollment larger than those for whites.

The one bright spot in the enrollment picture is that minority women continued to make significant gains in many professional schools. Unfortunately, this has little impact on the pool from which college faculty are drawn. However, these women can hardly be faulted for responding to market forces—higher starting salaries and, possibly, greater opportunities for advancement. Certainly the picture for minority women on college faculties has not been one of great optimism. Their share of faculty slots grew slightly over the decade, but their chances for achieving tenure seem to be lower than average. To some extent, this probably stems from their isolation from those faculty members who could serve as mentors and who could provide access to research funds and research opportunities. The same isolation reduces their chances of moving up to administrative positions where they can advance themselves and serve as mentors and advisers to other minority women. Instead of leading the charmed life of a "two-fer," minority women in higher education may be getting the worst of both worlds—as both minorities and women.

Notes

1. The recent immigrant group does not include those nonresident aliens who came to the United States solely for educational purposes, but those who came prior to entry into higher education and who had the intention of becoming permanent residents.

2. For discussion of some of these issues, see the National Institute of Education series on minority women: *Conference on the Educational and Occupational Needs of American Indian Women*, October 1980; *Conference on the Educational and Occupational Needs of Asian and Pacific American Women*, October 1980; *Conference on the Educational and Occupational Needs of Black Women*, April

1978; and *Conference on the Educational and Occupational Needs of Hispanic Women,* September 1980.

3. Alice Rossi and Ann Calderwood, eds., *Academic Women on the Move* (New York: Russell Sage Foundation, 1973).

4. Richard Freeman, *The Overeducated American* (New York: Academic Press, 1976), p. 137.

5. Constance M. Carroll, "Three's a Crowd: The Dilemma of the Black Woman in Higher Education," in Rossi and Calderwood, *Academic Women on the Move,* pp. 173–185.

6. Carroll, "Three's a Crowd," pp. 180–181.

7. Paula Quick Hall, *Problems and Solutions in the Education, Employment, and Personal Choices of Minority Women in Science* (Washington, DC: American Association for the Advancement of Science, August 1981).

8. See Michael E. Borus, ed., *Tomorrow's Workers* (Lexington, MA: Heath, 1983); and John R. Shea, *Years for Decision: A Longitudinal Study of the Educational and Labor Market Experience of Young Women,* vol. 1 (Columbus: Center of Human Resource Research, Ohio State University, 1971).

9. It should be noted that among the 18-to-24-year-olds, female high school completion rates are higher except among Asians.

10. To some extent enrollment rates for men during this period were influenced by changes in the nation's military manpower policies. In the early 1970s the draft was ended and replaced by an all-volunteer system of armed forces recruitment. Educational exemptions under the draft no longer provided an incentive for men to enroll or remain in school.

11. Lorenzo Morris, with Floyd Hayes and Doris James, *Equal Employment Opportunity Scoreboard: The Status of Black Americans in Higher Education, 1970–79* (Washington, DC: Institute for the Study of Educational Policy, 1981).

12. There is some evidence that lack of sufficient financial aid for blacks was a major factor in failure to pursue or complete graduate programs. Also, the aid available was in fields where blacks were already overrepresented. See National Advisory Committee on Black Higher Education and Black Colleges and Universities, *A Losing Battle: The Decline in Black Participation in Graduate and Professional Education* (Washington, DC: U.S. Office of Education, October 1980).

13. See National Advisory Committee on Black Higher Education and Black Colleges and Universities, *Admission and Retention Problems of Black Students at Seven Predominantly White Universities* (Washington, DC: U.S. Office of Education, October 1980).

14. Betty M. Vetter and Eleanor L. Babco, *Professional Women and Minorities* (Washington, DC: Commission on Professionals in Science and Technology, 1987).

15. National Research Council, *Summary Report 1985: Doctorate Recipients from United States Universities* (Washington, DC: National Academy Press, 1986), p. 39.

16. National Research Council, *Minority Groups Among United States Doctorate-Level Scientists, Engineers and Scholars, 1973* (Washington, DC: National Academy of Sciences, 1974); and unpublished data, National Research Council, Office of Scientific and Engineering Personnel, Doctorate Records File, 1986.

17. National Research Council, *Minority Groups.*

18. Paula Quick Hall, "Minority Women in Science—A Statistical View," *Newsletter of the National Network of Minority Women in Science* (undated).

19. National Research Council, *Humanities Doctorates in the United States, 1985 Profile* (Washington, DC: National Academy Press, 1986).

20. Hall, "Minority Women in Science."

21. Beverly Guy-Sheftall, "Black Women and Higher Education: Spelman and Bennett Colleges Revisited," *Journal of Negro Education* 51 (Summer 1982):278–281.

4

Re-entry Women

Historical Overview

The story of continuing education for women in the 1970s is essentially the story of women's changing life experiences during that period. Demographic and political indicators of social change—rising age at first marriage, rising divorce rates, falling birth rates, increased participation in the labor force, increased attention to women's rights—were accompanied by internal changes in the way women viewed themselves and their place in society. This chapter deals with the effect of these changes on the educational needs and aspirations of women as reflected in their decisions about further education and with the response of the educational system to those needs.

For the purpose of this discussion, re-entry women are those who have returned (or considered returning) to higher education in a college or university setting to begin or complete degrees after an interruption of greater or lesser duration. Usually the interruption, and there may be more than one, results from the assumption of adult responsibilities. Returning women are usually older than the traditional student, though not always; they are not usually residential, but they may be; they may be full- or part-time students. They are, in short, infinitely varied in their situations and their goals. As a population they have been identified for a variety of special programs and support systems. We are not concerned here with adult education or other nondegree courses, valuable though they may be. Our focus is on access to the mainstream curriculum.

As a first step it is essential to identify and describe re-entry women and the reasons for their return to higher education in large numbers in the early 1960s and since. We begin our account with this task.

The Context: Balancing Work and Home

As Mirra Komarovsky reminded us 35 years ago, to raise the question of women's education is to face the whole problem of women's role in society.[1] The fundamental problem for contemporary women is rooted in the separation of the sexes in the home and the workplace and in the resulting patterns of parental responsibility for the nurturance of children. Well before World War II Alva Myrdal and Viola Klein began collecting data for their study published in 1956, *Women's Two Roles: Home and Work*.[2] Klein, a British sociologist, developed a structural theory that allowed women to visualize their life span as a succession of three phases, each dominated mainly by one function: a period of training and education, followed if possible by years devoted to raising a family, with these in turn being succeeded by a period during which past training and experience are put to wider social use. Myrdal and Klein, like others before and since, did not resolve in their own minds just what the balance should ideally be between family and career (or employment). On the one hand, they extolled the possibility of careers compatible with family responsibilities as a postulate dictated by common sense "disappointing though it may be to many an idealist who . . . hoped for complete and unconditional equality between the sexes." But, immediately, they assert that discrimination will not be abolished until and unless women are able to compete with men on equal terms.

Although their formulation was not a challenge to the traditional understanding of sex roles, the "new establishmentarian two-role policy" had an impact on American practice. In the 1968 revision of *Women's Two Roles*, Myrdal and Klein discuss ways to keep the vocational spirit alive and include as an outstanding example the "Continuing Education schemes which many American colleges have set up in recent years."[3] For example, the University of Michigan established in 1964 a Center for Continuing Education of Women with three major goals: to help women return to education; to help the University *change* in response to their special needs; and, when time and resources allowed, to help women at home keep up with their career fields and to encourage undergraduates to look ahead to the probable patterns of their work and family lives. It was designed, in other words, to accommodate a sequential pattern of home and work.

The Myrdal and Klein formulation was influential as a model, but it was not the only one. President Bunting of Radcliffe College, in launching the Radcliffe Institute for Independent Study (now the Bunting Institute) in 1960, was not guided by a theory that projected interruptions in education as normative for women. In spite of the separation of the Radcliffe Institute from the Harvard-Radcliffe degree-granting process, Bunting's goal was to keep women in the academic mainstream—to make it possible through educational and institutional support for outstanding women *not* to endanger a developing career by interrupting their educations during the child-bearing years.[4]

Elizabeth Cless, another of the pioneers in continuing education for women, makes clear in *Some Action of Her Own,* edited by Helen Astin, that the educators who developed the early experiments were not seeking to create alternative systems, but rather to explore possible ways of making higher education available part time or full time as needed throughout a woman's life.[5] *Some Action of Her Own* gives an account of the continuing education movement of the 1960s. In a review of the book, the movement was referred to as an early effort to combat both sexism and ageism in colleges and universities.[6] It should be noted, however, that "sexism" and "ageism" were not words in the vocabularies of those who led the movement.

Although not captive to easy assumptions about sequential stages for women's life choices, these educators of women *were* time bound and aware of women's participation rates in the workforce. In 1960 women in the child-bearing years *were* out of the labor force (see Figure 4.1). Providing special programs for their re-entry to education after the interval at home made sense, especially since trained personnel, including college teachers, were in short supply and in "post-Sputnik" demand. But Figure 4.1 also tells us why efforts to build a model for educational planning that fits the real lives of women are at risk. Within a short 20 years women were fairly evenly distributed in the workforce across age groups. As Jessie Bernard has pointed out, the rate of social and economic change has consistently outdistanced theorizing about how to manage the variables of marriage and children, workforce preparation, and work.[7]

Special Programs: What Is Equity?

By the early 1970s a number of assessments of continuing education programs, both general and institutionally specific, appeared. The Women's Bureau in 1971 listed 375 institutions as illustrative of programs established with a specific concern for adult women.[8] The American Association of University Women in 1970 surveyed 750 colleges and universities of which 454 responded.[9] Ninety-five percent "offered opportunities" for mature women to complete degrees, but only 49 percent

Figure 4.1 Labor Force Participation Rates, by Age and Sex: 1950–1980

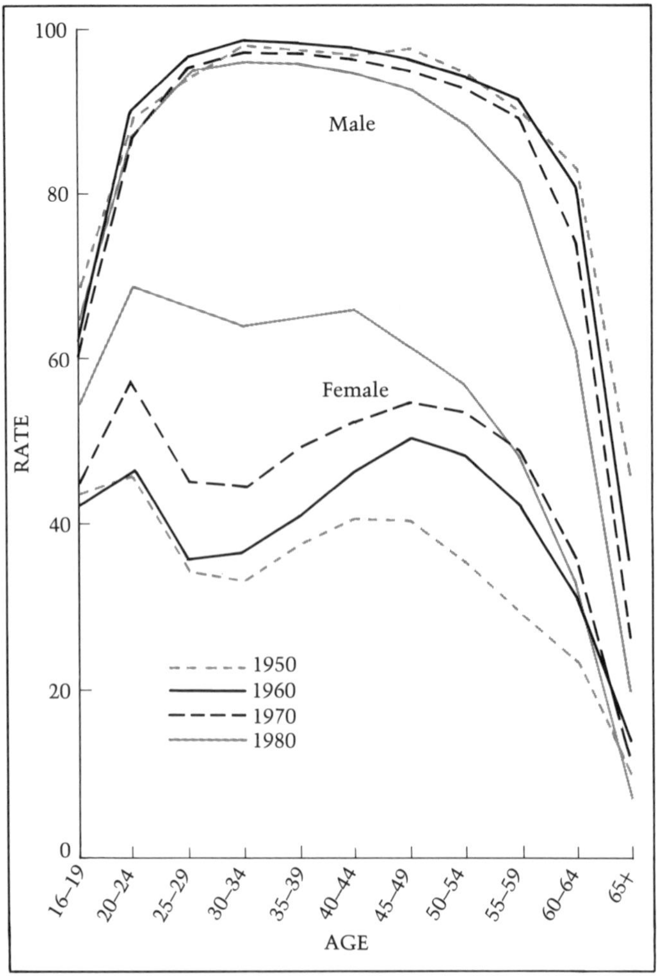

Source: Suzanne M. Bianchi and Daphne Spain, *American Women in Transition* (New York: Russell Sage Foundation, 1986), p. 144.

reported institutional concessions, and no one knew how many women were involved. Jacquelyn Mattfeld, in an unpublished report in 1971, examined more closely the 156 institutions that the Women's Bureau had identified as programs admitting or facilitating the admission of adult women into degree programs.[10] She concluded that the AAUW 95 percent had doubtful meaning, noting that the "lustrous names in private education" were "conspicuous by their absence" and that "it has fallen to the larger state universities and a smaller number of private ones to carry out on a considerably broader scale the policies and practices introduced by early planners of continuing education for women." Moreover, Mattfeld observed that even these programs for women were not considered central to the institutions that host them. Nevertheless, she attributed real if modest success to continuing education programs in achieving their potential for moving women into nontraditional careers, for addressing career changes and upgrading women in the marketplace, for improving women's position in academe, for offering sensitive personal counseling and support, and for encouraging research on women, while continuing to advocate for the institutional flexibilities needed for recurrent education. Mattfeld, too, was prescient. All of these purposes in varying combinations are the province of today's continuing education programs, melded, in many cases, in programs and centers under other titles.[11]

Mattfeld's 1971 assessment was corroborated in 1976 with the publication of *Some Action of Her Own*. In it, Carole Leland describes continuing education programs as "academic misfits which lasted" and which "reflect the heritage of committed, visionary leadership."[12] She is generous in evaluating the leadership and the programmatic successes of the programs, but candid in noting their limited, even threatened, resources and their academic marginality. More pointedly, she warns, ". . . if continuing education programs for women are to be maintained or expanded, the successes they claim, the problems they face, and the priorities of their financially beleaguered institutions must be closely scrutinized."

The assessment and the warning were all but academic as the women's movement asserted an alternative view of equity in higher education, a view which submerged for a time the voices urging structural changes to accommodate the special needs of women. The cry for equality of the sexes without regard for difference enabled the strategies which produced the protections of the law against discrimination. As a result of the evolving understanding, women's centers became even more diverse. The older programs benefited from the ferment; those that survived the economic strains of the time enlarged their responsibilities or shifted their priorities. A few, like the University of Michigan Center, have done both but have also remained vigorous in their response to the special needs of women who are balancing their domestic roles with education or work.

During the 1970s the number of women students increased rapidly and by 1979 they represented the majority of total enrollment in higher education. They postponed marriage and children and moved into all the professional fields in ever larger numbers. They did not, however, press institutions to provide any kind of structural response to assist them in achieving their aspirations; rather they accepted the institutional status quo.

Currently, women educators are debating strategies for educational equity. Some contend that gender differences should be de-emphasized while others continue to advocate special educational programs and support systems. In 1981 the Project on the Status and Education of Women of the Association of American Colleges published a set of 15 papers identifying the barriers to education experienced by re-entry women and recommending measures which institutions can adopt to provide equal access to this population.[13] The reports were directed to degree-granting institutions, and they came at a time when the number of traditional age students was declining, making re-entry women and men an important pool from which to draw to maintain enrollments. Among the measures recommended were special recruitment programs, credit for prior learning or credit by examination, refresher courses, academic and career counseling services, financial aid for part-time students, and child care and other support services.

There are no comprehensive studies to indicate the extent to which institutions of higher education offer such programs and services at the present time. A summary of the most recent available data is provided by Carol Tittle and Elenor Denker in their 1980 volume, *Returning Women Students in Higher Education.*[14] Although a majority of colleges and universities offer some types of services or programs for returning women, ·the number of institutions with fully developed programs to recruit, orient, and support returning women students for degree-credit courses is probably less than 30 percent and possibly as little as 10 percent. Such programs are more likely to be found in two-year colleges where they frequently serve low-income women with no prior degree. In this respect they differ from the earlier programs of continuing education that were established at major universities and women's colleges with a clientele that was middle class for the most part and included a significant proportion who already held the first degree.

It is clear that higher education has not yet adjusted to the differences in life patterns of men and women. In an issue of the *Journal of the National Association of Women Deans, Administrators, and Counselors* devoted to the continuing education of women, Joy Rice, associate professor at the University of Wisconsin–Madison, states that the challenge is "to develop the institutions and structures that will enable both men and women to have choices and options."[15]

Theoretical Perspectives

There are several lines of inquiry relating to adult development that may in time influence the adjustment of higher education to the changing lives of women and men. Janet Giele, associate professor of Sociology at Brandeis University, has defined a concept that she calls "crossover," which posits variations from prescribed notions of the normal life sequences of education, family, and work. Instead, Giele sees individual differences in the major phases of life. For some, education may come after child-bearing and early work experience; for others, the sequence will be reversed or follow an intermittent pattern. Giele says that educational policies should be designed to permit maximum crossover and maximum flexibility so that persons can take up developmental tasks according to their own schedule and their own individual life history.[16]

A second exploration with a bearing on educational policy is the work of Jacqueline Eccles,[17] a developmental psychologist at the University of Michigan. She and her students are constructing a model of achievement choices based on values which free them from explaining women's achievement patterns in male achievement terms. They reject the presumption that career development patterns of women that are different from those of men are "deficient" in some sense. They may be equal without being identical.

These theories suggest a context for thinking about re-entry women in higher education. They raise issues of educational equity on which much remains to be done. Centers for continuing education of women have played an important role in encouraging and engendering relevant research. In 1967 leaders of a number of centers with varying charters from their institutions banded together as the National Coalition for Research on Women. As educational program designers and counselors, they hoped to collect information about career needs and achievements of women and to collect national data about women returning to education. These plans were overwhelmed by the broader economic and social changes brought about by the women's movement and were not carried out. However, the coalition was instrumental in securing support from the Carnegie Corporation for the study of 15 prototypical continuing education centers and their participants and alumnae reported in *Some Action of Her Own*. It was the culminating activity related to the coalition, whose functions were subsequently absorbed in part by the American Council on Education Office of Women's Programs.[18] The coalition was succeeded over a decade later by the National Council for Research on Women, which emerged from the women's studies movement of the 1970s (see chapter 13). Several leaders of the earlier coalition became active members of the council.

National Trends in Higher Education Enrollment

The increase in the enrollment of women represents nearly 80 percent of the growth of total enrollment in institutions of higher education from 1970 to 1985.[19] In particular, striking increases in the number of older students, of part-time students, and of students in two-year institutions all primarily reflect increased numbers of women students. Between 1970 and 1985 the total number of students aged 25 and over in higher education increased from 2.4 million to 5.1 million. The number of women in that group more than tripled during the period, while the number of men less than doubled. The figures are shown in Table 4.1.

During the same period (1970 to 1985) the number of part-time students increased from 2.4 million to 5.1 million. Of the total number of part-time students in 1984, 57 percent were women. Older students are far more likely to be enrolled part time. In 1985, 73 percent of all students and 74 percent of women students aged 25 and over were enrolled part time. The number of students enrolled in two-year institutions rose from 2.2 million in 1970 to 4.5 million in 1985, of which the proportion of women was 41 percent in 1970 and 56 percent in 1985. A majority of all students, men and women, attending two-year colleges do so part time.[20]

While the period between 1970 and 1985 saw rapid increases in the numbers of women enrolled in professional degree programs, they nevertheless remained considerably behind the men. Returning women in particular were unlikely to enroll in nontraditional professional areas. Such programs, at least at the major elite institutions, enrolled few stu-

Table 4.1   Enrollments in Postsecondary Institutions, by Sex and Age Group: 1970 and 1985 (in thousands)

Age Group	1970		1985	
	Female	Male	Female	Male
18–24 Years	2,528	3,408	3,421	3,494
25–34 Years	471	1,091	1,649	1,565
35 Years and Over	409	415	1,246	639
Total	3,408	4,914	6,316	5,898
Percentage Aged 25 Years and Over	25.8%	30.6%	45.8%	38.7%

Source: National Center for Education Statistics, *Digest of Education Statistics, 1987* (Washington, DC: NCES, 1987).

Table 4.2   Enrollment in Institutions of Higher Education,
by Sex, Age, and Attendance Status: 1970 and 1985

Sex and Age	Numbers (in thousands)		Percentage Part-Time	
	1970	1985	1970	1985
Total	8,581	12,247	32.2%	42.2%
Male	5,044	5,818	30.5	38.8
14–17 Years	129	121	3.9	15.7
18–19 Years	1,349	1,230	6.2	9.9
20–21 Years	1,095	1,216	9.6	15.5
22–24 Years	964	1,048	32.6	30.3
25–29 Years	783	991	58.2	59.8
30–34 Years	308	574	76.6	73.9
35 Years and Over	415	639	81.9	84.8
Female	3,537	6,429	34.6	46.1
14–17 Years	129	113	9.3	10.6
18–19 Years	1,250	1,370	8.8	11.4
20–21 Years	785	1,166	16.3	18.7
22–24 Years	493	885	53.1	43.9
25–29 Years	292	962	72.6	68.8
30–34 Years	179	687	84.4	76.7
35 Years and Over	409	1,246	85.6	80.1

Source: National Center for Education Statistics, *Digest of Education Statistics, 1987* (Washington, DC: NCES, 1987), p. 123.

dents on a part-time basis and generally enrolled fewer students at older ages than did graduate or professional programs in more traditional fields for women.

Although women and men are now enrolling in essentially equal numbers at ages 18–19 and 20–21, the drop-off among women is still evident in the 22–24 age group, as indicated in Table 4.2. The drop-off was not as severe in 1985 as it was in 1970, but there continues to be a greater likelihood that women will return to campus after a break in their education. Moreover, a cumulative educational deficit of women continues to show in the adult population. In 1985, 23 percent of men but only 16 percent of women aged 25 and over had completed four years or more of college.[21]

This discrepancy in educational attainment also shows clearly in the comparative education of husbands and wives. Among most married couples, the husband's educational attainment is significantly greater than that of the wife. This discrepancy is the reality that women have faced as they sought to enter or re-enter the labor force.

Recent decades have seen a dramatic surge in the number of women in the paid labor force. More to the point, this increase is primarily a result of increased participation by married women, particularly married women with children. Most of these women are concentrated in a narrow range of occupations, primarily clerical, service, and lower-paying professional and technical work, especially health care and primary and secondary school teaching. The median earnings of women have remained about two thirds of the earnings of men. It seems clear that correcting women's educational deficit must be a major part of any strategy to upgrade employment opportunities for women and to reduce the difference in earned income between men and women.

Demographic Characteristics of Returning Women— The Early Years

Who are the returning women? How has the population of women seeking to enter or re-enter mainstream degree programs, graduate or undergraduate, changed since the mid 1960s? What characteristics have remained the same? Since 1964 the Center for Continuing Education of Women (CEW) at the University of Michigan has maintained annual records describing the women who have come to the center for counseling and other services. These records provide perhaps the best available profile of women returning for baccalaureate or graduate degrees.

By the end of 1968, data were available for 1,752 women who had come to the center since it opened in the autumn of 1964. Three fourths of these women were married; the rest were widowed, divorced, or single. Three fourths of the women had children. Their average age was 35; a third of them were over 40 years of age, with only 13 percent under age 25; 57 percent were in the 30–50 age range. Among those who were married, half had husbands who were in professional occupations; 14 percent of the husbands were still students. At the time of their first appointment at CEW, 29 percent had done some graduate work and 30 percent had had some college, but did not have a four-year degree. Very few had no more than a high school education. (This situation is consistent with national education statistics, which indicate that women who do not go on to college immediately after high school are much more likely, if they later resume their education, to enroll in community colleges than in major four-year colleges or universities.)

At the point of their first interview, nearly half of the early participants were homemakers, not employed and not in school. Thirty-one
percent were employed, full time or part time. Over half of these early
participants indicated that they wanted to pursue further education in
order to seek employment in a new field in the future. A fifth indicated
that they wanted further education in preparation for future employment in their present field (or one they had worked in in the past).
They were primarily interested in traditional fields for women: for example, 57 percent mentioned an interest in some aspect of the field of
education.

There were gradual shifts in these figures over the next five years,
and by 1973 the number married had decreased from three fourths to
about one half. The number employed full time had increased somewhat and the proportion of participants who were already in school also
increased, so that the number who were neither employed nor in school
decreased from nearly 50 percent to 34 percent by 1973. The diversity
with respect to level of education at the first interview, however, remained much the same. The interest in traditional professional and
liberal arts fields also persisted. Among nearly 5,500 women who came
to the center in the 1964–1973 period, only 10 percent indicated a possible interest in biological and physical sciences and 4 percent an interest
in mathematics or engineering. These figures did not vary greatly over
this entire period.

Current Characteristics of Returning Women

In recent years the CEW population has included fewer women aged 40
and over. In the early 1980s nearly half of the first-time CEW participants were in the 25–34 age range, with roughly one fifth under age 25.
In 1983 only one sixth of the women were aged 40 and over compared
with one third in the early years of the center. Today, the older women
who come to the center are more likely to be concerned with immediate
employment issues and less likely to be thinking of returning to school
than are the younger participants. Increasingly, of course, younger
women of high academic ability stay in school longer, or return sooner,
so that they will have less need to be completing degrees at age 40 and
over. And the younger the returning woman student, the more closely
she resembles the "normal" student population.

However, the diversity of educational attainment at the time of the
first appointment which was characteristic of the early participants continues to be the case. Their educational goals also reveal a wide range,
with respect to both level of aspiration and clarity of goals. In 1983, of

575 first-time participants who were not enrolled at the time of their first appointment, 34 percent were uncertain of what degree they wished to earn; many were debating among several fields, most of which would involve earning a graduate degree. Twenty-five percent wanted to earn a specific graduate degree, 16 percent wanted to earn a bachelor's degree, 10 percent wanted to take some courses but were not necessarily interested in earning a degree, and 15 percent were concerned with employment or career development issues not involving further enrollment.

Returning women may be at any stage of career development; clarity of career goals is essentially unrelated to prior educational attainment. In recent years, CEW participants have fallen in roughly equal numbers into four different categories of career development, according to counselors' descriptions. In 1983, 24 percent were pursuing a clear educational or career goal; 21 percent were in the process of formulating a new goal which appeared to be a natural development or outgrowth of their experience thus far (such as returning to school for a higher degree in the field in which they had been employed); 19 percent were changing career fields or goals, in a move away from an earlier choice which no longer seemed appropriate (12 percent were changing fields because of poor job prospects in their old field); and 24 percent were attempting to establish a clear career goal for the first time. The career goals women form as they are growing up are more severely constrained by sex-role stereotypes about appropriate occupations than are men's. The need for skilled and knowledgeable counseling, as such women contemplate entering or re-entering the job market, is attested to by the experience of thousands of women.

The two most striking changes in the demographic characteristics of the women coming to CEW over the years have already been alluded to: the number of women who are already employed has increased steadily, and the number who are married has decreased steadily. In the 1980s more than three fifths of the annual participants are employed compared with less than one third in the early years. And roughly 35 percent are married compared with nearly 80 percent in the mid-1960s.

As a consequence of these changes, financial problems are a significant issue for increasing numbers of women who wish to return to school. In contrast to the early years, when many of the women who returned to school were married to professional men with stable incomes, the prospective returning woman today is more likely to be self-supporting. Earning a further degree, therefore, must frequently be accomplished either by combining employment and going to school or by leaving established jobs in order to enroll in programs that require enrollment in daytime classes or do not encourage part-time study. In 1981, 20 percent of the CEW participants were both enrolled and employed compared with 8 percent of the participants from 1964 to 1970. Of the student participants in 1983, 56 percent were employed—16 percent full time and 40 percent part time.

The use of the center by minority students has increased in the last five or six years to approximately 20 percent. They are not analyzed separately in the follow-up studies discussed in the next section because there were relatively few minority participants prior to 1977–1978. In general, minority participants are more likely to be in school, less likely to be married, and much more likely to need financial help than nonminority participants.

Many women return to school without special services, but the Michigan data, far from indicating a lessening need for such services, strongly suggest that the issues for re-entry women today are more complex than they have been at any time in the past. Other studies of returning women students, including those returning to two-year colleges, indicate similar needs.

Follow-Up Surveys of CEW Participants

1977 Follow-Up Survey of Early Participants

CEW's annual participant records provide a picture of the demographic characteristics of re-entry women. They do not, however, provide any outcome data; they do not reveal what has happened in the lives of the participants in later years. Did they enroll and complete degrees? Did they then seek employment? How satisfied are they with their lives and careers? This sort of information can be obtained only in follow-up studies. In 1977, therefore, with the aid of a grant from the Ford Foundation, a 10-page questionnaire was mailed to all women who had come to CEW between 1964 and 1973 for whom a current address could be located. The questionnaire asked about educational and employment histories and aspirations, career orientation, advantages and disadvantages of working, how they viewed themselves, what was missing in their lives, what they would do differently if they could start over. In all, 1,145 women responded, ranging in age from 22 to 83, with a fairly even distribution across the life span.[22]

Had the respondents actually followed through with their plans for further education? Of 1,118 women aged 22 to 69, 52 percent held graduate degrees compared with the 14 percent cited in the previous section for the early participants. Fifteen percent of the respondents were enrolled in school at the time of the survey. Thus, it appears that substantial numbers of the women who came to CEW in its early years did in fact enroll and complete degrees in subsequent years. Approximately 20 percent had obtained their highest degree at age 40 or over and 46 percent at age 30 or over. Half of the respondents had had an interruption of five or more years in their education, and half of them said that they had not yet completed as much education as they would like to.

Nearly three fourths of the respondents were employed—45 percent full time and 29 percent part time. Their work histories reflected a recent resumption of labor force activity; nearly half of those who were employed had been employed continuously for less than six years. Most of the women had had some work experience early in their lives, typically either before marriage or before having children. More than half (53 percent) had had an interruption of five years or more in their employment histories. Almost all of the women intended to work in the future, whatever their current employment status. About three fourths of the women said that they thought of themselves as having, or planning, a career.

Career orientation was clearly related to age: 87 percent of the women aged 25–34, 80 percent of those aged 35–44, 66 percent of those aged 45–54, and 45 percent of those aged 55–64 described themselves as having or planning a career. There was also a clear age trend in the relative emphasis placed on career concerns compared with more traditional homemaker concerns (such as giving priority to husband's career, the importance of having children, and not letting work interfere with family activities). Women who thought of themselves as having careers placed relatively greater emphasis on career concerns than did noncareer women in each age group; among the career-oriented, younger women gave greater emphasis to career concerns than did older women. Among the middle age ranges—35 to 54—those women who thought of themselves as having or planning careers were more satisfied with their lives, and showed higher self-esteem, than were the noncareer women. (Among the younger women, almost all were interested in careers; among the older women—those aged 55–64—the career versus noncareer distinction was not particularly important. It was not uncommon for older women who were employed full time in interesting jobs to say that they did not think of their work as a career. Their attitudes were reflected in such comments as, "It just gradually developed" or "I didn't really plan to do this.")

Among respondents in the 35–54 age range, those who thought of themselves as having or planning a career were more likely to be employed full time than part time; those who did not think of themselves as having a career were more likely to be employed part time than full time. Among the career women, those who were employed full time expressed greater satisfaction with their lives than did those who were employed part time; among the noncareer women, those who were employed part time were more satisfied than those who were employed full time. Career women who were employed part time were more likely to give a job-related response, in describing what was missing in their lives, than were those in full-time jobs.[23]

Earning graduate degrees contributed to a successful transition to employment; women who had earned graduate degrees were more likely to be employed than women who had not earned such degrees. More specifically, employed career women who were satisfied with their lives were more likely to have earned graduate degrees than were the career women who were not satisfied with their lives or than the noncareer women, whether satisfied or not. Women who were interested in careers, but were not employed, were less apt to have finished graduate degrees and more likely to say that they had not finished their education. Furthermore, it appeared that women who had earned graduate degrees as returning women were more likely to be employed than those who had earned graduate degrees at an earlier point in their lives—right after college, for example, or before marriage.

Among the women who had made a successful transition to employment after a significant period as a homemaker, there appeared to be a great variety of patterns in the actual chronological sequence in which they moved through various steps or stages. For those who had married and had not experienced any marital disruption, the most typical sequence appeared to be the following: graduation from college, marriage, employment, a period as a homemaker with young children, then a return to school to earn a graduate degree, followed by a return to employment. But many women went through far more complicated sequences, with several transitions into and out of the labor force, and sometimes several periods of enrollment in school. The histories of such women do not suggest some sort of "mid-life crisis" as the genesis of their return to school. Rather, they suggest persistence in pursuit of goals, despite interruptions, or periodic changes in goals, in accordance with changing circumstances and interests.

Seventy percent of the women said that they would do something different, if they could start all over again, about getting an education (most frequently, that they would finish their education sooner); 63 percent would do something different about planning a career (again, most frequently that they would think about a career sooner); 41 percent would do something different about getting married (most frequently, that they would wait longer to marry); and 38 percent would do something different about having children (again, most frequently that they would wait longer to have children). The greater satisfaction among women who were employed full time at higher salaries is corroborated by the fact that they were less apt to say that they would do something different about getting an education, planning a career, and having children than were the housewives, while there was no difference between these two groups with respect to mentions of marriage.[24]

1981 Survey of CEW Participants and Other Degree Recipients

Because of the changes described earlier that were taking place in the population of returning women—increased levels of employment, greater numbers of single or divorced women, greater concern with immediate employment or career issues—and because of the increasing numbers of younger women moving into nontraditional professional fields, researchers and counselors interested in women's lives felt a need to know more about what was happening in the early years of career development among these newer generations of educated women. In 1981, therefore, with further funding from the Ford Foundation, the Center for Continuing Education of Women at Michigan conducted a second survey, drawing the respondents from two different sources: women who had come to CEW between 1974 and 1977 and women and men who had received graduate or professional degrees from the University of Michigan in 1977 or 1978. The degree recipients were selected to represent a broad range of fields, from traditionally female- to traditionally male-dominated professions. In all, there were 1,182 respondents, including 588 former CEW participants, and 457 women and 137 men from the degree recipient sample. The questionnaire covered many areas, including satisfaction with educational and employment experience thus far, plans for the future, and measures of psychological well-being and attitudes, with particular emphasis on the effects of marital and parental status and on the interfacing with the spouse's career concerns and development.

Of the 588 respondents who had come to CEW between 1974 and 1977, 49 percent had earned graduate degrees by 1981, 40 percent had earned bachelor's degrees, and 11 percent had completed less than four years of college. Again, these figures suggest a considerable change in educational attainment since their first contact with CEW. According to annual participant records for 1976 and 1977, about 17 percent of the first-time participants in those years had earned graduate degrees, 41 to 43 percent had earned college degrees, and 41 percent had completed less than four years of college. Similarly, there was an increase in employment levels. Among the CEW respondents to the 1981 survey, 77 percent were employed compared with 55 or 56 percent in the annual participant data for 1976 and 1977.

How successful in the job market have these women been who returned to earn degrees after a period of time as a homemaker or in other employment? Using 1981 data for women who had earned graduate degrees, women who had received their last degree at age 30 or over were compared with those who had received their last degree when they were under age 30. These comparisons were made separately for women in four different degree groups: those with PhDs; those with graduate degrees in nontraditional professional fields (business, law, medicine, dentistry, architecture, engineering, and several planning fields); those with master's degrees in traditional professional fields (social work, nursing, library science, and public health); and those with other master's degrees across the broad range of humanities, social sciences, and physical sciences. In none of these degree groups were there significant differences between the two age-at-degree categories with respect to various measures of career satisfaction: satisfaction with career development thus far, how occupationally successful respondents felt themselves to be, how much they enjoyed the work they were doing, how satisfied they were with their jobs (based on an index composed of ratings of 14 different job characteristics), their current salary, or how satisfied they were with their lives in general.[25]

Conclusions

Patterns of education and work are evidently changing, so much so that they challenge prevailing theoretical ideas about life stages and the institutional policies that follow from them. We observe that women continue to drop out of education at a higher rate than men do, but more of them are completing their education before marriage and children than was true for an earlier generation. Women who now re-enter mainstream degree programs are on the average younger, much more likely to be single or divorced, and more likely to be employed than were the re-entry women of 20 years ago. While there is still a tendency for women to interrupt their education or career for marriage or to have children, the patterns for withdrawal and return have become increasingly varied. As the normal student population in graduate and professional schools includes more women, and as women return after briefer interruptions, re-entry women look less and less different from the rest of the student body, and they have more and more similar career aspirations. There is no evidence that one pattern in the timing of education and career is more desirable than another.

As students become more differentiated in terms of life stages and choices, but look more alike as students and potential professionals, distinctions in educational strategies and policy may be reduced. As opposed to stressing differences between cohorts of women and calling for institutional redress to accommodate women's concerns, as women's leaders have in the past, the higher educational establishment may better meet these concerns with more institutional flexibility for individual differences without regard to age or sex. Such flexible policies are conducive not only to greater equity but also to greater efficiency in higher education.

We have noted that re-entry women have constituted a significant and increasing share of the student population in postsecondary education during the last decade. Our data also show that although women predominate among students aged 25 and over and part-time students, there are also substantial proportions of men in these groups. By and large, we know less about the men in this population than we do about the women. The overall size of the group, however, has not escaped the attention of institutions of higher education, many of which made special efforts to attract such students to maintain enrollments when confronted with a slowdown in the rate of expansion of the population pool of college-going 18-to-24-year-olds during the latter part of the 1970s. Of the total fall 1985 enrollment of 12,247,000 students, fully 43 percent are aged 25 and over and 45 percent attend part time.[26] Even the most prestigious universities have begun to advertise continuing education, general studies, or other programs directed toward nontraditional students. The question, however, is how well the needs of such students are met.

Economic necessity may move higher education toward a more individualized response to all students, a trend to be encouraged. Certainly some of the support services that have been developed for re-entry women are equally applicable to men. The need for counseling, studies skills refresher courses, financial aid, and even day care is not limited to women only. However, marginal curricula and a few services do not represent the kind of "structural changes" envisioned by women leaders who planned for re-entry programs 25 years ago. Nor do they satisfy those today who still dream of a mainstream education that will assure both men and women choices and options as their individual life patterns may dictate.

Research in the 1960s and early 1970s stressed the institutional, situational, and personal barriers to education for women. Higher education was still responding to goals that were set in the 1950s and 1960s, and the excitement of planning new institutions for newly defined populations gave hope that an understanding of the barriers would inform these plans. In the research of more recent date reported here, changes in the women and their situations have been documented. These educated women assume that they will have careers whether they marry or not. They may postpone marriage and children, but they still intend to have children. They are, in the main, confident of their rights and choices. But their lives are more complex than they have ever been, and they have not yet achieved the institutional accommodation and the equity in education to which they are entitled.

Notes

1. Mirra Komarovsky, *Women in the Modern World* (Boston: Little, Brown, 1953).
2. Alva Myrdal and Viola Klein, *Women's Two Roles: Home and Work* (London: Routledge & Kegan Paul, 1956; 2nd ed., 1968).
3. See Myrdal and Klein, *Women's Two Roles*, 2nd ed., pp. 160ff.
4. Conversation between President Bunting and the University of Michigan Center for Continuing Education of Women staff on a visit to Ann Arbor, Spring 1967.
5. Elizabeth Cless, "The Birth of an Idea: An Account of the Genesis of Women's Continuing Education," in Helen S. Astin, ed., *Some Action of Her Own: The Adult Woman and Higher Education* (Lexington, MA: Heath, 1976), p. 6.
6. *Signs* 3, no. 4 (Summer 1978):921–922.
7. Jessie Bernard, *Women and the Public Interest* (Chicago: Aldine & Atherton, 1971), p. 151.
8. Women's Bureau, U.S. Department of Labor, *Continuing Education Programs and Services for Women*, Employment Standards Administration Pamphlet no. 10, 1971.
9. For a report on the AAUW survey of women in academe, see Ruth Oltman, *Campus 1970: Where Do Women Stand?* (Washington, DC: American Association of University Women, 1970).
10. Jacquelyn A. Mattfeld, "A Decade of Continuing Education: Dead End or Open Door?" unpublished manuscript, Sarah Lawrence College, 1971.
11. For a description of one such center, see Jean W. Campbell, "The Integration of Service, Advocacy and Research in a University Women's Center," paper presented at the International Interdisciplinary Congress on Women, Haifa, Israel, December 1981.
12. In chapter 2 of *Some Action of Her Own* (see note 5), Carole Leland discusses the case-study programs she analyzed for this seminal volume.
13. A series of 15 reports on continuing education for women is available from

the Project on the Status and Education of Women of the Association of American Colleges. (See bibliography for titles.)

14. Carol Tittle and Elenor Denker, *Returning Women Students in Higher Education* (New York: Praeger, 1980).

15. Joy K. Rice, "Operation 2nd Chance," *Journal of the National Association of Women Deans, Administrators, and Counselors* 46, no. 4 (Summer 1983): 3–10.

16. For a useful summary of developmental approaches, see Rita Weathersby and Jill Tarule, *Adult Development: Implications for Higher Education,* AAHE-ERIC/Higher Education Research Report no. 4 (Washington, DC: American Association for Higher Education, 1980).

17. Jacqueline Eccles discusses her model in "Sex Differences in Achievement Patterns," paper presented at the Nebraska Symposium on Motivation, Lincoln, October 1983.

18. Scholars who are interested in the record of the continuing education movement in the 1970s should read Astin, *Some Action of Her Own;* Tittle and Denker, *Returning Women Students in Higher Education;* and Ruth Eckstrom, Marjory Marvel, and Jean Swenson, "Educational Programs for Adult Women," in Susan Klein, ed., *Handbook for Achieving Sex Equity Through Education* (Baltimore: Johns Hopkins University Press, 1984).

19. National Center for Education Statistics, *Digest of Education Statistics, 1987* (Washington, DC: NCES, 1987), p. 123.

20. U.S. Bureau of the Census, *Statistical Abstract of the United States, 1986* (Washington, DC: U.S. Government Printing Office, 1986), p. 151.

21. National Center for Education Statistics, *Digest of Education Statistics, 1987,* p. 14.

22. Approximately 3,200 questionnaires were sent out, but there were many inaccuracies in the addresses used, so that it is difficult to estimate a true response rate. On the basis of an attempt to reach a sample of nonrespondents by telephone, it is estimated that at least 60 percent of the intended recipients who actually received the questionnaire returned it.

23. For an analysis of the relationship between employment status and psychological well-being of these women, see Jean D. Manis, "Relationships Among Career Orientation, Employment Status, Self-Esteem, and Life Satisfaction of Women: An Analysis of Age Differences," paper presented at the annual meeting of the American Educational Research Association, New York, March 22, 1982 (CEW Research Report no. 10).

24. See Jean D. Manis and Hazel Markus, "Combining Families and Careers: Views from Different Points in the Life Cycle," in *Changing Family, Changing Workplace* (Ann Arbor: Center for Continuing Education of Women, University of Michigan, 1980).

25. For a summary of findings from these two CEW surveys, see Jean D. Manis, "Some Correlates of Self-Esteem, Personal Control, and Occupational Attainment: An Overview of Findings from CEW Surveys of Educated Women," paper presented at the Center for the Study of Higher Education

and the Program in Adult and Continuing Education, University of Michigan, April 11, 1984 (CEW Research Report no. 18). See also Jean D. Manis, "Combining Professional Careers with Marriage and Parenthood: Preliminary Findings from a Survey of Recent Recipients of Graduate or Professional Degrees" (CEW Research Report no. 12) and "Professional Women Today: Interrelationships Among Career Satisfaction, Marital Satisfaction, and Division of Household Labor" (CEW Research Report no. 13).

26. *Chronicle of Higher Education,* September 4, 1985, p. 31. Source of data: National Center for Education Statistics.

5

Women's Centers

The establishment of women's centers on college and university campuses in the early 1970s was a direct response to the growth of the women's movement and an acknowledgment of the need for a new kind of support for women. They provide a meeting place and range of services for women both within and outside the academy. Some of these centers are student initiated, student run, and funded primarily by student associations or, on occasion, student support services. Others are administratively affiliated, with institutional funding, and are directed by a salaried faculty person or administrator with activist interests. It is this second group of women's centers that this chapter will discuss since they are usually more permanent and secure than student-run centers and more likely to have an impact on the campus and the larger community. We will examine the role of these women's centers in the academic community and the wider community, noting developmental changes up to the present time, and will assess the major problems and prospects they face in the future. In addition to the sources cited in the text, the information presented in the chapter draws on interviews with representatives from 25 women's centers throughout the country. (These centers are listed in Appendix 5.1.)

According to a 1979 survey of campus-based women's centers that are administratively affiliated, there were 600 at that time.[1] A more recent indicator of the prevalence of women's centers and the proportion of them that are administratively affiliated is provided by a 1982 survey of on-campus women's programs conducted by the Feminist Press in connection with the publication of *Everywoman's Guide to Colleges and Universities*. Of the 551 institutions which replied to an extensive questionnaire about the campus climate for women, approximately one third have women's centers of one kind or another. Of these, two thirds are administratively affiliated and one third student run.[2] These findings are also consistent with an estimate of 600 administratively affiliated centers for all higher education institutions. The total number of campus-based women's centers of all kinds is estimated to have been 2,500 in 1987.[3]

The most notable characteristic of university- and college-based women's centers is their diversity: a diversity of services and activities and a diversity with respect to their constituencies. A multi-service and multi-resource women's center is quite different from a research center, a women's studies program, an employment center, a counseling center, a continuing education center, or a center for battered women, although it may offer one or more of these services and resources. Women's centers' services and resources may also include organizing conferences, film showings, art exhibitions, seminars, workshops, and noncredit courses; producing publications; offering referral and counseling services; operating as a clearinghouse and repository of information and reference material on women's issues; setting up and running a child-care center; identifying emerging issues for women on campus; and serving as an advocate for campus women.

Some women's centers serve only women within their institution; some even are limited to young undergraduates. A few have alumnae support and participation; many include returning adult women students and women in the larger community. Most commonly, centers are funded by the Office of Student Services. Some come under the budget of the Office of Continuing Education or the Division of Academic Affairs. A few are under the aegis of the President's Office, the Division of Community Service, the Affirmative Action Office, or the Women's Studies Program. Wherever they originate, budgets are almost always small, sufficient to support full-time staffs of one, two, or three people.

Background

Women's centers of the 1970s were an outgrowth of the pioneer movement of continuing education for the women in the 1960s.[4] Starting in the late 1950s many middle-class educated women who had followed the national pattern of early marriage and staying home to raise young children began to show interest in completing their interrupted education or going on for graduate or professional training in order to return to a career or start a new one. This coincided with and was reinforced by labor market shortages in the post-Sputnik period and the growth of the service professions.

In the early 1960s a number of innovative continuing education programs for women were set up to accommodate these women and prepare them for jobs, often on a part-time basis. Such programs as the Continuing Education Centers for Women at Michigan, Minnesota, Syracuse, and Wisconsin universities; Sarah Lawrence College; and the Radcliffe Institute for Independent Study were quickly followed by programs throughout the country, including a number of special retraining programs in such areas as mathematics and chemistry. In all these programs, in the words of the director of the Michigan Center: "Emphasis was placed on institutional changes that would accommodate a combination of roles over a woman's lifetime. In this sense, continuing education meant adjusting the educational system to the demands of women's dual role, taking for granted interruptions in their formal education and providing as a matter of course for their reentry into the system."[5] Also taken for granted was the fact that women would marry and have children and take major responsibility for the family. What was new was the way in which women articulated their need and right to creative self-expression through education and work.

As a result of these innovative programs, mature women broke down most of the stereotypes about "mature" and "women" as they went back to school showing ability, perseverance, and energy, often while juggling full-time home responsibilities. Many of these returning women were in the forefront of the women's movement that emerged in the later 1960s. They posed new questions about women's lives and expectations for the 1970s.

The creation of women's centers in institutions of higher education in the early and mid-1970s represented in part a response to the needs and concerns of re-entry women, particularly in the area of education and employment, but their motivation went beyond that to include some of the more radical ideas of the growing women's movement. Besides acknowledging the extent and depth of discrimination against women at all levels of society, campus women's centers raised and examined new and more fundamental questions about women's lives, roles, and expectations. They were designed to raise women's consciousness regarding their socialization into narrow and circumscribed gender roles and to encourage them to raise and broaden their aspirations to achieve their full potential as individuals. This feminist resurgence on campuses throughout the United States was reflected in the charter of the Barnard College Women's Center written in 1973. It included the statement that the center should be

> an endeavor to foster a heightened sense of women's identity . . . to serve as a physical and psychological meeting ground for women . . . by encouraging the open sharing of knowledge and experience and increasing ties among diverse groups of women. Its further aim is to create an atmosphere and develop programs which will invest women with confidence and a sense of purpose.

As centers were established on campuses throughout the United States, they sought to provide, or to pressure the institution to provide, programs and services which would help women achieve equity in all aspects of their education and work. At the same time, they helped to develop a sense of community among women and to combat feelings of isolation. For the most part, women's centers started at large coeducational institutions rather than at small liberal arts or women's colleges, for it was here that women felt the most isolation and discrimination. An early unpublished study done in 1974 surveyed all known women's centers on U.S. college campuses (which then totaled 230, including student-run centers) and received a 40 percent response.[6] Of these, only 7 were at women's colleges. A separate questionnaire was sent to 142 women's colleges and replies from 49 revealed that they offered a more supportive atmosphere for women with many role models among faculty, administration, and alumnae. The responses also indicated that women's colleges often offered some of the services provided by women's centers, including, for example, abortion counseling and contraceptive information or a library of women's literature, as well as some not offered by women's centers in the beginning, such as personal, psychological, and vocational counseling and job placement. Hence, administrative or faculty-staffed women's centers at women's colleges were and still are rare.

When women's centers were created at women's colleges, they came as a response to special needs. At one such institution, a group of alumnae felt that their college needed a place for older alumnae whose needs were different from those of young students. At another, a coordinate women's college at a large university, a women's center was established to focus on career planning for women rather than having to rely on an insensitive university placement office. At still another, the creation of a women's center was conceived by a strong task force of alumnae, faculty, administration, and students, who insisted that their college respond to the challenge of the women's movement with new programs and services.

Interestingly, one institution, which had started in 1892 as a normal school for women and grew as a women's college to become part of the University of North Carolina at Greensboro in 1917, became coeducational in 1963 and subsequently suffered serious declines in the opportunities available to women. This was documented in several surveys of alumnae, faculty, administration, and students in 1978–1979. These surveys were instigated by a group of concerned alumnae who had graduated before 1963 and had become leaders throughout the state. The findings indicated clearly that when it was a women's college, it had been a significant training ground for women leaders. After 25 years as a coeducational institution, women students, faculty, and administrators were dramatically underrepresented in leadership positions on campus, despite the fact that student enrollment was 65 percent women. This discovery led to the establishment of a women's center in 1979 whose primary function was to promote leadership roles for women.

Patterns of Development

By 1970, as legal mechanisms were slowly being developed and put into place to end discrimination against women in higher education, there was at the same time a building up of explosive energy among women on campuses. Women were angry at the rigidities of their institutions, eager to see some immediate changes, and at the same time aware that an important first step in effecting change was to raise the consciousness of women. Unless women in general became fully aware of their second-class status, they would not act to change that status. On most campuses, however, there were no structures through which these feminist women could express their concerns. Typically, the only special office for women was a dean of women's office. There was no affirmative action office, rarely a women's studies program, only a sprinkling of women's studies courses and continuing education programs for women, and few women in top administrative positions or senior faculty levels. The time was ripe for the creation of new structures, but in most cases institutions were not receptive. The only immediate response came from a few of the established continuing education programs for women which broadened their focus to include the needs of all women on campus.

The emergence of the early women's centers followed a generally similar pattern. Varying slightly from institution to institution, small groups of women (including some combination of students, faculty, staff, administration, alumnae, and on occasion women from the larger community) met, established themselves as a committee or task force, and devoted months, even years, to preparing the necessary groundwork to convince their administration of the need for a women's center. Sometimes a rape incident on campus or a pending lawsuit by a faculty member speeded things up. In a few instances, the impetus came from a chancellor or president who, aware of new federal guidelines on affirmative action, appointed a task force to consider women's needs on campus. But often this process dragged on for years as reports and recommendations were enmeshed in the red tape of bureaucracy and caught up in changes in administration. At one institution the women's center was instigated and backstopped by an off-campus group, a strong community-based women's center.

Sometimes an administration was willing to make what it believed to be a temporary commitment, providing a small and inadequate budget and a little space, often one room in the basement of a remote building. But, if not, women learned to use some of the strategies and tactics which an earlier generation of students in the 1960s had used to move intransigent authorities. When an administration was unreceptive and when women felt that they had exhausted normal channels, they resorted to holding an all-campus rally, sitting in the president's office, taking over a building, or taking down the walls between offices to create "space" when they were told there was no space.

Although there has always been great diversity among women's centers, they shared certain common goals. All of them tried to address a broad range of women's issues, going far beyond immediate undergraduate needs. In addition, in the spirit of the larger women's movement, they opened their doors to all women, both on and off campus, partly in recognition of the fact that many women had never had the opportunity to go to college and to develop employment skills because of family responsibilities and partly because they felt that their programs and services would be enriched by including the full diversity of women's experience. Even the few centers that were started during this period as continuing education centers for women expanded their services to respond to the needs of a broader constituency.

Survival in the Early Years

With limited institutional support and in most cases no outside funding, women's centers were viewed by many administrators as a fad which would fade away after a few years. Unlike the continuing education centers which had a real place in the institutional framework and boasted respectable budgets, a staff of trained counselors, and a well-paid director, women's centers had almost no support. Nonetheless, their personnel functioned at an extremely high energy level, filling a new and important campus need. Directors managed on a shoestring, using enormous creativity: in one instance where a center was housed in an oversized closet, one of its first activities was to hold an open house, done lavishly with flowers, food, and drink. Large numbers of faculty, administrators, and students attended, overflowing into the halls. The point was well made and the center was given more suitable space.

In those early years, following the principles advocated by feminist groups, many centers functioned in a nonhierarchical manner. In some cases, all decisions were made collectively; in others, efforts were made to share decision making and responsibility extensively but not completely. Sometimes even the salary allotted for a director was shared. To supplement small staffs, centers depended on dedicated student workers and volunteers. Many centers developed internships and practicas for undergraduate and graduate students. One of the largest centers, Everywoman's Center at the University of Massachusetts at Amherst, has always had between 80 and 100 volunteers at a time; the Brooklyn College Women's Center had one of the first peer counseling programs, using some 30 volunteers, all working under the supervision of a professional.

For some centers, an important part of survival in those early years was the support of someone in top administration: a provost, a chancellor, a dean, or an associate director of athletics—often, but by no means always, a woman. On a few campuses, there was active support from the very beginning from tenured faculty women, but in the early 1970s this was rare.

The range of programs and services of women's centers in the early 1970s was very broad, with the emphasis on personal empowerment and identifying some of the emerging issues for women. Many offered lectures, workshops, seminars, conferences, films, poetry readings, and art exhibitions; some issued a community calendar of women's events; some served as a drop-in center with information and referrals on such subjects as health, housing, childcare, divorce, legal rights, and employment. A good number provided peer counseling and career counseling; a few provided professional counseling. Many organized consciousness-raising and support groups; some gave noncredit courses on the new scholarship on women as well as on many areas of women's rights and on such topics as self-defense and assertiveness training. Some centers operated libraries, which contained books, articles, periodicals, clippings, and other printed material on women's issues. Others published newsletters, bibliographies, and reports of presentations given at the center. A few centers got involved in campus safety for women, childcare, and improved health services for women, but most did not tackle these issues until later.

The handful of centers which had started as continuing education centers and shifted to become full-fledged women's centers had the largest budgets; thus, in addition to many of the above services, they gave financial aid to returning students and did research on many aspects of this particular group of women. At campuses where there were re-entry women students and no continuing education centers for women, women's centers served this group, either working with the re-entry program or adult education department for men and women on campus if there was one, or filling that role unofficially if there was no program or office. Because of the close relationship most centers had with women outside the academy, it was not unusual for a center to play a role in the recruitment of re-entry women. In addition, having regular brown bag lunches and providing other opportunities for re-entry women students to meet together proved to be important to the morale and, incidentally, to the retention of this group of students.

By reaching out and including community women and their concerns in center programs, women's centers developed strong ties between the institution and the larger community which proved to be an unexpected, inexpensive, and important public relations asset for the institutions. These activities have included programs co-sponsored with community groups; programs for high school girls or single parents, and task forces working with special community groups such as Third World women. One center, the Douglass Advisory Services for Women of Douglass College, Rutgers University, had as one of its major goals from the very beginning that of providing advice and counseling to women in the community through a special outreach center located off campus in the New Brunswick inner city. In addition, some centers have always had strong ties with local and state women's organizations.

The relationship between women's centers and the development of women's studies programs was often a close one. Center directors often served as the catalyst in setting up a women's studies committee and continued as a guiding force and administrative arm, compiling and publicizing existing women's studies courses on campus and performing many of the administrative details that went with the long credentialing process. Interestingly, some of the early well-established women's studies programs often performed many of the functions usually carried out by women's centers—even including community outreach—with the result that at some of these institutions there has never been a women's center, or if there is one it has usually not been fully supported by its institution.

From the beginning an important issue for women's centers was that of lesbianism. Lesbian women contributed a great deal of vitality and energy to the new women's movement in general, and they saw women's centers as an important advocacy agency. In the women's centers as in the larger movement, most lesbians devoted their attention to a full range of emerging women's issues. A minority elected to work on specifically lesbian issues: they created special programs and activities that would validate the lesbian experience, and they worked to eliminate discrimination on the basis of sexual preference.

It was important for women's centers to incorporate these interests within their mission and to find effective ways to work with lesbians and all other women who supported their basic goals. And most of them did. Most centers were extremely successful in minimizing division among their constituencies. At a time when women's centers were barely accepted by their institution and in a general atmosphere of homophobia which sought to divide the women's movement and threatened the very existence of women's centers, this took deliberate conscious effort.

Growth and Change

As the women's movement developed and became more sophisticated, women's centers added services and programs, often dealing with emerging issues or old issues which were being publicly identified for the first time: conferences, lectures, and workshops on such topics as health care for women, grass roots organizing for battered women, sterilization abuse and poor women, perceptions of black women writers, and the situation of women in other parts of the world. Discussions on topics which were on the cutting edge of the new scholarship on women were initiated, often in cooperation with other sectors of the campus, and they were well attended and well received. Centers also began to address issues of race and class, seeking out, wherever possible, minority women for active participation in their programs. The Everywoman's Center at the University of Massachusetts at Amherst insisted successfully that a minority person be added to its staff to reflect the demographic mix in the campus and the community population.

The mid-1970s saw both the establishment of new women's centers and the proliferation of women's groups on campuses. The centers were seen as the coordinating link between women's groups on campus and as the liaison between the administration and individual women and women's groups. Many of these groups turned to the centers for advice, support, co-sponsorship of programs, and, on occasion, the use of their space. This was particularly true of student groups where women students were beginning to seek their identity as women and wanted programs reflecting this concern. Hence, it was not unusual for a women's center to set aside a small part of its budget to help student groups put together programs on women's issues. These ranged from film festivals on women for the undergraduate anthropology club or the Latin American club, to a seminar on women for the pre-law society, to serving as a message center and evening meeting place for the Lesbian Activist Group or the campus student ERA group.

Many directors were able to negotiate increased space and higher budgets and benefit from work study and, for a short time, from CETA funds. This expansion in space and funding did represent an acknowledgment on the part of administrators that the centers were serving a function on their campuses; it also provided administrations with the opportunity to show an open-mindedness to new ideas. Nevertheless, budgets, paid staff, and space remained small and inadequate and in no way reflected the volume of services provided.

As the centers grew, many found that there was a conflict between the requirements of their institution and the practices which they had adopted from the feminist movement. They learned that collective decision-making was unwieldy and did not serve them well in negotiating with their institution. They learned that if they were to achieve salaries and fringe benefits commensurate with other administrative personnel in their institutions, they had to fit into existing job qualifications and adjust to the institutional structure. Nonetheless, most centers tried to preserve the nonhierarchical structure of governance where they could, using the process among volunteers and committees and, where possible, among part-time employees and students. This maintained the excitement of working in a new way and ensured the involvement of more than a few. It was also for some centers a guiding principle that there could be another way to reach decisions and effect change.

Gradually, the centers' emphasis changed from personal support and direct service to advocacy and institutional change. There were a handful of women's centers which had always played a strong activist role, but they were the exceptions. The Penn Women's Center at the University of Pennsylvania was a notable one. It was created with the help of

Women for Equal Opportunity of Pennsylvania (WEOUP), an organization founded in 1970 that included many tenured faculty and that, among other things, was supporting women who had sued the university after being denied tenure.[7] When, in 1973, the administration virtually ignored a gang rape that took place on campus, WEOUP used its strong and vocal network to support the demand for the formation of a women's center with a mandate to monitor security. Eventually, the Penn Center persuaded the administration to appoint a woman security officer to assume responsibility for women's safety on campus. The center also had a mandate to monitor affirmative action, health, and other programs and became a major force for women on campus.

Advocacy as a Central Purpose

Most women's centers, while continuing to offer short-term counseling for personal self-development, career counseling and programs for re-entry women, rap groups, and workshops on health care and self-defense, gradually began to play a much more important role in identifying emerging issues affecting women within the institution and providing leadership in setting up machinery to provide solutions. This was true with such issues as rape, childcare, health service, sexual harassment, and athletics.

Centers often play a dual role: on the one hand, working behind the scenes, cooperating with appropriate offices or departments on a problem, often getting an office, department, or top administration to take action. They also serve as a whistle blower when a chronic problem needs action or when incidents occur: they publicize the issue or incident, get speakers, hold forums, and organize the campus community around the issue. Over and over, directors stressed the need to know what works on their campus and the importance of being able to communicate well and being politically skillful. At the very least, women's centers' staff serve as an important resource on women's issues on campus: providing background information to students as well as administrators; speaking in classes, residence halls, sorority and, on occasion, fraternity houses; sponsoring or co-sponsoring programs with other departments; and doing training programs for residence staff and student peer counselors on how to identify and deal with a problem stemming from a women's issue. For example, when officials at Princeton University expressed concern about the institution's continuing difficulties in attracting more women students, the Women's Center at Princeton held a forum on the subject of female admissions in the fall of 1986. It was reported to have drawn more students than any other forum held at the center in years.[8]

As one director put it, wherever the center finds a problem, she goes to the appropriate office to discuss it and get help, whether it be in the area of affirmative action, student life, career planning, health services, or athletics. Examples of problem solving are plentiful and include playing a role in getting a half-time appointment on the status of women as part of faculty affirmative action; pressuring an administration to appoint an affirmative action officer; and, in a case where the appointment was given to an administrator who already had a full-time job and did little more than give lip service to this new function, getting an additional person appointed whose sole responsibility was affirmative action. At one institution a council of deans developed sexual harassment guidelines which were sexist. The women's center pressured the council to enlarge the input and redo the guidelines so that they were acceptable to the women on campus. One center was instrumental in getting the dean of student life to hire a feminist assistant director of psychological services, and another the appointment of a special counselor in the counseling service to work exclusively with lesbian and gay students.

Often women's centers have started or helped to start programs and services which have subsequently become institutionalized. This has happened with childcare centers, rape crisis centers, and the addition of free Pap and pregnancy tests to campus health services. To develop institutional policies, many centers took the initiative in setting up and often chairing committees which met for months—even years—developing a policy on sexual harassment or campus childcare which would be satisfactory both to the women on campus and to the administration and the board of trustees. Occasionally, the impetus came from the administration. At one institution, the women's center responded to a request from the vice chancellor's office to develop a sexual harassment education program. With funds from his office, a part-time coordinator was hired to train a group of peer resource educators and to present informational programs. A handful of women's centers have gone one step further and stated publicly that they not only serve as an advocate for women on their campus but also play an active role in the formulation of feminist legislation and social policy in the state. What could be accomplished and how varied greatly from campus to campus and depended on a number of variables such as the style of the director, the existence of other supportive women's groups, a sympathetic administration, and the seriousness and frequency of the problems women faced on a particular campus.

No issue was more explosive than rape, and here of course women's centers played an important role in bringing the issue to public view—often before institutions were ready to acknowledge it—and in pressuring institutions to set up educational programs, escort services, rape crisis centers, and machinery for reporting rape. Many of the large state universities have rape prevention and education programs, often located in their women's centers. Most have separate funding, often from the office of the chancellor or president. One of the oldest rape prevention and education programs is at the University of California at Berkeley. Started by a graduate student who herself had been accosted in the mid-1970s, the program was initially funded by her institution. The U.S. Law Enforcement Assistance Administration (no longer in existence) liked the program so much that she was asked to expand her proposal for all nine California campuses. Federal money was allotted to police chiefs on each campus to develop programs in cooperation with women's centers or other representative women's groups. The grant ended after two years, and since then each institution has continued the funding with close cooperation between the campus police force and the women's center.

Challenging Traditional Scholarship

An important component of institutional changes lies in the continuous challenging of the basic underpinnings of traditional scholarship. Many women's centers include programs and services which raise questions about traditional scholarship as it affects our understanding of women, questions which provide an opportunity for students and others to start thinking about women and their heritage in new ways. These programs and services present some of the current research on the new scholarship on women, and a few are actively engaged in some aspect of research.

Some centers have resource collections of books, articles, bibliographies, directories, pamphlets, special issues of journals, and subscriptions to large numbers of women's newsletters and periodicals. Although none of these collections is large, a few have been characterized as the size of a small special library. Unlike traditional libraries, material is usually catalogued according to women's issues. Emphasis is placed on significant material which might not easily find its way into traditional library collections, such as classic feminist writings often published by small presses or publications with brief lives. The heart of most of these collections is the vertical file material, which includes important research articles and a wide variety of published and unpublished material generally labeled as ephemeral by librarians. Some of the centers have sufficient space to set aside a separate room for their library collections, a room which is used by students and others doing research on some aspect of women's lives.

Many women's centers sponsor workshops, seminars, conferences, and lectures which are on the cutting edge of the new scholarship on women, often with the women's studies program or, if there is none, with one or more academic departments. At one institution the women's center brings in feminist scholars from other parts of the country to discuss their work in a faculty lecture series. This is done with the help of the affirmative action office, which contributes $5,000 a year. The Barnard Women's Center gives an annual conference entitled "The Scholar and the Feminist," each year examining a different aspect of the impact of feminism on traditional scholarship. These conferences are interdisciplinary and recognize the inextricable relationship between theory and practice and between scholarship and activism. A number of articles and publications have grown out of these programs and have contributed to the recognition of the validity and visibility of this new scholarship in traditional academic circles.

By the late 1970s a number of women's centers began to focus on research. Some of the newer centers set up during that period included a research component in their list of major goals, while a few of the older established ones added it to their many functions. For example, the newest chapter of the Higher Education Resource Services, HERS/West, which has among its services a research component, is located in the Women's Resource Center of the University of Utah, and the director of the center is also the director of HERS/West.[9]

Finding money to add a research wing to their programs has not been easy for the few multi-service women's centers which have tried to make the change: research requires a budget many times the normal, very limited women's center budget. In order to attract large foundation, corporate, and government grants as well as individual gifts of the size needed, centers have had to modify original goals and even scrap controversial programs. Even when grants have been awarded, the center has to constantly search for new funds that will enable it to continue its research once the first monies have been expended.

Two very different, well-conceived campus models can be found in the Spelman College Women's Research and Resource Center and the Pembroke Center for Teaching and Research. Both are relatively new centers. The first is an all-inclusive women's center with a strong research component, and the second is a teaching and research center which is affiliated with a strong women's center which has functioned since 1975.

The Spelman Center in Atlanta, Georgia, was started in 1981 to "do curriculum development in women's studies, research on Black women and community outreach to Black women."[10] In the few years it has been in existence, it has broadened its focus to include an international dimension; it has brought outstanding black women to Spelman on a regular basis and held major conferences on such issues as black women's health concerns and black women and public policy. The fact that the center is the first of its kind at a historically black women's college in the South and that it has already attracted major outside funding suggests that it will continue to flourish.

The Sarah Doyle Women's Center, which opened at Brown University in 1975, had as one of its six goals to facilitate research and instruction on sex roles, sex differences, and the status of women and men in society. On a small budget and staff of two professionals, this goal was initially more a dream than a reality. Within a few years, the center became an important part of the university, connecting with many academic and nonacademic departments, offering a wide range of programs and services and using a large number of students as volunteers and paid staff. In 1981, with strong support from the director of the Sarah Doyle Women's Center, the Pembroke Center for Teaching and Research on Women was established. A nationally known feminist historian was appointed to an endowed chair as its director, and the director of the Sarah Doyle Center became the associate director on a half-time basis. The two are coordinate organizations, co-sponsoring many programs but each maintaining its own identity and special functions. The Pembroke Center is funded by private and public agencies and a special effort is being made to interest alumnae in making sizable contributions, in the hope that they may find the Pembroke Center less controversial and hence more appealing than the Sarah Doyle Center.

Staff and Structure

Most of the women's centers established in the 1970s have survived but remain small. Few have budgets over $100,000 (in fact, the median is considerably less), and most have managed with tiny staffs, often with two or three full-time people.[11] Some centers operate with only one full-time person, either a director or the administrative assistant. When we look at the range and number of the services and programs centers provide, it raises the question of how all this can be accomplished with such restricted staffs and budgets.

The answer appears to lie in the dedication and drive of the person who directs the center and the creative ways in which the centers have solved their staffing problems. Most still maintain a high *esprit de corps*, characteristic of a pioneer venture testing its wings and not yet firmly entrenched in an institutional structure. Many of the directors have been in their jobs from the very beginning; most of the others at least five years. About half of the original directors had academic credentials; the rest had a background in administration or activism. Some of the original directors were tenured faculty members who were given released time and paid by their departments. There are still some directors—mostly with academic credentials—who hold other administrative or teaching positions within the institution while directing the women's center part time. As directors retire or leave, the tendency is to replace them with people with full academic credentials.

Besides energy, leadership, commitment to feminist issues, and political sensitivity to what works at an institution, women's center directors have had to be innovative and creative in administering their operation. They have designed internships, practica, and—where it works—simply volunteer programs for undergraduate and graduate students, which serve to provide the centers with trained advocates, peer counselors, and coordinators of special projects. In addition, directors have designed part-time jobs with specific functions, jobs which are often filled by students with special talents and/or interests. At one women's center, the director of the center's library, the art gallery coordinator, the calendar coordinator, the coordinator of the faculty lecture series, the graphic arts designer, and the publicity director are all students. At another, students are hired to organize task forces in the dormitories and sorority houses. On one campus where the women's center occupies an entire small house, answering the phone, keeping the log, making referrals, and taking reservations from other women's groups for the use of meeting rooms are all handled by a corps of close to 50 volunteer student staffers. Each student makes a commitment of between one and three hours a week plus attendance at a regular Friday afternoon staff meeting. At these meetings problems surrounding their tasks and pressing women's issues on campus are discussed. Student staffers share in some of the decisions on programming and on allocation of women's center funds to other student programs. At institutions where there is a high proportion of re-entry women, using students as volunteers and employees is particularly successful since many women are over age 25 and bring a degree of maturity and solid job experience to their work in centers.

Not only has the use of students, both paid and volunteer, made it possible for women's centers to perform all their functions; it has proved to be an important way of increasing visibility for the women's center and creating ambassadors throughout the campus. Perhaps even more important, it has proved to be an invaluable experience for those students who have participated either as volunteers, interns, or paid workers. For most, it has meant work with real responsibility and an opportunity to be exposed to the serious issues raised by the women's movement on a day-to-day basis. And, finally, as an unexpected by-product, it has given students the chance to work closely with and get to know faculty, administrators, and other adult women in a much more informal manner than is usually experienced by undergraduate students.

Accountability within the institution varies. Most directors report to an administrator in either student or academic affairs. Some centers have advisory or executive committees which are highly structured and meet regularly to set and approve policy. Most meet infrequently and irregularly, serving primarily as a public relations arm and as a support and information group.

Directors serve on a wide range of campus committees. These include committees concerned specifically with women, such as women's studies, affirmative action, sexual harassment, childcare, the chancellor's committee on the status of women, or the academic women's caucus. In addition, they may serve on the task force on drugs and alcohol, the presidential commission on planning and future mission of the university, or the prestigious faculty affairs committee of the university senate. Many directors also serve on committees and boards of community groups, in this way cementing ties between the institution and the larger community.

Most directors play an important role in building a support network with other women's groups on campus. They cooperate with these groups on programs, sit on their advisory boards or committees, and help present a united front where there are specific problems that affect all women on campus. Unless, for instance, there is rapport between the women's center, the women's studies program, the research center, the continuing education program for women, and the affirmative action office, each group appears more fragmented and its influence on the administration and on the campus is reduced.

The Current Status: Problems and Prospects

In assessing the current status and future prospects of the several hundred multi-service, campus-based women's centers, it is noteworthy that despite serious changes in institutional priorities, the political climate for women, and extensive budget cuts, almost all have survived. Essentially a phenomenon of the 1970s, they developed out of a determination to end the discrimination and isolation that so many women felt on campuses across the country and from the keen awareness of the need to set up new programs for women. Institutional funding was forthcoming, although in minimal amounts. Very few centers were started in the 1980s, partly because by then there was on most campuses a proliferation of other programs concerned with questions of equity for students, faculty, and staff; partly because of budget cuts; and partly because of increasing political conservatism. Yet, in spite of these current problems, most centers are in no imminent danger of being phased out; indeed, some are seen as a more integral part of their institution than they were in earlier years.

The centers share a number of problems, which defy easy solutions. These problems were brought out at two conferences, both held in 1979. The first was a conference on special programs for women in higher education, held at Arden House under the sponsorship of the Barnard College Women's Center. The second, a conference on women's centers and higher education, was the final stage of a several-phase National Women's Center Training Project of the Everywoman's Center at the University of Massachusetts at Amherst. In the report from the Barnard conference, participants representing women's centers described a kind of administrative schizophrenia on the part of institutions—on the one hand, giving minimal support to their women's centers and, on the other hand, turning to them to solve problems the institution was unequipped or unwilling to handle.[12] And the final report of the Everywoman's Center conference describes comparable problems that women's centers faced then and continue to face.[13] If anything, the problems dealt with by women's centers and the administrative problems of the centers themselves are more serious today than they were before.

Many centers have suffered severe budget cuts in the last few years. In some cases, this had reduced the full-time staff to one. At the same time, centers which used to receive outside funding for part of their programming have found that much of this funding has dried up and that they must now depend on their institutions for most or all of their funds. For the most part, directors have given up hope of expanding their activities but, instead, find that they must pare existing programs.

For example, some centers have been forced to limit their services to matriculated students and no longer open their doors to women from the larger community. Those few centers that can point to a supportive dean, vice chancellor, or other administrator at the policymaking level consider themselves fortunate because of the vast difference that support makes in the ease with which the center operates.

The role of women's centers today is much more limited than it was in the 1970s. Apart from budgetary considerations, many of their earlier functions have been institutionalized elsewhere on campus. The number of women's studies programs and research centers has increased and continues to increase. Most colleges and universities now have affirmative action offices, sexual harassment policies and procedures, counseling services, and rape prevention programs. Centers are now largely oriented toward student activities and concerns, concerns that are somewhat different from those of the 1970s. Students in the 1980s by and large reflect the prevailing climate of political conservatism and what has been called, correctly or not, a neo- or post-feminist era. They tend to regard the battles of the 1970s as having been won. In the words of one director, they are "conventional, careerist and complacent."[14] It seems to them that equal employment opportunity exists, that egalitarian marriages can be achieved, and that they can combine independence, productive careers, marriage, and children for a life of fulfillment. One cannot, of course, generalize about all students in the 1980s any more than any other period, and there are certainly young feminists on campus who are committed to the movement. But it is clearly the case that many of the women's center programs that attracted students in the 1970s do not attract the students of the 1980s. Women's centers are finding that students are less interested in women's issues that have to do with poverty, racism, reproductive rights, single parenting, and health hazards, but turn out for programs on careers and the combination of professional life with motherhood.

On the other hand, as women's centers have moved away from some of the provocative issues of the 1970s and moved from the margins to the mainstream of their institution, they have been able to achieve a degree of security that earlier women's centers lacked. Their position is also furthered by the fact that they are now represented on the national scene by two organizations. One is the Women's Centers/Services Caucus which operates within the National Women's Studies Association and represents campus-based centers. The other is the National Association of Women's Centers (founded in 1986), which includes both community and campus-based centers. At the same time, institutions are reassessing the place of women's centers on their campuses, and as directors leave they tend to be replaced by new directors more closely allied to the administration. There is a risk that in time centers may become a version of what used to be the dean of women's office, providing services for women students as an arm of the administration but not necessarily serving as advocates for women, particularly on subjects that are deemed to be controversial. Some directors have said that they no longer use the word "feminist" in their descriptive literature. In other cases, new directors are hired who do not see themselves as feminists, but rather as good administrators and part of a management team. One such director who manages a wide range of activities on a modest budget, including reaching out to men and doing programs on "dressing for success," was told by her chancellor that her center is "a jewel in his crown."

Conclusions

In sum, women's centers played a significant role in bringing feminism to the campus and serving as advocates for women in the 1970s. They were never well funded, but nevertheless were able to offer a wide range of services to students, faculty, and community women. They have survived and continue to survive during the 1980s, but their scope of activity has narrowed considerably as many of their earlier functions have been institutionalized in the form of women's studies programs, research centers, affirmative action offices, sexual harassment policies and procedures, counseling services, and rape prevention programs. Advocacy and activist functions have been reduced as centers have concentrated more on career planning and other student services. At the same time, there has been less participation by community women, not only because of the shift in focus of campus centers but also because of the development of off-campus community centers and services for women. Women's centers on campuses, in their early years, provided many services that were lacking in the community—personal and career counseling, rape crisis and sexual harassment counseling, referrals for displaced homemakers, and so on, but over the past six or seven years state and local funds have been used to provide such services through community centers and agencies. It was often campus students and faculty women who spearheaded these local programs, providing advice and technical assistance. Indeed, some of these community women's centers are run by former students who gained experience at campus-based centers.

Campus women's centers are clearly in a period of transition. Their historic role of advocacy and activism on feminist issues extending beyond the campus is not in doubt. What their eventual role on campus will be, however, is not yet certain.

Appendix 5.1
Women's Centers Interviewed

Women's Center
Barnard College
New York, NY

Women's Center
Brooklyn College
Brooklyn, NY

Sarah Doyle Women's Center
Brown University
Providence, RI

Center for the Study, Education
  and Advancement of Women
University of Calfornia
Berkeley, CA

Women's Resource Center
University of California
Los Angeles, CA

Women's Center
University of California
Santa Barbara, CA

Women's Center
Central Connecticut State College
New Britain, CT

Women's Center
University of Connecticut
Storrs, CT

Douglass Advisory Services for
  Women
Douglass College
New Brunswick, NJ

Women's Center
Jersey City State College
Jersey City, NJ

Emily Taylor Women's Resource
  and Career Center
University of Kansas
Lawrence, KS

Everywoman's Center
University of Massachusetts
Amherst, MA

Center for Continuing Education
  for Women
University of Michigan
Ann Arbor, MI

Women's Center
University of Minnesota
Minneapolis, MN

Women's Center
Montclair State College
Montclair, NJ

Women's Center
University of New Mexico
Albuquerque, NM

Women's Resource Center
University of North Carolina
Greensboro, NC

Women's Center
Oakland Community College
Detroit, MI

Women's Services
Ohio State University
Columbus, OH

Penn Women's Center
University of Pennsylvania
Philadelphia, PA

Women's Center
Ramapo College
Mahwah, NJ

Women's Research and Resource
   Center
Spelman College
Atlanta, GA

Newcomb Women's Center
Tulane University
New Orleans, LA

Women's Resource Center
University of Utah
Salt Lake City, UT

Women's Center
Vanderbilt University
Nashville, TN

Notes

1. Association of American Colleges, Project on the Status and Education of Women, "Women's Centers: Where Are They?" (Washington, DC: AAC, 1979).
2. Florence Howe, Suzanne Howard, and Mary Jo Boehm Strauss, eds., *Everywoman's Guide to Colleges and Universities* (Old Westbury, NY: Feminist Press, 1982).
3. This estimate is provided by the National Association of Women's Centers, a new organization which is referred to later in the text.
4. For a full description of the development of continuing education programs in the 1960s, see Jean W. Campbell, "Women Drop Back In: Educational Innovations in the Sixties," in Alice Rossi and Ann Calderwood, eds., *Academic Women on the Move* (New York: Russell Sage Foundation, 1973). See also chapter 4 in this volume.
5. Campbell, "Women Drop Back In," p. 96.
6. Judy Bertelson, "Women's Center Survey," in *Two Studies of Women in Higher Education*, unpublished, Ford Foundation, May 1974.
7. Karen Childers, Phyllis Racklin, Cynthia Secor, and Carolyn Tracy, "A Network of One's Own," in Gloria DeSole and Leonore Hoffman, eds., *Rocking the Boat* (New York: Modern Language Association, 1981).

8. *New York Times*, November 5, 1986, p. B1.

9. Established in 1972 with support from the Ford Foundation, the first Higher Education Resource Services (HERS) office was at Brown University; it later moved to Wellesley and was called HERS/New England. It was followed in a few years by HERS/Mid-Atlantic at the University of Pennsylvania. The newest chapter, HERS/West, located at the University of Utah, is funded by grants from the Ford Foundation, the Carnegie Corporation of New York, and the William Donner Foundation.

10. Spelman College, *Women's Research and Resource Center Newsletter*, vol. 1, no. 1, March 1982, p. 1.

11. Available budget data are not sufficiently precise to be measured. A few directors are paid by academic departments; a portion of operating expenses of some women's centers is paid by student life departments, and women's centers have no knowledge or control of routine operating costs. Sometimes the budget includes an extra stipend from the president's or chancellor's office to cover the cost of a special program such as the Rape Prevention and Education Program. Also, sometimes the budget includes an outside grant for a special one-time project such as a conference or publication. Although small budgets are the rule, a handful of centers—mostly former continuing education programs—have budgets well over $200,000, with extra outside funding for special projects.

12. Elizabeth Kamarck Minnich, in cooperation with the Barnard Women's Center, *Special Programs for Women in Higher Education, a Report from the Barnard Conference, March 14–16, 1979* (New York: Women's Center, Barnard College, 1979), pp. 43–44.

13. Kathryn L. Giraud, Patricia A. Sorce, and Joan L. Sweeney, *Increasing the Effectiveness of Women's Programs on College Campuses: A Summary of the Activities and Accomplishments of the National Women's Training Program*, pp. 41–55 (National Women's Training Project, Everywoman's Center, University of Massachusetts at Amherst, and the U.S. Department of Health, Education, and Welfare, unpublished, no date).

14. Alice Miller, "Wooing College Women in a Post-Feminist Era: The Challenge Facing Women's Centers," paper presented at the first annual convention of the National Association of Women's Centers, San Antonio, May 29–June 1, 1986, p. 2.

6

Women's Colleges

A study of the women's colleges in the last two decades reveals that they are declining in numbers and in overall enrollment. At the same time, however, individual women's colleges are characterized by a great vitality. This strength is apparent in their capacity to sustain a female tradition of intellectual excellence, in their promotion of women as scholars, and in their focus on a healthy educational climate for women. In order to understand the current status of women's colleges and their particular role in education, it is revealing to step back in time to the beginning of higher education for women in the United States and to see how prevailing cultural, economic, and social circumstances gave rise to these colleges and shaped their subsequent history.

The Beginnings of Higher Education for Women

When Harvard College opened in 1636, its chief function was to educate young men for the clergy and for other professions such as law and, to a lesser extent, teaching.[1] Since these professions were limited to men, formal higher education was not open to women. Indeed, throughout the colonial period, it was not considered necessary to provide *any* formal education for girls. Free public education was not generally available and in private schools boys were taught reading, writing, and arithmetic, while girls, if they attended at all, learned only reading. Girls were usually taught domestic skills. It was only in New England that girls learned to read, as it was considered important in Puritan society for women as well as men to read the Bible.[2]

Following the Revolutionary War, the idea of education for women gained acceptance as the founders of the republic saw the need to educate a populace capable of exercising democratic principles. When public schools were established, education was extended to girls as well as boys, on the rationale that educated wives and mothers were needed to raise their sons as informed and responsible citizens. During the early nineteenth century, secondary education spread rapidly, starting with private schools, first for boys and then for girls. Private schools for girls did not prepare them for college, but they did provide general cultural subjects including languages, history, and even some science along with the social graces. Public secondary schools, however, provided basically the same education for girls as for boys, thus contributing to the growing aspiration of girls for higher education.

Higher education for women first took the form of academies and seminaries, some of which were founded primarily to train students for teaching. Beginning in the 1830s female seminaries were established in New England and New York, later spreading to the West and the South. For example, Mount Holyoke Seminary, later to become Mount Holyoke College, opened in 1837 and its graduates went on to found new seminaries in other parts of the country. Colleges for women were first established in the South during the period prior to the Civil War. They were, of course, open only to white women. Coeducation began during the same period, initially at Oberlin in 1837, followed by a few private colleges and early state universities.

During the Civil War, women entered many occupations previously restricted to men, thus establishing precedents for women to work in those areas and creating pressures for the education needed. Other conditions during the war and its aftermath created an environment favorable to the admission of women in higher education. The extension of political and legal rights to black men inevitably raised the issue of the status of women, including access to education. The rapid expansion of public schools enlarged the need for teachers, one of the few occupations in which women were accepted. The establishment of public land grant institutions under the Morrill Act of 1862 opened up new opportunities for coeducation that were not previously available.

Notwithstanding these conditions, women did not move into higher education without a struggle. With a few exceptions, even the land grant institutions, which were not legally required to admit women, initially excluded women or greatly restricted their participation. Coeducation was not broadly accepted in these institutions until the 1870s, following a decade or more of pressure from women who demanded admission to schools receiving state funds.[3]

As higher education expanded during the latter part of the nineteenth century, a diversity of institutions came into being. They included, in addition to public coeducational institutions, women's colleges, normal schools, and other public vocational institutions. In this period the configuration of higher education became increasingly coeducational. In 1870 only 30 percent of colleges were coeducational; by 1900, 70 percent admitted both men and women.[4] Also, in this period many of the well-known women's colleges of today were founded. They were not uniform in purpose; rather they reflected two distinct perceptions of the higher education needs of women. Some women's colleges were based on the view that separate education was necessary because of women's special domestic, social, and professional spheres. Seminaries were the forerunners of some of these institutions, such as Mary Baldwin in Virginia and Agnes Scott in Georgia. Other women's colleges, such as Vassar, Smith, Wellesley, and Bryn Mawr, were designed to provide women with opportunities for education equivalent to that of men, opportunities that were denied to them by such prestigious institutions as Harvard, Yale, and Princeton.

By 1900 there was a diverse population of women's colleges throughout the country. They can be classified as follows:

Independent:
> *Seven Sisters colleges* (Vassar, Wellesley, Mount Holyoke, Smith, Bryn Mawr, Radcliffe, and Barnard)
> *Southern white women's colleges,* such as Sweet Briar, Randolph-Macon, Sophie Newcomb, and Goucher
> *Southern black women's colleges,* such as Spelman and Barber-Scotia

Parochial:
> *Catholic women's colleges,* such as Marymount, Emmanuel, and the College of New Rochelle

Public:
> Hunter, Douglass, and Texas Women's University

In the early twentieth century, the two-year junior colleges emerged, representing another set of institutions important in the history of women's education. In the 1920s and 1930s other independent women's colleges were also founded, notably Bennington, Sarah Lawrence, and Scripps. A brief history of these colleges follows.

The Pioneer Period: 1875–1920

The Seven Sisters

Seven independent schools for women, now commonly called the "Seven Sisters," were founded in the late nineteenth century to provide an education equal to that of men at the Ivy League colleges. Often the women's colleges were more experimental than the men's colleges, especially in their science curriculum. Mount Holyoke, Vassar, and Wellesley innovated laboratory research, provided expensive equipment, and emphasized new research methods. By the 1890s the Seven Sisters had pioneered in developing new social science courses as well.[5]

The women's colleges provided talented women intellectuals with the opportunity to do research and to teach. Historian Margaret Rossiter notes that the women's colleges employed the largest number of notable achieving women in science in this formative period. Women faculty at Wellesley had unusual power and status. However, at some of the women's colleges—Smith and Vassar, for example—where men served on the faculty, distinctions in titles, salaries, and housing arrangements made the women professors feel secondary in status.[6]

The women's colleges altered the conventional classical curriculum and the intellectual ethos that accompanied it. Because middle-class women were associated with teaching and with reform, the separate women's colleges upheld the norms of social service for their students. Studies of the careers of the first graduates of the Seven Sisters demonstrate that this generation was instrumental in establishing the agenda of social reform for the Progressive movement in the United States. For example, graduates founded settlement houses and initiated studies of slums and urban problems. Not every early graduate of the women's colleges departed from the expected social role, however. Some succumbed to the "family claim" and after college devoted their lives to domesticity.[7]

From the "bonds of womanhood," early women college students built a sense of community. After college many women lived together in dyads, or what Lillian Faderman terms "Boston marriages." Marriage rates for the first generation of students compared with the rest of the female population were quite low. By the 1920s, this generation of progressive women students, who grew up in a female world and who were bent on careers, was replaced by a new generation who were desirous of heterosexual unions and reconciling marriage with career. The women's colleges experienced a rift between the pioneer generation of career-minded faculty and the next generation of students. On the whole, however, the intellectual life was still held in high esteem by all.[8]

Southern White Women's Colleges

In the nineteenth century, the ideology of southern womanhood emphasized women's piety, purity, and submission to husband and to God.[9] Southern culture did not tolerate any questioning of slavery—the slavery of race or the slavery of sex. To challenge patriarchal authority would have been tantamount to overt rebellion. At the same time, however, southern white women were expected to rule the domestic sphere.

Rates of literacy for southern white women lagged behind those of their northern sisters. Still, there was a seminary movement that affected women's education in the South. Historian Thomas Woody suggests that Georgia Female College, which opened in 1839, thought of itself as a serious contender for the title of "the first women's college."[10] After studying the curriculum, and finding that it failed to require Latin and Greek, Woody concludes that it was not a genuine college. Woody notes that Mary Sharp College, which opened in 1851, in Winchester, Tennessee, required both Latin and Greek in a four-year curriculum leading to an AB degree and credits that institution as the first bona fide women's college. It is difficult to say for sure what was a seminary and what was a genuine college. The larger significance of the intellectual climate in the South is that by the late 1800s, white, middle-class women had opportunities to attend seminaries and get more than a decorous education. Also, the tradition of separate social spheres for men and women was very much the operating force behind the development of separate women's colleges.

Several independent women's colleges existed in the South prior to 1920. Among these were Goucher, Sweet Briar, Hood, Agnes Scott, Randolph-Macon, and Sophie Newcomb, the coordinate college of Tulane. Very little attention has been paid by scholars to the clientele, faculty, or curriculum of these institutions or to the career patterns of their alumnae. It should be noted that until 1921 these colleges were members of the Southern Association of Collegiate Women. This association controlled admissions to the organization and then promoted its members through fellowships and publicity. After 1921, the Association of Collegiate Alumnae, which represented eastern, midwestern, and western women's colleges, merged with the Southern Association to form the American Association of University Women, an organization which endures to this day.

Southern Black Women's Colleges

Prior to the Civil War, black men and women experienced slavery in the South and racial oppression in the North. It was illegal to educate slaves in the southern states. After the Civil War, education was viewed as a key to the emancipation of southern blacks and to the elevation of the status of blacks in the North. Thus, intrinsic to the aims of black women's higher education has been the concept of "race uplift."[11]

In the nineteenth century, black education was not rigidly divided along gender lines. The majority of black women were educated in coeducational institutions. A few single-sex colleges for black women, all located in the South, opened during the pioneer period. In 1881 in Atlanta, Georgia, Sophie B. Packard and Harriet Giles, two white women of strong New England abolitionist tradition, founded Spelman College. They emphasized the liberal arts curriculum, but with considerable attention paid to the practical skills of women students.

Bennett College in Greensboro, North Carolina, originally opened as a coeducational institution in 1873. In the early years, Bennett trained men and women for careers in education and the ministry. In 1926 Bennett was converted into a liberal arts college for black women. Two other women's colleges, both now coeducational, were founded in this period: Barber-Scotia in Concord, North Carolina, was founded in 1867, and Houston Tillotson in Austin, Texas, was founded in 1876.

Between 1900 and 1920, a vocational education movement swept through the United States, and a debate between liberal arts versus vocational education was a crucial issue for black women's colleges. Black education was particularly influenced by Booker T. Washington, who encouraged the development of vocational programs for blacks that would give them marketable skills in industry. W. E. B. Dubois rejected this notion of accommodation to what he perceived as a racist occupational system and preferred that blacks continue to acquire liberal arts degrees. Black women's colleges had commitments both to general enlightenment and to the pragmatic concerns of the black community. Both Spelman and Bennett colleges developed vocational programs for women in the form of home economic curricula in the 1920s.[12]

Catholic Women's Colleges

Most Catholic colleges before 1900 excluded women. During the pioneer period (after 1900), a variety of sisterhoods were instrumental in founding 19 women's colleges. While some drew their clientele from upper-class Catholic families and were located in suburban settings, many others educated the children of working-class families and were urban, commuter colleges. The Catholic women's colleges were also scattered geographically. Recent scholarship on Catholic women's higher education is nearly nonexistent. This is unfortunate since these institutions constitute over half of all the women's colleges in the United States.

What were the central purposes of Catholic higher education for women? Moral character was stressed, as well as intellectual development.[13] Service was also expected. In 1931 Marygrove College, in Detroit, stated that one of its principles behind the liberal arts was the "art of making a living." Every graduate at Marygrove was to be provided with the means for self-support. The occupations which the college considered appropriate for women included college or high school teaching, social work, banking, secretarial work, journalism, library work, music, and being a successful wife and mother in an ideal Catholic home.

In 1921 the College of St. Catharine in St. Paul, Minnesota, listed 70 percent of its graduates as teachers. This figure had fallen to 30 percent by 1931, reflecting a variety of new careers which Catholic women pursued, including business and social work. In 1929 the College of New Rochelle, in New York, listed its graduates in the following occupations: teaching—college, high school, and elementary; business—executive, secretarial, statistical, sales, and insurance; journalism—editorial, publicity, and advertising; architecture; dental hygiene; law; library science; social services; dietetics; and stage.[14] Possibly because the Catholic women who attended these colleges were more often than not from working-class backgrounds, these colleges promoted careers as a source of mobility for their clientele.

Diversity and Expansion: 1920–1950

After the pioneer period, women's colleges continued to grow in numbers. The period of the 1920s and 1930s saw the founding of many more Catholic women's colleges. Additionally, there was a drive to establish two-year women's colleges with more vocational objectives, known as the junior college movement. Finally, several innovative four-year, elite private women's colleges such as Sarah Lawrence, Bennington, and Scripps were founded in this era.[15]

To a large degree, the colleges founded in the 1920s were influenced by the Progressive education movement. Progressive education emphasized child-centered or student-centered learning. It put a great priority on creativity and independence in the classroom. Art and music were considered as intellectually important as the humanities, social sciences, and the physical and biological sciences.

Sarah Lawrence College (in Bronxville, New York), which graduated its first class in 1934, emerged from this context of emphasis on creative higher education; it was committed to experimental learning. Bennington College (in Bennington, Vermont) also emphasized independent learning and the arts. Scripps College (in Pomona, California) broke with traditional departmental structures, as did the other two colleges, and grouped fields around intellectual interests. By World War II, then, the women's colleges were highly diversified.[16]

Continuity and Change: 1950–1960

The period from the end of World War II until 1960 has been viewed as a retrogressive one for educated American women. Betty Friedan talked about the era in terms of the "feminine mystique." The gains that women made in the labor force in World War II were largely eradicated by the social pressure to have women return to the home to resume their domestic roles. In the main, the women's colleges tried to keep the beacon of feminism alive during this period. The Seven Sisters continued to resist attempts to add home economics to their curriculum and continued to inspire some women to go on to graduate school. Nonetheless, maternity and childcare were widely viewed as women's social destiny. Sensing the possible frustration of their graduates, leaders of the elite women's colleges began in the 1950s to talk about a "new design for living." What this meant in the particular has never been clear. In general, they argued that women should return for advanced degrees after their children grew up. This provided the pool of older talented women who were later to make their "comebacks" in the 1960s and 1970s, continuing their education and moving into the professions.[17]

Recent scholarship takes issue with the idea that the women's colleges were wholly attuned to the ideology of the feminist movement. In the late 1950s and 1960s the president of Mount Holyoke spoke of its students as "uncommon women," women whose aspirations should remain high, and one study showed that 25 percent of Mount Holyoke's graduates majored in sciences or mathematics. Nevertheless, such "uncommon women" were clearly given to understand that they were mostly expected to marry and to devote themselves to volunteer community affairs or the teaching profession.[18]

During this post–World War II period, many of the women's colleges consciously courted male faculty members in the hope of raising the status of their departments. Very few of the women's colleges accommodated married women with children. In a study done of the Radcliffe PhD in 1956, several respondents who were teaching at women's colleges expressed deep frustration with the barriers which confronted even the most talented of faculty women.[19] One woman noted that women's colleges were still a "man's world" in terms of hiring, salaries, promotions, and the esteem granted by the institution. By 1960 in the Seven Sisters (except for Wellesley College), male presidents predominated, and many men filled the ranks of faculty and administrators.[20]

In 1961, at her inauguration as president of Radcliffe, Mary I. Bunting referred to the "climate of unexpectation" for American women. Women, she argued, were dissuaded from significant intellectual involvement, and she expressed the view that women's colleges should give more attention to women's special needs. Acting on her own principles, Bunting opened the Radcliffe Institute in 1961 to accommodate women who wanted to come back to careers in the academic and medical professions. But as one study noted, the prospect of coming back involved the "necessity of catching up. Ten or twenty years is a long time to be away from one's profession . . . and women realize it."[21]

Challenges and Creative Adaptations: 1960–1985

The contemporary feminist movement that emerged in the United States in the 1960s posed new challenges to women's colleges. They came to be viewed as institutions which had been victims of patriarchy, and as such they were seen by many as anachronistic. During the 1960s, the number of women's colleges declined sharply as some shifted to coeducational status, some merged with coordinate or other institutions, and a few small and marginal schools closed their doors.

Beginning in the 1970s, however, women's colleges took on a new lease on life. After years of acting like "sleeping beauties," they saw themselves once again as leaders in articulating the educational needs of women just as they had in the pioneer period. If we look at women's colleges and their institutional responses to the pressure for coeducation between 1960 and 1985, we find that the early years were characterized by a "flight" pattern that later changed to a "fight" pattern. After losing some of the brightest women students to the newly coeducational Ivy League schools such as Yale and Princeton, the women's colleges rebounded, recruited students more aggressively, and strengthened their commitment to the production of high-achieving women.[22]

The continuation of the historically significant role in providing an equal opportunity for women to become the producers as well as the consumers of knowledge characterizes the contemporary portrait of women's colleges. Yet, this portrait must be put in the context of the broader trends in higher education and the roles of women in society.

Women's greater access to colleges and universities and their admission to historically male institutions, including the military academies, have diverted potential students away from women's colleges. These changes have necessitated modifications in the position and mission of these colleges within the structure of higher education. Gender desegregation has meant that women's colleges no longer provide the sole or primary access to higher education for their traditional clientele. However, desegregation also means that these colleges have new opportunities to explore additional roles and define their particular missions. Consequently, the contemporary portrait of women's colleges is often a study in contrasts—contrasts between decline and vitality, between relevancy and obsolescence, between innovation and conservatism.

A Statistical Portrait of Women's Colleges

In 1986 there were 90 women's colleges, including 17 junior colleges. These institutions are so designated because their self-identity, mission, and enrollment are principally female and they are dedicated to collegiate instruction.[23] Women's colleges constitute 2.7 percent of all U.S. colleges and universities. They are located in 21 states and the District of Columbia, with 50 percent situated in the Northeast and another 21 percent in the South. As Table 6.1 shows, independent or private institutions constitute 44 percent of the total. There are only two public institutions—Douglass College of Rutgers University and Texas Women's University. The majority of these women's institutions have some

Table 6.1   Number and Types of Women's Colleges: 1960–1986

	1960	1970	1980	1986
Total Institutions	2,000	2,525	3,231	3,388
Women's Institutions	233	255	117	90
Independent				40
Catholic				32
Other Parochial				16
Public				2

Sources: 1987 Directory of Higher Education (Washington, DC: Higher Education Publications, 1987); Peterson's Guide to American Colleges and Universities (Princeton, NJ: Peterson's Guides, various years); and Women's College Coalition, Profiles of Women's Colleges, (Washington, DC: WCC, 1980–1981).

explicit affiliation; 36 percent of the total are Catholic and 18 percent are affiliated with a variety of Protestant denominations. As previously noted, the Catholic women's colleges play a significant role in the education of women and in the women's college community.

Given the importance of various religions in women's higher education, it is interesting to note that there are few institutions for Jewish women. While there are numerous seminaries, rabbinical colleges, and proprietary institutions for men, there is only one seminary for Jewish women among the women's colleges. The absence of a college curricular tradition for Jewish women, with the one exception, is significant and most probably the result of orthodox Judaic teaching. The belief in the separate, yet complementary, roles of the sexes has historically defined scholarship and study (especially of the Torah) as the province of men.[24]

The level of education and types of degree programs vary among the women's colleges, but the predominant mode is the four-year liberal arts college (see Table 6.2). Nearly half of the institutions offer the Bachelor of Arts or Science degree as their highest degree, and most of them define themselves as liberal arts institutions. The 17 junior, or two-year, colleges represent 19 percent of the total. Approximately a third of the institutions offer graduate degrees. However, this high proportion is somewhat misleading. Most of the graduate programs at women's colleges offer master's degrees only, particularly in teaching, social work, and nursing. Doctorates are awarded only at Bryn Mawr, Simmons, Smith, and Texas Women's University.

The enrollment of women in higher education for 1986 totaled more than 5.9 million, and they represented 52 percent of all college enroll-

TABLE 6.2   Level of Educational Degree Programs in Women's Colleges: 1986

Level of Degree Programs	Number of Colleges	Percentage
Two-year	17	18.9%
Four-year	43	47.8
Graduate	29	32.2
Nondegree	1	1.1
Total	90	100.0

Source: National Center for Education Statistics, *1987 Directory of Higher Education* (Washington, DC: Higher Education Publications, 1987).

Table 6.3   Enrollment at Women's Colleges: 1986

Number of Students	Number of Colleges	Percentage
Fewer than 100	1	1.1%
100–499	22	24.4
500–999	29	32.2
1,000–1,499	15	16.7
1,500–1,999	14	15.6
More than 2,000	9	10.0
Total	90	100.0

Source: National Center for Education Statistics, 1987 Directory of Higher Education (Washington, DC: Higher Education Publications, 1987).

ments. That same year, women's colleges enrolled approximately 100,000, or less than 2 percent of all women attending college. Over 80 percent of these women were enrolled in undergraduate programs. Women's college enrollment is predominantly undergraduate and predominantly full time. However, the majority of graduate students in these institutions attend part time.[25]

The size of women's colleges as indicated by student enrollments ranges from 200 at Hartford College for Women in Connecticut to well over 8,000 at Texas Women's University. Table 6.3 shows the 1986 distribution of institutional size, with a third enrolling between 500 to 1,000 students and another third in the 1,000–2,000 range. Generally, women's colleges tend to be smaller in size than the national average for institutions.

There is only limited demographic information about the women who attend women's colleges. A 1980 comparative study of freshman women at 50 women's colleges and all freshman women reports that almost 99 percent of first-year students at women's colleges were under age 25 compared with 61 percent nationwide, and a larger proportion (18.4 percent compared with 16 percent nationwide) were minority women. Among freshman women at women's colleges, blacks represented 11 percent, Asian Americans 2.2 percent, Mexican Americans 1.8 percent, and Native Americans and Puerto Ricans both approximately 0.8 percent. In Profile II: A Second Profile of Women's Colleges, it was reported that the first-year women at women's colleges tended to come from families with a higher than average level of educational attainment, with more dependents, and with more siblings in college.[26] The median family income was $24,999 compared with a median of between $15,000 and $19,999 for women at all institutions.

In summary, the women's college is usually seen as a small to medium size, predominantly white, private, four-year institution located in the Northeast, the kind of institution typified by the Seven Sisters and other elite institutions. This view, however, does not convey the diversity among women's colleges. It neglects Catholic, public, and two-year institutions, as well as the two historically black women's colleges, Spelman in Atlanta and Bennett in Greensboro, North Carolina. It also overlooks institutions with other religious affiliations, Protestant and Jewish. Keeping in mind that diversity, we now turn to a consideration of the debate over the contemporary relevance and strength of education at women's colleges.

The Forces of Decline

The late 1960s and the 1970s were difficult for women's colleges. They experienced declining enrollments, decreased financial support, and a decrease in their representation as an institutional form of higher education. But perhaps most troubling was the use of these statistics as evidence in what was a growing criticism of women's colleges as institutions. Social observers pointed to the dropping enrollments of women's colleges and the decline in the number of these institutions as indicative of their fundamental nonviability in contemporary times.

The empirical evidence clearly reveals that the 1960s and 1970s were a period of distress and contraction. From 233 women's colleges in 1960, there remained only 90 in 1986, a decline of over 60 percent. Women's colleges constituted 11.6 percent of the institutions of higher education in 1960 and only 2.7 percent in 1986. Moreover, additional declines are in store. Wheaton College and Goucher College, both stalwarts among women's colleges, announced plans to admit men: Goucher in 1987 and Wheaton in 1988.[27]

The contraction in women's colleges is also evident in the enrollment patterns during those two decades. In 1960 approximately 106,000 women attended women's colleges, and they represented approximately 10 percent of all women attending college in that year. By 1986, while their total enrollments were approximately the same, proportionally women's colleges were enrolling less than 2 percent of all college women. On the basis of these statistics, it has been argued that women themselves no longer view those institutions as serving their

higher education needs. With expanding opportunities in other institutions of higher education, more women are choosing coeducational over
single-sex institutions.

It is important, however, to review these arguments and the data
used to support them. Part of the explanation for why women's colleges
are contracting is related to broader trends in higher education. First,
there is an ongoing realignment of institutional types. While the total
number of colleges and universities has increased, many of the newly
established institutions have been public two-year colleges which have
made postsecondary education more accessible and less expensive. Private institutions, including women's colleges, have been adversely affected. The pattern of decline of women's colleges between 1968 and
1984 is shown in Table 6.4. The loss of parochial schools, especially the
Catholic ones, accounts for the greatest decrease—58 percent of the
total.

Colleges with smaller than average enrollments and junior colleges
were also likely to drop from the women's colleges population. In addition to the movement from private to public education, they were particularly hard-hit by the financial pressures caused by rising inflation.
Profile II: A Second Profile of Women's Colleges notes that women's colleges,
like most small colleges, are critically tuition-dependent and "derive
approximately 49 per cent of their total current revenues from tuition
and fees."[28] Consequently, declining enrollments and financial uncer-
tainty have been particularly hard on these colleges.

The decline in the number of women's colleges since the 1960s is part
of a general trend away from single-sex colleges and universities,
whether for women or men. In fact, the decline of single-sex institutions

Table 6.4   Pattern of Contraction in Women's Colleges: 1960–1984

Type of Institution	Number Decreased 1960–1984	Percentage of Decline
Public	5	3.5%
Independent	54	38.3
Parochial	82	58.2
Total	141	100.0

Sources: Peterson's Guide to American Colleges and Universities (Princeton, NJ: Peterson's
Guides, 1960, 1984); and National Center for Education Statistics, *1987 Directory of Higher
Education* (Washington, DC: Higher Education Publications, 1960, 1984).

for men has been much greater than that for women. In 1960 there were 139 men's colleges, which constituted about 7 percent of higher education institutions. In 1986 the number was down to 94, and most of these were small Catholic or rabbinical seminaries. A few were military institutions and only three were liberal arts colleges. The total enrollment of men's colleges of all types was little more than 22,000 in 1986.[29] That represents a decrease of over 97 percent. In today's society, men's colleges are all but nonexistent. In comparison, women's institutions have fared well.

The fate of the 141 institutions which disappeared from the roster of women's colleges between 1960 and 1984 is presented in Table 6.5. Fifty-five colleges, or 39 percent of the total, became coeducational. Five merged with other institutions. The situation of the remaining 81 institutions is unknown, and it is presumed that most have ceased operation. Generally, the four-year and graduate institutions were more likely to admit males, while the two-year colleges and Catholic women's colleges were mainly among the institutions that appeared to have closed their doors.

The decline hypothesis is concerned not only with the statistical trends of women's colleges, but also with the issues of their educational role and significance. Contemporary criticism of women's colleges is based on two quite different arguments. On the one hand, women's colleges are seen as outdated and no longer needed in modern times as a consequence of the shift to coeducation. On the other hand, women's colleges are seen as needed but no longer playing a significant role in higher education because they have not maintained their special historic role and promise. The former perspective doubts the continuing neces-

Table 6.5   **Nature of the Decrease in Women's Colleges: 1960–1980**

Nature of Decrease	Number	Percentage
Became Coeducational	55	39.0%
Merged with Another College	5	3.5
Unknown (Presumed to Have Ceased Operation)	81	57.4
Total	141	99.9

Sources: National Center for Education Statistics, *Directory of Higher Education* (Washington, DC: Higher Education Publications, 1960, 1980) (Washington, DC: U.S. Government Printing Office); and the *Peterson's Guide to American Colleges and Universities* (Princeton, NJ: Peterson's Guides, 1960, 1980).

sity of women's colleges as a special institutional form in higher education. The latter does not. Rather, it represents the position of those
who advocate a stronger role for women's colleges. Feminists such as
Catharine Stimpson, a graduate of Bryn Mawr, and Betty Friedan and
Gloria Steinem, both graduates of Smith, have criticized their alma ma-
ters for their moribund stance vis-à-vis the women's movement during
the 1960s and 1970s.[30] The 1980s appear to have introduced a period of
consolidation and a new sense of purpose.

The Seeds of Vitality

Although women's colleges have continued to decline in number, the
rate of decline has been stemmed and some of the remaining institutions
report increasing enrollments during the 1980s. What accounts for the
renewed interest in women's colleges at a time when more and more
women are entering coeducational institutions? Proponents of women's
colleges contend that, unlike coeducational institutions, they give particular attention to the educational needs of women. They attribute the
appeal of women's colleges to four main factors: the academic environment, presence of women faculty members, leadership development,
and program innovations.

Traditionally, women's colleges have sought to provide a normative
and supportive environment in which women could develop their intellectual and career potential. Extensive research on the impact of college
environments clearly shows that the nature of the learning environment
produces important differences in students' aspirations, confidence,
and career performance.[31] In 1973 Elizabeth Tidball, a professor of physi-
ology at George Washington University and a trustee of Wellesley College, published the first of a series of articles reporting on the baccalaureate origins of high-achieving women.[32] Based on information
provided in *Who's Who of American Women,* Tidball found that women's
colleges were almost twice as effective as coeducational colleges in producing graduates who obtained doctorates and were high career achievers. Moreover, she found that the higher the proportion of faculty
women, the greater the number of achievers among the graduates of the
institution. She attributed this outcome to the influence of women faculty members as role models or mentors.

Understandably, the Tidball studies were widely quoted by advocates
of women's colleges, and they were given considerable attention in the
media during the 1970s. The findings did not go unchallenged, how-

ever. One of the questions raised had to do with the selection of the sample of individuals from a *Who's Who*. It was argued that this sample represented women from a much earlier era and would not necessarily be representative of the graduates of women's colleges during the 1970s when admission to prestigious, formerly all-male institutions opened up. Studies by other scholars indicate that factors such as selective recruitment and self-selection of students may account for the greater number of achievers among graduates of women's colleges.[33] In a study of approximately 1,800 freshmen women enrolling in both women's and coeducational colleges, Linda Lentz found that the enrollees of the women's colleges were more career oriented and assigned greater priority to career over other endeavors. Alexander Astin et al. report similar characteristics. First-year students at women's colleges had higher high school performances, higher aspirations, and a more nontraditional pattern of major and career choice.[34] The implication of these studies is that the relationship between the number of female faculty members and achievers may not necessarily be a causal one. Nevertheless, there can be no doubt that women's colleges provide a more supportive educational environment for women, whether they are among the highest level of achievers or not, than do coeducational institutions. At the very least, in women's colleges students are not subject to the kind of subtle discrimination described in chapter 2. In addition, of course, they have more opportunities to participate in student government and to assume other leadership positions. On this point, the experience of those women's colleges that changed to coeducational status is revealing. It has been reported that male students, even if they constituted a numerical minority, came to dominate classroom and informal discourse, as well as to assume leadership of student activities.[35]

A second factor that is often quoted to justify women's colleges is the representation of women in faculty and administrative positions. Women constitute 55 percent of the faculty at women's colleges compared with only 26 percent at other institutions, according to the 1981 *Profile* report of the Women's College Coalition. Moreover, in women's colleges women constitute about half the faculty at every rank compared with other institutions where they are disproportionately in the lower ranks. (See Figure 6.1.) Also, in women's colleges, unlike other institutions, women faculty members are evenly distributed across the academic disciplines. They represent more than half of the faculty in the humanities, social sciences, and science division at women's colleges compared with 42 percent, 37 percent, and 18 percent, respectively, at other colleges and universities. In short, women's colleges offer a more

Figure 6.1   Percentage of All Full-Time Instructional Faculty Who Are Women at Four-Year Women's Colleges and Other Four-Year Colleges and Universities, 1978–1979

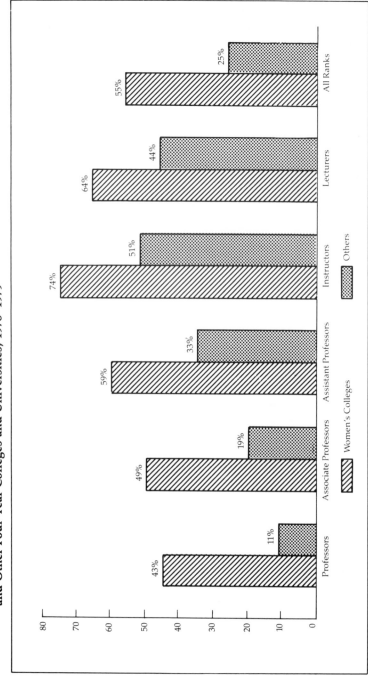

Source: Women's College Coalition, *Profile II: A Second Profile of Women's Colleges* (Washington, DC: Women's College Coalition, 1981), p. 83.

favorable opportunity structure for faculty women than do other institutions. From the viewpoint of students, this means a larger number and wider diversity of women to serve as role models or mentors.

At the administrative level, approximately 66 percent of the women's college presidents are female compared with 8 percent nationally. Of the women's colleges, Catholic institutions are most likely to be female-headed; they represent approximately 40 percent of all women's college presidents.[36] The Women's College Coalition reported in 1982 that in nearly half of the colleges, three of the previous five presidents were women, and in a quarter of the colleges all of the previous five were women.[37] The coalition also reported that in more than two thirds of the women's colleges, three or more of the top five administrative positions were held by women. Women are also more likely to hold positions on the board of trustees of women's colleges than of other institutions. In 1981 women constituted 48 percent of all board members and 28 percent of all board chair positions.[38] Clearly, women's colleges have demonstrated a commitment to women's leadership and control of institutional resources and objectives.

In terms of program innovations, women's colleges have developed a broad array of curricular, extracurricular, and support programs for women. For example, Simmons College founded a graduate management program for women, the first of its kind, in 1973. Subsequently, similar programs were introduced in schools of business administration and other institutions. Mills College was instrumental in the establishment of the Math/Science Network in the San Francisco Bay area in 1976. This is a joint program with the Lawrence Hall of Science at the University of California, Berkeley, to encourage young women to study more mathematics and science and to consider nontraditional occupations. Radcliffe College established the Bunting Institute in 1960 as a center of independent scholarship by women. While many institutions of higher education initiated new degree and nondegree programs for returning women during the 1970s, women's colleges were more hospitable in the treatment of these students and in the provision of support services. The Ada Comstock Scholars Program at Smith College is a case in point. It offers an opportunity to women beyond the traditional college age whose studies have been interrupted to complete their degree. The program offers a flexible course schedule, financial aid, housing, childcare, and other support.

It seems curious that women's colleges have not been at the forefront of the women's studies movement as it developed during the 1970s. On the other hand, it is logical that a major new area of scholarship should emerge in graduate research universities rather than liberal arts colleges.

Women's colleges did not at first see the need for women's studies at institutions such as theirs that were already committed to the needs of women. The early resistance of women's colleges to women's studies has also been attributed to two other reasons. One was the fear of being, in any sense, inferior to men's colleges, and the other was the fear of being labeled lesbian institutions.[39] There were, of course, exceptions. Gerda Lerner at Sarah Lawrence and Annette Baxter at Barnard were among the first to offer courses in women's history. Women's colleges are now active supporters of women's studies. In 1980 Wheaton College, under President Alice Emerson, embarked on a campus-wide program to incorporate the new scholarship on women into the curriculum. Radcliffe, Wellesley, Smith, Barnard, and Spelman house research and resource centers for women's studies (see chapter 13). Women's studies are undoubtedly an important factor in the continued vitality of women's colleges.

A Research Agenda for Women's Colleges Today

What is the contemporary role of women's colleges in higher education? What is their significance to higher education in general and to the education of women in particular? The case for women's colleges has three main elements. First, it is argued that they contribute to the diversity of the higher educational system and provide an alternative institutional model for women whose needs are not well served by the prevailing environment in coeducational colleges and universities. Second, women's colleges are seen to be needed to provide standards of educational equity for women, including treatment of students inside and outside the classroom and representation of women on the faculty. Third, women's colleges are viewed by some as an important social institution for female empowerment and mutual support. In contemporary society, women's colleges represent one of the few remaining female worlds. They provide a structural and ideological base from which to address the concerns of women not only in education but in society at large.

To what extent are the arguments for present-day women's colleges valid? What are the actual and potential contributions of women's colleges in the predominantly coeducational world of higher education in the 1980s? Much of the scholarship on women's colleges during the last decade has been historical.[40] There has been comparatively little in-depth research on the contemporary scene. Among the few recent examples of such research are Mirra Komarovsky's study of Barnard

undergraduates and the study of the intellectual and ethical development of Wellesley students by Blythe Clinchy and Claire Zimmerman.[41]

The future of women's colleges will depend in part on their ability to
define and articulate their modern roles persuasively. To do that will
require more data and research than is now available. First of all, we
need to know more about the diverse institutions that make up the
current population of women's colleges, their clienteles, their programs,
and the career patterns and achievements of their graduates. In compiling data and designing studies we need to differentiate between the
Seven Sisters and institutions in other parts of the country; we need to
give more attention to Catholic women's colleges, which represent a
large proportion of the total; and we need to take into consideration the
differences between urban and residential institutions. For example, at
Marymount Manhattan College a majority of the students are over 25
years old. Similarly, at Alverno College, in Milwaukee, nearly half of the
students are "older" or returning women.[42]

In addition to institutional characteristics, we need further information about the clientele of women's colleges. Who are the entering freshmen who opt for women's colleges in the 1980s? How do women students choose between Barnard and Columbia or between Bryn Mawr
and Swarthmore? One way to approach this question is to utilize data
collected in the annual freshmen surveys of the Cooperative Institutional Research Program (CIRP). These surveys, conducted by the
Higher Education Research Institute of UCLA, cover approximately
280,000 students each year at 550 two- and four-year colleges and universities. The survey questionnaires include an array of demographic,
experiential, and attitudinal issues as well as degree aspirations, major
and career plans, and expectations about college. It would be possible to
compare the profile of freshmen entering women's colleges with the
national norms for all freshmen.

A third and more difficult area of research would involve a comparison of the curricula of women's colleges and those of other institutions.
How are women's studies programs being implemented? Do women's
colleges offer any educational programs not elsewhere available? How
well do they serve the needs of nontraditional or returning women
students? Finally, how does the learning environment of women's colleges today differ from that of other institutions? Some of the foremost
women's colleges maintain cooperative arrangements with adjacent
coeducational institutions. Radcliffe is, of course, integrated with Harvard. Smith and Mount Holyoke are part of a Five College Consortium
with Amherst, Hampshire, and the University of Massachusetts at
Amherst. The five institutions share classes, library resources, faculty,

and cultural events. Other institutions with coordinate relationships include Barnard with Columbia, Bryn Mawr with Haverford and Swarthmore, and Scripps with the Claremont colleges. For all intents and purposes the campus climate at these institutions is coeducational. How do role models and mentors function under these circumstances? What particular supportive programs and services do the women's colleges offer to their students?

Conclusions

To spell out a research agenda for women's colleges is to emphasize how difficult a task they face to maintain an important role in higher education for women. At the present time there are only 90 such institutions left, and there is no expectation that the historical decline in numbers will reverse itself. It may well be that women's colleges will continue to produce professional and high-achieving women out of proportion to their numbers. Even so, it seems likely that their future role will be primarily that of resource or conservator rather than pioneer or leader in the higher education of women.

Notes

1. Mabel Newcomer, *A Century of Higher Education for American Women* (New York: Harper & Brothers, 1959), pp. 5–6.
2. Barbara Miller Solomon, *In the Company of Educated Women: A History of Women in Higher Education in America* (New Haven: Yale University Press, 1985), p. 3.
3. Solomon, *In the Company of Educated Women,* pp. 51–53.
4. Joyce Antler, "Culture, Service and Work: Changing Ideals of Higher Education for Women," in Pamela J. Perun, ed., *The Undergraduate Woman: Issues in Educational Equity* (Lexington, MA: Lexington Books, 1982), p. 19.
5. Newcomer, *A Century of Higher Education for American Women;* Margaret Rossiter, *Women Scientists in America: Struggles and Strategies to 1940* (Baltimore: Johns Hopkins University Press, 1982); and Patricia A. Palmieri, "Here Was Fellowship: A Social Portrait of Academic Women at Wellesley College, 1895–1920," *History of Education* 23, no. 2 (Summer 1983):195–214.
6. Rossiter, *Women Scientists;* Patricia A. Palmieri, "In Adamless Eden: A Social Portrait of the Academic Community at Wellesley College, 1875–1920," doctoral dissertation, Harvard Graduate School of Education, 1981.
7. Joyce Antler, "After College, What?: New Graduates and the Family Claim," *American Quarterly* 32, no. 4 (Fall 1980):409–435.

8. Elaine Showalter, *These Modern Women: Autobiographical Essays from the Twenties* (Old Westbury, NY: Feminist Press, 1978).

9. Ann Firor Scott, *The Southern Lady: From Pedestal to Politics, 1830–1930* (Chicago: University of Chicago Press, 1970).

10. Thomas Woody, *A History of Women's Education in the United States*, 2 vols. (New York: Octagon Books, 1966).

11. See Linda Perkins, "The Education of Black Women: A Historical Perspective," paper presented at the annual meeting of the Organization of American Historians, April 4–7, 1984; and "Black Feminism and 'Race Uplift': 1890–1900," Radcliffe Institute Working Paper, 1981.

12. Patricia Bell-Scott, "Black Women's Higher Education: Our Legacy," *Sage* 1 (Spring 1984):8–11; Patricia Bell-Scott, "Schooling Respectable Ladies of Color: Issues in the History of Black Women's Higher Education," *Journal of the National Association of Women Deans, Administrators, and Counselors* (Winter 1979):22–28; Jeanne L. Noble, *The Negro Woman's College Education* (New York: Columbia University Press, 1956); Florence Read, *The Story of Spelman College* (Princeton, NJ: Princeton University Press, 1961); Florence Read, "The Place of the Women's College in the Pattern of Negro Education," *Opportunity* 15 (September 1937):267–270; and Constance H. Marteena, "A College for Girls—Bennett College," *Opportunity* 16 (October 1938):306–307. Also see *Journal of Negro Education* 51 (Summer 1982): Special Issue on the Impact of Black Women in Education.

13. Sister Mary Mariella Bowler, "A History of Catholic Colleges for Women in the United States of America," doctoral dissertation, Catholic University of America, Washington, DC, 1933.

14. Bowler, "History," p. 94.

15. See Helen Horowitz, *Alma Mater: Design and Experience in the Women's Colleges from Their Nineteenth Century Beginnings to the 1930's* (New York: Knopf, 1984).

16. Patricia A. Palmieri, "The Matter of Difference: The Women's College Tradition in Higher Education," paper presented at the Mount Holyoke Sesquicentennial, Fall 1984.

17. Marian Elizabeth Stroebel, "Back Home for Keeps?: Women in Higher Education in the 1950s," *Furman Studies* 19 (December 1983):1–21.

18. Elizabeth Green, *Mary Lyon and Mount Holyoke: Opening Its Gates* (Hanover, NH: University Press of New England, 1979).

19. Radcliffe College Committee on Graduate Education for Women, *Graduate Education for Women: The Radcliffe Ph.D.* (Cambridge, MA: Harvard University Press, 1956).

20. See Palmieri, "Matter of Difference."

21. Radcliffe College Committee, *Graduate Education for Women*.

22. Alice Rossi and Ann Calderwood, eds., *Academic Women on the Move* (New York: Russell Sage Foundation, 1973); Alice Rossi and Ann Calderwood, "Women's Colleges Make a Comeback," *McCall's*, April 1980, pp. 56–57;

and Elizabeth Stone, "What Can an All-Women's College Do for Women?" *Ms.*, May 1979, pp. 61–63.

23. Sources of statistical data about women's colleges are Women's College Coalition, *A Profile of Women's Colleges*, and *A Profile of Women's Colleges— Analysis of the Data; Profile II: A Second Profile of Women's Colleges* and *Profile II: A Second Profile of Women's Colleges—Analysis of the Data* (Washington, DC: Women's College Coalition, 1980, 1981); National Center for Education Statistics, *Digest of Education Statistics, 1983–84; Fall Enrollment in Higher Education*, various years; *Education Directory for Colleges and Universities* (Washington, DC: U.S. Government Printing Office, 1961–62 to 1981–82; and *1987 Directory of Higher Education* (Washington, DC: Higher Education Publications, 1987).

24. For general materials on Jewish women, see Elizabeth Koltum, *The Jewish Women: An Anthology* (Waltham, MA: Schocken Books, 1973); Charlotte Baum, Paula Hyman, and Sonya Michel, *The Jewish Woman in America* (New York: New American Library, 1977); and Natalie Bein, *Daughters of Rachel* (New York: Penguin, 1980).

25. Women's College Coalition, *Profile II—Analysis*, p. 4.

26. Women's College Coalition, *Profile II—Analysis*, pp. 6–7.

27. *New York Times*, May 6, 1986, and January 30, 1987. The total number of women's colleges peaked in 1963–1964 at 279 before starting to decline.

28. *New York Times*, May 6, 1987, and January 30, 1987.

29. Data compiled from National Center for Education Statistics, *1987 Directory of Higher Education.*

30. Catharine R. Stimpson, "Women at Bryn Mawr," in Editors of Change, *Women on Campus: The Unfinished Liberation* (New Rochelle, NY: *Change* Magazine, 1975), p. 194.

31. See Women's College Coalition, *A Study of the Learning Environment at Women's Colleges* (Washington, DC: WCC, 1981); Roberta M. Hall and Bernice R. Sandler, "The Classroom Climate: A Chilly One for Women?" (Washington, DC: Project on the Status and Education of Women, Association of American Colleges, 1982); and Brown Project, *Men and Women Learning Together: A Study of College Students in the Late 70's* (Providence: Brown University, April 1980).

32. M. Elizabeth Tidball, "Perspective on Academic Women and Affirmative Action," *Educational Record* 54 (Spring 1973):130–135; and "The Search for Talented Women," *Change* 6 (May 1974):51–52. Also see M. Elizabeth Tidball and Vera Kistiakowsky, "Baccalaureate Origins of American Scientists and Scholars," *Science*, August 20, 1976, pp. 646–652.

33. Linda P. Lentz, "The College Choice of Career-Salient Women: Coed or Women's?" *Journal of Educational Equity and Leadership* 1 (1980):28–35; and "College Selectivity, Not College Type, Is Related to Graduate Women's Career Aspirations," paper presented at the annual meeting of the American Educational Research Association, New York, March 1982.

34. Alexander W. Astin, "The American Freshman: National Norms for Fall 1978," in Women's College Coalition, *Profile of Women's Colleges*, pp. 33–58; and *Four Critical Years* (San Francisco: Jossey-Bass, 1977).

35. See David A. Karp and William C. Yoels, "The College Classroom: Some Observations on the Meaning of Student Participation," *Sociology and Social Research* 60 (July 1976):421–439; Barrie Thorne and Nancy Henley, eds., *Language and Sex: Difference and Dominance* (Rowley, MA: Newbury, 1975); J. Farley, "Co-Education and College Women," *Cornell Journal of Social Relations* 9 (1974):87–97; Florence Howe, *Myth of Co-Education: Selected Essays, 1964–1983* (Bloomington: Indiana University Press, 1984); and Sarah Sternglanz and Shirley Liberger-Ficek, "Sex Differences in Student-Teacher Interactions in the College Classroom," *Sex Roles* 2 (1979):321–343.

36. Jean Lipman-Blumen, *Gender Roles and Power* (Englewood Cliffs, NJ: Prentice-Hall, 1984), p. 47.

37. Women's College Coalition, *A Profile of Women's College Presidents* (Washington, DC: WCC, 1982); and Susan Nall Bales and Marcia Sharp, "Women's Colleges—Weathering a Difficult Era with Success and Stamina," *Change* 13 (October 1981):53–56.

38. Bales and Sharp, "Women's Colleges," p. 53.

39. Jane S. Gould, "Personal Reflections on Building a Women's Center in a Women's College," *Women's Studies Quarterly* 12 (Spring 1984):4–11.

40. Foremost among the recent historical studies bearing on women's colleges are Horowitz, *Alma Mater*; and Solomon, *In the Company of Educated Women*.

41. Mirra Komarovsky, *Women in College* (New York: Basic Books, 1985); and Blythe Clinchy and Claire Zimmerman, "Epistemology and Agency in the Development of Undergraduate Women," in Pamela J. Perun, ed., *The Undergraduate Woman: Issues in Educational Equity* (Lexington, MA: Lexington Books, 1982).

42. *New York Times*, Education Supplement, January 5, 1986.

7

Women's Studies and Curricular Change

The evolution and growth of women's studies as a formal area of teaching and research is one of the major achievements of women in higher education over the last 20 years. The idea of women's studies emerged in the late 1960s under the impetus of the women's movement, and its progress since then has been extraordinary. Against all odds—financial, political, and intellectual—a cadre of committed feminist scholars, joined by a few men, succeeded in gaining recognition for the legitimacy of the subject area and led the way to the establishment of courses and degree programs in colleges and universities throughout the country. The proportion of all institutions offering women's studies courses already exceeds 40 percent, and the number is still growing. Long before the 1980s, moreover, women's studies crossed national boundaries to appear in various forms in many other countries, including developing countries.

The world of feminist scholarship as it exists today also includes research centers or institutes and professional journals, books, working paper series, and other publications for the dissemination of the new knowledge. Research centers and their role in the development of women's studies are dealt with at length in chapter 13. Here we are concerned with teaching and issues relating to the curriculum.

The Genesis and Growth of Women's Studies

Beginning in 1968, feminist scholars on several U.S. campuses began to question a simple reading of discrimination in academe and to seek the underlying causes. Certainly, fewer women than men were associate and full professors on any campus, including women's college campuses. Only a handful of women served as college presidents. But the more persistently difficult question was why so many women, even in traditionally female-typed undergraduate majors, had chosen not to go on to graduate school? In English, for example, while a majority of undergraduate majors were female and a minority male, the statistic at the PhD level was precisely reversed.[1]

These questions coincided with the appearance of one pioneering study of the elementary school curriculum, published in Princeton as a pamphlet called *Dick and Jane as Victims*. The authors were a group of NOW members, some of whom were faculty wives. The study of 134 widely used elementary reading texts revealed consistent stereotypes of mothers as housewives only, and mainly unintelligent ones at that; of fathers as briefcase-carrying white-collar workers who came home to solve problems for the whole family; of a family of two children, an older male and a younger female; and two pets, a male dog older and larger than a female cat.[2] Academics reading this study turned to their own texts to find, not surprisingly, similar stereotypes or the absence of women altogether.

In 1969 a group of feminists at Cornell University organized a conference which resulted in a faculty seminar, to examine the portrayal of women in the social and behavioral sciences. The seminar led to the establishment of an interdisciplinary course on women, followed in 1970 by a coordinated female studies program of six courses from different departments of the university. At about the same time, a similar effort was under way across the continent, where a women's studies program was started at San Diego State University. Included were such courses as Women in Literature, Women in Comparative Cultures, and Contemporary Issues in the Liberation of Women.

From 1970 on, women's studies courses and programs spread rapidly, fostered chiefly by two strategies and two factors and impelled by the fact of the women's movement that continued to keep women in the media—on the front page of newspapers, on the cover of magazines, and on the television screen. The two factors were the presence among the student body of women students eager for knowledge about themselves; and the presence among the faculty, albeit at lower ranks, of a sizable percentage of women, enough at least to make a difference. Many of these women in the vulnerable positions of temporary faculty or on tenure lines risked tenure by developing and teaching new women's studies courses. A handful of senior faculty, among them Gerda Lerner, Alice Rossi, and Florence Howe, risked their reputations and did likewise.

Given the body of students eager for the new scholarship on women, and the numbers of faculty eager to begin the teaching that would lead of necessity again and again back to the scholarship, how then to proceed? What was needed to move women's studies forward? There was no national meeting until 1977. There were not even regional meetings until 1973. And yet, even without discussion, two strategies emerged that were key to dissemination of the idea and details of its practice.

The first was the most obvious strategy of all academics: to use the professional association and its annual meetings for discussion and dissemination of new ideas. The Modern Language Association (MLA), for example, established a Commission on the Status and Education of Women in the spring of 1969, its charge both to study the status of women faculty in 5,000 English and modern language departments and to review the content of the curriculum in those departments. In 1970, at the MLA's annual meeting, the commission offered to an audience of more than 1,000 women and men a forum that included a paper on the status of women faculty, another on the literary curriculum's male biases and female stereotypes, and two of the first lectures in feminist literary criticism to be heard.

Also in 1970 the second and ultimately key strategy appeared, a strategy that was responsible for the rapid early spread of women's studies courses as well as for the spread of the idea of establishing women's studies *programs*. This was the strategy, first carried out under the direction of Sheila Tobias, then associate provost at Wesleyan University, of printing course syllabi for distribution at professional associations' annual meetings. *Female Studies I*, a collection of 17 course syllabi, was distributed at the American Psychological Association's annual meeting in the fall of 1970; and *Female Studies II*, a collection of 64 course syllabi, at the 1970 post-Christmas meetings of the MLA. In this volume, its editor, Florence Howe, also included more than a dozen manifestoes of newly established Women's Studies Programs at such institutions as the University of Washington, Barnard College, and San Francisco State University. In each case, more than 200 copies were sold at the meeting, and several thousand in the next several years, when *Female Studies* III to X also appeared and were widely distributed to academics.[3]

It is not surprising, therefore, to find the numbers of women's studies courses rising dramatically through the early 1970s. In December 1970, at its annual meeting, the MLA's commission on the Status of Women published the first guide to women's studies, under the title "Current Guide to Female Studies," listing over 110 courses. The second guide, published only a year later, listed 610 courses, of which more than a dozen were graduate courses. The guide also listed 15 organized women's studies programs, five of them degree-granting and one at the MA level.[4]

We shall have more to say about the idea and the importance of *programs* as distinct from courses. But it is important to note here that part of the strategy for early dissemination of the idea of women's studies included the publication in the *Female Studies* series of not only course syllabi, bibliographies, and brief essays from such teacher-scholars as Gerda Lerner, but also the entire and often lengthy manifesto-like documents that accompanied the establishment of programs, including their rationale, their requirements, the strength of their faculty, their curricular designs, and their goals for students.

In 1974 the Feminist Press, with a small grant from the Ford Foundation, carried out a survey of women's studies courses and programs and published a comprehensive directory entitled *Who's Who and Where in Women's Studies*, which listed 4,490 courses taught by 2,225 faculty members at 995 institutions.[5] At that time, there were 112 organized women's studies programs on campus. Unfortunately, there are no later figures available for the total number of courses offered or the number of faculty members teaching women's studies courses. Since 1974 the Feminist Press has maintained an annual update of women's studies programs in the *Women's Studies Quarterly*. As of 1986, there were 482 programs and the number was still growing. More than two thirds of those programs offer either a minor or an undergraduate major, in addition to more than 60 graduate programs leading to either the MA (50) or the PhD (16). Sixteen institutions offer the new graduate minor as part of traditional doctoral programs.

Data are not available for total enrollments, but partial data based on case studies suggest that the size as well as the number of women's studies programs has increased. In 1975 the National Advisory Council on Women's Educational Programs, a federal committee, authorized a formal study of 15 women's studies programs, published as *Seven Years Later: Women's Studies Programs in 1976*. The 15 programs chosen were both representative and "mature,"[6] that is, begun during the decade's first three years. Enrollments in these programs showed continuous growth. For example, at San Francisco State University where there were 160 students in 4 women's studies courses in 1970, there were over 2,000 students in 68 courses in 1976. At the University of Washington, the program grew from 282 students in 9 courses in 1971 to more than 2,500 students in 60 courses in 1976. A series of monographs published by the National Institute of Education in 1980 also chronicled the growth in number and profusion of courses offered in women's studies during the first decade of its existence.[7] During the 1980s more than 150 new programs in women's studies came into being, including those at Yale, Stanford, Princeton, and, more recently, in 1986, at Harvard.

A survey of campus trends conducted by the American Council on Education (ACE) in 1984 provides an overview of the place of women's studies in the curriculum of colleges and universities after nearly a decade and a half of growth. Its report indicates that undergraduate women's studies courses not leading to a major are now offered at 1,099 of 2,623 institutions, or 41.9 percent.[8] The breakdown by type of institution is as follows:

	Number	Percentage
All Institutions	1,099	41.9%
Universities	390	68.1
Four-Year Colleges	361	48.9
Two-Year Colleges	348	26.5

As the data indicate, women's studies courses are most available on university campuses. Over two thirds of all universities and nearly half of all four-year colleges offer women's studies courses. By comparison, only a quarter of two-year institutions offer such courses, notwithstanding the preponderance of women students at those institutions. One should add, for the record, that the statistic is quite understandable in the context of higher education generally. Faculty members at two-year institutions teach almost twice the number of courses as faculty on doctorate-granting campuses and do not have the research facilities or the resources, including graduate students and research leaves, with which to prepare to teach women's studies courses. The ACE survey also reports that 71 institutions offer an undergraduate major in women's studies, most of them universities. (This figure differs from the women's studies program total cited above in that it refers to programs offering women's studies degrees directly and does not include "individual majors," collateral majors, majors within such other programs as American Studies, certificate, or graduate programs.)

Beginning in 1983–1984 the National Center for Education Statistics of the U.S. Department of Education listed women's studies as an interdisciplinary field for purposes of reporting degrees awarded. In that year 126 BAs were reported, of which 11 were awarded to men. In addition, there were 9 MAs, all of them to women, and 2 PhDs, both to women.[9] Since these figures refer only to women's studies as an interdisciplinary major, they do not capture all of the earned degrees relating to women's studies, since many of these are subsumed as specialties under such other categories as history or psychology or American studies. At the PhD level, for example, we know that the Woodrow Wilson National Fellowship Foundation receives an average of 175 applications annually for its dissertation fellowship in women's studies. Further evidence is provided by information on dissertations on file at University Microfilms. A total of 441 dissertations in women's studies have been reported to date, beginning with 5 in 1978 and increasing to 92 in 1985. The number of dissertations on women's studies subjects, inclusive of those within regular departments, was 2,154 between 1981 and 1984.[10]

A recent survey of women's studies programs indicates that in the decade since the 1975 report there has been dramatic growth in the size and enrollments of women's studies programs and courses and dramatic increases in the size of some budgets, especially on the doctorate-granting university campuses. Individual course enrollments, for example, in the ubiquitous Introduction to Women's Studies have reached as high as 900 at Ohio State University, 720 at the University of Southern California, 548 at the University of Maryland, and 350 at the University of Colorado.[11]

The Process of Institutionalization

In the very early stages of women's studies, courses were often introduced on campus on an experimental basis or as informal seminars or colloquia rather than as regular departmental offerings. Unlike such other fields as foreign area studies or urban studies, no external funding for curriculum development was available to women's studies, and the new courses were solely the result of voluntary efforts by pioneering feminist scholars on the faculty. By the early 1970s, it was possible to gather 300 course syllabi from as many different faculty members, all of whom were interested in sharing them. The willingness to share new teaching information in a new field was in itself unique to academe—we know of no precedent here. We read this willingness as an indication of the strength of the feminist ideology that had spawned women's studies in the first place. While a majority of these courses were in English, sociology, and history, most other academic disciplines were also represented, along with the interdisciplinary "introduction" to women's studies, labeled in a variety of ingenious ways, depending on the departmental umbrella that had offered it the necessary academic shelter. After an initial period of a year or two, on some campuses some of these courses were reviewed by an instructional committee before becoming an established part of a departmental academic curriculum. If a women's studies program had by then been established, the course might also be cross-listed in women's studies.

The excitement of teaching these new courses deserves notice. Whatever a faculty member's proper discipline, she had to read in other fields to be able to present material clearly and in appropriate context. For example, teachers of a course called Images of Women in Literature would need to introduce the concept "women" through the use of sociological, historical, and even economic and political ideas and contexts. While many literature faculty commonly use concepts outside their discipline, focus on "women" was entirely new. Perhaps as important, for the first time in her academic career, this faculty member had to focus on something directly relevant to her own life. Further, and still more important, the students came into class with a "readiness" for this kind of serious study of material directly and immediately relevant to their lives—thus, the classroom as a living space. That there were few tests and few precedents mattered not at all ultimately. Faculty used what they could find, even putting to effective use a sexist text when the ideal one wished for was unavailable. The needed texts, on occasion, appeared largely through the energies of a "network" of pioneers, not only in the United States, but in Canada. Many faculty members, for example, taught from an early version of *Our Bodies, Our Selves*, published first in Canada on newsprint in the shape of a magazine. Manuscripts of essays that would not appear in print until years later also circulated through the early network of women's studies practitioners and were often xeroxed for students. A further stimulus for the pioneer faculty were the students themselves, for the early growth of women's studies coincided with the growth in enrollments of "returning" or "older" women students, coming to college with the express purpose of "changing their lives." What better instrument to effect that change than women's studies, an effort to change the institution responsible for teaching women and men about women's lives?

The single most important factor in the institutionalization of women's studies was the decision, on campus after campus, by a handful of faculty feminists in each case, to attempt to organize courses in the form of a program and not a department. The model was not home economics, nor even black studies, but rather American studies. What was sought was a coordinator and office, some clerical assistance, a small budget, and the right to organize a coherent curriculum through the use of faculty who would be stationed and tenured or tenurable within their respective departments. The form resembled the spokes of a wheel, or what was referred to as a center and a "network." This strategy of institutionalization served another important objective of women's studies—that of changing the traditional curriculum throughout the university. And it was common knowledge that a separate department could not be an "agent of change" for the broader curriculum.

The 1976 study *Seven Years Later* established that mature women's studies programs had passed through an initial phase dubbed "creative anarchy" and had by mid-decade entered a second phase of institutionalization. The attributes of the second phase included a paid coordinator, a formal budget or access to a dean's formal budget, a formal curriculum that passed through a women's studies committee for review by a more general campus-wide curriculum committee, and a "line" relationship for all the program's activities between the coordinator and some administrator, typically a dean or vice president of arts and sciences or, on smaller campuses, the dean of faculty.

The curricular form adopted by women's studies programs included an introductory interdisciplinary core course, followed by a selection of courses offered by various departments, but reviewed by the women's studies faculty as appropriate to their program. These were, for majors, often followed by a senior seminar and an integrative field work experience or an internship. Even in 1976, a few of the largest programs had already begun to offer, on budgets established by the university, an internal series of core courses in addition to the two already mentioned. These were taught either by faculty hired as adjuncts for this purpose or by regular faculty on release time from their departments. In the past decade, an increasing number of programs have adopted this format, including increasingly specific and rigorous requirements for the bachelor's degree. We shall have more to say about the content of women's studies courses and programs in a later section.

While most programs began life under the rubric of a committee (a committee at Harvard University, for example, functioned for more than half a decade before establishing a formal women's studies program in 1986), institutionalization also has included the continuation of a governing committee, often with student representation, as well as with connections to other feminist groups on campus—the women's center, for example. While only three programs in the country have department rather than program status, and can recommend their own faculty for tenure in women's studies rather than in departments, women's studies programs sometimes have been able to influence appointments informally through contributing to a review process, and in a significant number of instances faculty hold appointments jointly in a department and in women's studies. Of necessity, therefore, women's studies must have close ties to departments. As we shall make clear, the benefits include the ability to get on with the major goal of changing the entire traditional curriculum.

While the autonomy of women's studies programs is severely restricted with regard to the tenuring of faculty, it has not been restricted with regard to the granting of degrees to students. Programs coast to coast have had the same procedures open to them as to departments for the establishment of minors, BAs, MAs, and PhDs, and they have taken advantage of those rights.

Several additional factors were strategic for the development of women's studies. We have already mentioned the support of women's commissions within professional associations. During the late 1960s and early 1970s, there were also many caucuses and committees organized both within and as splinter groups outside professional associations. The activities of these groups are described in chapter 12. Although much of the work of these committees was devoted to advancing the professional status and career opportunities of women, they also directed attention, chiefly through programming at the annual meetings, to women as subject of teaching and research in the disciplines.

Also early in the 1970s, strategic support for the recognition and institutionalization of women's studies came from the establishment of national fellowship programs for research on women by major national foundations—notably Ford to begin with and then Carnegie, Rockefeller, and Mellon. Other foundations, such as Russell Sage, have been major supporters of scholars engaged in social science research relating to women. As of 1983, nationwide there were ten fellowship programs for women scholars or scholarship about women.[12] Further support for individual or project research was also forthcoming from government agencies such as the National Endowment for the Humanities, the Fund for the Improvement of Postsecondary Education, the National Institute of Education, and the Women's Educational Equity Act Program.

Important in the process of institutionalization was the founding of the National Women's Studies Association (NWSA) in 1977. The process began in 1972, when the *Women's Studies Newsletter* (now the *Women's Studies Quarterly*, published by the Feminist Press) attempted to connect a national constituency of teachers interested at least locally in the new curricular reform. In those years, elementary and secondary school teachers, as well as college faculty, were not only in communication, but dreamed of working together to overthrow the male-centered curriculum. Thus, when the founders of NWSA stated the organization's purpose, not surprisingly it was broad-based: "to further the social, political, and professional development of women's studies throughout the country and the world, at every educational level and in every educational setting."[13] From the beginning, NWSA drew a large and diverse membership consisting not only of scholars but also administrators, community activists, and other women's studies practitioners as well as of school teachers, though not as many as had been anticipated. As of 1987 its membership was about 3,000. NWSA holds an annual meeting and publishes a quarterly newsletter. It is also planning a scholarly quarterly to begin publication by the end of the 1980s. Its overall activities are designed to serve as a network and mechanism for mutual support among its constituencies and also to disseminate information about women's studies as widely as possible.

Although NWSA has played an important role in the development of women's studies, it is the association of generalists, and of persons committed to such reforms as "mainstreaming" or "balancing" the curriculum, rather than to faculty committed to scholarship in their own discipline. Its sessions serve teachers and women's studies program directors as much as, or more than, the historian or the economist. No single association represents scholarship in women's studies. Nor could such an association exist without subsuming all the professional associations that already exist. Rather, much of the function of representing and spreading scholarship in women's studies rests with the academic disciplines and their professional associations, and, at times, with women's caucuses, commissions, or committees within those associations. Women's studies scholars are much more likely to attend and present papers at the annual meetings of the Modern Language Association, the American Economic Association, or the American Sociological Association, for example, than those of the National Women's Studies Association. The Berkshire Conference on the History of Women, which is interdisciplinary in orientation, is the largest gathering of feminist scholars in the United States. It is an informal organization of feminist historians which was founded in 1928 and revitalized in 1972, when its first conference was held on the campus of Douglass College. Its triennial meetings have been held consistently on the campuses of women's colleges—in 1984 at Smith and in 1987 at Wellesley.

Probably the most strategic factor in the institutionalization of women's studies in its second decade has been the establishment of organized centers for research. As of 1986, there were more than 50 such centers across the country, the majority of them campus based. They are described more fully in chapter 13. Suffice it to note here that their purpose was and is to provide resources for research about women, strengthening the efforts of individual scholars. They offer such facilities as libraries, staff support, forums for exchange of ideas, and assistance in project development and funding. Collectively, they have made a crucial contribution to the position of women's studies, its capacities, and its recognition in the academic community and beyond.

An essential element in the establishment of a new field is, of course, the development of a body of literature. When the earliest women's studies programs were instituted there was little by way of appropriate textbooks or other course material. The growth in volume of publications since then has been nothing short of spectacular. New journals such as *Women's Studies* and *Feminist Studies* appeared in 1972 and *Signs: Journal of Women in Culture and Society* made its debut in 1975. *Signs,* published by the University of Chicago Press, with Catharine Stimpson as its founding editor, has become the most widely known of the new journals in women's studies circles in the United States and abroad. New presses were created to serve the unmet needs of various women's studies constituencies. The largest and most successful of these, as well as the first, is the Feminist Press, which was established in 1970. Since then the Feminist Press has grown with the women's studies movement, reflected its concerns, and contributed to its growth. It has published curricular material for the school and college level; has reprinted fiction, autobiography, and other books by women authors to restore the lost history, culture, and literature of women; has anticipated curricular needs by producing original texts and anthologies; and has served as a resource for reference material relating to women's studies.

Today, articles relating to women regularly appear in professional journals of most disciplines, and university presses and most trade presses commonly have a section on women's studies. Women authors and reviews of feminist literature and scholarship appear in increasing numbers in the *New York Review of Books, New York Times Book Review, Atlantic Monthly, Harper's,* and *Times Literary Supplement.* In the mid-1980s two new feminist periodicals were founded to review the growing body of literature—the *Women's Review of Books* and *Belles Lettres.* Textbooks, previously nonexistent, are now available for women's studies courses across the disciplines, including history, law, psychology, economics, and literature, as well as for interdisciplinary introductory courses.

A further milestone in the institutionalization of women's studies was its formal recognition as a degree specialty in 1983 by the U.S. Department of Education. The annual statistics of earned degrees conferred will henceforth provide a significant measure of the progress of women's studies, even though, as we have noted, it does not include subspecialties within disciplines.

Thus far, we have traced the institutionalization of women's studies from the establishment of courses and degree programs to national fellowship programs; the formation of a National Women's Studies Association; the development of a network of research centers; the publication of new scholarly journals, texts, and other literature; and formal recognition of the women's studies degree in the official statistics of the Department of Education. There is one further step to be noted: the establishment during the 1980s of endowed chairs in women's studies. This is another sign of the maturity and acceptance of the field. There are now upwards of a dozen chairs already in existence, including those at the University of Southern California, the University of Wisconsin, Brown University, and Rutgers University.

Objectives and Curriculum

In the early years of women's studies, few onlookers saw the field as a serious area of study. Many saw the effort as part of a "fad" that would fade as the women's movement faded or failed, and others ignored it, also expecting it to disappear quickly. Probably the most serious charge was made by opponents who saw women's studies as "political," and hence not properly academic or especially "objective." For many reasons—among them, that the 1970s saw the erosion of belief in the "objectivity" of all learning, including that of the hard sciences—the charge of "political" proved not to be a serious threat. It allowed feminist scholars to say publicly that the absence of women from the curriculum was also "political," that all education understood as the control of information and the hegemony of knowledge was "political." Ultimately, the charges and countercharges were silenced by the extraordinary outpouring of scholarship that even some hardened male chauvinists could not ignore.

Probably it was just as well that in the earliest years women's studies was largely ignored by faculty and administrators alike, for the early manifestoes of women's studies programs were ambitious political and intellectual statements. From a study of more than 50 of these written before 1973, five goals emerge:

1. to raise the consciousness of students—and faculty alike—about the need to study women, about their absence from texts and from the concerns of scholarship, about the subordinate status of women today as in the past
2. to begin to compensate for the absence of women, or for the unsatisfactory manner in which they were present in some disciplines, through designing new courses in which to focus on women, thus to provide for women in colleges and universities the compensatory education they needed and deserved
3. to build a body of research about women
4. with that body of research, to re-envision the lost culture and history of women

5. using all four goals, to change the education of women and men through changing what we have come to call the "mainstream" curriculum[14]

From the outset, though the words "consciousness" and "consciousness-raising" appeared in all program manifestoes, it was also clear from the course syllabi that the single most important instrument with which to raise consciousness was the new scholarship about women. Of course, in many introductory courses, then and now, students are encouraged to discuss their own experiences and comprehensions of the world (often in small groups arranged expressly for that purpose), but the content of women's studies courses from the first also included an awareness that one had to gather information about many persons' experience before one had what could be called "knowledge." For many women's studies faculty pioneers, those early years in the first part of the 1970s were halcyon, despite the fact that much of the teaching was done on overload and certainly without release time for the new preparation or the new demands of large enrollments and the desire for small discussion groups in addition to lectures. The intellectual excitement was compensation enough.

While none of the goals disappeared, by the mid 1970s the strategic goal—to "change the education of all women and men"—had some focus, and there was a new goal as well. The new goal was "to open additional career options for students through development of coherent academic programs." This goal suited the process of institutionalization, for it responded to the need to justify the establishment of women's studies as a "major" through the naming of vocational areas that in our times majors need to serve. It also responded to an academic clientele increasingly focused on status, money, and vocation, rather different from the service-oriented undergraduates of the 1960s and early 1970s. Women, moreover, were being told on every side to prepare for careers. Women's studies programs said that they, too, could provide especially valuable career options, such as careers in personnel, social work, or working with the elderly; in short, any field that deals with women.

From the beginning, women's studies pioneers held that studying women was as useful a preparation for the workplace as studying history or literature or economics. If one organized this study as a dual major, moreover, one would be more richly equipped than other students for a career in many fields, as well as for graduate study. With women's studies, one would have, in addition to the traditional major, the valuable new scholarship on women. Further, for those going directly to the workplace, women's studies offered fresh perspectives on the history and contemporary condition of women to be used especially within such institutions as social work agencies, schools, or publishing houses. Less obvious even to the students themselves, and certainly to those in control of the workplace, was the fact that women were the major consumers, the major readers of books and periodicals, the major church-goers and volunteers, and that, thus, much of the curriculum of women's studies might be seen as directly relevant to the world of work, especially within institutions that served women.

In the 1980s women's studies programs often announce their curriculum in the manner of the University of Illinois Circle Campus—as "valuable background if you plan careers that deal with women's issues or with women as clients." Such a description may be said to cover all areas of work, including teaching, law, medicine, and psychiatry, as well as social work. At Stanford University, the elegant brochure of the Feminist Studies Program declares:

> A degree in Feminist Studies prepares a student for any career requiring the ability to read with critical analysis and to write with clarity of thought. Feminist Studies stresses analytical thinking. At the same time, it encourages the development of personal interpretation, an asset to any profession.

> Feminist Studies qualifies a student for entry into fields of graduate study and for immediate non-academic work in areas such as the following: education—teaching and administration; writing and editing; affirmative action; management; human resource development; politics; personnel and counseling; consulting.

> Examples of jobs held by recent graduates in Feminist Studies include: Women's Health Center Administrator; Educational Coordinator, Rape Crisis Center; intern, feminist newspaper; journalist; fundraiser; financial consultant; scientist.

A private two-year college in California publishes a large 32-page magazine, on heavy paper, richly illustrated with photographs, called *Women's Studies Program*, the last ten pages of which describe a "Vocational Program—Women and Non-Traditional Careers." These are named as follows: graphics (computer graphics, graphic design, graphic production); telecommunications (radio broadcasting, television broadcasting, cable television, industrial television, sound recording); photography (photographer, photo journalist, studio assistant); information systems (computer operator, junior programmer); laser-optic technology; administration of justice (police officer, detective).

With regard to the strategic goal of changing education, by the mid-1970s some mature programs were beginning to do two kinds of new work. They were trying to reach schoolteachers, either through funded summer institutes (at the University of Arizona and at Sarah Lawrence College, for example) or through ongoing evening courses or one- or two-day conferences especially for teachers (as at Indiana University or at SUNY/College at Old Westbury). This effort was part of the early vision that women's studies would grow at all levels of education. In general, its success has been limited.

More successful has been the effort to reach out to faculty not involved in women's studies at all, but who were principally responsible for large introductory courses. By the early 1980s, more than 40 women's studies projects of this kind were in place. They were called variously efforts to "mainstream," to "balance" the curriculum, or to "integrate" women into the curriculum.[15] The results of a recent survey suggest that more than 25 percent of all women's studies programs sponsor some work in "balancing" the curriculum.

In the nearly 20 years since its beginning, the women's studies curriculum has grown in complexity as well as in size and scope. It would not be possible today for most institutions to offer a course called the History of Women or Literature by Women. Courses have become as differentiated with respect to nation, chronology, genre, theme, or issue as the traditional curriculum. Indeed, on some campuses one can find in the catalog a course, for example, called the History of Colonial America and another called Women in Colonial America. Similarly, economics departments may offer Labor Economics (ignoring women), and cross-list another course with women's studies called Women in the Labor Force.

As important, the curriculum has differentiated among the various populations of women within the United States. From the first, women's studies programs very self-consciously declared themselves as wanting to include race and class along with gender in each course taught. In addition, many of the largest programs from the first offered at least a single course on the black woman; fewer courses were offered that focused attention directly on working-class women, but there were some. And Chicanas, Puerto Rican women and other Hispanic women, Native American women, and Asian American women also continue to be the focus of some women's studies courses. In the recent survey of women's studies programs, 50 percent offer at least one course on minority women; 13.6 percent offer three to six courses.

Several other shifts in curriculum are worth noting. From the beginning, the focus was solely on the United States, or, more rarely, on Europe as precursor. The rationale was understandable: It was difficult enough to avoid the usual white, middle-class focus of U.S. education and include minority and working-class women within the already stretched curriculum. There was little room for the rest of the world. But beginning early in the 1980s, perhaps because of the high percentage of women's studies faculty attending the U.N. Mid-Decade conference in Copenhagen, one can discern a noticeable increase in courses focused on Third World women. The 1985 survey, for example, indicates that more than 60 percent of all programs offer at least one course on Third World women; and 16.8 percent of all programs offer from two to seven courses.

A third development worth noting here is the increased number of courses devoted to methodology, especially in interdisciplinary research, at both the undergraduate and graduate levels. Almost all large programs offer at least one course in feminist "theory." In general, there are now more core courses offered by the programs themselves, with faculty teaching both from social science and humanist perspectives, the goals of which are to prepare students for complex thinking and analysis, as well as for activist futures.

Some of this new curricular development comes as a result of an effort to deal with the general problem of what to do at the graduate level in women's studies. The entire development of women's studies is a curious amalgam of undergraduate educational focus and extraordinary new research scholarship. Because women's studies is an enormous area for scholarship, the focus of graduate study has tended, not surprisingly, to remain disciplinary; though often in the social sciences history can be combined easily with economics or political science when the study is demographic, women-centered, and, for example, focused on employment. The establishment of graduate minors by 16 programs allows for a traditional disciplinary doctoral program to be enhanced and given particular direction by the inclusion of women's studies research methodology seminars and other courses at the graduate level.

A recent informal survey of women's studies programs by Deborah Rosenfelt, the director of San Francisco State's program, concludes that only one institution offers a truly interdisciplinary MA degree in women's studies—the University of Illinois at Chicago. She has also found that many programs are offering very sophisticated graduate courses in theory and methods of feminist scholarship.

Whether programs are in their first or second decade of life, their curricular offerings are similarly dependent upon the resources of their particular campuses. Women's studies majors often complain that all courses are not offered every year, dependent as they are on the schedules of faculty members who are also committed to departmental needs. No program in the country offers all the courses that it would be possible to offer, though some of the largest and most distinguished university-based programs may offer 100 different courses throughout a single academic year. One needs to be clear at the outset, of course, that women's studies programs both "offer" courses and "coordinate" courses. There is, moreover, substantial variation among programs as to the control over these coordinated offerings. On some campuses, a program's curriculum committee reviews course syllabi and interviews faculty who want their courses cross-listed in women's studies. On other campuses, the women's studies coordinator routinely lists all those courses given by or about women, regardless of their content and perspective. In general, however, the program itself is responsible for the introductory/interdisciplinary course and for other courses designed especially for majors. Some large programs offer a body of "core" interdisciplinary courses. At San Francisco State University and at Ohio State University, for example, these program-developed courses may number as many as 15 a semester. In addition, several dozen other courses, based in traditional departments or in ethnic studies programs, are coordinated by these women's studies programs.

The best way to describe this curriculum is to note its inclusivity. No area of the social sciences and humanities remains uninvaded by women's studies; and certain areas of the sciences—biology, biochemistry, physical anthropology, geology and geography—have begun to be touched by women's studies.

One way to catch the flavor of the curriculum is to note the most popular courses. In many instances, these are versions of the ever-present Introduction to Women's Studies. In other cases, these are introductory courses called more specifically Women, Culture, and Society or Woman: Self and Others. More specialized still, and possibly still serving an introductory function, are Sociology of Sex Roles; Writing: Women in America; Anthropology: Women, Sex Roles, and Culture; and Women and Health.

One may also describe this curriculum in terms of the disciplines it is in the process of revising or in terms of interdisciplinary topics. The following list cuts through both types of categories, as do the titles of courses offered or coordinated by women's studies programs.

1. *Patriarchy*. While this is an overriding theme in all women's studies courses, some courses, including the Introduction to Women's Studies in its various guises as well as courses in theory and methods, focus especially on this theme. The focus may take the form of the study of philosophy, theology, sociology, or psychology (Women and Philosophy, Women and Theology, and so on); however organized, a course of this kind will examine the patterns of a gender-based organization of

social, economic, political, and cultural life, to describe the construction of reality that insists on male dominance and female subservience, its history, perhaps even including its origins in some prehistorical past, its contemporary construction, and the slight shifts that have begun to occur in the past 20 years both in consciousness and in action.

2. *Sex-role stereotyping.* This is a second overriding theme in women's studies courses, especially in the Introduction to Women's Studies. It often takes the form of a study of images of women and men—in literature, for example, in advertising and the media, in film, or in the Bible. The point of such study is dual: to hone the analytic abilities of students to see gender-typed stereotypes prejudicial to either women or men and to consider as well how such stereotypes might be changed, and to what visions of human potential.

3. *Sex differences.* This aspect of the curriculum emerges in such courses as the Psychology of Sex Differences, Psychology of Sex Roles, Psychology of Gender, or, more rarely, Psychobiology of Sex Differences. A course of this sort is a staple in all large programs, and sometimes, as at the University of Washington, for example, one that is cross-listed in psychology for majors, or to fulfill a science requirement, and that attracts enrollments of more than 150 students each year. Such courses are by nature comparative, and they serve to dispel certain deeply held myths about women's alleged emotionality and men's alleged rationality.

4. *Sexuality (and health).* Even more than the courses on sex differences, those on sexuality, especially when they are called Human Sexuality and are team-taught by a woman and a man, attract very large enrollments. Such a course at the University of South Florida, offered by the women's studies program and called Human Sexual Behavior, for example, reports enrollments of more than 500 each term. In the 1980s courses on women and health now include sexuality as a subtheme. In all cases, sexuality includes both homosexual and heterosexual behavior, as well as the sexuality connected with pregnancy and childbirth.

5. *History.* While some growing number of departments of history include at least one specialist in "women's" history who offers several courses in a particular specialization, it would be possible to replicate the entire male-centered curriculum in history with courses focused on the other half of the human race. At present, however, programs offer only selected courses in aspects of U.S. women's history, or aspects of British, or European, or Chinese, to name several of the myriad possibilities. By and large, most women's studies programs feel an obligation to include at least an introductory course in the history of women in the United States, though it has become increasingly awkward to cram

200 or more years of history—and of women of various races and classes and ethnicities—into a single course or even two. Thus, specialization, especially on major university campuses, has grown, and courses called American Women in the Twenties or German Women Under Hitler, for example, are not unusual. At the same time, one needs to note with regard to the women's studies curriculum that the influence of history on all courses and disciplines has been ubiquitous. Women's studies faculty, whether in literature, economics, or sociology, teach with a strong sense of historical change in the status of women and the condition of their lives.

6. *Literature and the other arts.* As in history, it would be possible to teach a women's studies curriculum parallel to all that currently exists in the male-centered curriculum. In departments of English and in foreign language departments, that process is under way; and in art history and musicology, the process is just beginning. General courses called Women Writers, Women Painters, or Women Composers are commonplace, though some major universities with faculty resources offer courses as specific as Nineteenth-Century Women Novelists in the United States or Twentieth-Century French Women Poets, as well as courses on such individual writers as Virginia Woolf, Colette, Zora Neale Hurston, and Willa Cather. Women's studies courses also focus on newly recognized genres especially important to women artists: Quilts, for example, is a new area of study, as is the Diary Literature of Women and Women's Autobiography.

7. *Psychology.* Critiques of Freud's view of the psychology of women, along with those of Erik Erikson and other male theorists, provide material for courses called Women and Psychology or the Psychology of Women. By the early 1980s, such courses were also focusing attention on several new perspectives about female psychology and female development from such feminist scholars as Jean Baker Miller, Nancy Chodorow, and Carol Gilligan.

8. *The family.* Courses on women and the family are found in departments of history, sociology, psychology, and elsewhere. Women's studies courses emphasize the various forms the family has taken throughout history and into the contemporary period, and cross-culturally as well. Courses typically also focus on the ideology of egalitarian families and the social structures needed to bring such institutions about.

9. *Work.* Courses on women and work, like courses on the family, may be found in a variety of departments, including history, economics, sociology, and even literature. Such courses have redefined the work of women to include such unpaid activity as childcare and housework as well as community activity outside the home. Courses on women and/or

in the labor force may be found in even some of the more conservative departments of economics. The History of Women and Work may focus on working-class women and their records in factories, fields, and mines, or on professional women and their inroads into law, medicine, teaching, and other areas once denied them. This aspect of the curriculum may have had a particularly profound effect on the expectations of both younger and returning women students, since prior to women's studies there was nothing in the curriculum to encourage the idea that women might work as well as marry and rear children.

10. *Education.* Departments and schools of education have not been in the vanguard of women's studies scholarship. Relatively few institutions offer courses for prospective elementary and secondary school teachers on sex-role stereotyping in the schools, and still fewer offer courses on the history of women's education, an area rich in possibilities for fresh scholarship. As with the family, education is an institution that has both kept women in a subordinate position—especially through the use of a male-centered curriculum—and also provided a vehicle for change. Women's studies courses in this area focus on the dual nature of educational institutions in a democratic society. Some courses are just beginning to include a review of the history of women's studies itself.

11. *Law and social movements.* Among the earliest women's studies courses was Women and the Law, offered, for example, by a practicing Philadelphia lawyer for the women's studies program at the University of Pennsylvania in the early 1970s. Such a course was unique not only because of its focus on women, but also because it was offered in an undergraduate curriculum, not a law school. It is interesting to note that male undergraduates, interested in studying law, elected such courses for that reason. Obviously essential to an understanding of the status of women, women's history, and women's participation in social movements to change that history, such courses may also have been instrumental in suggesting to a whole generation of women students that their future lay in legal study and practice. In the mid 1980s the study of women and the law has become of major importance in developing countries interested in organizing women's studies curricula at the undergraduate level.

Associated with the study of law has been the study of women and social movements, in particular the nineteenth-century and twentieth-century abolitionist and civil rights movements. More recently, scholars interested in peace studies and the history of women and international law and international feminist movements have been constructing courses about women and peace movements.

12. *Black women's studies, Chicana studies, working-class women's studies, Jewish women's studies.* While, in principle, women's studies teaching should ideally include the study of race and class as well as gender, the curriculum has, from the start, included at least occasional courses called the Black Woman, or the Puerto Rican Woman, or Jewish Women Writers, to allow for focus on the scholarship of a particular group, sometimes in a particular era as well. In large programs, especially on campuses with sizable ethnic studies programs, such courses may multiply.

13. *Women and development.* The study of women in developing countries has grown, especially since 1980, and on many campuses women's studies programs have made efforts to include such courses in their curriculum. Some of these courses focus on particular parts of the world—for example, Women in Sub-Sahara Africa, Caribbean Women, or Women in Central America. Others focus on aspects covered topically in the curricular themes described above—for example, Women and the Economy of Development or Women, Kinship, and Family Structures in China. In Third World countries now constructing women's studies curricula for use in schools and colleges, the opening theme may be this one, and all other themes reviewed here may follow from it.

Two final caveats bear repeating: first, the women's studies curriculum ideally and idealistically aims to include a focus not only on gender, but also on the intersections of gender with race, class, ethnicity, and other relevant characteristics of individuals and groups. Further, while the focus is unabashedly on women, there is constantly present, visibly and occasionally subtly, a comparison with men.

Paralleling the shift in emphasis of women's studies courses has been a shift in research emphasis. During the early 1970s a substantial amount of research was devoted to documenting discrimination against women and identifying sexism or patriarchy throughout society, in space and time. An early shift to survivors of that patriarchy augmented research by presenting what Gerda Lerner has called "contribution" history, including the history of prior women's movements, not only in the United States and the West, but in almost every country throughout the world. While these tasks continue, increasing attention is being given to the impact of the new knowledge on the fundamental assumptions of the disciplines, on public policy issues such as the impact of new technologies on the work and family roles of women, and on gender differences in general. Indeed, there is, in some quarters of the women's studies research and teaching worlds, a new shift to the study of gender that runs parallel to the study of women. While the study of gender may seem to include men more readily than women's studies per se, and while funding agencies may be more sympathetic to the study of gender than to the study of women, feminists are alert to the fact that gender per se narrows what has been until now a very broad area of study. Gender narrows the field to discrimination and the study of differences between men and women, leaving to one side the major thrust of the women's studies movement from the beginning, the development of a body of knowledge that restores the lost history and culture. While women's studies has made inroads into the development of such a body of knowledge, the field is only at the beginning of its development. Further, only when such bodies of knowledge are extensive, can scholars begin to review history or other areas of scholarship—including men as well as women in their purview.

Women's studies in the 1980s has also given more attention to the international dimensions of women's issues. While feminist scholars on both sides of the Atlantic had been in touch with one another throughout the 1970s and had shared ideas and controversies, the women's studies community in the United States did not at first address the concerns of women in developing countries. There were, of course, exceptions, particularly among anthropologists who were stimulated by the women's movement to examine women's roles more closely than had been customary. Among the earliest and most influential books on women in developing countries were *Women's Role in Economic Development*, by Ester Boserup; *Women, Culture and Society*, edited by Michele Rosaldo and Louise Lamphere; and *Toward an Anthropology of Women*, edited by Rayna Reiter.[16] In her groundbreaking work, Boserup, a Danish economist, studied development policies based on the then prevailing Western models and showed how in the process of "developing" (or industrializing) a nation, the traditional division of labor between the sexes was disrupted, generally depriving women of their productive work while offering men new training. As a result, the whole process of economic growth was retarded. There is now a substantial literature on the critical work of women in the economic systems of developing countries and of the significance of such work for development policy.

The establishment of the U.N. Decade for Women from 1975 to 1985 gave further impetus to the study of women's roles worldwide. In May 1980 UNESCO convened a meeting in Paris of a committee of experts on research and teaching relating to women. In its final report, the committee recommended that UNESCO cooperate in the creation and development of both women's studies programs and research as part of university curricula and in other relevant institutions.[17] In so doing the committee expressed the view that programs for teaching and research in women's studies are one of the means to securing women's complete equality. The committee report goes on to state: "Women's studies, which has developed independently in various countries, has already shown that it can enrich both scholarship and social policy, demonstrating a dynamic force in the development of new forms of knowledge. We believe that comparative studies will be of special value" (p. 2).

UNESCO responded in a limited way to the recommendations of the committee, supporting regional meetings and seminars. In Latin America these meetings were instrumental in the formation of a Latin American Women's Studies Association. Similar associations have been attempted, with some UNESCO support, in the Middle East and in the Far East, as well as in Africa.

A far more potent force in extending women's studies to countries throughout the world was the program of Women's Studies International presented at the U.N. Mid-Decade Conference in Copenhagen in July 1980. This program, organized by the Feminist Press in collaboration with the National Women's Studies Association, the Simone de Beauvoir Institute of Canada, and the SNDT Women's University in India, consisted of a series of 35 seminars and workshops over a 10-day period attended by more than 500 representatives from 55 countries. Many learned about women's studies for the first time. Others came to exchange views on theory, pedagogy, research methodology, and policy analysis. The result was the formation of a worldwide network of women's studies scholars and practitioners called Women's Studies International. Following the Copenhagen conference, women's studies moved ahead rapidly in some parts of the world such as India and the Caribbean. Elsewhere, a beginning was made. The full extent of the international progress of women's studies was demonstrated at the U.N. End of Decade Conference, held at Nairobi, Kenya, in July 1985. The second program organized by Women's Studies International, held in conjunction with that conference, was co-sponsored by 26 organizations and institutions in 15 countries. There were over 1,000 participants in the sessions, all of them active in some way in women's studies. African countries were well represented and are now among those making notable advances in women's studies.

Current Status

After a period of substantial growth since 1970, women's studies courses and programs are now firmly entrenched on college and university campuses. They have grown in sophistication as well as in size and number, and they have made their influence felt abroad as well as in the United States. Yet they do not reach directly more than a small segment of the student body, most of them women. We have noted that it is one of the objectives of women's studies to integrate the new knowledge into the mainstream curriculum, thereby affecting the education of all men and women. To what extent has women's studies been successful in achieving this goal?

The first effort to measure the impact of women's studies on the liberal arts curriculum was undertaken by a group of women faculty members at Princeton in 1976. The project was limited to an examination of the introductory courses in four disciplines that have been among the most active in women's studies. Lois Banner, the project director, collected and analyzed 355 syllabi from 172 departments in a variety of institutions. Supplementary information was gathered through questionnaires sent to department chairmen, directors of women's studies programs, and publishers of textbooks. It was found that with few exceptions little or no attention was being given to women in these courses.[18] The situation in sociology was somewhat better than in the other fields largely because of the availability of an introductory text—*Sociology*, by Suzanne Keller and Donald Light—which covered a wide range of research relating to women. Department chairmen reported that the presence of women in their departments and, to a lesser extent, the existence of a women's studies program on campus were important in determining whether individual faculty members were taking heed of the new scholarship on women and incorporating it into the basic curriculum. Based on these findings, Banner concluded that methods of persuading faculty to revise their existing syllabi and to incorporate material on women were called for. And they were not long in coming.

One was the outcome of a recommendation of the Princeton project itself, namely, the preparation of a monograph, *Teaching Women's History*, written by Gerda Lerner and widely distributed by the American Historical Association.[19] The monograph provides a guide to relevant topics and source material including material from other disciplines, making it easier for faculty members to incorporate women's history into existing courses. This is only one of several kinds of curriculum integration activities that have been undertaken since the latter part of the 1970s. A variety of approaches have been used, including workshops, summer institutes, conferences, faculty development grants, consultations, and curriculum revision programs. Many of these have been funded by government agencies or private foundations.

By 1981 a directory of curriculum integration programs prepared at the Center for Research on Women at Wellesley College listed nearly 50 projects.[20] In that year, the Southwest Institute for Research on Women at the University of Arizona, one of the leaders in the mainstreaming movement, convened a conference of directors of curriculum integration projects to share information and pass on the results of their efforts to others. The conference, which was held at Princeton, resulted in the formation of an informal network and a conference report that was designed as a handbook on strategies for instituting integration projects.[21] One of the most ambitious projects during this period was an institution-wide effort at Wheaton College to integrate the study of women into the liberal arts. The Wheaton project culminated in a national conference in 1983 attended by 250 women and men who were involved in curriculum integration projects or were interested in initiating them. The conference and the ensuing report were intended as "both a spur to the process of gender balance in the curriculum of American higher education and a means of expanding the network of those undertaking this effort."[22] Among the more promising recent mainstreaming efforts are several that deserve mention. One program, initiated in 1985 with support from the Ford Foundation, has introduced new perspectives on women into the curriculum of ten formerly all-male colleges. For example, Columbia University is in the process of redesigning its well-known contemporary civilization curriculum to integrate the new perspectives. At Towson State University in Maryland, a three-year project, established with a grant from the Fund for Improvement of Postsecondary Education, provided workshops, mentors, conferences, and other supportive strategies to several hundred faculty in various departments. This project has raised additional funding for outreach to faculty in a dozen nearby campuses as well as in local secondary schools, public and private.

We use the word "integrate" advisedly, rather than the word "add," since one cannot as a rule simply add new perspectives without changing traditional ways of thinking. As feminist scholar Elizabeth Minnich has pointed out, one cannot simply add the idea that the world is round to the assumption that it is flat. One must revise the whole conceptual framework. In that sense, women's studies scholars speak of new paradigms and of "transforming" the curriculum. In what ways and to what extent has the new scholarship influenced the disciplines? In recent years several volumes of essays on this subject have appeared. *The Prism of Sex*, edited by Julia Sherman and Evelyn Beck, shows how feminist research has challenged the premises and content of six disciplines— history, literature, psychology, sociology, philosophy, and political science. A similar volume, *Men's Studies Modified*, edited by Dale Spender, looks at the impact of feminism on a number of other academic disciplines including anthropology, economics, and biology, as well as fields such as education and law. A third volume, *A Feminist Perspective in the Academy*, edited by Elizabeth Langland and Walter Gove, examines feminist scholarship in the humanities and social sciences and seeks to assess the difference it has made in the mainstream curriculum.[23] The conclusion reached is that feminist scholarship has indeed begun to alter the state of knowledge of the disciplines but that women's studies has yet to have any substantial influence on the traditional curriculum.

There has been some further progress in the integration process during the six or seven years since these assessments were made. Nevertheless, it is the consensus among those engaged in integration efforts as well as others that change has been slow in coming. In a sense, this is hardly surprising. Curriculum change is never rapid, and it certainly cannot be expected to be rapid when basic assumptions are being challenged. In the case of feminist scholarship, the speed of acceptance also relates to the number of women in faculty positions. While all faculty women are not necessarily feminist in outlook, they are more likely than men to be sympathetic to women's studies. Until women are better represented in faculty positions, particularly tenured faculty positions, it will continue to be difficult to transfer the new insights of women's studies to the traditional curriculum.

Future Prospects

At the present stage of women's studies, the number of degree programs is still growing and the process of integration is under way. There is no reason to expect a reversal in these trends in the immediate future. It will be increasingly difficult for institutions that do not have women's studies courses or programs to ignore so substantial and significant a field of scholarship. It will be particularly difficult on campuses where women in the student body outnumber men. With respect to graduate and professional schools, women's studies has not yet begun to reach full growth. Graduate programs are needed to produce teachers of women's studies. Among the professional schools, law is the most advanced, whereas education and social work, the traditional women's fields, are still in the early stages of developing women's studies courses and integrating women's issues into their curricula.

For these reasons, the prospect is for further expansion of women's studies beyond the 1980s. There are and will continue to be problems, however. One problem has to do with the lack of departmental status of women's studies. As we have noted, in nearly all cases women's studies is structured as an interdisciplinary program rather than as a separate department. There has been much debate about the pros and cons of this arrangement. The advantage of departmental status is that it provides control over faculty appointments and budgets. On the other hand, women's studies as a department runs the risk of being marginalized and generally ignored by the rest of the university. Underlying the debate is the issue of whether women's studies is a discipline, with its own theory and methodology, or whether it is a new area of study that is integral to the existing disciplines.[24] The preponderant structure of women's studies programs as they now exist and continue to be formed suggests that the case for women's studies as a discipline has not yet been made. At the same time, women's studies programs apart from but integrated with the disciplines are seen as essential, and that appears likely to continue for the foreseeable future. Programs continue to have two crucial functions. One is to coordinate the course offerings of the various disciplines, providing guidance and support for students who choose women's studies as a major. The other is to ensure the continued development of new perspectives, ideas, and knowledge by providing a sympathetic and stimulating environment for faculty and graduate students from a variety of departments who are at the forefront of the new scholarship on women. The environment for women's studies scholars in traditional departments is still likely to be one of indifference, if not disdain. But even if in the long run this was no longer the case, women's studies would still be needed to coordinate research efforts and curriculum development across the disciplines.

Problems aside, even at the conclusion of close to two tumultuous decades of development, one may still find undergraduates claiming that women's studies "changed my life" and one may still find graduate students and more established scholars making discoveries that will not only change one aspect of the curriculum or the discipline from whence it springs, but also the lives of women and men. The work of women's studies has only just begun. Generations of committed scholar-teachers will need to continue both the development of the curriculum and scholarship if academe is ever to offer a truly coeducational higher education to students. We are still discovering "lost" women writers, still trying to write or rewrite women's history, still puzzling over socialization patterns and the intransigence of sex stratification in the workforce, still arguing with men and with women about basic human needs in a gender-free world. Perhaps most important for the future is the comprehension gained during these two decades of the essential relationship between knowledge about women and the possibilities for changing the patterns of women's lives.

Notes

1. Florence Howe, "A Report on Women and the Professions," *College English* 32 (May 1971):847–854. This essay was given as the opening lecture in the forum offered by the Commission on the Status and Education of Women at the Modern Language Association's annual meeting in December 1970.

2. Women on Words and Images, *Dick and Jane as Victims: Sex Stereotyping in Children's Readers* (Princeton, NJ: Women on Words and Images, 1972). Pre-publication versions were available far earlier.

3. *Female Studies I, II, III, IV, V,* and *VIII* were published by KNOW, INC. in Pittsburgh, between 1970 and 1973; *Female Studies VI, VII, IX,* and *X* were published by the Feminist Press between 1972 and 1975.

4. Florence Howe, "Women's Studies and Social Change," in Alice Rossi and Ann Calderwood, eds., *Academic Women on the Move* (New York: Russell Sage Foundation, 1973), p. 393.

5. Tamar Berkowitz, Jean Mangi, and Jane Williamson, eds., *Who's Who and Where in Women's Studies* (Old Westbury, NY: Feminist Press, 1974).

6. Florence Howe, *Seven Years Later: Women's Studies Programs in 1976*, a Report of the National Advisory Council on Women's Educational Programs, 1977.

7. The series includes, among others, the following: Elaine Reuben and Mary Jo Boehm Strauss, *Women's Studies Graduates;* and Florence Howe and Paul Lauter, *The Impact of Women's Studies on the Campus and the Disciplines* (Washington, DC: National Institute of Education, 1980).

8. Elaine El-Khawas, *Campus Trends, 1984*, Higher Education Panel Report no. 65 (Washington, DC: American Council on Education, February 1985).

9. Unpublished data, National Center for Education Statistics.

10. *Women's Studies: A Catalogue of Selected Doctoral Dissertation Research* (Ann Arbor: University Microfilms International, 1986).

11. In 1985 Florence Howe surveyed the nearly 500 women's studies programs with a brief questionnaire. The new data cited in this paper come from that survey's return of 58 percent.

12. Catharine R. Stimpson, with Nina Kressner Cobb, *Women's Studies in the United States* (New York: Ford Foundation, 1986).

13. Preamble to the NWSA Constitution.

14. Florence Howe, "Feminist Scholarship: The Extent of the Revolution," *Change*, April 1982, pp. 14–15.

15. Peggy McIntosh, with Katherine Stanis and Barbara Kneubuhl, "Directory of Projects: Transforming the Liberal Arts Curriculum through Incorporation of the New Scholarship on Women," *Women's Studies Quarterly* 11, no. 2 (Summer 1983):23–29. Some of the other projects were sponsored by such professional associations as the American Historical Association and the American Political Science Association, or by such nonprofit educational institutions as the Wellesley College Center for Research on Women and the Feminist Press.

16. Michele Rosaldo and Louise Lamphere, eds., *Women, Culture and Society* (Stanford: Stanford University Press, 1974); and Rayna R. Reiter, ed., *Toward an Anthropology of Women* (New York: Monthly Review Press, 1975). These collections of essays by leading feminist anthropologists exploring new ways of analyzing the place of women in a wide variety of social systems have become classics in the field.

17. UNESCO, *Final Report and Recommendations*, Document SS-80/Con.626/9, Research and Teaching Related to Women: Evaluation and Prospects meeting, Paris, May 20, 1980.

18. Princeton Project on Women in the College Curriculum, *Final Report*, March 1, 1977.

19. Gerda Lerner, *Teaching Women's History* (Washington, DC: American Historical Association, 1981).

20. Martha Tolpin, *Directory of Programs: Integrating Women Into Higher Education Curricula* (Wellesley, MA: Center for Research on Women, 1981).

21. Myra Dinnerstein, Sheryl R. O'Donnell, and Patricia MacCorquodale, *How to Integrate Women's Studies into the Traditional Curriculum,* paper no. 9 (Tucson: Southwest Institute for Research on Women, University of Arizona, 1981).

22. Bonnie Spanier, Alexander Bloom, and Darlene Boroviak, eds., *Towards a Balanced Curriculum: A Sourcebook for Initiating Gender Integrating Projects,* based on the Wheaton College Conference (Cambridge, MA: Schenkman, 1983), p. 5.

23. Julia A. Sherman and Evelyn Torton Beck, eds., *The Prism of Sex* (Madison: University of Wisconsin Press, 1981); Dale Spender, ed., *Men's Studies Modified* (New York: Pergamon Press, 1981); and Elizabeth Langland and Walter Gove, eds., *A Feminist Perspective in the Academy* (Chicago: University of Chicago Press, 1981).

24. For a discussion of this issue, see Judith B. Walzer, "New Knowledge or a New Field Discipline?" *Change*, April 1982, pp. 21–23; and Gloria Bowles and Renate Duelli Klein, eds., *Theories of Women's Studies* (London: Routledge & Kegan Paul, 1983).

PART III

Women as Faculty Members and Scholars

8

Affirmative Action

If the campus issue of the 1960s was student protest, surely the cry of the 1970s was "affirmative action." In that decade, academic women became more and more aware that a benign neutrality would not be enough to achieve equality on campus. Reasoned expositions of the facts apparently would not be enough to change the dismal pattern of continuing pay differentials, discrimination in hiring and promotion, and the many related phenomena which contributed to institutionalized, systemic discrimination against women. In fact, it became increasingly apparent that the first step was to establish unequivocally that a problem did exist, with regard to both hiring and research.[1] Women's initial objections seemed to meet with lengthy rationalizations of the status quo rather than with active help, or even understanding of the problems.[2] More was needed, and more became available, through a legal system already attuned to civil rights and through the administrative action of the federal government in connection with the large amounts of federal money being directed into colleges and universities.

As noted earlier, in the 1970s numerous federal laws were passed which for the first time extended the requirement of nondiscrimination to faculty and administrators in higher education.[3] More important for affirmative action, the Executive Order which outlawed sex discrimination in all federally financed employment was actively applied to higher education for the first time.[4] In addition, more and more lawsuits were filed asking for equitable treatment and restitution of lost benefits.[5] All of these active efforts to bring women into the mainstream of higher education came to be associated with the term "affirmative action."

While purists will rightly object that "affirmative action" refers only to a form of legal redress stemming from the equitable power of the courts and is limited to certain well-recognized principles, a realistic appraisal of affirmative action for women in higher education requires an assessment of both the technical legal remedy and the larger societal concept. Both concepts are systematically misdefined by opponents of wider academic opportunities for women, and even by some who support the widening of opportunities but fear the loss of academic autonomy. This may be a reaction to the incredibly difficult task of making academics face the fact that there has been systematic discrimination in academe. Most academics do not want to discriminate consciously, and the inescapable conclusion that they may have done so can give rise to feelings of guilt and consequent self-justification.[6]

Whether the continuing misdefinition of affirmative action is only a classic conservative response to a new social movement, or a more conscious misdirection of thought, it has had the effect of requiring every discussion of affirmative action to begin with lengthy definitions, both for the sake of accuracy and in the heretofore vain supposition that it will be possible to stop arguing about issues that do not exist and that all involved will agree on a common definition. This effort does not presume so much. When the U.S. Civil Rights Commission, under the Reagan administration, moves from supporting the idea of quotas in limited circumstances to an investigation of the adverse effect of affirmative action on higher education, it is clear that the definitional struggle is not at an end. The Supreme Court has only added to the confusion by supporting affirmative action in education in both *Bakke* and *Wygant*, but failing to agree on a definition or majority opinion in either case.[7] Given these ongoing definitional struggles, this chapter will attempt some assessment of how "affirmative action" came to be focused on higher education in the 1970s and what that focus has meant for the institutions, for the women in them, and for affirmative action itself.

The Context of the University as an Organization

While the university is often on the frontier of social organization from a theoretical point of view, it would seem to be the most inert of institutions in regard to its own internal organization. Edward Shils has pointed out that certain currently existing universities are the oldest continuously existing institutions on earth, with the sole exception of the Roman Catholic Church.[8] The earliest universities were not created by either church or state; they created themselves.[9] For both historical and policy reasons, institutions of higher education have guarded this independent status assiduously and subtly ever since.[10] Thus, much of the initial opposition to affirmative action may have been more opposition to the governmental interference involved in enforcement than to the underlying social idea. However, it may also be that sounding the clarion call for autonomy and academic freedom was to some degree a ruse to avoid full integration of women on campus.

From the beginning, universities were male. Women were never considered as students and were not accepted as faculty. This tradition was probably a simple transfer from the church since students had to be at least nominal members of clerical orders to attend a university, even if this only meant a tonsured haircut.[11] This tradition, long observed and deeply embedded, seemed to become a myth with a life of its own. Even the advent of scientific rationalism in the nineteenth century failed to dispel it. At that time it was decided that women should not be allowed into higher education because the mental energy necessary for higher education would be drained directly from the uterus and would therefore weaken women's reproductive capacity and destroy the race.[12] As late as 1958 Caplow and McGee could write: "Women tend to be discriminated against in the academic profession, not because they have low prestige but because they are outside the prestige system entirely. . . . Women scholars are not taken seriously and cannot look forward to a normal professional career."[13]

Discussion of affirmative action should distinguish between the right which women assert and the methodology used to remedy violations of that right. It seems clear that many are not convinced of the existence of the right itself, although the attack of affirmative action would appear to center primarily on the question of the remedy. The whole issue of "quality" would appear to dispute the fact that women are as intelligent and as capable of becoming scholars, teachers, and administrators as are men. If that issue can be resolved, the discussion becomes clearer. By any other standard, the increase in the availability pool would *raise* the quality of those selected. If neither religion nor biology supports that exclusion, perhaps psychologists can explain, if not justify, the reluctance to use brains attached to female forms. Thus, when discussing the inappropriateness of preferences, or so-called reverse discrimination, it is well to remember that for centuries men have been given an absolute preference on university campuses. Since women were rarely if ever considered as colleagues, men have had the privilege of competing only against each other in the continuing determination of the best and the brightest.

In their essay "Legal Structures and Restoring Equity,"[14] Macauley and Walster discuss primarily psychological, rather than legal, equity.

They define "harmdoing" as committing an act that creates an inequitable relationship. Harmdoers, they say, experience distress and will try to restore equity to a relationship through (1) restitution to the victim or (2) rationalization of the harm through derogation of the victim, denial of responsibility, and minimization of the harm.

Given the history of the university and its inherent nature—an organization which seeks to make itself the most enlightened institution in society—it is not hard to see why rationalization of the exclusion of women came more comfortably than restitution. Probably without thinking very deeply about it, traditionalists tended to assume that the university practice must be correct. Academic women have striven valiantly to destroy various rationalizations for inequity with factual studies, and even succeeded in some measure, but it is a slow process at best. "Affirmative action" began as it was recognized that something more was needed to enter the academic corridors of power; some active method to establish restitution as the means to destroy the imbalance in the relationship was required. So, affirmative action can be defined, in one sense, as the various means used on campus to effectuate restitution, leading to a balanced relationship between the sexes in higher education. In another sense, it means a way of gaining attention for the presentation of rational argument.

As has been noted, much of the controversy over affirmative action is a war of words, and the relentless urge to define is hard to escape. However, perhaps some variation is possible. "Affirmative action" as used by the courts is generally a form of equitable remedy. Therefore, it is really necessary to begin by defining equity, particularly since affirmative action, as an equitable remedy, finds itself in the middle of a much larger controversy concerning the overuse of the equity jurisdiction of the courts, the structure of our judicial system, and our whole societal system of social justice. As Abram Chayes pointed out in his seminal article in the *Harvard Law Review*,[15] equity, which began as a corollary jurisdiction to soften the inflexible nature of the common law courts, now threatens to take over the judicial system as a method to restructure society.

Affirmative Action and Equity

Equity is a very old concept. It is referred to in the Old Testament[16] and in Aristotle's *Nichomachean Ethics*. Aristotle writes, "That which is equitable then, is just, and better than one kind of justice, not indeed better than absolute justice, but better than the error of justice which arises from legal generality. *This is in fact the nature of the equitable; it is a rectification of law, where it fails through generality.*"[17] [emphasis added]

Centuries after Aristotle, the English established courts run by the king's chancellor—the "Courts of the King's Conscience"—to dispense equity. Interestingly, the Chancery Courts were the only courts which allowed a married woman to appear before them to pursue her legal rights. The equity courts also evolved the idea of the trust, a device originally used to protect married women's property. The Chancery Courts administered relief where the remedy at common law was inadequate, generally because the common law had become too inflexible in its application. The Chancery Courts were known for their more flexible procedures and more pliable decrees. The injunction is probably the best-known equitable remedy, and affirmative action is a form of affirmative injunction.

The great English jurist Frederic Maitland wrote that equity acted where, "although there was a remedy at law, for some reason it was inadequate to grant the relief required," adding that the chancellor might also choose to act affirmatively in the petitioner's behalf,[18] something a common law judge would never do. Claimants at equity often alleged that they could not obtain justice at law because their opponent was too rich and too powerful. The power of the Chancellor would act as a counterbalance to give them some redress, even as today the power of the courts can balance the power of the university against the individual, to some degree.

The equity courts became a part of the American legal system when, in 1787, the Constitution (Art. III, Sec. 2) provided that the judicial power of the federal government "shall extend to all cases at law or in equity arising under the constitution and laws of the United States. . . ." An American legal scholar, commenting on the growth of equity, wrote, "This capacity of moulding a decree to suit the exact exigencies of a particular case is indeed one of the most striking advantages which procedure in chancery enjoys over that in common law. . . ."[19]

Given the idea that equitable remedies were flexible and affirmative, it is not surprising that they were applied by the federal courts in the 1960s to continuing evasions of civil rights law. An example is the series of voting rights cases in which southern states continually passed new legislation to evade the latest federal court judgment endeavoring to enforce federal law. This use of equity jurisdiction was directly challenged in the Louisiana voting rights cases, where the state acted continually to create new evasionary laws as the old ones were struck down by the court.

Equity and Civil Rights

The first Louisiana lawsuit was filed because blacks were not allowed to vote under a state constitutional provision allowing only those whose grandfathers had voted to vote. When that clause was invalidated by the federal court, an "interpretation test" which every voter had to pass was enacted. When the interpretation test was invalidated, a white primary system was established. As that system was before the federal district court which ultimately invalidated it, the Louisiana legislature enacted a new law requiring every voter to pass a "citizenship test." Even though the citizenship test law had been passed *after* the suit was filed, the District Court enjoined the state from applying it, retained jurisdiction, and ordered monthly reports to be filed with the court on the number of black voters registered. The state appealed to the U.S. Supreme Court on the grounds that the actions taken by the District Court exceeded the equity jurisdiction and powers of that court.

In 1965 the Supreme Court strongly reaffirmed the equity power of the federal trial court, stating:

> The need to eradicate past evil effects and to prevent the continuation or repetition in the future of the discriminatory practices shown to be so deeply ingrained in the laws, policies, and traditions of the State of Louisiana, completely justified the District Court in entering the decree it did and in retaining jurisdiction of the entire case to hear any evidence of discrimination in other parishes and to enter such order as justice from time to time might require.[20]

Thus, with the question squarely before it, the Supreme Court affirmed the equitable power of the federal courts to take affirmative action to enforce federal law, and that decision has stood. The equity function of the federal courts in civil rights cases, particularly the school integration cases, has been vital to the progression of civil rights in this country. "Affirmative action" became the new name for this exercise of equitable jurisdiction to enforce the law where the remedy at law was inadequate.

Affirmative Action as a Remedy

In court cases, the use of affirmative action as a remedy is almost always preceded by a formal finding of past discrimination.[21] If past discrimination cannot be proved, affirmative action cannot be used as a remedy. In the transfer of the use of the affirmative action remedy to the Executive Orders applicable to federal contractors, the existence of prior discrimination in employment was assumed.[22] In all other respects the idea was the same, except that the specific form of the remedy was promulgated and enforced by the executive branch of government. For those critics of the courts who feel that the exercise of equitable jurisdiction has gotten out of hand and changed the function of the courts as it was originally envisioned under the concept of the separation of powers, the use of affirmative action as a regulatory device by the administrative agencies is certainly a more appropriate method to effect social change.

One problem with the use of the Executive Orders to enforce affirmative action is that the orders are not enacted by Congress; they are purely executive acts by the President. However, by the same token, Executive Orders apply only to federal contractors. It is possible to avoid affirmative action requirements by refusing to take any federal money or by showing that there is no underutilization of protected groups.

The currently effective Executive Orders, 11246 and 11375, are the last in a long series of Executive Orders applying to federal contractors and initiated by President Franklin Roosevelt during World War II when A. Philip Randolph, president of the Brotherhood of Sleeping Car Porters, convinced him that such an order would lower defense costs by enlarging the labor pool (and avoid a march on Washington by blacks seeking greater employment opportunities). The original Executive Order pertaining to nondiscrimination in federally funded employment was amended and expanded by every subsequent president until Lyndon Johnson signed Executive Order 11375 in 1968, adding sex discrimination to the list of prohibited practices. The formal use of affirmative action was added by President Kennedy in Executive Order 10925. Numerous cases have upheld the constitutionality of affirmative action under the Executive Orders; relatively few have considered the question of whether the President has the power to require affirmative action of federal contractors. Such cases as do exist establish that the primary legal justification for the exercise of affirmative action is the executive responsibility to effect cost savings.[23] Thus, in higher education terms, affirmative action is actually just one more facet of cost accountability. From the government's standpoint, opening the field to all applicants regardless of race or sex should lower the cost and improve the quality of federal grants to universities in just the same way as for defense contracts.

Throughout this time the legal characteristics of affirmative action have been characterized primarily by flexibility and continuing judicial supervision, or a definite time period after which the affirmative action remedies were no longer required. Affirmative action is inherently a temporary measure, both in the courts and in administrative agencies.

Numerous lawsuits have tested the constitutional and statutory validity of the affirmative action remedy for employment discrimination. Some of the better known cases are in the construction industry. In these cases, several federal courts validated the use of affirmative action as constitutional and in harmony with the nondiscrimination statutes. Various subsidiary points such as the use of some form of numerically expressed goals were also upheld. Through these cases, the validity of the affirmative action remedy for employment discrimination became firmly entrenched in federal case law.[24] One form of this validation was the approval of the use of affirmative action plans as defenses to charges of employment discrimination in the so-called reverse discrimination cases. This issue reached the Supreme Court in 1979 in *United Steel Workers of America* v. *Weber*, 443 U.S. 193 (1979). In that case the Supreme Court specifically validated an affirmative action plan adopted by an employer to remedy patterns of race discrimination in employment, even though there had been no suit filed charging or establishing employment discrimination.[25] The Supreme Court made clear that it did not intend to validate all affirmative actions plans, but only the one under consideration.[26] At the same time, the Court gave some guidelines for determining whether a given plan would be permissible under the Civil Rights Acts and Constitution, as follows:

1. The purpose of the affirmative action plan should follow that of the Civil Rights Act, to break down old patterns of segregation and hierarchy and to open employment opportunities which had been traditionally closed.
2. In order not to "unnecessarily trammel" the interests of other employees, no discharge could be required, nor could any absolute barriers to advancement by other workers be set up.
3. The plan should be limited in time, seeking not to maintain a balance, but to eliminate a manifestation of imbalance.[27]

These guidelines have remained in place and are useful for assessing affirmative action plans in higher education as well.

Affirmative Action and Higher Education

How did the enforcement of the Executive Order against sex discrimination in federally related employment get transferred from construction contractors to colleges and universities? Largely through the legal and political efforts of the Women's Equity Action League (WEAL), and especially through the work of Dr. Bernice Sandler, chair of the WEAL

Action Committee for Federal Contract Compliance, who, in 1970, filed a class action complaint against institutions of higher learning, charging an industry-wide pattern of discrimination against academic women. Subsequently, specific charges were brought against more than 250 institutions, and additional charges against other institutions were brought by individual women and women's groups on campus. A national letter-writing campaign requesting congressmen to ask the Secretaries of Labor and Health, Education, and Welfare (HEW) why the Executive Orders were not being enforced on campus brought a wave of congressional letters to the Secretaries. The end result was increased enforcement attention to the university community.[28]

Why did academic women respond with such vigor to WEAL's efforts? At the beginning of the 1970s, women's participation in faculty and administrative ranks in higher education was definitely pyramidal, and those women who did hold faculty positions typically had salaries substantially less than their male colleagues. Women also complained of unequal treatment in teaching assignments and the granting of tenure. Only 42 percent of women held tenure, while 60 percent of men did.[29] Equality was an idea whose time had come, or at least so academic women thought.

To the genuine surprise of many academic women, universities did not see it that way. Tradition continued to be the dominant value on campus, even to the exclusion of rational analysis. Further, the appearance of federal enforcement officers on campus posed the kind of unheard-of threat to institutional autonomy which was not to be countenanced for any reason. Affirmative action became juxtaposed in the minds of many with the cause of academic freedom—an unfortunate entanglement of issues which has been difficult to unsnarl. The university tradition of autonomy would have resisted governmental pressures in any context, but the administrative realities of affirmative action were particularly unfortunate. The Secretaries of HEW and Labor, in order to respond promptly to congressional pressure to accelerate enforcement efforts, were often forced to use officers and agents from other areas of government who were less than totally familiar with academic customs and mores. To have to begin with a definition of academic tenure was almost unthinkable to some university officials. The initial enforcement efforts struck some university administrators as more suited to a factory assembly line than to the rather different employment conditions in institutions of higher education. The resulting well-articulated objections led to a federal effort to draft special guidelines for the enforcement of affirmative action in higher education.

Early drafts of *Guidelines for Higher Education* highlighted four major substantive disagreements between the higher education community and HEW: curriculum, including textbook content; athletics; vocational education; and single-sex scholarships. Due largely to the efforts of the then president of Stanford University, all attempts to regulate curriculum or textbook content were eliminated in order to protect academic freedom. Single-sex scholarships remained a violation of the Higher Education Guidelines, although the idea of pooling the total number of each type of scholarship in order to compare the total number of dollars going to men and women was accepted. Attempts by vocational educators to exempt their activities from affirmative action requirements were also unsuccessful, and the Vocational and Rehabilitation Education Act of 1976 contained strong provisions mandating specific administrative measures to enforce affirmative action.

The most difficult issue, for a number of reasons, was athletics. Athletic directors argued strongly that their programs, and more specifically their budgets for revenue-producing sports, ought to be exempted. However, once the attempt to amend Title IX to exempt contact sports had failed, the agencies held firm in their refusal to exempt any aspect of athletics from the requirements of affirmative action under the Executive Order.[30] The enactment of Title IX,[31] specifically prohibiting sex discrimination in education and thereby extending the nondiscrimination requirements to students for the first time, has been in fact a great help in the general movement of affirmative action for women on campus, despite the dampening effect for a time of the limiting ruling in the Grove City decision by the Supreme Court.[32] The full effect of this powerful statute is yet to be felt.

The battle over "goals" versus "quotas," a continuing contrapuntal theme in the affirmative action discussion, deserves mention as well. Quotas, defined as absolute numerical hiring requirements, had been approved as a temporary measure in several contractor cases and in some cases concerning police and fire departments where earlier efforts had brought no results.[33] According to these cases, quotas are a remedy to be used only when other methods have been tried and have failed. Goals, on the other hand, were not absolute requirements, but rather a numerical standard by which to judge substantive progress toward sex equity. When the higher education community objected to absolute numerical hiring goals, for any number of legitimate reasons, HEW offered the alternate idea of goals based on numerical analysis of availability pools as a standard to determine whether real progress was being made. Many educators immediately objected that the difference between goals and quotas was only semantic; that both meant the hiring of unqualified people. In 1972, at the American Council on Education's annual meeting in Miami, Florida, Robben W. Fleming, then president of the University of Michigan and a distinguished labor lawyer, stood up in a public meeting to state that he thought that the difference between goals and quotas was more than semantic, that he was glad HEW had adopted the former, and that he, for one, was willing to try to work with it. Most responsible administrators have taken the same position in the intervening years. Here again, the discussion is a red herring. Quotas have never been asked for and have certainly never been enforced in higher education. Like many arguments against affirmative action and sex equity, opponents have set up a bogus issue which has never existed. Any meaningful discussion of goals themselves has thus been avoided. Higher education's initial impulse to defend itself by asserting that availability pools for various disciplines and departments were so difficult to determine as to become almost impossible has only resulted in more complex and precise recordkeeping. These data, while initially expensive to compile, are actually of great benefit in studying higher education for any number of other reasons.

Once the furor over overall issues posed by the Higher Education Guidelines had settled down, and memoranda from chief enforcement officials had made clear that comprehensive affirmative action plans and yearly recordkeeping would be required of higher education institutions, discussion turned to the nature of the recordkeeping, the amount of statistics which had to be kept, and the extent of the yearly reports. Many universities have complained bitterly over the administrative, recordkeeping, and duplicating expenses. At the same time, affirmative action requirements have undoubtedly provided the impetus to modernize university personnel practices and regularize recordkeeping. The generation of much better recordkeeping has greatly improved our ability to study and understand higher education in all its aspects. The advent of the computer, along with private and public fiscal crises of the 1970s, and the state legislators' demand for greater cost accountability all made better, more uniform personnel procedures inevitable in any event. Further, external pressures gave administrations the ability to overcome faculty resistance to being treated as mere employees. As any good affirmative action officer knows, affirmative action, in its procedural aspects on campus, is just good personnel policy.

The Higher Education Guidelines, issued in 1972 by HEW and based on the more generally applied Revised Order No. 4 issued by the Labor Department in 1971,[34] had this to say about the meaning of affirmative action: "The premise of the affirmative action concept of the Executive Order is that unless positive action is undertaken to overcome the effects of systemic institutional forms of exclusion and discrimination, a benign neutrality in employment practices will tend to perpetuate the *status quo ante* indefinitely."

Under the guidelines, the implementation of affirmative action began in academe, as in industry, with institutional determination of underutilization of the protected classes. "Underutilization" was defined as having fewer women or minorities in a particular job than would be reasonably expected by their availability. To determine availability, institutions had to find out the number of women who might be available for any given job opportunity. Definition of these "availability pools" by academic discipline, cross-discipline, and quality of degree-granting institution of the candidates became complex. Yet, this requirement has caused the higher education community to know itself in a way it never had before. Further, the increasingly sophisticated and extensive data on candidate availability had a strong impact on many open-minded, research-oriented faculty members who had been genuinely convinced that adequate women candidates did not exist. The requirement to advertise positions created an additional method, often outside the traditional networks, of bringing women to the attention of search committees.[35]

Although there has been some objection to the difficulty and costs involved, generally this approach to hiring has been accepted, fitting easily into the research tradition of the university. The major failure is that on some campuses the availability information does not reach the search committee until after the search is completed, when it is used to justify a decision already made. On well-run campuses, these figures are the most useful at the time the "short list" is determined. Effective administrators genuinely interested in implementing affirmative action can then hold up the conduct of personal interviews if the departmental list diverges greatly from the availability pool. Requiring departments to interview additional women candidates at this point is extremely important, because experience shows that personal interviews often have more positive effects for women and minority candidates because of unconscious stereotypical evaluations based solely on paperwork.[36]

If affirmative action is to be effective in the individual hiring process, close cooperation between the senior administrator, such as the dean, who controls the interview and travel budget, the affirmative action office which maintains the availability pool information, and the department chairman or search committee chairman is paramount. While some small, well-financed institutions have been able to accomplish this, on too many campuses a relatively small affirmative action office has acted only to add statistical reports to job decisions which have already been made. Any complex system is subject to the possibility of evasion. Universities, in insisting on their uniqueness, have succeeded in establishing a system which is not only expensive, but also easy to avoid. Thus, the success of affirmative action depends on the institutional willingness to make it succeed, and that in turn depends on executive leadership.

A second requirement under the guidelines is the establishment of hiring goals and timetables for the entire institution. Goals are defined as "projected levels of achievement resulting from an analysis by the contractor of its deficiencies, and of what it can reasonably do to remedy them, given the availability of qualified minorities and women and the expected turnover in its workforce."

This statement seems too clear to dispute or misunderstand, yet it resulted in advertisements asking specifically for minority or women candidates, and in numerous letters to unsuccessful male candidates telling them that they might have been hired were it not for affirmative action requirements. Whether caused by overzealous campus enforcement or a calculated overreaction, HEW moved to stop these practices by including a statement in the guidelines that such preferential treatment of candidates regardless of merit was clearly illegal and therefore not only not required, but prohibited.

As in industrial applications, the Higher Education Guidelines also cover promotion, but they have never had much effect on the tenure system. It is commonplace on many campuses for the dean to say: "We have affirmative action in hiring, but not in promotion." What is usually meant by this is that while the administration is willing to support and finance extra efforts to find women and minority candidates, and even to hire them, they are unwilling to give any special consideration in the promotion process. This view equates special treatment with unfair advantage, assumes that the tenure system works flawlessly without any personal biases, and assumes that the problems of systemic discrimination which make affirmative action necessary in hiring have miraculously disappeared in six years. The ultimate concern is said to be institutional quality, but that concept is narrowly defined and traditionally applied. Even at that, some campuses have developed specific written policies encouraging affirmative action in promotion and tenure, for example, allowing women candidates who are single parents to request an extra year to prepare their work for review.

It has been considered a satisfaction of the guidelines and the Labor Department requirements if the *percentage* of women assistant professors who make tenure is the same as the *percentage* of the male assistant professors who make tenure, but many institutions do not yet make the effort to achieve even this modest goal, while others show a remarkable consistency in promoting only the minimum percentage. At the same time, in most instances the numbers are so small within individual departments that statistical comparisons become insignificant. By and large, the tenure system, based on a confidential, subjective analysis, has remained untouched by affirmative action under the Executive Order. That is to say, during the second decade of women in academe, many departments were willing to *hire* women, but not necessarily to tenure them. Even individual orders or court decrees requiring a better tenuring pattern tend to require tenure *or* a valid explanation for the failure to do so, and the latter alternative is by far the more popular.

Tenure, Lawsuits, and Affirmative Action

The problem of hiring women but refusing to tenure them is so widespread nationally that it has been given a name: the Revolving Door Theory.[37] It has not been difficult for faculties to hire women as assistant professors, particularly given the increasing numbers of PhDs granted in the 1970s and 1980s in languages and literature, psychology, and several other disciplines. As Dr. Hornig's studies show, even in mathematics, the sciences, and engineering there is a steadily increasing number of doctorates being granted to women. Tenuring-in appears to be much more difficult.[38] Part of the problem comes from the nature of the tenure process; it is very difficult to monitor. Faculties are also extraordinarily sensitive on the quality issue at this point. However, the fact is that if a majority of male faculty members desire not to tenure a female colleague simply because she is female, there is still little that can be done about it, short of a signed statement to that effect by the department members. On most campuses, there is no necessity for justifying such a decision, to anyone. The problem lies almost as much with the tenuring system as with any inherent or subconscious tradition of sex discrimination. The tenure system assumes that all faculty members are objective and devoid of prejudice or unconscious bias of any kind. As John Adams might have said, it assumes that they are angels, not men.[39]

However, tenure itself is not an absolute value; it is only a method to protect the academic freedom of the individual professor. Whatever job security may result is clearly secondary to that goal. Unfortunately, the legitimate goals of the peer review process for promotion to tenure, as it has evolved, have resulted in a system whereby a very small number of people make this major decision with little accountability to anyone. It is an absolute power of academic life or death. Further, faculties seem to have convinced themselves, society, and, most important, the courts that this subjective, secret, unaccountable process is always carried on, by all faculty members at all institutions, in the most high-minded and ethical way, solely for the benefit of the institution. While published accounts of the internal mechanisms of tenure review are hard to come by, academic fiction is replete with them, with C. P. Snow's *The Masters* being one of the more illustrative examples. During the second decade of women in academe, the more realistic social conclusion seemed to be that since no nonmember could adequately perceive the arcane matters of academe, it would be better to risk some discriminatory exclusion than a dilution of academic autonomy stemming from affirmative action. However, this rather questionable conclusion may be swinging ever so slightly in the favor of women in some institutions where questionable tenure decisions have been reviewed and on occasion reversed by the president or other higher authority.[40]

The Tenure Process and Affirmative Action

First, there is the question of whether the overall tenure process is granted too much reverence. Peer review is a human institution, and, like other human institutions, it can be analyzed and evaluated. It seems at the very least paradoxical that an institution devoted to rationality and clear thought should surround one of its basic processes with such mysticism. It is uncomfortable for any human being or group of human beings to be evaluated. No one knows that better than teachers. But in the long run, evaluation may be preferable to a destruction of the whole process. Tenure, while not the whole of academic freedom, is vital to it. A threat to tenure is also a threat to academic freedom. Even now it is being argued that, at least in public institutions, academic freedom is unnecessary since all citizens possess the rights of free speech and free press, and academic freedom cannot give professors more rights than those they already possess as citizens.

Second, in many institutions the reliance on peer review as the exclusive measure of value is misunderstood, and hence misapplied. The reason for the unwillingness to question peer review, it is said, stems from a recognition that only a specialist in the same field can accurately assess the value of an assistant professor's work. However, those who actually make the decision, both on the departmental faculty and the campus-wide review committee, may not understand the candidate's work any better than a court might. It is common for a faculty member to be hired precisely because he or she fills a gap in the department's instructional and research offerings which no existing faculty member can adequately fill. It is true that departments at major institutions routinely ask for outside reviews by specialists in the same field as the candidate; however, the question is still decided by departmental faculty. Admittedly, there are other factors, such as teaching and service to the university, but these are often evaluated on a less stringent basis. The real peer review is by specialists in the candidate's own field, and the departmental use of these reviews can and should be more thoroughly evaluated in the case of allegations of discrimination. As noted above, it would be better to open up the tenure process a little than to lose it entirely.

Third, the confidentiality of the tenure review process is questionable. In the Blauberg case,[41] a senior professor was willing to go to jail rather than reveal his vote on a tenure decision, defining that personal privacy as a part of academic freedom. That is not the purpose of academic freedom; it is to allow faculty members to do research and teach freely without fear of dismissal for political or other irrelevant reasons. The basic question raised by the Blauberg case, and by numerous other faculty suits asking for information, is whether secrecy in the tenure evaluation process is such an integral part of academic freedom that its abolition would seriously undermine the academic and social value of academic freedom. Here again, secrecy allows the possibility of abuse, and liberties which are abused tend to be destroyed, or at least strongly regulated. That risk in itself should be reason enough to lift the veil of secrecy and let in the light of public responsibility. The tenure decision is not just an individual matter or a private club decision of an individual faculty. It is very much a social decision. The make-up of our faculties is too important a matter to be conducted in secrecy or subjectivity.

Professors are used to public criticism in the evaluation of articles for juried journals and in the exchange of views in these journals. The same standards of professional evaluation should apply to tenure review, and there is no reason for the one to be public and the other private.

Finally, professors, like judges, need to avoid inaccuracy, arbitrariness, and the "lack of consideration" referred to in *Gray* v. *NYU*[42] by rendering written opinions. The AAUP Statement, adopted in part by the Second Circuit in the Gray case, should be a minimum requirement. Surely professors are not less professionally responsible than judges, and there is no less need for accountability.

By and large the problem of tenure has not been touched by affirmative action under the Executive Orders during this period. The challenge came through individual lawsuits under other legislation. Yet these lawsuits set standards for administrative affirmative action and are a part of the larger movement.

Litigation, Lawsuits, and Class Actions

As noted above, the 1970s were an outstanding time for the passage of laws designed to eliminate sex discrimination on campus, yet until very recently the lawsuits brought under these statutes were largely unsuccessful. Athena Theodore's study of 470 women who filed some form of discrimination charges makes this painfully obvious.[43] Only two or three cases with special circumstances resulted in decisions for individual plaintiffs. In *Kunda v. Muhlenberg College*, 621 F.2d 532 (3rd Cir. 1980), a case mandating tenure for a physical education instructor if she fulfilled certain conditions of which she had not had prior notice, was decided by a woman judge and former law professor. *Sweeney v. Keene State College*, 569 F.2d 269 (1978) involved a situation in which the decision had already been made by the faculty; the only question was whether the plaintiff should have been promoted two years earlier. A further positive factor in the Sweeney case may have been the presence of Judge Tuttle, a retired "civil rights" judge from the South who wrote the decision the first time around for the First Circuit. Judge Tuttle's perspective is fairly unique. In commenting on the string of unsuccessful cases brought by academic women, Judge Tuttle wrote:

> . . . we voice misgivings over one theme recurrent in those opinions, the notion that courts should keep "hands off" the salary, promotion, and hiring decisions of colleges and universities. This reluctance no doubt arises from the courts' recognition that hiring, promotion and tenure decisions require subjective evaluation most appropriately made by persons thoroughly familiar with the academic setting. *Nevertheless, we caution against permitting judicial deference to result in judicial abdication of a responsibility entrusted to the courts by Congress. That responsibility is simply to provide a forum for the litigation of complaints of sex discrimination in institutions of higher learning as readily as for other Title VII suits.* [emphasis added]

The doctrine of judicial noninterference or academic abstention is not confined to sex discrimination cases; it applies to all cases brought against colleges and universities. The courts have traditionally refused to interfere in the basic academic process of the university, particularly in the evaluation of students or faculty. When this doctrine has been combined with the rather difficult burden of proof imposed by the courts on plaintiffs in these cases, the effect has been to leave the victims of sex discrimination in higher education without a remedy in the courts. It is true that some class actions have been successful, such as the *Lamphere* case at Brown, the *Rajender* case at the University of Minnesota, and the less well known *Muhlenberg* case, but the end result for the individual women on campus has been less than was hoped even in these cases. In *Rajender*, for example, the lead plaintiff got a substantial award, but all other cases had to be tried administratively on campus on an individual basis, and many were denied. While these initial determinations can be appealed, it is as yet unclear whether the individual plaintiffs will have the resources to do so. Although there have been a few encouraging signs, such as the opinion in *Lynn v. University of California–Irvine*, 656 F.2d 1337 (9th Cir. 1981), by and large the legal process has remained closed to academic women. Early in the period under discussion, John Johnston, Jr., and Charles Knapp documented the generalized judicial bias against women.[44] This bias, combined with the heavy burden of proof required in employment discrimination cases under the McDonell Douglas-Burdine standard[45] and the pervasive doctrine of academic abstention, gives academic women little hope of redress through the courts. Comparable worth, while a tremendous breakthrough for working women generally, does not particularly apply to the problems of academic women. Joel Friedman has suggested that the remedy lies in a shift in the burden of proof in discrimination cases from the plaintiff to the institution, in line with similar standards where one of the parties controls most of the relevant information and is much more powerful.[46] This, indeed, would be more realistic and would undoubtedly forward the position of women in academe, *if* it could be accomplished—particularly since even in cases such as that brought at Cornell where the university opened all its procedures to the court, the court weighed only the sufficiency of the academic procedure, not the correctness of the decision itself. It is relatively easy to cloak bad decisions in good procedure, and evidently that will pass muster with the courts since they are unwilling to look at the substance of the matter. Academic abstention still prevails, to the detriment of individual rights on campus.

If the courts were uniform in their reluctance to deal with sophisticated factual evidence, this might be more understandable. But the elements of a tenure decision are no more complex than the facts with which a court must grapple in a multi-district antitrust case, or a complex patent or tax case. There is no real reason why the courts should abdicate their statutory mandate in academic employment cases; but given the dozens of cases to date in which some way was found to avoid a decision against an institution, it seems unlikely that the courts will provide an adequate avenue for the establishment of the rights of academic women.

Quality and Individual Merit

One of the major criticisms of affirmative action is that it denies individual merit and establishes the concept of group rights. This is an extraordinary criticism when the purpose of affirmative action is just the reverse. Affirmative action itself is nothing but an attempt to have considerations based only on group attributes set aside so that individuals can be judged on their own merits. Women and minorities have clearly been excluded from faculty and administrative positions in higher education solely because of their group identifications. Such well-established behavior patterns are not quickly or easily changed. Centuries of group discrimination demand a consideration of group identity when attempting to obliterate that discrimination. While the arguments are sophisticated, surely they can be well understood in the academic community.

Thus, affirmative action *furthers* the concept of individual merit, rather than denying it. Of course, coerced consideration of individual women does not automatically cancel entrenched mental assumptions; it only presents opportunities for the individual woman to open the minds of her colleagues and opportunities for entrenched biases to become more subtly expressed. It seems rather strange that the assertion that discrimination is subtle, sophisticated, and complex and therefore needs remedies of a like kind should meet with such resistance from the academic community. Surely if any sector of our society could deal with sophisticated, intellectual analysis, it would be academe. Perhaps, since there has been no motivation to explore the complexities, it has not been done. Here again, there are certainly new heartening individual exceptions to this old rule.

In sum, it is important to remember that just the reverse of the widely voiced allegations is true, both in theory and in practice. The purpose of affirmative action is to require fair consideration of individual women on their individual merits. The practices and procedures of affirmative action require no more; in fact they have succeeded in achieving considerably less, particularly in the tenure process.

The second major criticism of affirmative action is that it lowers the quality of institutions by requiring them to hire unqualified or less qualified people—specifically, women. Here again, assertions are not supported by research findings or other scholarly evidence, but depend on faculty evaluations, which are neither rationalized nor explained. In any other endeavor, it is generally recognized that increasing the absolute number of qualified candidates *increases* the quality of those at the top. Top SAT scores are pushed up, for example, when very large numbers of students take the test. In simple numbers, the addition of women can double the pool of qualified applicants for a university faculty, thereby greatly increasing the potential quality of the institution. Here again, affirmative action results in the very opposite of what its critics ascribe to it.

Entrenched attitudes are not easily changed, even with the best intentions. It is these ingrained subconscious attitudes with which we all struggle. The important research done on this subject at the University of Delaware, published popularly under the title *Seeing and Evaluating People*, demonstrates that most evaluators, both men and women, still seem to see primarily the group characteristics of an individual woman, rather than her particular merits.[47] In one sense, the charge that affirmative action fosters group consideration rather than individual merit is itself an admission that individual women are still being judged primarily on their group identity rather than on individual merit. The court cases and other evidence which indicate that women doing scholarly work in women's studies or on women's issues in their own disciplines inevitably have their research discounted by evaluators underscores the reality of the persistence of group identification for women.

The Remedies

In "Affirmative Action 1972–1982: A Decade of Response,"[48] Helen Astin and Mary Beth Snyder make four recommendations for future enforcement of affirmative action: (1) simplified recordkeeping and more effective recruiting, (2) better mentoring for new faculty, (3) increased leadership pressure, and (4) better consideration of affirmative action requirements during recruitment.

These recommendations are reasonable and instructive; whether they are adequate for all institutions is another question. And they do not reach the difficult issue of tenure, which is a crucial issue for several reasons. First, in the many institutions which customarily tenure only a percentage of all assistant professors, even if all vestiges of discrimination were eliminated, the system would still work to keep down the absolute number of women of the faculty for some years to come.

Second, while some may argue that criteria for tenure are fairly straightforward and perfectly susceptible to quantitative measurement, others regard the process as too subjective to analyze. The fact that many review groups make every effort to avoid discrimination only makes it the more difficult to reach those bodies or individuals which do use the confidentiality of the tenure process to cloak discrimination.

Third, the tendency to downgrade the value of women's studies research in the tenure process undermines an extremely important area of intellectual development at a crucial period.

Finally, the continuing failure of large numbers of women to make tenure and the past failure of the courts to offer any remedy to them nullifies all prior affirmative action efforts for students and junior professors and thereby jeopardizes not only the progress of equitable treatment for women, but also the true progress of equal opportunity for achievement in academe.

To consider the Astin-Snyder remedies further: Simplified record-keeping is always to be desired, but care must be taken to avoid using cost as an excuse for reducing enforcement efforts. As the judiciary often notes, the *cost* of justice is not a valid objection. At the same time, ignorance of actual requirements combined with underbudgeting and poor program management can lead to a morass of rules and forms which accomplish little. Intelligent and informed enforcement which is adequately budgeted is the best protection against undue complexity. To some extent, effective recruiting itself depends on extensive record-keeping and information gathering, exactly as do alumni giving or athletic recruiting programs. The emphasis on data collecting should be to improve recruitment efforts rather than to justify "good faith efforts."

More effective recruiting needs to be followed by better retention, and here mentoring for new faculty is extremely important. Although mentoring is not uncommon in the sciences (where there are relatively few women), very few institutions have mentoring or orientation programs for faculty members in general, male or female. Such programs, where instituted, have been conducive to improved faculty morale.[49]

To date, increased leadership pressure seems to offer the most hope for meaningful change. Major institutions which have benefited from strong leadership and imaginative initiatives have achieved tangible results both in numbers and in campus morale. MIT is often cited in this context. The problem is that if campus leadership elects not to act, relatively little can be done about it.

More attention to affirmative action during retrenchment is vital to preserve the progress that has already been made, as the courts have recognized in public school education. However, the Supreme Court decision in the Wygant case, ambiguous and divided as it is, will probably work against much further implementation of this goal.

As the Astin-Snyder recommendations imply, the best hope for rea-sonably effective affirmative action measures lies in the understanding and goodwill of those in decision-making positions on campus. The past decade has provided a shock to the academic system, but in the long run it is to be hoped that new attitudes will prevail and the need for regula-tory intervention and lawsuits will diminish.

Conclusions

Affirmative action has been a premier force in theory and practice for women in higher education in their efforts to secure fair and equal treatment and to awaken community thought to the inequities inherent in long-accepted practices. The Executive Order and the court decisions upholding affirmative action as a legitimate exercise of courts' equity power in applying the Fourteenth Amendment not only gave women courage to go forward and claim their rightful place on campus; they also modified the behavior of those on campuses and, most important, acted as an educating mechanism, forcing faculty and administrators to pay attention to and begin to understand the meaning of true equity in higher education in all its complexity. The establishment of permanent affirmative action offices and the modernization of personnel practices and recordkeeping, and most particularly the advertisement of open positions, guarantee that the process of behavioral modification and education will continue on campus.

Women's studies scholars and others who have published research papers on affirmative action and equity in academe have also helped to establish the tide of change in the collective campus consciousness. Although affirmative action as a tool for sex and race equality is only beginning to be defined by the courts, and although some cases which have come down (such as the Jackson, Michigan, case disallowing affirmative action in lay-offs unless there had been a prior judicial finding of discrimination) have restricted its scope, the opinions as a whole, including the U.S. Supreme Court opinions, have consis-tently reaffirmed the legitimacy of affirmative action as a necessary legal tool to combat systemic discrimination and effectuate the Fourteenth Amendment.

While affirmative action may not have accomplished all that was orig-inally claimed for it and has not been able to shed the shibboleths of anti-merit and anti-intellectual bias attached to it by opponents and defend-ers of the status quo, it has nevertheless been a major force for good on campus and a foundation stone for the rightful progress of women and minorities. Even if the federal government continues to deny affirmative action by nonenforcement, even if the Executive Order is rescinded or modified, the activities of the past decade have succeeded in establishing the idea of sex equity on campus, and affirmative action will go forward, perhaps even more strongly by choice, rather than by force.

In fact, the greatest foe to affirmative action in the next decade may be complacency, a feeling that the battle is over when it has simply entered a new phase. It is now the time to reaffirm and reassert the principles, to continue analysis and monitoring, to develop new ways of exposing subtle forms of discrimination, and, above all, to support those who continue their untiring efforts to put theory into practice.

Notes

1. An analysis of some of the reasons for this attitude may be found in the following: Morris, B. Abrams, "Affirmative Action: Fair Shakers and Social Engineers," *Harvard Law Review* 99 (April 1986):1312; and Randall Kennedy, "Persuasion and Distrust: A Comment on the Affirmative Action Debate," *Harvard Law Review* 99 (April 1986):1327. Kennedy writes, "What is so remarkable—and ominous—about the affirmative action debate is that so modest a reform calls forth such powerful resistance."

2. Kennedy notes the further interesting fact that the question of whether prejudices might be responsible for the opposition to affirmative action is almost totally lacking from many of the leading articles on the subject; "Persuasion and Distrust," p. 1337.

3. Title IX of the Education Amendments of 1972, 20 U.S.C. sec. 1681. The Equal Opportunities Employment Act of 1972 extended Title VII of the Civil Rights Act of 1964 to educational institutions for the first time; see P.L. 92-26. The *Higher Education Guidelines: Executive Order 11246* was also issued by the Office for Civil Rights at HEW in 1972; the Equal Pay Act of 1963; 29 U.S.C. sec. 206(d)(1), was extended to professional employees for the first time by an amendment to the Fair Labor Standards Act, 29 U.S.C. sec. 213(a), effective July 1, 1972. The Health Professions Educational Assistance Act of 1976, 42 U.S.C. sec. 292 et seq., also contained prohibitions against various types of sex discrimination.

4. Executive Order 11375 amended Executive Order 11246 by adding sex discrimination to prohibited practices by federal contractors; 3 C.F.R. 169.

5. See Joel M. Friedman, "Congress, the Courts and Sex-Based Employment Discrimination in Higher Education: A Tale of Two Titles," *Vanderbilt Law Review* 34 (1981):37. All of the early cases, about 30 or so, brought by individual women against universities were unsuccessful, primarily because of the doctrine of academic abstention. See Harry T. Edwards and Virginia Davis

Nordin, *Higher Education and the Law* (Cambridge, MA: Institute for Educational Management, Harvard University, 1979), p. 14. Class actions, such as those against Brown University and the University of Minnesota, have been more successful. The first major successful individual case was *Sweeney* v. *Trustees of Keene State College*, 604 F.2d 106 (1st Cir. 1979); cert. den., 444 U.S. 1045 (1980).

6. See Stewart Macauley and Elaine Walster, "Legal Structures and Restoring Equity," in June Tapp and Felice Levine, eds., *Law, Justice and the Individual in Society: Psychological and Legal Issues* (New York: Holt, Rinehart, & Winston, 1977).

7. In *University of California Regents* v. *Bakke*, 98 S.Ct. 2733 (1978), the Supreme Court upheld the idea of affirmative action in student admissions while striking down the particular policy under consideration. In that case there were two opposing groups of four justices each, with Justice Powell writing the one decision all were able to concur in. In *Wygant* v. *Jackson Board of Education*, 54 L.W. 4479, U.S. (1986), a case concerning layoff patterns for public school teachers, there were three separate "majority" opinions, and four justices dissented in two separate opinions. Once again, the Court affirmed the use of affirmative action, disallowed the application in the particular case at the bar, and gave very little in the way of guidelines for future cases. In *United Steel Workers of America* v. *Weber*, 443 U.S. 193 (1979), the Court denied a reverse discrimination charge in employment and validated the use of an affirmative action plan in a company where there had been no formal finding of past discrimination. The legality and constitutionality of affirmative action were definitely established in *Local 28, Sheetmetal Workers' International Association* v. *U.S.*, 54 L.W. 5000 (1986), a case with a number of rulings which are highly significant for higher education. In that case, the Supreme Court rejected the argument that intentional discrimination against an individual was necessary to support affirmative action and, based on a finding of discrimination under Title VII, validated the application of a numerical goal for admission of apprentices into permanent membership (like tenure). It rejected the argument that the affirmative action plan, including a court-appointed administrator, constituted an unjustified interference with the union's statutory right to self-governance, stating that, "while the administrator may substantially interfere with the petitioner's membership operation, such 'interference' is necessary to put an end to petitioners' discriminatory ways." The Court also reaffirmed its right to abridge a bona fide seniority system, thereby limiting its prior decision in *Firefighters* v. *Stotts*, 467 U.S. 561 (1984) (at 4997). The Court stated that the numerical requirement for membership was a means by which to measure compliance, "rather than . . . a strict racial quota" (at 4999).

8. Edward Shils, *Tradition* (Chicago: University of Chicago Press, 1980).

9. F. M. Powicke and A. M. Emden, eds., *Rashdall's Medieval Universities*, vol. 1 (Oxford: Oxford University Press, 1936).

10. Alexander Murray, *Reason and Society in the Middle Ages* (Oxford: Clarendon Press, 1978). Justice Frankfurter made a strong statement in support of uni-

versity autonomy in *Sweezy* v. *New Hampshire*, 354 U.S. 234, 262 (1957) concurring opinion, and Justice Powell picked up this same idea in *Bakke;* see note 7.

11. Powicke and Emden, *Rashdall's Medieval Universities*. Prior to the evolution of universities in the twelfth century, learning was promulgated by individual, often ambulatory, teachers. As Abelard has taught us, this form of education was not successfully extended to women.

12. In 1872 Dr. Edward Clarke, a member of Harvard's Board of Overseers and former member of the medical faculty, warned an audience at the Boston's Women's Club that exposing women "to the rigorous intellectual exercise of a Harvard education would seriously threaten their future reproductive capacity." Rosalind Rosenberg, *Beyond Separate Spheres: Intellectual Roots of Modern Feminism* (New Haven: Yale University Press, 1982), p. 5. Rosenberg adds, ". . . foremost among the difficulties women still face is the fact that belief in the inevitability of separate sexual spheres endures and has even intensified in recent years as a consequence of the writings of sociobiologists." See also Evelyn Fox Keller, *Reflections on Gender and Science* (New Haven: Yale University Press, 1985); and Dorothy Geis McGuigan, *A Dangerous Experiment: 100 Years of Women at the University of Michigan* (Center for Continuing Education of Women, Ann Arbor: 1970), chap. 2.

13. Theodore Caplow and Reece McGee, *The Academic Marketplace* (New York: Basic Books, 1958), pp. 111, 226.

14. See note 6.

15. Abram Chayes, "The Role of the Judge in Public Law Litigation," *Harvard Law Review* 89 (May 1976):1281.

16. See, for example, Psalms 98 and 99.

17. Aristotle, *Nichomachean Ethics*, book 5, chap. 14, Weldon trans. (New York: Macmillan, 1897).

18. Frederic Maitland, *Equity*, 2nd ed. (London: Cambridge University Press, 1936), pp. 3–6.

19. Joseph Story, *Equity Jurisprudence* (Boston: Little, Brown, 1939), sec. 27. This rationalization is still used. An equity decree "will go as far as possible to remedy past violation as well as bar violation in the future." *In re Koch*, 471 F.Supp. 175, 179 (SDNY 1979).

20. *Louisiana* v. *U.S.*, 380 U.S. 145, 156 (1965). This opinion also describes the history of this case.

21. One of the few exceptional cases was *Germann* v. *Kipp*, 429 F.Supp. 1323, 1333 (8th Cir. 1978). However, the Supreme Court emphasized the need for such a prior finding in the Wygant case; see note 7.

22. "Unlike the affirmative action provision of Title VII of the Civil Rights Act of 1964, which may be invoked by a court after finding that an employer has unlawfully discriminated, the Executive Order's affirmative action requirement is not based on proof of individual acts of discrimination. Instead, it is founded upon the strong national policy and possible constitutional imperative that the Federal Government, in expending its moneys, should not

subsidize invidious discrimination in employment." Peter G. Nash, "Affirmative Action Under Executive Order 11246," *New York University Law Review* 46 (1971):225, 229.

23. See "Note, Imposition of Affirmative Action Obligations on Non-Consenting Governmental Contractors (*U.S.* v. *N.O. Public Service, Inc.*)," *Harvard Law Review* 91 (1977):506; "Comment, E.O. 11, 246: Presidential Power to Regulate Employment Discrimination," *Missouri Law Review* 43 (1978):451.

24. See, for example, *U.S.* v. *Elevator Constructors,* 538 F.2d 1012 (CA 3 1976); *Associated General Contractors of Massachusetts* v. *Altschuler,* 490 F.2d (CA 1 1973); *Southern Illinois Builders Association* v. *Ogilvie,* 471 F.2d 680 (CA 7 1972); and *Contractors' Association of Eastern Pennsylvania* v. *Secretary of Labor,* 442 F.2d 15 (CA 3 1971).

25. In *Weber,* the Supreme Court specifically validated the legality of the affirmative action plan adopted by the employer-defendant, which reserved 50 percent of the openings in an in-plant craft training program until the percentage of minority craft workers was commensurate with the number of black workers in the availability pool.

26. Like the *Bakke* and *Wygant* decisions, discussed in note 7; however, the Wygant case, decided in 1986, picks up strongly on the Weber idea that no affirmative action plan should require the *discharge* of any worker.

27. *United Steel Workers of America* v. *Weber.*

28. For additional information on the political history of affirmative action, see A. Fishel and J. Pottker, *National Politics of Sex Discrimination in Education* (Lexington MA: Lexington Books, 1977).

29. Committee to Study the Status of Women in Graduate Education and Later Careers, *The Higher the Fewer: Report and Recommendations* (Ann Arbor: University of Michigan Graduate School, March 1974).

30. On December 11, 1979, HEW issued regulations pertaining to Title IX and intercollegiate athletics, 44 Fed. Reg. 71413. See also 47 Fed. Reg. 20809, 20822 (May 14, 1982); Fishel and Pottker, *National Politics,* pp. 82–83, pp. 95ff.

31. 20 U.S.C. secs. 1681–1686 (1976). The enactment of Title IX, in the context of effective enforcement by the executive branch of the federal government of other anti-discriminatory measures, seemed to so alarm some opponents to equity on campus that special legislation was passed to allow Congress to review the administrative regulations promulgated under this and all subsequent statutes. See Fishel and Pottker, *National Politics,* p. 95ff.

32. *Grove City College* v. *Bell,* 82-792 (February 28, 1984).

33. See the discussion concerning *Sheetmetal Workers* v. *U.S.* in note 7.

34. "Revised Order No. 4," 41 C.F.R. sec. 60-2.10, issued by the Office of Federal Contract Compliance.

35. As a bonus, advertising revenues provided much needed financial support to the *Chronicle of Higher Education* at a time when its continued existence as a resource for educational information and communication was in doubt.

36. See L. S. Fidell, "Empirical Verification of Sex Discrimination in Hiring Practices in Psychology," *American Psychologist* 25, no. 12 (1970); 1094–1098.

37. Dr. Jacqueline Macauley of Madison, Wisconsin, publishes yearly descriptions of this phenomenon at the American Psychological Association meetings and probably originated the term.

38. See chapters 9 and 11 herein.

39. Adams wrote, "If Socrates and Plato, Cicero and Seneca, Hutcheson and Butler are to be credited, reason is rightfully supreme in man. . . . But the nature of mankind is one thing, and reason of mankind is another; and the first has the same relation to the last as the whole to the part. The passions and appetites are parts of human nature, as well as reason and the moral sense . . . although reason ought always to govern the individual, it certainly never did since the Fall, and never will, till the Millennium; and human nature must be taken as it is, as it has been, and will be." John Adams, *Works...*, edited by Chas. Francis Adams (Boston, 1851), vol. 4, p. 402, quoted in *The People Shall Judge* (Chicago: University of Chicago Press, 1949), pp. 209–210.

40. A recent example is the decision regarding the appointment of Theda Skocpol at Harvard. See "A Question of Sex Bias at Harvard," *New York Times Magazine*, October 16, 1981. Skocpol was eventually granted tenure by the president of Harvard.

41. *In re Dinan*, 310 (1980) 24 Empl. Prac. Dec. (CCH) par. 31, 310. See also Michael R. Smith, "Protecting Confidentiality of Faculty Peer Review Records: *Department of Labor* v. University of California," *Journal of College and University Law* 8 (1981–82):20–53. The U.S. Supreme Court, by refusing to review a case regarding access to records in the 1985–1986 term, left this issue unresolved legally on a national basis, since the circuits were definitely split on this issue.

42. *Gray* v. *NYU*, 30 F.E.P. Cases 302 (2d Cir. 1982).

43. Athena Theodore, *The Campus Troublemakers: Academic Women in Protest* (Houston: Cap and Gown Press, 1986).

44. John D. Johnston, Jr., and Charles L. Knapp, "Sex Discrimination by Law: A Study in Judicial Perspective," *New York University Law Review* 46 (1971):675.

45. See *Texas Department of Community Affairs* v. *Burdine*, 450 U.S. 248 (1980).

46. Friedman, "Congress."

47. A monograph by F. L. Geis, M. R. Carter, and D. J. Butler, published by the Office of Women's Affairs, University of Delaware, 1982.

48. *Change*, July-August 1982.

49. For further discussion of the mentorship role, see Mary R. Rowe, "Building Mentorship Frameworks as Part of Our Equal Opportunity Ecology," in Jennie Farley, ed., *Sex Discrimination in Higher Education: Strategies for Equality* (Ithaca: New York State School of Labor Relations, Cornell University, 1981).

9

Nontraditional Fields for Women

One of the most fundamental changes in women's higher education since 1970 is the shift away from the conventional "women's fields" and into the sciences, engineering, medicine, other health professions such as veterinary medicine and dentistry, law, business and management, theology, architecture, and numerous smaller specialties. Such a large-scale movement into the traditionally male-dominated fields calls into question a number of long-cherished beliefs on the part of both women and men regarding the "differentness" of women, their presumed preferences for people over things, for emotion and intuition over rigorous logic and rational thought. For those scientists and other scholars who have argued the nature versus nurture problem of apparent sex differences in intellectual inclinations and achievements, the magnitude of the overall effect as well as the structure of its details provides a rich source of evidence which still remains largely unexplored. Although the interpretation of some of this evidence remains ambiguous, the major trends to which it testifies are clear and should affect the thinking and planning of faculty and administrators in academe and the decisions of policymakers.

A comparison of the numbers of degrees earned by women in traditional and nontraditional fields serves to illustrate the magnitude of some of these effects. In 1986, for example, there were about 68,500 women PhDs in the sciences, including the social sciences, and 28,600 in the humanities in the total active stock of U.S. doctorate holders.[1] Among the total of 31,770 new doctorates awarded in 1986, 11,244 went to women; 5,422 of these were in engineering and the sciences and 1,565 in all humanities fields combined, with the remainder in education and other professional fields such as business, architecture, and theology. One thousand of the women science PhDs were in the physical, mathematical, and engineering sciences—the most rigorously quantitative fields—compared with about 400 women English PhDs, the single largest humanities field for women.[2] In 1985 more than 14,400 women earned law degrees, an almost eleven-fold increase since 1970, and nearly 4,900 women graduated from medical schools, seven times the number in 1970.[3] In 1971 just over 1,000 women earned MBAs; by 1986 that number had grown to nearly 21,000.[4] Similar shifts in field distribution occurred at the undergraduate level. In 1970 women earned about 38,000 bachelor's degrees in English and only 338 in engineering, but in the mid-1980s the number of female English graduates had dropped to about 15,000, while the number of engineering graduates had climbed to about 11,000. Between 1970 and 1984, the aggregate number of women baccalaureates in business management increased more than nine-fold to 100,122, and those in education (that quintessentially female field) shrank by almost 50 percent, to about 70,000, despite the concomitant increase of 144,000 (41 percent) in the annual total of women college graduates.[5]

The juxtaposition of such figures comes as a surprise to most people partly because the contrasts run so precisely counter to stereotypic beliefs and partly because most presentations of education data use percentages rather than numbers. Proportions of women by field are indeed the operational quantity for analysis of employment data, but they tend to obscure the underlying trends in women's behavior because proportions are of course also affected by what men are doing, and men's educational choices have also undergone considerable change since 1970. Male graduates have *decreased* in total number by about 5 percent, and are now only 48 percent of all baccalaureates; their shares of education, social sciences, and humanities degrees have declined by about half. Their biggest gains occurred in engineering, computer fields, and business.[6] Some of the changes in sex/field distributions of bachelor's degrees are summarized in Figure 9.1.

Although the overall trends are clearly all in the direction of equalizing male and female educational patterns, field differences in the onset, rate, and extent of change allow us to identify many of the factors that contribute to women's educational decision-making and their large-scale movement into nontraditional disciplines and professions. Such an analysis is the subject of this chapter.

Figure 9.1   Selected BA/BS Degrees by Sex: 1972 and 1986

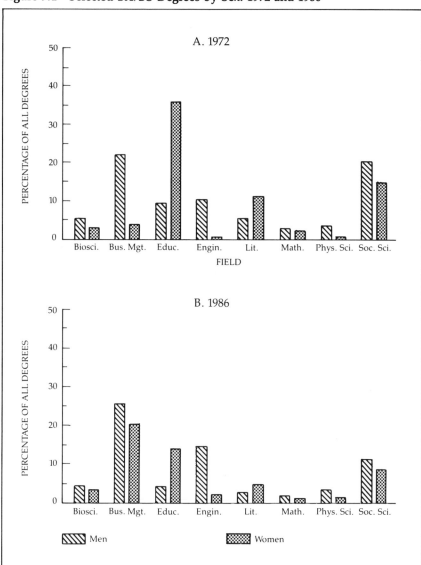

Sources: Lois Weis, "Progress But No Parity," *Academe* (November–December 1983):30; *Manpower Comments* 23, no. 9 (November 1985):24; and Betty M. Vetter and Eleanor L. Babco, *Professional Women and Minorities* (Washington, DC: Commission on Professionals in Science and Technology, 1987), table 2-15.

Women as Students

The 1970s were a period of rapid expansion in women's participation at advanced degree levels as well as at the undergraduate level. By the mid-1980s women's share of master's degrees grew to nearly half, and among PhDs their proportion grew from 16 percent in 1972 to over 35 percent by 1986. These changes are shown in Figure 9.2.

As we have noted above, some increases in professional degrees were even more striking; proportional changes are shown in Figure 9.3.

Baccalaureate Degrees

The significance of the various degree levels differs for different fields and is related to their usefulness as career entries. For example, bachelor's degrees in engineering, education, business and management, nursing and certain other health professions, and a few smaller specialties serve as a primary entry into a profession, although some of these

Figure 9.2   Proportion of Degrees Earned by Women: 1972–1986

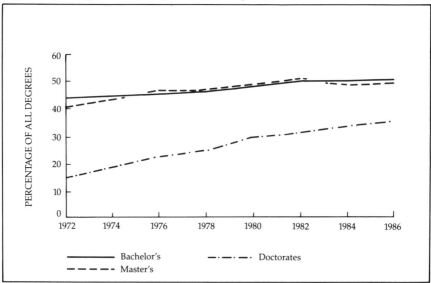

Sources: National Center for Education Statistics, U.S. Department of Education, "Degrees and Other Formal Awards Conferred," annual surveys; National Research Council, *Summary Report: Doctorate Recipients from United States Universities* (Washington, DC: National Academy Press, 1982 and 1986); and Betty M. Vetter and Eleanor L. Babco, *Professional Women and Minorities* (Washington, DC: Commission on Professionals in Science and Technology, 1987), table 2-15.

Figure 9.3   Selected Professional Degrees Awarded to Women: 1970–1985

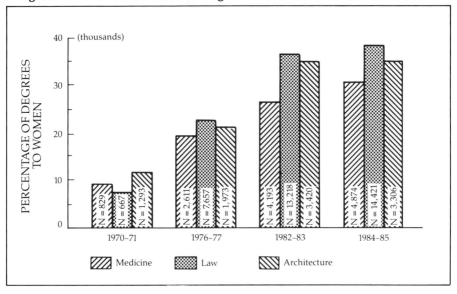

Source: Betty M. Vetter and Eleanor L. Babco, *Professional Women and Minorities* (Washington, DC: Commission on Professionals in Science and Technology, 1987), table 3-2.

do require additional certification. In many other fields—prominently so in the sciences, the humanities, and especially the learned professions— a doctorate or equivalent advanced degree is the most desirable or sole career entry. However, a master's degree may serve as an intermediate step, providing access to less prestigious versions of the career—for example, as a technician or research assistant instead of a research scientist or as a college teacher instead of a university professor. Students who are aiming for full professional careers customarily pursue graduate work to the doctorate or equivalent. Because of the differences in length and cost of study, the distribution of both men and women among undergraduate fields responds more quickly to structural change in education and to the ups and downs of the labor market than does distribution among most graduate fields. Engineering offers the classic illustration of the latter point, with the growth and decline in enrollments generated from year to year by market conditions, and a resulting "feast or famine" oscillation between unfilled demand and oversupply.

Even a cursory review of education statistics such as has been presented here reveals a close correlation of women's educational choices with occupational possibilities. The preferred major fields of college women have long been those that offered hope of some rewarding employment, however restricted the latter choices may have been. The massive swing to nontraditional fields that we have already documented at the undergraduate level reflects, first and foremost, women's new perception that equal opportunity mandates opened new occupations to them. Both women and men have retreated from the social sciences because adequate employment was not available. This was also the case in mathematical sciences, where women continue to be almost as well represented as men, long-established conventions to the contrary notwithstanding. Mathematical sciences remain among the most sex-neutral undergraduate majors, where they have been for many years. In the physical sciences, the rate of growth in women's participation remains fairly steady, though not spectacular. Men, on the other hand, have barely maintained their numbers in the core fields of physics and chemistry and hence their proportion of these baccalaureates is declining steadily. Psychology is currently the only major social science field where women's enrollments and degrees are holding steady, although the number of men has continued to decline from its high in 1974. A sex-neutral major since the 1940s, psychology is turning into a female-dominated field even as the total numbers of degrees drop back to their 1970s levels.

Graduate and Professional Degrees

In the majority of academic disciplines, a master's degree is an intermediate stop-off between the baccalaureate and the doctorate rather than an end in itself, although the purposes and significance of the degree have varied over time and by field. Until the 1970s the master's degree provided an adequate, if not distinguished, entry to college teaching in most humanities areas, though rarely in the sciences. The doctorate was and is required for full faculty status at universities and first-rank colleges as well as for most nonacademic professional positions in the sciences, although in engineering the master's degree is adequate for many nonacademic research positions and the doctorate necessary mainly for university faculty.

Master's degrees in management are the major exception to these generalizations; they are the professional degree of choice for virtually all practitioners intending to enter or advance in management, except for a small percentage who earn doctorates to gain faculty positions. The rapid growth in numbers and proportions of women MBAs is shown in Table 9.1. It is evident that despite an almost twenty-fold increase in women's participation, a similar though relatively smaller growth for men still keeps the proportion of women graduates below one third.

Table 9.1   **MBA Degrees Awarded to Women: 1971–1986**

Year	Number	Percentage Women
1971	1,045	3.9%
1972	1,207	4.0
1973	1,533	4.9
1974	2,161	6.6
1975	3,080	8.4
1976	4,974	11.6
1977	6,664	14.3
1978	8,216	16.9
1979	9,698	19.1
1980	12,355	22.3
1981	14,513	25.0
1982	17,069	27.8
1983	18,862	28.9
1984	20,088	30.1
1985	20,869	30.9
1986	20,849	31.0

Sources: Betty M. Vetter and Eleanor L. Babco, *Professional Women and Minorities* (Washington, DC: Commission on Professionals in Science and Technology, 1984), table 3-13; *Scientific, Engineering, Technical Manpower Comments* 22, no. 9 (November 1985):26; 23, no. 9 (November 1986):24; and unpublished data, National Center for Education Statistics.

In the conventional "women's fields" of nursing and social work, the MA or MS is generally reserved for specialized training and is relatively uncommon. Averaged across all fields, women earn a slightly higher proportion of master's degrees than men, a result of their somewhat different field distributions. Field for field, however, women are slightly less likely to earn a master's than a bachelor's degree, but substantially more likely to do so than to earn a doctorate.[7] The only significant exception occurs in nursing, which is almost totally dominated by women and where the few male participants are less likely than women to persist to advanced degrees.

Women earn about two thirds to three quarters of all master's degrees in the humanities and in education, and even higher proportions in various health professions and in library science. At the doctoral level, on the other hand, most of these relationships are reversed and men earn the majority of the most advanced degrees. Home economics is the only field in which women have consistently earned as much as 70 percent of doctorates for the last decade, although women now earn the

Figure 9.4   PhD Recipients by Field Group and Sex: 1974–1986

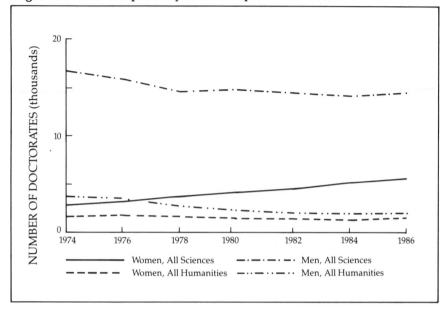

Source: National Research Council, *Summary Report: Doctorate Recipients from United States Universities* (Washington, DC: National Academy Press, 1984 and 1986).

majority of doctorates in English, modern languages, art history, and some social sciences.

Since about 1970, the numbers and proportions of doctorates earned by women in various academic disciplines have served as a popular yardstick for measuring women's progress in higher education. Figure 9.4 displays some of the changes that have occurred in both men's and women's educational behavior. Total numbers of doctorates awarded annually have dropped somewhat from their peak in 1973 owing entirely to declining numbers of men in both the humanities and the sciences. Women's participation has remained essentially constant in the humanities but increased steadily in all science fields; the number of women science PhDs more than tripled between 1970 and 1986, and conservative projections based on undergraduate participation predict continued growth in the near future.[8] These figures, however, reflect some important differences in underlying behavior over time. Most significant of these is that the graduate participation rates and consequently the graduate degree attainment rates of both sexes declined sharply in the mid 1970s and began a slow recovery in the early 1980s. The decline was far greater for men than for women;[9] most observers ascribe the lowered interest to the poor prospects of academic jobs and the concomitant explosion of attendance in professional schools. Because of the much greater decline in male participation, use of *proportions* of degrees rather than numbers may overestimate the actual rate of change, as mentioned earlier. Another confounding factor is that all these changes in rates differed by field. Additionally, doctorate completion times vary widely among fields, depending primarily on the amount and kind of financial aid available.[10] We may correct for these factors by calculating the true degree attainment rate or *parity index* for women in various fields. The parity index for PhD attainment is termed PI_2 to distinguish it from certain other indices.[11] It is defined as the ratio between the percentage of PhDs earned by women in a given field and year and the percentage of baccalaureates earned by them in the same field, lagged by the number of years appropriate to each field.[12] The PI_2 values for several major field groups are shown in Table 9.2 for 1970–1986. It should be noted that PI_2 approaches unity as women's likelihood of earning a doctorate in a given field and year approaches men's. Inspection of the values in Table 9.2 shows that women have attained such parity in social sciences and are approaching it in biosciences, while in mathematical sciences they are not only far less likely than men to attain PhDs but their rate of progress is also very slow. Engineering represents a rather special case in that until about 1980 the numbers of women PhDs were too small to yield very reliable results. Women's high degree attainment rate in this field may reflect their comparatively favorable test score position (see below), greater difficulty in finding appropriate employment, or other factors that remain to be explored. The

Table 9.2 Parity Index Values for Selected Broad Fields and Years

Field	1970	1982	1984	1986
Physical Sciences	.39	.71	.68	.73
Mathematical Sciences	.22	.34	.43	.40
Engineering	.80	1.27	.70	1.00
Life Sciences	.58	.93	.95	.88
Social Sciences (including Psychology)	.54	.89	.92	1.00

Sources: National Science Foundation, *Women and Minorities in Science and Engineering* (Washington, DC: NSF, January 1984), pp. 167–168, 174; and National Research Council, *Summary Report: Doctorate Recipients from United States Universities* (Washington, DC: National Academy Press, various years).

decline in PI_2 for physical sciences in 1984 was due primarily to chemistry, a field which suffers from a greater than average number of sex inequities whose causes remain unexplained.[13] Comparable PI_2 data in the humanities show attainment of parity in 1983;[14] in education this milestone was passed in 1979 and has been exceeded annually since then.[15]

In the last year or two, as attention has begun to focus on the increasing proportion of PhDs in engineering and sciences who are foreign citizens, it has become evident that most of the statistics concerning U.S. women's participation must be revised, generally upward. This is the case because the sex/field distributions for foreign citizens differ considerably from those for U.S. citizens. A comparison of these distributions over the last decade, calculated from *Summary Report* tables, illustrates the nature and magnitude of the corrections. In 1976, for example, women earned 16.8 percent of all science and engineering doctorates and 18.7 percent of the total for U.S. citizens, while the corresponding figures for 1986 are 27.5 percent and 33.1 percent. The relative disparities are greatest in engineering, mathematics, and physics. In engineering, U.S. citizens earned 62 percent of women's degrees but only 39 percent of men's degrees. These differences are significant from a policy perspective, since non-U.S. doctorate recipients generally are not permanently available to the U.S. labor force. Further, since women are better represented among U.S. PhDs, affirmative action goals must be revised to take their greater participation into account. Additionally, of course, since the citizenship differences have grown over time, U.S. women's participation rates have increased at a faster rate than the overall data have indicated.

Progress in women's attainment of professional degrees, as already mentioned, has in some areas outpaced even the gains in doctorate attainment and has almost become a synonym for women's general advance since 1970. Although law and medicine are by far the most popular professional fields for both sexes and women's progress in these is most often cited, spectacular advances have also occurred in veterinary medicine, dentistry, architecture, theology, and other areas. Some of these are displayed in Figure 9.3. Unfortunately, no value strictly comparable to PI_2 can be calculated for these fields, since they have no unique baccalaureate-origin fields on which to base an analysis. Just because students enter most of these professional fields from a variety of undergraduate backgrounds, however, it is also reasonable to assume, as a first approximation, that women's proportion of professional degrees will be related to their presence in the overall (rather than a field-specific) baccalaureate pool. Consequently, PI_p, the parity index

Table 9.3 Parity Indices in Law, Medicine, and Veterinary Medicine

Year	JD	MD	DVM
1967	.10		
1968		.20	
1969	.10		
1970		.21	.19
1971	.17		
1972		.22	.23
1973	.19		
1974		.26	.26
1975	.35		
1976		.37	.41
1977	.51		
1978		.48	.56
1979	.63		
1980		.51	.73
1981	.68		
1982	.68	.53	.75
1983	.74	.56	.85
1984			
1985	.76	.60	.95
1986		.61	
1987		.64	

Sources: National Center for Education Statistics, *Digest of Education Statistics, 1980* (Washington, DC: NCES, 1980), p. 129; *Scientific, Engineering, Technical Manpower Comments 22,* no. 9 (November 1985):26; 24, no. 7 (September 1987):27; Vetter and Babco 1984, pp. 3–4, 8–37; and *Chronicle of Higher Education* 34, no. 9 (October 28, 1987):2.

for professional degrees, is defined as the ratio between the percentage of law (or medicine, veterinary science, and so on) degrees earned by women in year x and the percentage of all baccalaureate degrees earned by them in year x-3 (or x-4, and so on). Some representative PI_p values are shown in Table 9.3.

If we compare plots of some parity indices in professional fields with those in PhD fields, as in Figure 9.5, we can gain an improved understanding of the processes at work in determining the rates at which women continue to advanced degrees in nontraditional fields.

Professional fields exhibit a pattern that differs significantly from those in academic fields: An initial stagnant period (the continuation of a historic pattern) ends abruptly in 1974 in law and more gradually in 1975

Figure 9.5 Parity Indices, Selected Academic and Professional Fields: 1968–1983. Data points are given in Tables 2 and 3 of the text.

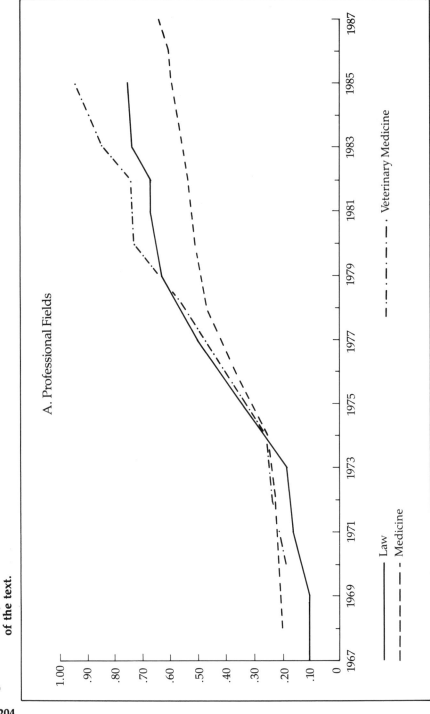

A. Professional Fields

Law ——————

Medicine — — — —

Veterinary Medicine — · — · —

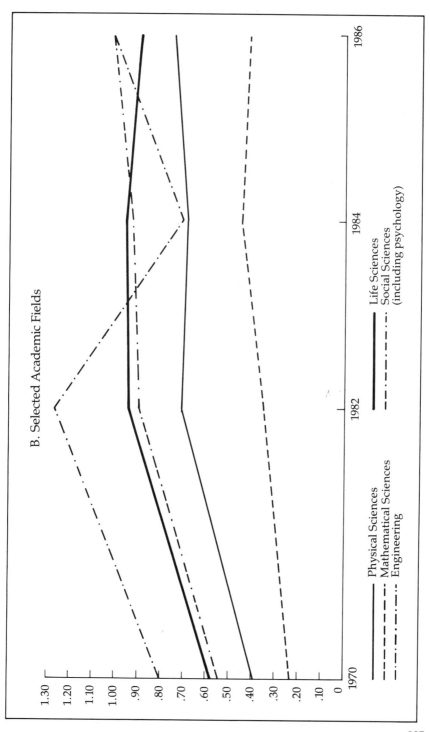

B. Selected Academic Fields

Physical Sciences
Mathematical Sciences
Engineering

Life Sciences
Social Sciences
(including psychology)

in medicine and veterinary science, followed by consistent growth through most of the 1970s and then some leveling of growth in the early 1980s. Such characteristics have useful counterparts in physical phenomena, where an initial slow increase or build-up is called an *induction period* and the slowing of growth observed about 1979 is said to suggest *saturation*. The induction period in our case reflects two different conditions: (1) whether or not graduate study requires highly specific preparation and (2) the standard length of time needed for degree completion. Thus, law requires no specific undergraduate major and only three years for degree completion; admission to law schools became more available to women in 1971, and in 1974 a sharp rise in women's degrees is evident. In medical schools, admissions were expanded at the same time and with a four-year curriculum the effect is visible in 1975, although it continues to build while more women undergraduates take more of the necessary science courses throughout the 1970s. In veterinary schools, the opening of admissions to women, who had previously been excluded by especially restrictive practices,[16] almost certainly overshadowed all other factors. Causes of the saturation phenomenon are less readily identified. If it occurred to the same degree in all three fields, that would suggest strongly the dominance of "women-related" factors such as unwillingness to curtail or sacrifice family life. However, since the induction period depended so clearly on external or institutional factors (admissions policies/quotas) it is reasonable to suppose that saturation is similarly externally produced. The likeliest cause for different degrees of saturation in different fields lies in the labor market; it is a general rule of occupations that women approach equality in them when employment prospects decline. Indeed, the legal profession and veterinary medicine have both become rather crowded in the last few years; some law schools have already suffered considerable decreases in enrollment, and under such conditions women students become more sought after. In medicine, although there are now only two applicants for every place in medical school where there were three a decade ago, the profession still obviously remains highly selective. The data suggest that some brake on women's participation continues to be imposed, most likely in admissions (since completion rates do not differ greatly between women and men).

Parity indices behave very differently in academic fields, starting with the fact that the initial levels differ enormously by field.[17] In all fields we have examined *except* mathematics, the induction period which is observed throughout the 1960s has ended by 1971 or 1972 and is followed by a consistent rise, slower than in the professions but also less subject to saturation in the 1980s; parity—that is, an equal doctorate completion rate with men, with the baccalaureate as starting point—is clearly only a matter of a few years in most fields and has essentially been achieved in biosciences, behavioral sciences, and some humanities fields. Mathematics remains in a class by itself in having high female undergraduate participation but very low doctorate attainment rates and parity indices, which additionally fall well below all other fields in the rate of improvement. Sex discrimination in mathematics has been noted as especially marked by various authors[18] and is also reflected in unusually sex-biased graduate support patterns.[19] None of the closely related nontraditional fields such as computer science or engineering show a similarly low and flat parity index.

Although this analysis does not rule out "personal" factors that may affect women's decisions to pursue advanced degrees and unconventional careers, the variations across fields suggest that structural factors such as access to financial aid are far more significant influences, a view also supported by the findings of the National Commission on Student Financial Assistance.[20] The details of these issues can be better understood after we have examined the relative quality of women and men emerging with new graduate degrees and the uses they are able to make of their training.

Quality Comparisons of Female and Male PhDs

A wealth of evidence exists regarding the quality of students at receipt of the doctorate, even though no direct measure of total professional ability and/or performance has yet been invented. (Unfortunately, strictly comparable data for students in the professions are not available.) Several commonly used proxies for such a measure include scores on standardized tests, prior academic performance, doing graduate work in an excellent department, completing graduate study in as brief a time as possible, being young, and having plans for a normal professional career in one's field. The discerning reader will understand that these proxy measures are interrelated and that several of them are somewhat subjective. Since the early 1970s, when indeed a few differences existed between male and female PhDs on such dimensions as time to degree completion, age, and future plans, these two groups have become essentially indistinguishable on paper.

With respect to testable "ability," probably better described as achievement (see below), Harmon[21] showed some years ago in a retrospective study of PhDs that women doctorates, field for field, had better test scores and school records than men. Again controlling for field, Graduate Record Examination (GRE) scores show a general trend for women to score 30–35 points below men on the quantitative test; generally higher than men by varying amounts on the verbal test, with the biggest difference—44 points—occurring in engineering; and significantly higher, by up to 50 points (again in engineering), on the analytical tests.[22] Among all academic fields, engineering has the most favorable test outcome for women relative to men, while behavioral and social sciences show the least advantage (or greatest disadvantage) for women.[23] The sex difference on the quantitative test is very similar to the one observed on the so-called Scholastic Aptitude Test (SAT) with respect to both field distribution and magnitude. The latter test has come under increasing criticism since about 1980 for a number of reasons, most dealing with the issue that it is in fact a test of achievement and not, as the College Entrance Examination Board (a commercial organization despite its title) has insisted, a test of aptitude. The difference in definition is critical to women, who are only one half to two thirds as likely as men to have taken advanced mathematics in high school and hence to be equally well prepared for the test.[24] When course-taking is held constant, the sex difference in test scores almost disappears. Contributing further to the observed and highly publicized sex differences on the SAT are totally unpublicized differences in size and demographic characteristics between the groups of men and women who take the test, all of them in the direction of increasing the observed differentials in quantitative scores. These differences include the basic facts that in the mid-1980s the number of women test-takers annually exceeded the number of men by over 50,000, or about 12 percent, and the female group contained some 17,000 (23 percent) more minority individuals than the male. Other differences—in family income, parents' education, type of high school attended, and similar variables—accurately track the important demographic distinctions.[25] A complete analysis of the extent to which sex differences in scores are in fact ascribable to these basic demographic differences remains to be done.

Other possible "quality" differences between male and female PhDs were explored by the Committee on the Education and Employment of Women in Science and Engineering (CEEWISE) of the National Academy of Sciences. CEEWISE found that women were as likely as men to have graduated from departments rated "excellent" or "very good," that with only a few exceptions (discussed below) they graduated as fast as or faster than men, that they were about the same age, and that at least by the end of the 1970s they had identical plans for employment or postdoctoral study.[26]

Other Factors Affecting Women's Participation

A variety of factors other than simple ability to do particular kinds of intellectual work influence students' decisions to pursue graduate work and professional careers. Among these may be a range of more or less personal factors including family and other relationships that affect both men and women, though generally in opposite senses, and a number of structural factors that most prominently include institutional access and money. Although the vast majority of research papers within the rich literature on women's higher education and participation in nontraditional fields deals with personal, often psychological, factors, both access and money are probably more important, as we have been suggesting. Without them, no combination of excellent ability and unswerving devotion to goals will be rewarded with advanced degrees and professional careers.

Access to particular education programs, at any level, has historically been regulated in several ways, most prominently by complete exclusion, limited quotas, and denial of financial aid. Women, minorities, Catholics, Jews, and students who came from poor families were the traditional targets of all these practices. The strictures against women were the last to be eliminated, with passage of Title IX of the 1972 Higher Education Amendments and their subsequent implementation beginning in 1974. Equal access to graduate and professional programs was by no means a certainty before then, although most formerly all-male institutions had begun admitting women about 1969–1970 in the hope of being able to make fuller use of their humanities faculties in the lean years ahead.[27] Ways of regulating women's access through quotas were varied, an extremely common method being to require higher grade point averages and test scores from women than from men. Such practices have been confirmed, for example, for the Veterinary School of the University of Pennsylvania,[28] for the University of Michigan,[29] and for Cornell.[30] In the case of Cornell, the ingenious mechanism of assigning arbitrary numbers of "female beds" to specific departments or units of the university made it a simple matter to regulate admissions to engineering or other technical curricula.

Money is unquestionably also a dominant factor in manipulating women's participation. With few exceptions, however, the matter of financial aid to women students has remained either neglected or misinterpreted. An interesting example of misinterpretation has to do with which families send their children to college. Until the late 1960s it was widely recognized that college women came from somewhat wealthier backgrounds than their male counterparts, an observation that was universally explained on the grounds that wealthy families thought education important enough to offer it even to daughters, who would make little economic use of it, while poorer families considered it worthwhile only for sons. The possibility that less financial aid for women would produce the same result and that the outcome indeed indicated a problem that had not even been examined seems never to have occurred, at least in print, to the many analysts who pontificated on the subject. Since then, various reasonably sex-neutral student support mechanisms have been developed, although we still await a comprehensive analysis of the topic. As noted above, college women now come from somewhat poorer families than men. Presumably, now that aid is more equally available, these families have come to the very reasonable conclusion that poorer women may need an education even more than similar men.

The major discriminatory practices were phased out in the early 1970s, but higher education has a long time scale. Women who were not admitted to college or granted financial aid in 1970 were also missing from the ranks of law graduates in 1977, from those of physicians or veterinarians in 1978, from physics and chemistry PhDs in 1980 and 1981, or from life scientists in 1982.

In graduate education in the sciences, sizable sex differences occur in amount and kind of financial aid, and all of them are disadvantageous to women. First, there are enormous differences among fields in the amount of public funds available, chiefly federal. Mathematical, natural, and engineering sciences generally enjoy a high level of federal support in the interests of maintaining national security, the nation's health, and an economically competitive position. Students in such fields therefore find adequate sources of financial support throughout graduate training, unlike colleagues in most social sciences and especially in the humanities; accordingly, the proportion of self-help required of students is small in physical sciences and rises steeply in the humanities and education. Since the latter are fields with high female participation, the curious relationship between high need for self-support and high proportions of women that is shown in Figure 9.6 emerges.[31]

It is not possible to ascertain from existing data what, if any, causal relationship underlies this correlation. Overall, however, 52 percent of women graduate students compared with only 40 percent of men report primary support from self-help sources (which include family and spouse's contributions as well as own earnings). Women are additionally more likely than men to support themselves by loans—again the reverse of most beliefs. Some of the difference in the need for self-support arises because almost 5 percent of male PhDs as late as 1985 still derived primary support from the G.I. Bill, while only 1 percent of women had access to this source.[32]

Figure 9.6 Women PhDs (U.S. Citizens Only) in Selected Fields, and Proportion with Self-Support as Major Source of Graduate Support: 1985

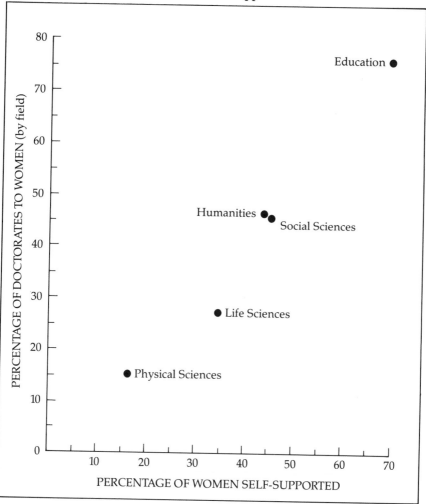

Source: Susan L. Coyle, *Summary Report 1985: Doctorate Recipients from United States Universities* (Washington, DC: National Academy Press, 1986), pp. 25, 50–51.

Although we have no direct information about systematic sex differences in the dollar value of graduate financial aid, such differences do exist in the sources of support and hence in the effect on individuals. A research assistant, for instance, while nominally paid for work performed for a professor, is also doing the work for a dissertation and thus loses no time toward a degree. The opposite is true of a teaching assistant, whose work in instructing undergraduates or grading papers results in lost research time. Additionally, the two support mechanisms have very different effects on the professional socialization process that is considered such an important component of graduate training. A research assistant spends most of his or her time in contact with peers and mentors, maximizing both informal and formal learning. In contrast, a teaching assistant who is spending significant amounts of time with and for undergraduates is not only physically removed during that time from a productive learning environment, but is also much more likely to be alienated from the mainstream activities of the field. Sex differences in the award of teaching and research assistantships (over and above the inherent field differences) exist in virtually every field, but are of most concern in a few science fields.

Larger differences of this type occur primarily in computer sciences and earth, environmental, and marine sciences, but patterns disadvantageous to women take other forms still. In mathematics, for example, where research assistantships play only a small role in financing students, about 10 percent more women than men are teaching assistants but men are almost five times more likely to hold fellowships. Eight of eleven major science fields require more self-support from women, and in humanities the count is three out of four.[33]

The impact of such practices on women already in graduate school is undoubtedly unfavorable in pragmatic terms, but may be even more damaging in terms of lowered self-esteem, declining interest in the profession, and similar effects that have been widely documented.[34] It is harder to say whether they also affect prospective women students, and no empirical evidence speaks to that point in other than the most general terms.

The more individual or personal factors affecting women's educational decisions (that is, personal relationships, family needs, geographical location, and so on) are, unlike the foregoing, not field-specific except that in most professional fields a practitioner is thought to have more freedom with respect to relocating, and so on, than someone in an academic field who needs a job in an institution. At this writing, entry-level positions in the professions are not especially easier to find than academic ones in the nontraditional fields, and there is no evidence to confirm or reject such a conjecture.

Academic Employment

So far, we have examined women as students in nontraditional fields. It is characteristic of students in these fields in general that they do not undertake graduate or professional study without a well-developed intention to pursue the career for which that education is intended. The educational experience itself is seldom as joyful as students always hope, and the cost in money, foregone earnings, postponed personal gratification, and sometimes personal relationships is too high for anyone to undertake frivolously. The goal of study is a career, though not necessarily an academic one, especially in the case of the professions. However, since our concern is with higher education, that is the sector we will examine.

The rapid growth in women's participation as students is not reflected in their presence as faculty in the graduate and professional schools that trained them, even allowing for some reasonable lag time. For example, in 1986–1987 women were 20.4 percent of full-time faculty in law schools, at a time when women's share of law degrees was more than twice that figure and had exceeded it for about eight years.[35] However, faculty positions in academic fields (as distinct from professional schools, which had been living in boom times until lessened demand became apparent about 1984) are limited in number by a variety of factors, the most compelling of which is money. Growth in faculty positions since the early 1970s has been limited almost entirely to a few fast-growing fields like computer sciences. Prior discrimination had left most faculties, at least in the pace-setting colleges and universities, with no women in most science fields and only a few in other areas. A steady-state philosophy in most institutions left little room for improving the proportions of faculty women, and most prognoses in the early 1970s were pessimistic with regard to whether affirmative action policies could in fact increase the number of female faculty. Nonetheless, by 1984 the numbers and proportions of women faculty had grown compared with the very low levels of the early 1970s. In the last of its four reports, CEEWISE analyzed the increase in total faculty positions and in those held by women in all science and engineering fields combined, finding that between 1977 and 1981 the number of positions at the three professorial ranks had increased, at all two- and four-year colleges and universities combined, by 13,495, or 12.2 percent, while the number of such positions held by women had increased by 3,240, or 24.1 percent. These totals are compared with a grand total of 123,660 faculty positions in science and engineering fields. The top 50 institutions (ranked by federal research and development expenditures) were better than average in employing women faculty, increasing their numbers by 28.1

percent compared with only 22.9 percent in all other institutions.[36] CEEWISE further found that the characteristic sex differences in academic rank, with the majority of men at full professor rank and the single largest block of women in assistant professorships, remained in place, as shown in Figure 9.7.

Further analysis showed that, field by field, the proportion of women among assistant professors slightly exceeded their presence in the relevant PhD pools.[37] However, the rate of promotion for male assistant professors was markedly higher—by more than 50 percent in the case of the top 50 institutions, as shown in Figure 9.8.

Pursuing this clue further, CEEWISE found that women assistant professors held non–tenure-track posts almost twice as frequently as men (Table 9.4). The apparently generous hiring of women assistant professors, then, is at best an artifact of data collection and at worst a deliberate deception by universities.

A case of particular interest occurs in chemistry. The field exhibits one of the largest discrepancies between availability of women PhDs and women on faculties, and in addition both the data on all aspects of employment and its reputation mark it as one of the most biased of fields.[38] The Women Chemists Committee of the American Chemical Society has conducted periodic surveys of women chemistry faculty. In 1983 it found that, surveying only departments granting baccalaureate and master's degrees, women held 546, or 11 percent, of a total of 4,944 faculty positions in the three professorial ranks, an increase of 0.5 percent in three years and virtually unchanged since 1965. (Faculty members in this group of institutions were not necessarily doctorate holders.)

Table 9.4 **Tenure-Track Status of Assistant Professors by Sex: 1981 (Doctoral Scientists and Engineers)**

	Number of Assistant Professors		Percentage Not Tenure Track	
	Women	Men	Women	Men
All Four-Year Colleges and Universities	5,826	20,882	22.5%	13.7%
Top 50 Institutions	1,428	4,652	15.0	11.0
Other Institutions	4,398	16,230	24.5	14.3

Source: Committee on the Education and Employment of Women in Science and Engineering, *Climbing the Ladder: An Update on the Status of Doctoral Women Scientists and Engineers* (Washington, DC: National Academy Press, 1983), chap. 4, p. 15.

**Figure 9.7   Faculty Rank Distribution of Doctoral Scientists and Engineers
by Research and Development Expenditures
of Institution and Sex: 1981**

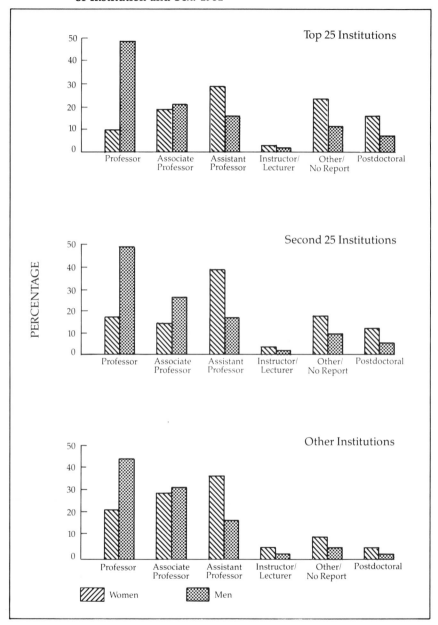

Source: Committee on the Education and Employment of Women in Science and Engineering, *Climbing the Ladder: An Update on the Status of Doctoral Women Scientists and Engineers* (Washington, DC: National Academy Press, 1983), figure 4.2.

215

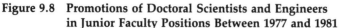

Figure 9.8   Promotions of Doctoral Scientists and Engineers in Junior Faculty Positions Between 1977 and 1981

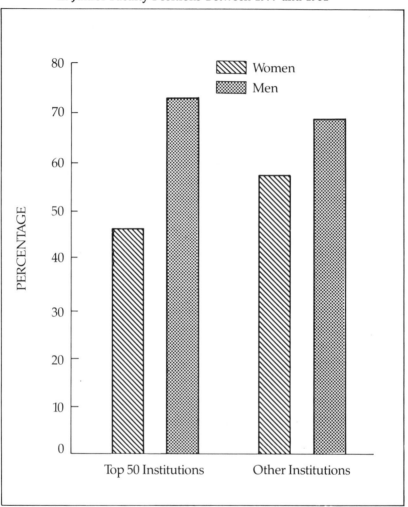

Source: Committee on the Education and Employment of Women in Science and Engineering, *Climbing the Ladder: An Update on the Status of Doctoral Women Scientists and Engineers* (Washington, DC: National Academy Press, 1983), chap. 4, p. 13.

Note: Based on survey responses in 1977 and 1981 from a common set of individuals. The sample sizes for women and men who were assistant professors in 1977 and who reported rank in 1981 are (a) in the top 50 institutions, 125 women and 200 men; and (b) in other institutions, 411 women and 601 men. For both men and women, the median year of receipt of the doctorate was 1973.

A similar survey of faculty in doctorate-granting departments showed a slightly better rate of increase, from 61 women faculty of a total of 4,091 (1.5 percent) in 1970–1971 to 180 of 4,470 (4.1 percent) in 1982–1983. During the same period, the number of doctorates awarded to women annually in the field grew from 189 (9.9 percent) in 1972 to 272 (16.1 percent) in 1982. In biochemistry, where women have earned 25 percent of all doctorates awarded between 1973 and 1982, they were only 8.5 percent of full-time faculty in graduate departments, a decrease of over 1 percent since 1979.[39]

In line with such significant differences in rank and tenure status, the mean salaries of women scientists are well below those of men, a finding corroborated by every study of the subject ever conducted. Because of the various ways in which salary data have been gathered, aggregated, or disaggregated by a number of authors, it became difficult to arrive at statistically valid sex comparisons. CEEWISE therefore sponsored a large matched-sample study of male and female PhDs which focused heavily on salary comparisons. Even when the men and women carefully matched for field, doctoral cohort and department, academic position, type of employing department, and years of experience were compared, large salary differentials remained in nearly all cases.[40]

Factors Affecting Career Paths

In considering women's participation in nontraditional fields at the various levels of education, we found the major influences that determined women's field choices, ability to attend college or graduate school, and likelihood of degree completion to be predominantly external. Despite long-established stereotypes and generally accepted rationales such as women's lack of interest in quantitative, rigorously logical, or highly competitive fields, the most compelling reason for women's comparative absence from these areas lies in the collection of methods by which educational institutions have restricted their participation over most of the last century. We have also seen that similar external factors contribute to women's continued underemployment in the academic sector; while determined opposition such as has been demonstrated in chemistry is probably not universal, it is widespread enough so that even in most humanities fields, where women have been very well represented among PhDs for many years, they remain largely absent from the ranks of senior faculty, especially in research institutions.[41]

Such pronounced institutional bias against women faculty has for many years been justified on a variety of grounds, among which the most apparently persuasive is often believed to be the "fact" that women's research productivity (conventionally measured in numbers of publications per unit time) falls below men's in every field. Research publications are, of course, one of the most significant measures used to determine faculty performance. In its first report, CEEWISE reviewed studies of sex differences in research productivity and concluded that "[they] have yielded ambiguous and sometimes contradictory results."[42] The committee continued:

> *For the specific case of science faculty*, factors such as access to appropriate research facilities, division of time between undergraduate and graduate teaching responsibilities, and especially availability of graduate and other research assistants may be of far greater significance to productivity than rank or other variables which have been controlled in the studies cited above. We have not found any studies that control for these factors or indeed considered them. [emphasis added]

(We do have such studies that are applicable to social sciences faculty members, as reported in chapter 11.) Returning to the topic of sex differences in career outcomes ostensibly based on differences in productivity, the committee concluded: "It appears likely that comparisons of this type serve more as indicators of inequality in initial appointments and later promotions, with attendant differences of access to graduate students, facilities, and funding, than as measures of inherent sex differences in research capability."[43]

These issues were also argued to some extent by Jonathan Cole, who noted in passing (in a highly controversial study) the absence of productivity studies that control for the important variables mentioned above, but concluded nonetheless that sex differences in scientific productivity are "real" and that the academic reward system correctly accounts for them.[44]

The argument is unlikely to be resolved until women become tenured faculty members in at least the major science fields in sufficiently large numbers that adequate comparisons of productivity can be carried out in the manner outlined above. As long as the number of women full professors in doctorate-granting (that is, research-producing) departments nationwide averages out to less than one per department, as in chemistry, it will be quite impossible to perform a meaningful study. Further, at the rate of progress in that field and others, the possibility may not be realized in the next century.

When all of the evidence is weighed, including factors such as geographic mobility that restrict job choice for women much more often than for men, about half of the overall sex difference in career outcomes can be accounted for. The only rational explanation for the remainder is discrimination.

Conclusions

There is a wealth of data available on women in nontraditional fields and professions, of which we have had space to review only a portion. Nevertheless, the general outlines of women's position in these fields are quite clear. On the one hand, the rate at which women enter or prepare for these fields has risen dramatically over the last two decades, especially in areas such as law and medicine which demonstrably limited their participation in the past. On the other hand, the gains in academic positions, especially in graduate departments, have not kept pace either with the sanguine expectations of the early 1970s or with the increased production of women doctorates. Further, by the mid 1980s the rate of increase had begun to level off across all nontraditional areas. A "glass ceiling" appeared somewhere around one third of advanced degrees, and the proportion of women who attained top-level professional positions continued to fall short of the numbers to be expected on the basis of equal opportunity.

Such a phenomenon raises several questions. First, are women's achievements in these fields limited in some fundamental way by ability and motivation? The data do not speak unambiguously to this question, since ability measures are imperfect, and in any case do not point to significant gender differences, since motivation depends heavily on incentives and is not readily quantified. One might speculate that the lure of equal expectations overcame for a time the limitations imposed by geography or family responsibilities, but that eventually a more realistic perception of opportunity caused women to adjust their aspirations downward again. The trouble with such an argument is that the data on the whole do not support it. A growing number of studies show that married women with children do better professionally than women who are unencumbered by families. Further, if the career differences are due to women's lesser or different ability they should vary by field. The most striking generalization, however, is that the degree to which women's success falls short of men's is, proportionately, about the same across the entire spectrum of academic and other learned professions. The difference is most clearly expressed in the fact that, with all measurable factors such as education, experience, ability, and type of employment held constant, the ratio of women's to men's salaries for full-time, year-round employment is approximately .85.

The data consistently draw a sharp distinction between women as students and as faculty or other practitioners—a distinction which is by no means limited to this group of disciplines but which has been noted as existing across the spectrum of professions. The functional difference between students and faculty, from an equity perspective, is straightforward: Students of either sex create jobs and other benefits for faculty, but women who seek faculty positions (or other professional positions) are competing with men for a very scarce and highly valued resource and are not welcome.

Events external to central academic purposes have played some role in how women students have been viewed since 1970. It has been a period of almost unremitting tension in academic institutions, beginning with the trauma of Kent State and Cambodia and continuing, once the political crises were past, in a draining succession of developing financial problems and threatening predictions of worse to come. The anticipated decline in the young adult population, with its attendant implication of a 25 percent reduction in the college-going cohorts, hung like a deadly shadow over most academic planning of the 1970s. In the event, the decline has had relatively little effect on student enrollments, which are becoming increasingly dependent on older students, the majority of whom are women. It is also the case, however, that the extended education necessary in most nontraditional fields holds less appeal for the mature student who has fewer years left in which to make such an investment pay off. Young students have remained the mainstay of such programs and will probably continue to do so.

The young white men who are the traditional students in such programs, however, are in relatively short supply. Their participation in most basic science fields—most markedly in mathematics, physics, and chemistry—has either actually declined or barely held steady numerically while declining as a proportion of all students. This underlying trend is rarely recognized but readily documented since shortly after the end of World War II.[45] By the 1970s there was considerable excess capacity of both faculty and facilities in many of these departments, making them obvious targets for cutbacks in an academic economy under pressure. Women were indeed a welcome new phenomenon in their student populations and were for a time encouraged, not to say wooed, with an assortment of special programs, counseling, career days, and, in the case of engineering, sometimes extensive recruitment efforts.[46] The same situation that produced a demand for students operated to depress opportunities for faculty of either sex. In spite of recruitment schemes, at least on paper, women faculty remain few in number, often isolated, held in lower ranks, and underpaid. If academic employment were the sole career path in science, engineering, and other nontraditional fields, it is likely that women's participation would be much lower than it is in fact. Still, the extent of change that has occurred even in academe since 1970 should not be undervalued. Perhaps the greatest promise lies in the fact that 25 percent or more of the young, most highly trained scientists and other professionals are now women—an enormous change from the 5 percent or so with which we began the 1970s. They are at the cutting edge of their fields, they have traveled into space and explored the oceans, and they will unquestionably also change the face of academe.

Notes

1. Betty D. Maxfield and Mary Beslisle, *Science, Engineering, and Humanities Doctorates in the United States: 1983 Profile* (Washington, DC: Office of Scientific and Engineering Personnel, National Research Council, National Academy Press, 1985), pp. 1, 6; and National Research Council, *Summary Report: Doctorate Recipients from United States Universities* (Washington, DC: National Academy Press, 1984, 1985, 1986).

2. National Research Council, *Summary Report: 1986.*

3. Betty M. Vetter and Eleanor L. Babco, *Professional Women and Minorities* (Washington, DC: Commission on Professionals in Science and Technology, 1986), table 3-3; and *Scientific, Engineering, Technical Manpower Comments* 24, no. 7 (September 1987):27.

4. Vetter and Babco, *Professional Women and Minorities,* table 3-14.

5. Lois Weis, "Progress But No Parity," *Academe* 71, no. 6 (November-December 1985):29–33; *Scientific, Engineering, Technical Manpower Comments* 23, no. 9 (November 1986):24.

6. Weis, "Progress," p. 30.

7. Vetter and Babco, *Professional Women and Minorities,* table 2-11.

8. Committee on the Education and Employment of Women in Science and Engineering (CEEWISE), *Climbing the Ladder: An Update on the Status of Doctoral Women Scientists and Engineers* (Washington, DC: National Academy Press, 1983), pp. 1.14–1.15; and National Research Council, *Summary Report 1986,* early release.

9. National Science Foundation, *Women and Minorities in Science and Engineering* (Washington, DC: NSF, January 1986), pp. 173–174; see also CEEWISE, *Climbing the Academic Ladder: Doctoral Women Scientists in Academe* (Washington, DC: National Academy Press, 1979), p. 21.

10. Peter D. Syverson, *Summary Report 1981: Doctorate Recipients from United States Universities* (Washington, DC: National Academy Press, 1982).

11. CEEWISE, *Climbing the Ladder: Update,* pp. 1.5–1.12.

12. CEEWISE, *Climbing the Ladder: Update*, pp. 1.11–1.12.

13. CEEWISE, *Climbing the Academic Ladder*, p. xiv.

14. Lilli S. Hornig and Ruth B. Ekstrom, *The Status of Women in the Humanities*, forthcoming.

15. Computed from National Center of Education Statistics, *Earned Degrees* series; and National Research Council, *Summary Report: Doctorate Recipients from United States Universities*, annual series.

16. Personal communication to Lilli S. Hornig from Dr. Robert Davies, University of Pennsylvania.

17. PI$_2$ values for such "feminine" fields as English, foreign languages, and psychology are almost identical to the biosciences; see Hornig and Ekstrom, *Status of Women*.

18. CEEWISE, *Climbing the Academic Ladder*, p. xiv; *Climbing the Ladder: Update*, p. xv, tables 1.2 and 2.2.

19. Syverson, *Summary Report*, pp. 15–16.

20. National Commission on Student Financial Assistance, *Signs of Trouble and Erosion: A Report on Graduate Education in America* (New York: NCSFA, 1983), pp. 79–80.

21. Lindsey R. Harmon, *High School Ability Patterns—A Backward Look from the Doctorate*, Scientific Manpower Report no. 6 (Washington, DC: National Academy of Sciences, August 1965).

22. National Science Foundation, *Women and Minorities*, pp. 167–168.

23. National Science Foundation, *Women and Minorities*.

24. National Science Foundation, *Women and Minorities*, p. 154.

25. Leonard Ramist and Solomon Arbeiter, *Profiles, College-Bound Seniors, 1982* (New York: College Entrance Examination Board, 1984), p. 1.

26. CEEWISE, *Climbing the Academic Ladder*, pp. 23–28; *Climbing the Ladder: Update*, pp. 2.2–2.9.

27. Hornig and Ekstrom, *Status of Women*.

28. Robert Davies, private communication.

29. Dorothy G. McGuigan, *A Dangerous Experiment: 100 Years of Women at the University of Michigan* (Ann Arbor: Center for Continuing Education of Women, 1970).

30. Charlotte Williams Conable, *Women at Cornell: The Myth of Equal Education* (Ithaca, NY: Cornell University Press, 1977), pp. 110–117.

31. Susan L. Coyle, *Summary Report 1985: Doctorate Recipients from United States Universities* (Washington, DC: National Academy Press, 1986), table L.

32. Coyle, *Summary Report*, pp. 25, 52.

33. Syverson, *Summary Report*, text table D.

34. Saul D. Feldman, *Escape from the Doll's House* (New York: McGraw-Hill, 1974), pp. 37–75.

35. Vetter and Babco, *Professional Women and Minorities*, pp. 80–81.

36. CEEWISE, *Climbing the Ladder: Update*, p. 4.6.

37. CEEWISE, *Climbing the Ladder: Update*, p. 4.12.

38. CEEWISE, *Climbing the Academic Ladder*, p. xiv; and Margaret W. Rossiter, *Women Scientists in America: Struggles and Strategies to 1940* (Baltimore: Johns Hopkins University Press, 1982), pp. 249–258, 304, 362.

39. Vetter and Babco, *Professional Women and Minorities*, p. 146; and *Scientific, Engineering, Technical Manpower Comments* 21, no. 2 (March 1984):24–25.

40. Nancy C. Ahern and Elizabeth L. Scott, *Career Outcomes in a Matched Sample of Men and Women Ph.D.s* (Washington, DC: Committee on the Education and Employment of Women in Science and Engineering, National Academy Press, 1981).

41. Hornig and Ekstrom, *Status of Women*.

42. CEEWISE, *Climbing the Academic Ladder*, p. 87.

43. CEEWISE, *Climbing the Academic Ladder*, p. 88.

44. Jonathan R. Cole, *Fair Science: Women in the Scientific Community* (New York: Free Press, 1979), pp. 62–69.

45. Hornig and Ekstrom, *Status of Women*.

46. Jane Z. Daniels and William K. LeBold, "Women in Engineering: A Dynamic Approach," in Sheila M. Humphreys, ed., *Women and Minorities in Science: Strategies for Increasing Participation*, AAAS Selected Symposium no. 66. (Washington, DC: American Association for the Advancement of Science, 1982).

10

Transitional and Traditional Fields for Women

The last chapter chronicled the massive shift of women from the traditional "women's fields" to the sciences and other male-dominated professions over the last decade and a half. At the same time, women have continued to enter the traditional fields in large numbers. These fields consist of two widely disparate groups—on the one hand, the academic disciplines within the humanities, primarily history, languages, and literature; and on the other hand, the professional fields of teaching, social work, library science, and nursing. The humanities are counted among the learned professions and, as such, they are directed toward scholarly careers or cultural activities, inside academia or outside. By contrast, teaching, social work, library science, and nursing as a group can readily be recognized as service professions, leading to careers for the most part outside academic life. They are, of course, of lower status than the traditionally male-dominated professions of medicine, law, and engineering. In addition to the more traditional disciplines and professional fields, women have continued to move into the social sciences, significantly increasing their representation in those fields.

Historically, women have been relatively well represented in the social sciences, although there are marked differences within specific disciplines. Economics, for example, is as nontraditional an area for women as is physics, whereas psychology has been a popular field for women for a long time. Since 1970, the social sciences in general have been in a period of transition, moving rapidly toward sex-neutral status. This chapter focuses on the changes that have taken place in

225

the transitional fields as well as in the humanities and traditional professions for women.

The Social Sciences

Compared with the scientific fields and the humanities, the social sciences are young disciplines. Formal college and university teaching in
these subjects dates only from the late nineteenth or early twentieth
century. This was a period in which women were entering higher education in large numbers, and many were attracted to the social sciences,
particularly psychology. During the 1920s, women earned 17 percent of
the total doctorates awarded to the social sciences. Since that time the
number of doctorates awarded to women in these fields increased steadily. However, the increase did not keep up with the growth in the
number of degrees awarded to men, so that until the 1970s the share of
social science doctorates awarded to women declined. As shown in
Table 10.1, the proportion dropped to 14 percent in the 1960s and did
not surpass the 1920s rate until the 1970s.

Table 10.1 also shows the number and percentage of degrees earned
by women in the major disciplines within the social sciences. The largest
field by far, both in the number and proportion of women, is psychology. The proportion of women in anthropology and sociology over the
past decade has reached the same level as that for psychology, but the
numbers are much smaller. In 1986 the number and percentage of doctorates awarded to women in the social sciences was as follows:

Field	Number	Percentage
Anthropology	191	51.2%
Economics	157	19.9
Political Science	115	26.2
Sociology	227	45.0
Psychology	1,591	51.5
Other Social Sciences	295	34.7
Social Sciences, Total	2,576	42.6

The number of doctorates awarded to women in sociology exceeded
that of men in 1985 but fell below 50 percent in 1986. Despite such year
to year fluctuations, it seems clear that the social sciences in general—
and psychology, sociology, and anthropology in particular—are in the
process of transition from predominantly male fields to what might be
regarded as sex-neutral fields, so far as doctoral degree attainment is
concerned. There are, however, significant sex differences in fields of

Table 10.1   Doctorates Awarded to Women in the Social Sciences, by Field and Decade: 1920–1986

	1920–1929		1930–1939		1940–1949		1950–1959		1960–1969		1970–1979		1980–1986	
	Number	Per-centage	Number	Per-centage	Number	Per-centage	Number	Per-centage	Number	Per-centage	Number	Per-centage	Number	Per-centage
Social Sciences, Total*	325	17.1%	562	15.8%	580	14.5%	1,510	11.0%	3,604	14.3%	14,641	24.5%	16,413	39.4%
Anthropology and Sociology	40	16.4	117	20.4	121	17.0	311	15.4	660	18.6	3,258	33.7	2,774	44.1
Economics	52	8.5	71	6.4	83	7.1	125	4.2	245	4.6	734	8.8	833	15.1
Political Science and Public Administration	26	9.0	45	8.5	45	7.8	87	5.4	257	8.2	1,043	14.8	899	19.8
Psychology	189	29.4	290	26.0	302	24.1	911	14.3	2,264	20.7	1,361	32.2	10,512	51.1

Source: Betty M. Vetter and Eleanor L. Babco, *Professional Women and Minorities* (Washington, DC: Commission on Professionals in Science and Technology, 1986), p. 34; National Research Council, *Summary Report 1985: Doctorate Recipients from United States Universities* (Washington, DC: National Academy Press, 1986), p. 41; and unpublished data, National Center for Education Statistics.

*The social science total includes a variety of other specialized fields not shown here, such as area studies, criminology, and geography.

specialization within the disciplines. For example, in psychology the number of doctorates awarded to men and women is roughly equal in clinical psychology and counseling, but men outnumber women in cognitive, experimental, industrial, and organizational psychology. On the other hand, women outnumber men in developmental, educational, and social psychology.

Minority women accounted for 9 percent of the doctorates awarded to U.S. women in 1985. This figure represents an increase from 5 percent in 1975. For black and Hispanic women, as for white women, the total number of degrees awarded in the social sciences was second only to that for education. For Asian women the pattern of field selection was somewhat different. The largest concentration of doctorates is in the life sciences, followed by education, with the social sciences third. The figures for the social sciences are as follows:[1]

	1975	1985
American Indian Women	2	9
Asian Women	10	28
Black Women	47	95
Hispanic Women	9	59
White Women	1,258	1,826
Total U.S. Women	1,326	2,017

Although the social sciences may have become relatively sex-neutral if one considers only degree attainment, the representation by gender in faculty positions is another matter. Here women have made some gains since the 1970s, but the changes have not been commensurate with degree attainment. In 1985 women constituted 21 percent of full-time faculty members in the social sciences compared with 16 percent in 1974.[2] The breakdown by field is as follows:

	1974	1985
Economics	8.0%	11.4%
Sociology	23.6	26.6
Political Science	10.3	14.4
Psychology	21.3	28.1
Other Social Sciences	20.9	27.6
All Social Sciences	15.8	19.9

The increase in the number and proportion of social science doctorates awarded to women over the ten-year period has translated into considerable improvement at the entry level but not in the upper reaches of the faculty. In economics, the share of assistant professors has tended to mirror the share of PhDs, but progress to the top academic ranks of the profession has been slow or nonexistent. Only 3 to 4 percent of all full professors were women, both in 1974 and 1985.[3] Over the same period, the number of male PhD recipients who entered academic employment increased from 54 to 61 percent while the proportion of women declined sharply from 58 to 49 percent.

Unlike economics, sociology was a declining field of enrollment during the past decade. The number of sociology majors dropped precipitously from a peak of approximately 35,000 in 1974 to less than half that in the 1980s.[4] Notwithstanding the difference in underlying conditions, however, the employment pattern for women in sociology was similar to that in economics. Overall, they made slight gains in faculty positions, but they were overrepresented in entry-level positions and underrepresented in tenured positions. In 1981 women represented 14 percent of full professors in sociology, 24 percent of associate professors, and 40 percent of assistant professors.[5]

Women are also underrepresented in departmental administrative positions in sociology although, again, there has been a slight improvement since 1970. In 1981 women represented 10 percent of the chairs of PhD-granting departments and 15 percent of BA-granting departments, proportions that are below their representation on the faculty. Women represented an even smaller minority of directors of graduate study, 7 percent overall.[6]

Employment patterns in sociology since 1975 show a significant shift out of academia and into industry and government for both men and women. The figures are as follows:[7]

Type of Employment	Men		Women	
	1975	1981	1975	1981
Education	85.8%	75.6%	78.7%	70.5%
Business and Industry	1.1	5.4	1.8	3.8
Nonprofit Organizations	2.7	4.9	5.9	9.8
Government	5.2	7.4	4.7	8.1
Other	0.3	0.5	—	—
Not Employed	4.9	6.1	8.9	7.7

As can be seen, women are consistently more likely than men to be unemployed or employed outside the education sector. Particularly striking is the proportion of women sociologists employed in nonprofit organizations, nearly 10 percent in 1981.

Psychology has been one of the fastest growing disciplines since World War II. As a proportion of all doctorates awarded, psychology increased from 4 percent in 1945 to over 10 percent in 1986. At the same time, major changes have taken place in the nature of the field. Psychology consists of a number of subfields which fall into two main categories, those that are primarily academic and those that are service-oriented. The academic subfields are experimental, comparative, physiological, social, and developmental psychology, along with personality and psychometrics. The service provider subfields are clinical, counseling, and school psychology. Much of the growth of psychology came in the so-called health-service-provider fields, mainly clinical, counseling, and school psychology. In contrast, the academic subfields, after a period of growth to the mid 1970s, have experienced a sharp decline since then. Prior to World War II, experimental psychology dominated the discipline, accounting for 70 percent of doctorates awarded in psychology. By 1986 the percentage had dropped to less than 10 percent. Thus, there has been a marked shift in the field composition of psychology from academic to practice-oriented concentrations. Clinical, counseling, and school psychology now account for more than half the doctorates awarded in psychology.[8]

Employment patterns in psychology since 1975 reflect the shifts in field composition. During this period the proportion of doctorate recipients in psychology entering academic employment declined from 50 to 24 percent. In part, these low percentages also reflect the limited number of faculty positions available due to the high rate of tenuring in during the previous decade. In this situation, women in psychology, as in other fields, have been able to increase their representation in faculty positions, but they have not achieved parity. As of 1985–1986, according to a survey by the American Psychological Association, women represented 23 percent of faculties in 331 graduate departments, or 22 percent of full-time and 37 percent of part-time faculty.[9]

In the social sciences as a group, it is clear that economics and political science will continue to be male-dominated for some time. What the prospects are for anthropology, sociology, and psychology is less clear. Notwithstanding the higher rate of degree attainment by women, movement into positions of power and influence remains low, and it is not likely that these fields will be female-dominated, or even sex-neutral in any real sense, over the next decade.

The Humanities: Degree Attainment

The humanities have long been considered a traditional area for women because of the substantial number of women who have entered the various disciplines in the field. By no means, however, have women dominated those disciplines. The number and proportion of degrees in the humanities awarded to women now exceeds that of men at the bachelor's and master's degree level, but, as with the other learned professions, the doctorate is the main point of career entry. At that level the number of degrees awarded to men overall still exceeds that for women, although the differential has narrowed substantially since the early 1970s. The exception is the subfield of languages and literature where the number of doctorates awarded to women has exceeded that of men since 1980.

Both men and women have shifted away from the humanities as a field of concentration since 1970, but the decline in the field has been greater for men than for women. At the undergraduate level, women earned 64,310, or 47 percent, of all bachelor's degrees in the humanities and arts in 1970. By 1986 the number had declined to 55,338, but this represented 62 percent of the bachelor's degrees awarded in the humanities in that year.[10] Another way of looking at the shift is to compare the proportion of women majoring in the humanities in 1970 and 1986. The humanities represented 26 percent of the bachelor's degrees awarded to women in 1970 but only 11 percent in 1986. The comparable figures for men were 13 percent and 7 percent.

At the master's level, the total number of degrees awarded in the humanities and arts declined from over 27,260 in 1970 to less than 17,000 in 1986, a drop of over 35 percent. Women earned a majority of the master's degrees in the field in both years, 51 percent in 1970 rising to 59 percent in 1986. As a proportion of all master's degrees, humanities and arts declined from 13 percent in 1970 to 6 percent in 1986.

Although the master's degree in the humanistic fields may lead to some kinds of academic positions, it is more commonly an intermediate step to the PhD. The same is not true of the arts, which represent a substantial component of the master's degrees in the humanities and arts. The master's degree in fine arts, music, and other visual and performing arts is the terminal degree for careers in these fields, with the possible exception of careers in teaching. The relatively few doctorates in these fields are primarily research-oriented. The number of master's degrees in the arts increased from 7,800 in 1970 to 8,742 in 1983, an increase of 12 percent. Relative to all master's degrees in the humanities and arts, this represents a significant increase—from 21 percent in 1970 to 45 percent in 1983. Thus, the arts in general and women in the arts in particular are holding their own as far as degree attainment is concerned.

At the doctoral level the humanities have declined in both number and proportion of total number of doctorates awarded since 1970. As

Table 10.2   Doctorates Awarded in the Humanities: 1970–1985

Year	Total	Men	Women	Percentage Women
1970	4,067	3,095	972	23.8%
1971	4,366	3,309	1,057	24.2
1972	4,701	3,430	1,271	27.0
1973	5,361	3,815	1,546	28.8
1974	5,170	3,594	1,576	30.5
1975	5,046	3,359	1,687	33.4
1976	4,881	3,208	1,673	34.3
1977	4,562	2,903	1,659	36.4
1978	4,231	2,635	1,596	37.7
1979	4,139	2,547	1,592	38.5
1980	3,867	2,335	1,532	39.6
1981	3,748	2,200	1,548	41.3
1982	3,558	2,049	1,509	42.4
1983	3,495	1,964	1,531	43.8
1984	3,528	1,942	1,586	44.9
1985	3,428	1,939	1,489	43.4
1986	3,461	1,896	1,565	45.2

Source: National Research Council, Summary Report: Doctorate Recipients from United States Universities (Washington, DC: National Academy Press, 1970–1986).

shown in Table 10.2, the total number of doctorates in the humanities dropped from 4,067 in 1970 to 3,461 in 1986. This represents a decline from 13 percent to 11 percent of the total number of doctorates awarded annually. Table 10.2 also shows a substantial increase in the proportion of doctorates in the humanities awarded to women, from 24 percent in 1970 to 45 percent in 1986. Doctorates in the humanities earned by men reached a peak in 1973, the peak year for all doctorates, and declined steadily thereafter. For women in the humanities the number of doctorates continued to increase until 1975, declined somewhat during the rest of the 1970s, and turned upward again in the 1980s. Two of the principal areas in the humanities are history and languages and literature. In 1986 women were the recipients of 34 percent of the doctorates awarded in history and 58 percent of those awarded in languages and literature.

Members of minority groups, both men and women, represent less than 10 percent of the doctorates awarded in the humanities. Although all minority groups have increased their percentage of doctorates earned over the last decade, they have tended to concentrate in fields other than the humanities. The largest field for blacks, Hispanics, and American

Indians is education, followed by social sciences. The predominant fields for Asians are the physical sciences and engineering.

The Humanities: Employment

Careers in the humanities are by no means limited to higher education; a substantial amount of scholarly work and writing takes place outside. Normally, however, careers in arts and letters outside academic life do not require the doctoral degree. Those who seek the doctorate aspire primarily to teaching and research in higher education. Indeed, that is more true of doctoral recipients in the humanities than those in any other field. The humanities are basic to the liberal arts curriculum and the demand for humanities doctorates is closely tied to faculty needs on the part of higher education institutions. Compared with other fields, there are fewer obvious alternative career options.

In 1970 well over 80 percent of doctoral recipients in the humanities planned employment in educational institutions.[11] In the two largest fields—history and English and American literature—the figures were 84 percent and 88 percent, respectively. By comparison, the figure was 52 percent in psychology, 69 percent in mathematics, and only 24 percent in physics, to choose examples from the social and physical sciences. Since 1970 there has been a steady decline in employment prospects in colleges and universities as higher education entered a period of financial stringency. The slowdown in the rate of growth in higher education, combined with the high rate of faculty tenuring during the 1960s, severely restricted the number of academic positions available. By 1986 the proportion of doctorate recipients in the humanities with planned employment in educational institutions had dropped to 46 percent compared with 26 percent for the social sciences and 11 percent for the physical sciences.[12] There was some increase in the number of those entering employment in the business, government, and nonprofit sectors, but the proportions were small relative to the other fields, 13 percent overall. Nearly 28 percent of the new PhDs in the humanities in 1985 were still seeking employment at the time the degree was awarded.

According to figures compiled by the National Center for Education Statistics of the Department of Education, the total number of full-time faculty members in higher education grew from 163,656 in 1960 to 369,000 in 1970 and reached a peak at 469,0000 in 1983. Since then the number has declined to 440,000 in 1986.[13] A profile of the humanities faculty in 1983 is provided in Table 10.3, showing academic position by doctoral cohort, field, and sex. With each successive cohort the number and proportion of women in academic positions increase.

Table 10.3 Academic Position of Humanities Doctorates, by Year of PhD, Field, and Sex: 1983

| | Field of Doctorate and Sex | | | | | | | | | |
| | All Fields | | English and American Literature | | History | | Other Languages and Literature | | Other Humanities | |
1983 Academic Position and Year of PhD	Male	Female	Male	Female	Male	Female	Male	Female	Male	Female
Total, 1940–1959 PhDs (N)	6,900	900	1,700	300	2,200	200	1,100	200	1,900	200
Faculty	95.3%	86.1%	99.2%	82.6%	90.0%	87.1%	95.0%	88.7%	98.1%	86.3%
Professor	86.6	73.2	90.6	70.7	82.2	75.3	86.3	71.8	88.2	76.9
Associate Professor	8.5	10.0	8.6	8.5	7.8	11.8	8.7	13.2	9.1	5.5
Assistant Professor	0.2	2.4		3.5				1.9	0.8	3.8
Instructor		0.6						1.9		
Nonfaculty	1.5	1.9			3.5	1.1			1.0	2.2
Teaching Staff	0.8	1.6			2.2	1.1	0.6	4.1	0.1	0.5
Research Staff	0.6	0.3			1.2		0.6	4.1	0.9	1.6
Postdoctoral Appointment	0.8	0.3	0.4		1.3		2.1	1.1	0.1	
Other	2.1	9.6	0.4	14.3	5.2	8.1	2.2	6.0	0.8	9.9
No Report	0.2	2.0		3.1		3.8				1.6
Total, 1960–1969 PhDs (N)	14,100	3,200	3,700	1,200	4,100	400	2,400	900	3,900	700
Faculty	93.5%	87.2%	90.0%	83.2%	97.6%	89.2%	92.9%	87.6%	92.9%	92.1%
Professor	69.0	53.6	67.2	54.3	76.6	52.7	58.3	45.7	69.4	62.9
Associate Professor	22.5	28.1	22.8	24.4	18.6	31.6	30.3	35.9	21.5	22.6
Assistant Professor	1.5	3.6		2.9	2.4	4.9	3.6	3.9	0.8	3.7
Instructor	0.5	1.9		1.6			0.8	2.2	1.2	3.0
Nonfaculty	1.8	1.6	2.9		0.7		2.4			4.0
Teaching Staff	1.5	1.1	2.5		0.7		1.4	2.7	1.5	1.6
Research Staff	0.3	0.5	0.4				1.0	2.7	1.5	2.4
Postdoctoral Appointment	1.5	1.0		1.4	0.8	1.8	1.3	0.5	3.8	0.3

234

Other	2.2	7.7	5.2	12.0	1.0	6.7	2.4	6.4	1.4	2.9
No Report	1.1	2.5	1.9	3.4		2.2	1.0	2.8	0.5	0.7
Total, 1970–1975 PhDs (N)	14,600	5,400	3,800	1,900	3,800	800	2,600	1,500	4,400	1,200
Faculty	93.4%	84.7%	93.8%	85.8%	94.1%	82.7%	95.8%	85.5%	91.0%	83.4%
Professor	31.4	19.1	27.7	17.3	39.2	23.0	27.1	20.4	30.2	17.7
Associate Professor	50.7	45.5	55.2	47.1	46.9	39.6	53.7	44.8	48.4	47.5
Assistant Professor	9.5	16.4	9.6	19.0	4.9	12.9	13.0	15.2	11.1	16.4
Instructor	1.9	3.7	1.3	2.5	3.1	7.2	2.0	5.1	1.3	1.7
Nonfaculty	1.6	4.3	0.7	4.4	1.5	3.9	1.2	2.3	2.9	7.0
Teaching Staff	1.3	2.8	0.7	2.7	0.7	3.3	1.0	1.5	2.4	4.2
Research Staff	0.3	1.5		1.7	0.8	0.7	0.2	0.8	0.4	2.8
Postdoctoral Appointment	0.9	1.1	0.6	0.1	0.8	0.3		2.8	0.8	0.9
Other	3.0	7.6	3.4	7.5	2.9	11.0	1.7	7.3	3.6	6.0
No Report	1.1	2.3	1.6	2.2	0.7	2.1	1.4	2.2	1.7	2.7
Total, 1976–1982 PhDs (N)	9,600	6,400	2,300	1,900	2,000	600	1,500	1,900	3,800	2,000
Faculty	86.6%	76.3%	82.7%	74.5%	82.8%	79.9%	87.8%	75.4%	90.5%	77.8%
Professor	9.0	4.3	11.2	6.4	11.9	0.3	3.9	2.9	8.2	4.7
Associate Professor	30.0	17.9	25.2	23.5	28.3	13.8	26.5	12.5	35.2	18.9
Assistant Professor	43.6	48.6	40.6	36.6	37.2	61.4	55.6	55.4	43.9	49.5
Instructor	4.1	5.6	5.7	8.0	5.5	4.3	1.8	4.5	3.3	4.7
Nonfaculty	3.5	4.8	2.8	5.2	5.8	1.7	2.3	6.1	3.3	4.1
Teaching Staff	3.1	3.5	2.8	3.9	3.9	0.2	1.7	5.1	3.3	2.7
Research Staff	0.5	1.3		1.3	1.9	1.5	0.6	1.0		1.4
Postdoctoral Appointment	1.1	3.4	1.1	1.3	1.5	1.7	2.2	4.5	0.3	4.7
Other	6.1	13.2	6.9	15.2	9.1	16.7	6.5	12.6	3.9	11.0
No Report	2.7	2.3	6.5	3.8	0.9	1.1	1.1	1.4	1.9	2.4

Sources: Betty M. Vetter and Eleanor L. Babco, *Professional Women and Minorities* (Washington, DC: Commission of Professionals in Science and Technology, 1986), p. 108; and National Research Council, *Science, Engineering and Humanities Doctorates in the United States—1983 Profile* (Washington, DC: National Academy Press, 1984).

Note: Other Languages and Literature = Classical Languages and Literature and Modern Languages and Literature. Other Humanities = Art History, Music, Speech/Theater, Philosophy, and "Other" Humanities.

The same holds true for each of the main fields in the humanities. Women in the humanities are now being appointed to faculty positions in proportion to their representation among new PhDs, but as Table 10.3 clearly shows, once in academia women do not advance as rapidly as men to tenure positions. Moreover, they are more likely to hold part-time positions or positions in community colleges.[14] A study of full-time humanities faculty in 1982 conducted by the American Council on Education (ACE) found that, in general, with regard to institutional setting, the higher the level of educational offering the lower the representation of women. Women account for 41 percent of the full-time humanities faculty at two-year colleges, but only 24 percent at universities.[15]

The ACE study provides information about minority status as well as gender for full-time humanities faculty. The figures for all institutions are shown in Table 10.4. Overall, women represented 30.7 percent of total faculty; of these 3.5 percent were minority women. At the full-professor level the proportion of women was 15.5 percent, of which 1.3 percent were minority women. There are significant differences in the way faculty are distributed by discipline. Compared with the average for the humanities as a whole, the proportion of women faculty is higher for English and languages and lower for history and philosophy. This distribution, of course, reflects the representation of women among the doctoral recipients in those disciplines.

The evolution and development of women's studies during and since the 1970s have created new opportunities for teaching and research careers in academic life. Scholars in the humanities, primarily women but also a few men, have been among those at the forefront of the phenomenal growth of the field, notwithstanding the slowdown in the rate of growth and conditions of financial stringency in higher education generally. We do not have data on the total number of faculty members teaching departmental or interdepartmental courses in women's studies, but in view of the size of programs, the number must be substantial. The formation of centers for research on women, chronicled in chapter 13, has provided opportunities for scholarly work both for faculty members and for nonmembers. The establishment of the National Endowment for the Humanities in 1965 greatly expanded resources for research in the humanities. Research centers in the humanities grew dramatically during the 1970s, precisely at a time when large numbers of PhDs in the humanities were unable to find places in the university. There are now well over 100 humanities institutes in the United States.[16] A leading example of the newly formed institutes is the National Humanities Center at Research Triangle Park, North Carolina.

Humanities scholars other than those in academic life or independent research centers have entered a variety of occupations. Some, particu-

Table 10.4 Gender and Minority Status of Full-Time Humanities Faculty, by Rank and Tenure: 1982

Rank	Total Faculty	Men	Women		Minority Women	
			Number	Percentage	Number	Percentage
Total Faculty	58,682	40,680	18,014	30.7%	2,064	3.5%
Tenured						
Professor	17,377	14,680	2,689	15.5	242	1.3
Associate Professor	15,291	11,410	3,880	25.4	349	2.3
Other	10,200	6,237	3,965	38.8	622	6.1
Subtotal	42,867	32,328	10,534	24.6	1,213	2.8
Nontenured						
Tenure-Track	8,306	4,688	3,622	43.6	467	5.6
Non–Tenure-Track	7,503	3,642	3,860	51.4	384	5.1
Subtotal	15,809	8,330	7,483	47.3	851	5.4

Source: Irene L. Gomberg and Frank J. Atelsek, *Full Time Humanities Faculty, Fall 1982* (Washington, DC: American Council on Education, 1984), p. 15.

larly those in the languages, are teaching in elementary and secondary schools. The nonprofit world has attracted an increasing number, and women are relatively well represented there. The government has also provided alternative careers, particularly for those in history. A growing proportion of humanities doctorates have found employment in business and industry. Among 1986 doctorate recipients in the humanities, 5 percent took jobs in the nonprofit sector, 3 percent in government, and 6 percent in business and industry. Careers in business are not unusual for PhDs in science, economics, or psychology, but there is no tradition of work in corporations by historians, literary critics, or philosophers. The kinds of positions that humanities scholars filled, how they prepared for those positions, and what their experiences were are described in *Corporate Ph.D.*, based on a study conducted under the aegis of the Institute for Research in History in New York.[17] Case studies are presented in which a literary critic becomes a vice president for public relations, a philosopher operates as an account executive, and a historian serves as a strategic planner.

As of 1986 there are signs of reversal in the downturn of the academic job market, particularly in the humanities. Colleges and universities are beginning to plan for a bulge of faculty retirements in the 1990s because of the high rate of tenuring in during the growth period of the 1950s and 1960s. At the same time, demographers are predicting an undergraduate enrollment increase beginning about 1995 when the children of the baby-boom generation will be old enough for college. The possibility is there for women scholars to move up into senior academic ranks, but it will not come about automatically. Concerted efforts will be required to turn the possibility into a reality.

The Traditional Professions for Women

The foremost professions that have long been dominated by women are teaching, social work, library work, and nursing. Sixty percent or more of each of these professions have been staffed by women since the turn of the century or, in the case of nursing, before. While women have made gains in the last two decades in professions traditionally dominated by men, they have also increased their concentration in the so-called women's professions. These are, of course, the helping professions of slighter prestige, lesser training, and lower income. Although the Bureau of the Census classifies them as professional and technical fields, they are often referred to as semiprofessions or paraprofessions.[18]

In 1973 women constituted 70 percent of elementary and secondary school teachers, 61 percent of social workers, 82 percent of librarians, and 98 percent of registered nurses. In 1985 these proportions had increased to 73 percent for teachers, 68 percent for social workers, and 87 percent for librarians. The percentage for nurses declined slightly to 95 percent, but remains the highest of any of the professions.[19] In terms of numbers, teachers and nurses far exceed other professions in the employment of women, including minority women. In 1985 there were 2.6 million teachers and 1.4 million nurses as against 292,000 social workers and 175,000 librarians. Minority women represented 9.4 percent of teachers, 8.6 percent of nurses, 15.5 percent of social workers, and 6.9 percent of librarians. These proportions are significantly higher than they were in the 1960s.

Within the traditional female professions, men and women tend to enter different areas of specialization. Men gravitate toward the administrative or technical aspects of the profession rather than direct services, and they advance more rapidly than women to supervisory and managerial positions.

Education

Entrance into a career in education, other than higher education, is primarily through the bachelor's or master's degree. Most school teachers are certified by state regulations governing public education, but in some circumstances teachers may begin with the baccalaureate in fields other than education while returning to college for the required specialized courses or a master's degree in education. In the past, the vast majority of public school teachers did not hold a degree beyond the bachelor's, but over the last two decades the bachelor's degree has gradually been replaced by the master's as the entry-level credential. In 1971 the baccalaureate was the highest degree held by 70 percent of public school teachers. By 1983 the proportion had dropped to less than 50 percent. The majority of public school teachers now hold the master's or other advanced degree, including the doctorate.[20]

Trends in degree attainment in the field of education are shown in Table 10.5. As indicated, the total number of degrees awarded at all levels has declined since the peak years in the 1970s, reflecting the decline in public school enrollment and reduced opportunities for teaching during that time. At the bachelor's and master's degree level, the number of degrees awarded to both men and women has declined sharply. The proportion of bachelor's degrees awarded to women has

Table 10.5 Degrees Awarded in Education, by Sex and Level of Degree: 1970–1971 to 1985–1986

Year	Bachelor's Degree			Master's Degree			Doctorate		
	Total Both Sexes	Women Only	Percentage Women	Total Both Sexes	Women Only	Percentage Women	Total Both Sexes	Women Only	Percentage Women
1970–71	177,638	132,236	74.4%	89,067	50,020	56.2%	6,398	1,355	21.2%
1971–72	192,368	142,492	74.0	98,280	56,355	57.3%	7,041	1,660	23.6
1972–73	195,640	143,816	73.5	105,646	61,450	58.2	7,314	1,813	24.8
1973–74	186,623	137,088	73.5	112,739	67,553	59.9	7,293	1,977	27.5
1974–75	168,749	123,703	73.3	120,233	74,733	62.2	7,443	2,296	30.8
1975–76	156,528	114,026	72.8	128,410	82,591	64.3	7,769	2,593	33.4
1976–77	143,658	103,740	72.2	126,375	83,201	65.8	7,955	2,769	34.8
1977–78	137,742	99,842	72.5	118,957	80,548	67.7	7,586	2,956	39.0
1978–79	127,853	93,568	73.2	111,834	76,734	68.6	7,731	3,263	42.2
1979–80	120,680	89,214	73.9	103,720	72,762	70.2	7,940	3,521	44.3
1980–81	108,265	81,196	75.0	98,381	70,301	71.5	7,900	3,736	47.3
1981–82	101,063	76,678	75.9	93,104	67,333	72.3	7,676	3,727	48.6
1982–83	97,991	74,321	75.8	84,853	61,621	72.6	7,551	3,787	50.2
1983–84	92,382	70,167	75.9	77,187	55,606	72.0	6,780	3,457	50.9
1984–85	88,161	66,897	75.9	76,437	55,492	72.6	6,717	3,480	51.8
1985–86	87,221	66,235	75.9	76,353	55,634	72.9	7,110	3,795	53.3

Sources: Betty M. Vetter and Eleanor L. Babco, *Professional Women and Minorities* (Washington, DC: Commission on Professionals in Science and Technology, February 1986), p. 256; and unpublished data, National Center for Education Statistics.

held more or less steady at about 75 percent, while the proportion of master's degrees awarded to women has increased from 56 percent in 1970–1971 to nearly 73 percent in 1985–1986. The growing emphasis on the master's degree rather than the bachelor's degree as the professional qualification for teaching can be seen in the change in relative numbers of degrees awarded. The total number of master's degrees awarded was 50 percent of bachelor's degrees in 1970–1971 and 88 percent in 1985–1986. At the doctoral level the number of degrees awarded to men and the total number of degrees have declined since 1976–1977, while the number awarded to women has increased steadily. As a result, the proportion of doctorates in education awarded to women has increased from 21 percent in 1970–1971 to 53 percent in 1985–1986.

The doctorate in education is designed primarily for educational administration at the school or college level or for teaching and research in schools or departments of education. Of those receiving the doctorate in education in 1986, roughly 42 percent had postgraduate plans for administrative positions and 38 percent for teaching and research positions.[21] Minorities doctorates are heavily concentrated in education, and minority men and women represented 12 percent of the degrees awarded in that field in 1986. More than half the minority doctorates in education were earned by women.

Women have not yet reached positions in school and college administration commensurate with their degree attainment. Higher education administration is dealt with in chapter 14. In public school administration, the upward progress of women has been slow, notwithstanding their preponderance as teachers and their attainment of advanced degrees. As of the early 1980s, women represented 83 percent of elementary school teachers, 46 percent of secondary school teachers, but only 18 percent of elementary school principals, 7 percent of secondary school principals, and 1.8 percent of district superintendants.[22] At the college and university level, women represent 28 percent of deans of schools of education[23] and 25 percent of faculty members in schools and departments of education.[24]

Social Work

Women played an important role in the evolution of social work as a profession in the early 1900s, and since that time social work has been seen as a female field. In the past, however, the degree of concentration of women in social work was less than that in elementary school teaching, nursing, or library work. In 1970 and the decades preceding, the ratio of women to men in social work was roughly two to one.[25]

During the 1970s significant shifts took place in the patterns of education for social work. Until 1974 the two-year master's degree was the recognized professional qualification for careers in social work. In that year, the Council on Social Work Education, responding to pressures arising from the growing need for social work personnel, adopted minimal accreditation standards for undergraduate social work education.[26] This action legitimated undergraduate education for social work, which was already growing rapidly relative to graduate work.

During the same period, there was a substantial increase in the concentration of women in the field. Between 1970 and 1986 the number and proportion of degrees in social work earned by women increased at all levels, while the number of degrees awarded to men remained essentially constant at the baccalaureate level, declined significantly at the master's level, and varied at the doctoral level.

These shifts in the profession are shown in Table 10.6. The number of bachelor's degrees awarded in social work surpassed the number of master's degrees in 1972–1973 and has remained higher since then. The proportion of women among degree recipients increased between 1970–1971 and 1985–1986 from 75 to 85 percent at the bachelor's level, from 60 to 80 percent at the master's level, and from 37 to 64 percent at the doctoral level.

As in other fields, the representation of women in faculty and administrative positions in schools of social work has not kept up with the rate of degree attainment. In a statistical survey of graduate schools of social work conducted by the Council on Social Work Education in 1984–1985, it was found that men held 56 percent of the administrative positions and were concentrated in the upper ranks. They held 71 percent of the deanships and 60 percent of the associate deanships, while women were more likely to have the two lowest paying administrative positions, namely, field directors (59 percent women) and assistant field directors (68 percent women).[27] In faculty positions, the overall numbers of men and women are roughly equal, but men are concentrated in the tenured ranks, while women predominate at the assistant professor level and below. The figures are shown in Table 10.7. The current position of women on faculties represents some improvement over 1972, but not a great deal. In 1972 women were 45 percent of all faculty members compared with 50 percent in 1985. At the tenured level there has been no increase in the proportion of women.

Members of minority groups are a significant presence in social work. Of all social workers in 1985, 18 percent were black and 6 percent were Hispanic. Minorities represent 23 percent of the faculties of schools of

Table 10.6 Degrees Awarded in Social Work, by Sex and Level of Degree: 1970–1971 to 1985–1986

Year	Bachelor's Degree				Master's Degree				Doctorate			
	Total	Men	Women	Percentage Women	Total	Men	Women	Percentage Women	Total	Men	Women	Percentage Women
1970–71	4,690	1,152	3,538	75.4%	6,148	2,438	3,710	60.3%	126	87	39	36.9%
1971–72	6,223	1,562	4,661	74.8	6,656	2,607	4,049	60.8	99	68	31	31.3
1972–73	8,182	2,147	6,035	73.7	6,896	2,543	4,353	63.1	111	82	29	26.1
1973–74	9,960	2,845	7,115	71.4	7,974	3,009	4,965	62.3	109	76	33	30.3
1974–75	10,784	2,735	8,049	74.6	8,852	3,325	5,527	62.4	135	87	48	35.5
1975–76	11,032	2,682	8,350	75.7	9,002	2,990	6,012	66.8	163	90	73	44.8
1976–77	11,673	2,638	9,035	77.4	9,596	3,047	6,549	68.3	131	76	55	42.0
1977–78	12,672	2,725	9,947	78.5	9,986	2,988	6,998	70.1	138	72	66	47.8
1978–79	13,180	2,572	10,608	80.5	9,893	2,868	7,025	71.0	136	75	61	44.9
1979–80	12,870	2,367	10,503	81.6	10,158	2,832	7,326	72.1	162	81	81	50.0
1980–81	12,410	2,107	10,303	83.0	10,240	2,614	7,626	74.5	193	89	104	53.9
1981–82	11,813	1,867	9,946	84.2	9,959	2,295	7,664	77.0	198	90	108	54.6
1982–83	11,445	1,798	9,647	84.3	9,456	1,969	7,487	79.2	215	91	124	57.7
1983–84	8,824	1,248	7,576	85.8	8,547	1,759	6,788	79.4	227	95	132	57.3
1984–85	8,063	1,164	6,899	85.6	8,900	1,717	7,183	80.7	218	79	139	63.7
1985–86	8,094	1,186	6,908	85.3	9,101	1,830	7,271	80.0	225	81	144	64.0

Sources: Betty M. Vetter and Eleanor L. Babco, *Professional Women and Minorities* (Washington, DC: Commission on Professionals in Science and Technology, 1986); and unpublished data, National Center for Education Statistics.

Table 10.7 Social Work Faculty, by Rank and Sex: 1985

Rank	Male		Female		Total	
	Number	Percentage	Number	Percentage	Number	Percentage
Professor	595	72.0%	231	27.9%	826	100.0%
Associate Professor	666	56.8	507	43.2	1,173	100.0
Assistant Professor	413	37.7	683	62.3	1,096	100.0
Instructor	139	40.0	208	59.9	347	100.0
Lecturer	146	37.3	245	62.7	391	100.0
Other	101	35.4	184	64.6	285	100.0
Total	2,060	50.0	2,058	50.0	4,118	100.0

Source: Council on Social Work Education, *Statistics on Social Work Education in the United States: 1985* (Washington, DC: CSWE, 1986), p. 16.

social work.[28] The breakdown by ethnic group is as follows:

Ethnic Group	Percentage
Total Ethnic	23.1%
Asian American	2.3
Black	14.8
Chicano	1.9
Native American	.9
Puerto Rican	2.2
Other Minority	1.0
White	76.7
Foreign	0.2
Total	100.0

Nearly two thirds of black and Puerto Rican faculty members are women, and a little over one third of Asian American, Chicano, and Native American faculty members.

In the past, gender differences in leadership positions in the field of social work have been attributed to the fact that more men than women held doctorates. If present trends continue, that will no longer be true in the future. It is still true, however, that men and women tend to enter different areas of specialization within social work and that these differences favor more rapid career mobility for men. For example, women are more likely to concentrate in direct services or case work, whereas men constitute a higher proportion of those preparing for administration or community development. Disparities of this kind will need to be eliminated if women are to achieve equal status with men in the social work profession, let alone take over in leadership positions.

Library Science

Of the professions that have traditionally attracted a high proportion of women, library science is the smallest field overall and does not employ women in absolute numbers as large as teaching, social work, and nursing. Moreover, it is a field of declining employment owing in part to the rise of computer and information sciences during the last two decades and also to budgetary cutbacks on the part of educational institutions and public agencies.

The primary professional qualification for careers in the field is the master's degree in library science. Relatively few degrees are awarded at either the bachelor's or doctor's level. Table 10.8 shows the trends in degree attainment in library and archival work since 1970. The number of master's degrees awarded has dropped sharply over the period, with

Table 10.8 Degrees Awarded in Library and Archival Science, by Sex and Level of Degree: 1970–1986

Year	Bachelor's Degree				Master's Degree				Doctorate			
	Total	Men	Women	Percentage Women	Total	Men	Women	Percentage Women	Total	Men	Women	Percentage Women
1970–71	1,013	81	932	92.0%	7,001	1,311	5,690	81.2%	39	28	11	28.2%
1971–72	989	66	923	93.3	7,383	1,484	5,899	79.9	64	36	28	43.8
1972–73	1,159	87	1,072	92.5	7,696	1,676	6,020	78.2	78	54	24	30.8
1973–74	1,164	86	1,078	92.6	8,185	1,817	6,368	77.8	56	34	22	39.3
1974–75	1,069	81	988	92.5	8,123	1,722	6,401	78.8	56	33	23	41.0
1975–76	843	58	785	93.1	8,084	1,753	6,331	78.3	71	39	32	45.1
1976–77	781	71	710	90.9	7,572	1,544	6,026	79.6	75	35	40	53.3
1977–78	693	80	613	88.5	6,935	1,386	5,549	80.0	67	43	24	35.8
1978–79	558	30	528	94.6	5,930	1,161	4,769	80.4	70	34	36	51.4
1979–80	398	20	378	95.0	5,374	1,004	4,370	81.3	65	27	38	58.5
1980–81	375	22	353	94.1	4,859	841	4,018	82.7	71	31	40	56.2
1981–82	307	43	264	85.9	4,506	799	3,707	82.3	84	31	53	63.0
1982–83	258	28	230	89.2	3,979	735	3,244	81.5	52	21	31	59.6
1983–84	255	33	222	87.1	3,805	766	3,039	80.0	74	38	36	48.7
1984–85	202	26	176	87.9	3,893	758	3,135	80.5	72	33	39	54.2
1985–86	157	17	140	89.1	3,626	721	2,905	80.1	57	22	35	61.4

Sources: National Center for Education Statistics, Digest of Education Statistics, (Washington, DC: NCES, 1972–84); Betty M. Vetter and Eleanor L. Babco, Professional Women and Minorities (Washington, DC: Commission on Professionals in Science and Technology, 1986); and unpublished data, National Center for Education Statistics.

the proportion earned by women remaining more or less around 80 percent. The number of bachelor's degrees awarded has also declined sharply, with the proportion earned by women decreasing somewhat from 92 percent in 1970 to 89 percent in 1986. The number of doctoral degrees, while small and fluctuating from year to year, shows a generally upward trend, with the proportion awarded to women increasing significantly from 28 percent in 1970 to over 61 percent in 1986. Available statistics indicate that approximately 10 percent of degrees in library science at all levels are awarded to members of minority groups. The preponderant number of minority degree recipients were women.

Of 215,000 persons employed as librarians, archivists, and curators in 1985, nearly 85 percent were women. Six percent were black, mostly women, and 2.6 percent were Hispanic, about half of whom were women.[29] In research libraries, however, and in faculty and administrative positions in library schools, men held the dominating positions.

As women have increased their share of doctorates earned in library science, they have made significant gains as administrators in schools of library science. They have fared less well as faculty members. They have increased their representation as deans or directors of library schools markedly, from 19 percent in 1970 to 32 percent in 1985. The figures are as follows:[30]

Year	Number of Schools	Headed by Women	
		Number	Percentage
1970	52	10	19.0%
1980	67	14	20.9
1985	65	21	32.3

Since 1970 women have also increased their representation as academic library administrators. Among the member institutions of the Association of Research Libraries there were no women directors in 1970. By 1985 women held 23 percent of the directorships and over 50 percent of the associate and assistant director level positions, as shown in the following:[31]

Year	Percentage Women Directors	Percentage Women Associate and Assistant Directors
1970	0%	16%
1976	11	30
1984	20	51
1985	23	50

On the other hand, the overall gender composition of the faculty remained unchanged between 1975 and 1985. As shown in Table 10.9, there was a significant increase in the proportion of women at the assistant professor level and an equally significant decline in the proportion at the associate professor level. In all faculty ranks combined, women represented 43 percent in 1985, the same percentage as in 1975.

Annual salary surveys of the Association for Library and Information Science Education (formerly the Association of Library Schools) show that salaries for men consistently exceed those for women. There are also gender differences in areas of specialization within the library sciences. Women tend to specialize in service for children, cataloguing, and classification while men concentrate in more prestigious areas such as information science, research methods, and library automation. As long as such differences remain, men will continue to advance to the upper echelons of librarianship at rates that exceed their overall representation in the profession.

Nursing

Nursing is, and always has been, the most sex-typed of the female professions. Although the degree of concentration of women in the field has declined slightly since the early 1970s, it remains extremely high. Of 807,000 registered nurses in 1972, 98 percent were women.[32] In 1985

Table 10.9 **Full-Time Women Faculty, Schools of Library Science, by Rank: 1975–1985**

	1975		1985	
Rank	Number	Percentage Women	Number	Percentage Women
Professor	146	29.5%	176	32.2%
Associate Professor	199	45.7	223	36.2
Assistant Professor	248	46.0	167	61.1
Instructor	26	75.0	12	83.4
Lecturer	19	57.9	14	50.0
Total	638	43.5	592	43.3

Source: Association for Library and Information Science Education, *Library and Information Science Education Statistical Report 1986* (State College, PA: ALISE, 1986).

there were 1.4 million registered nurses, of which 95 percent were women, including 8 percent minority women.[33]

Nursing does not require college-level training for entry into the profession as such. College degrees are necessary, however, for advancement into positions of greater responsibility, authority, and leadership in the profession. In particular, of course, academic degrees are essential for careers in nursing education. Prior to the 1970s most registered nurses were graduates of nondegree diploma programs. Since then there has been a rapid increase in the number of graduates of RN associate and baccalaureate degree programs and a corresponding decline in the number of graduates of diploma programs. By 1980–1981 diploma programs represented only 18 percent of the graduates of all registered nurse programs, while associate degree programs represented 49 percent and baccalaureate programs 33 percent. Thus, there has been a substantial upgrading of the profession over the last two decades.[34]

Advanced degrees in nursing have also increased rapidly since 1970. As shown in Table 10.10, the number of master's degrees awarded in nursing rose from 1,549 in 1969–1970 to 6,050 in 1985–1986 and the number of doctorates from a total of 11 in 1969–1970 to 277 in 1985–1986. In both cases women represent well over 90 percent of the recipients.

Unlike teaching, social work, and library science, women in nursing predominate in faculty and administrative positions. Approximately 96 percent of the faculties of schools of nursing are women. However, they wield little influence in the university; indeed, they are struggling to maintain their autonomy against the male-dominated medical profession.[35] Whatever the outcome of the struggle, there is little reason to expect that the extreme sex-stereotyping of the nursing profession will change any more rapidly during the next two decades than it has during the past two.

Conclusions

While women have made dramatic inroads into the sciences and the traditional male professions, such as medicine, law, and business, they have also increased their representation in the social sciences and humanities. In some disciplines they have reached or exceeded parity with men in doctoral degrees earned, but not as yet in faculty positions at tenured levels. During the past two decades women have also continued to enter the traditional women's professions and their concentra-

Table 10.10 Degrees Awarded in Nursing, by Sex and Level of Degree: 1969–1970 to 1985–1986

Year	Bachelor's Degree			Master's Degree			Doctorate		
	Total Both Sexes	Women Only	Percentage Women	Total Both Sexes	Women Only	Percentage Women	Total Both Sexes	Women Only	Percentage Women
1969–70	11,280	11,120	98.6%	1,549	1,531	98.8%	11	10	90.0%
1970–71	12,283	12,029	97.9	1,542	1,511	98.0	7	6	85.7
1971–72	13,245	12,902	97.4	1,846	1,815	98.3	10	10	100.0
1972–73	15,526	15,063	97.0	2,093	1,983	94.7	17	13	76.5
1973–74	19,409	18,653	96.1	2,293	2,229	97.2	14	14	100.0
1974–75	23,813	22,709	95.4	2,220	2,154	97.0	16	16	100.0
1975–76	26,846	25,484	94.9	3,058	2,968	97.1	16	16	100.0
1976–77	28,402	26,870	94.6	3,257	3,155	96.9	24	22	91.6
1977–78	30,307	28,661	94.6	3,812	3,671	96.3	56	53	94.6
1978–79	31,808	30,002	94.3	4,256	4,088	96.1	68	65	95.6
1979–80	32,852	31,054	94.5	4,637	4,464	96.3	118	116	98.3
1980–81	32,794	31,140	95.0	5,096	4,899	96.1	113	109	96.5
1981–82	33,177	31,482	94.9	5,312	4,034	94.8	134	128	95.5
1982–83	31,442	29,965	95.3	4,451	4,298	96.6	124	117	94.4
1983–84	32,237	30,592	94.9	4,437	4,240	95.6	156	150	96.1
1984–85	33,654	31,717	94.2	5,761	5,303	92.0	177	170	96.0
1985–86	34,097	32,139	94.3	6,050	5,571	92.0	277	257	93.0

Sources: Betty M. Vetter and Eleanor L. Babco. *Professional Women and Minorities* (Washington, DC: Commission on Professionals in Science and Technology, 1986), p. 225; unpublished data, National Center for Education Statistics; and *Summary Reports: Doctorate Recipients from United States Universities,* 1984 and 1985.

tion in these fields remains high. Except for nursing, however, they do not hold faculty positions commensurate with their degree attainment.

Notes

1. Susan L. Coyle, *Summary Report 1985: Doctorate Recipients from United States Universities* (Washington, DC: National Academy Press, 1986), p. 19. The total number shown here is not entirely comparable to that on page 226 in that it does not include non-U.S. citizens or those for whom race or ethnicity is not known. Separate tabulations are not given for Native American women because of the small number involved. For all fields combined, including the social sciences, Native American women earned 54 doctorates in 1985 compared with 9 in 1975. Women accounted for 25 percent of the doctorates awarded to Native Americans in 1975 and 58 percent in 1985.

2. Betty M. Vetter and Eleanor L. Babco, *Professional Women and Minorities* (Washington, DC: Commission on Professionals in Science and Technology, 1986), p. 115.

3. Committee on the Status of Women in the Economics Profession, American Economic Association, "Annual Report, 1985," *Newsletter*, February 1986, pp. 2–3.

4. Bettina J. Huber, *Employment Patterns in Sociology: Recent Trends and Future Prospects* (Washington, DC: American Sociological Association, 1985).

5. American Sociological Association, *Guidelines for Incorporating Women into Departments of Sociology in the Eighties* (Washington, DC: ASA, 1984), p. 5.

6. Bonnie Thornton Dill, Evelyn Nakano Glenn, and Bettina J. Huber, "Women in Departmental Administrative Positions," *ASA Footnotes* 2 (August 1983):10–11.

7. The data are from Huber, *Employment Patterns*, p. 36.

8. Committee on Employment and Human Resources, "The Changing Face of American Psychology," *American Psychologist* 41, no. 12 (December 1986):1311–1327.

9. Georgine M. Pion, J. Paul Bramblett, Jr., and Marlene Wicherski, *Graduate Departments of Psychology, 1985–1986: Report of the Annual APA/COGDOP Departmental Survey* (Washington, DC: American Psychological Association, 1986).

10. Sources of data: for 1970, Carnegie Commission, *Opportunities for Women in Higher Education*, 1973; for 1986, National Center for Education Statistics, unpublished data.

11. National Research Council, *Summary Report 1970: Doctorate Recipients*.

12. National Research Council, *Summary Report 1986: Doctorate Recipients*, advance release tables.

13. National Center for Education Statistics, *Digest of Education Statistics, 1987* (Washington, DC: U.S. Government Printing Office, 1987), p. 158.
14. Howard R. Bowen and Jack H. Schuster, *American Professors* (New York: Oxford University Press, 1986), p. 56.
15. Irene L. Gomberg and Frank J. Atelsek, *Full Time Humanities Faculty, Fall 1982,* Higher Education Panel Report no. 61 (Washington, DC: American Council on Education, August 1984).
16. For a discussion of independent research institutions and their role in scholarly life in the humanities, see Institute for Research in History, *Outside Academe: New Ways of Working in the Humanities* (New York: Institute for Research in History and the Haworth Press, 1981).
17. Carol Groneman and Robert N. Lear, *Corporate Ph.D.* (New York: Facts on File Publications, 1985).
18. James W. Grimm, "Women in Female-Dominated Professions," in Ann H. Stromberg and Shirley Harkess, eds., *Women Working* (Palo Alto, CA: Mayfield, 1978).
19. U.S. Bureau of Labor Statistics, *Employment and Earnings, 1985* (Washington, DC: U.S. Government Printing Office, January 1986), p. 175.
20. U.S. Bureau of the Census, *Statistical Abstract of the United States, 1986* (Washington, DC: U.S. Government Printing Office, 1986), p. 138.
21. National Research Council, *Summary Report 1984: Doctorate Recipients,* p. 39.
22. Carol Shakeshaft, "Strategies for Overcoming the Barriers to Women in Educational Administration," in Susan S. Klein, ed., *Handbook for Achieving Sex Equity through Education* (Baltimore: Johns Hopkins University Press, 1985).
23. College and University Personnel Association, *1985–1986 Administrative Compensation Survey,* (Washington, DC: CUPA, 1986), p. 48.
24. U.S. Bureau of Labor Statistics, unpublished tabulation of employment by detailed occupation, annual averages, 1985.
25. Grimm, "Women in Female-Dominated Professions," p. 303.
26. Gary R. Lowe, "The Graduate Only Debate and Social Work Education, 1931–59, and Its Consequences for the Profession," *Journal of Social Work Education* 21, no. 3 (Fall 1985):52–62.
27. Elaine Norman, "A New Look at Salary Equity for Male and Female Faculty in Schools of Social Work," *Affilia: Journal of Women and Social Work* 1 no. 4 (Winter 1986):42.
28. National Council on Social Work Education, *Statistics on Social Work Education in the United States: 1985* (Washington, DC: NCSWE, 1986), p. 10.
29. Vetter and Babco, *Professional Women and Minorities,* p. 76.
30. Mary Niles Maack, "Women in Library Education: Down the Up Staircase," *Library Trends* 34, no. 3 (Winter 1986):421.
31. Betty Joe Irvine, "Differences by Sex: Academic Library Administrators,"

Library Trends 34, no. 2 (Fall 1985): 235–257. Also "Women in Librarianship," *ALA Yearbook of Library and Information Services '86*, vol. 11 (Chicago: American Library Association, 1986), pp. 325–327.

32. U.S. Bureau of the Census, *Statistical Abstract of the United States, 1984* (Washington, DC: U.S. Government Printing Office, 1984), p. 419.

33. Vetter and Babco, *Professional Women and Minorities*, p. 75.

34. Vetter and Babco, *Professional Women and Minorities*, p. 226.

35. *Chronicle of Higher Education*, October 4, 1976, p. 3.

11

Faculty Women: Preparation, Participation, and Progress

As we have seen, in the early 1970s numerous federal laws and regulations were passed that were aimed at equalizing opportunities for women in higher education: Title VII of the Civil Rights Act prohibiting discrimination in employment was extended in 1972 to include all educational institutions; the Equal Pay Act of 1963 was extended to cover executive, administrative, and professional employment; and Title IX of the Education Amendments of 1972 was enacted prohibiting sex discrimination in all federally assisted education programs. Also in 1972 guidelines were issued for implementing Executive Orders 11246 and 11375 requiring federal contractors to institute affirmative action plans to ensure equal treatment of all employees. Since these measures were passed, how far have women faculty members progressed toward equity in employment?

In determining what is a reasonable percentage of women faculty to set as a target figure, affirmative action plans have used as a standard the "availability pool" of women among doctorates awarded. For example, the target percentage of women full professors in a particular field was commonly based on the percentage of doctorates awarded to women in the field ten years earlier. For assistant professors the relevant pool is the proportion of doctorates awarded to women in the preceding five years.

In this chapter, we will first examine national trends in the representation of women among doctorate recipients and among college faculty. We will then describe the participation of academic women across the

255

various types of institutions and assess the extent to which there has been a change in the access of academic women to employment in higher education institutions. We will also examine changes in the patterns of promotion, attainment of tenure, and salary levels. This national profile will be supplemented by more detailed data collected directly from faculty at a sample of 92 institutions during 1972 and 1980. This second data set enables us to look at changes within institutions with regard to opportunities for advancement and differentials in academic rewards. Finally, we will analyze the characteristics of a particular subsample of faculty, high producers of published research, compared with the characteristics of faculty in general.

Trends in Doctoral Production

As we have seen, the number and proportion of doctoral degrees earned by women have increased dramatically over the last two decades. The overall number of doctorates awarded to women climbed from 1,759 in 1965 to 11,244 in 1986, representing an increase from 10.8 percent to 35.4 percent of total doctorates awarded. The number of doctorates awarded to men peaked in 1972 and has declined steadily since then, while the number awarded to women has continued to grow.

Table 11.1 provides a profile of doctoral recipients since 1972, showing comparisons between men and women with regard to age, marital status, and postdoctoral employment plans. Between 1972 and 1986 the median age at the time of receiving the PhD increased for both women and men and was higher for women than men by about two years. The proportion of doctoral recipients planning postdoctoral study increased during the period, both for men and for women, and was consistently higher for men than for women. The proportion of doctoral recipients planning or seeking employment in educational institutions declined for both men and women. Significantly, however, the proportion for women is considerably higher than that for men, while the reverse is true for those planning on seeking careers in industry. If the percentage of those seeking employment in educational institutions is combined with those planning postdoctoral study and presumably also headed for academic careers, the proportion for women is higher than it is for men throughout the period. This suggests that the availability pool is somewhat higher than is indicated by the proportion of doctorates awarded.

The increase in doctorates awarded to women was accompanied by shifts in the distribution of degrees by discipline and marked changes in

Table 11.1 Profile of New Doctorates: 1972–1986

	1972	1980	1986
Total Number	33,001	30,982	31,770
Male	84.0%	69.7%	64.6%
Female	16.0	30.3	35.4
Percentage Married	74.5	61.1	57.3
Male	78.4	64.8	60.4
Female	54.6	52.8	51.6
Median Age at Doctorate	31.1 years	32.2 years	33.5 years
Male	30.9 years	31.7 years	32.7 years
Female	32.9 years	33.5 years	35.4 years
Percentage Planning Postdoctoral Study	15.5%	18.4%	22.0%
Male	16.0	19.7	24.2
Female	12.5	15.4	18.0
Percentage Planning Postdoctoral Employment	77.6	75.3	69.0
Male	77.4	74.1	66.1
Female	79.1	78.2	74.1
Educational Institutions	55.3	45.5	40.0
Male	53.8	41.9	36.0
Female	63.6	53.1	47.5
Industry	7.7	12.9	14.0
Male	8.7	14.8	15.9
Female	2.3	8.3	10.4
Government	8.7	8.9	7.1
Male	9.6	10.0	7.5
Female	4.3	6.3	6.4
Nonprofit	2.7	4.8	4.5
Male	2.6	4.7	4.1
Female	3.3	4.8	5.1
Other	3.2	3.5	3.3
Male	2.8	2.6	2.5
Female	5.6	5.6	4.8
Postdoctoral Status Unknown	6.9	6.3	9.0
Male	6.5	6.2	9.6
Female	8.4	6.4	7.8

Sources: National Research Council, *Summary Report: Doctorate Recipients from United States Universities* (Washington, DC: National Academy Press, 1972, 1980, 1986); unpublished data, National Research Council, Office of Scientific and Engineering Personnel, Doctorate Records File.

the relative proportions of doctorates earned by men and women. Table 11.2 displays the number of degrees awarded between 1982 and 1986 by broad field and by the percentage going to women. The largest proportionate increases for women have occurred in the professional fields, physical sciences, and life sciences. In numerical terms, however, the largest increases came in education, the social sciences, and life sciences. The number of doctorates awarded to women in the field of education has begun to decline, although the social sciences continue to show strong growth. In several fields the annual number of PhDs awarded to women now exceeds the number by men, as we have noted earlier.

Trends in Academic Employment, Promotion, and Salaries

The proportion of women as full-time faculty members of institutions of higher learning was 22.3 percent in 1972–1973 and increased to 27.1 percent in 1982–1983. A large proportion of these women, however,

Table 11.2   Doctorates Awarded by Broad Field: 1972–1986

	1972	1980	1986
Total Number	33,001	30,982	31,770
Women	16%	30.3%	35.4%
Physical Sciences	5,538	4,114	4,808
Women	6.6%	12.1%	16.1%
Engineering	3,503	2,479	3,376
Women	0.6%	3.6%	6.7%
Life Sciences	4,957	5,325	5,720
Women	6.7%	25.2%	34.0%
Social Sciences	5,611	6,253	5,841
Women	18.8%	34.5%	45.2%
Humanities	4,714	3,863	3,461
Women	27.0%	42.1%	45.2%
Professional Fields	1,526	1,345	1,936
Women	12.0%	27.9%	34.0%
Education	7,085	7,576	6,602
Women	23.2%	44.5%	54.3%

Sources: National Research Council, *Summary Report: Doctorate Recipients from United States Universities* (Washington, DC: National Academy Press, 1980, 1986).

were in low-ranked and nontenured positions such as instructors and lecturers. They were also concentrated in two-year institutions. A profile of women faculty members by rank and type of institution showing changes from 1972 to 1983 is provided in Table 11.3. Although women made substantial gains during the period at the assistant and associate professor levels, they remain underrepresented at the full professor level particularly in the major universities. Overall the percentage of women full professors increased only slightly, from 9.8 percent in 1972–1973 to 10.7 percent in 1982–1983. Approximately 11 percent of women faculty members are minorities, and this figure has changed very little over the past ten years.

With respect to the attainment of tenure, academic women continue to lag behind men. In the mid-1970s, 64 percent of all academic men compared with 46 percent of academic women were tenured. By the mid-1980s the percentage of faculty men who were tenured had increased to 69 percent, while the percentage for faculty women increased to only 47 percent. Data for selected years during this period are presented in Table 11.4. Thus, it appears that the differential between men and women has increased somewhat, although this may be due in part to the higher proportion of women newly appointed as assistant professors during this period.

In the early 1970s there was a pronounced disparity in the salaries of men and women faculty members. The record since then has been mixed. After some initial improvement in percentage terms during the 1970s, there was a slippage in the 1980s to the point where by 1986–1987 the disparity had, if anything, widened.[1] The figures are shown in Table 11.5. In 1972–1973 the average salary for women at the assistant professor level was 94 percent that of men. In 1986–1987 the percentage was 90 percent. At the full professor level, salaries for women were 88 percent of that for men in 1972–1973 and in 1986–1987 the percentage was the same. In dollar terms the salary gap widened significantly between 1972–1973 and 1986–1987. In 1986–1987 the gap was $2,730 at the assistant professor level and $5,440 at the full professor level compared with $680 and $2,283 in 1972–1973.

As with the tenure differential, the continuing disparity may be attributable to the increased rate of entry of women into academic positions during the period. The consequence of this is that women faculty members are likely to have less seniority and experience than their male counterparts. Other factors influencing the disparity include the distribution of faculty by discipline. In general, the differentials are wider in private institutions than in public institutions. By discipline the differen-

Table 11.3 Women as a Percentage of Total Full-Time Instructional Faculty on Nine-Month Contracts in Institutions of Higher Education, by Academic Rank and Level of Institutional Unit: 1972–1973 to 1982–1983

Academic Rank and Year	All Institutions	Public				Private			
		Total	Universities	Four-Year Institutions	Two-Year Institutions	Total	Universities	Four-Year Institutions	Two-Year Institutions
All Ranks									
1972–73	22.3%	22.7%	17.1%	23.2%	32.3%	21.2%	14.5%	23.6%	45.4%
1974–75	24.1	24.8	19.3	24.4	32.7	23.5	16.3	25.6	44.1
1976–77	25.2	25.7	18.9	24.6	34.4	23.7	17.0	26.0	42.4
1979–80	25.9	26.4	20.0	26.4	34.7	24.8	18.2	27.4	48.6
1980–81	26.7	26.9	19.5	25.8	35.9	26.1	19.0	28.4	47.1
1981–82	27.1	27.3	19.9	26.2	36.4	26.2	19.2	28.6	46.9
1982–83*	26.9	27.1	19.0	26.4	36.6	26.6	20.2	28.0	45.2
Professors									
1972–73	9.8	10.0	6.7	12.7	21.2	9.5	5.4	12.3	31.5
1974–75	10.3	10.5	6.6	12.7	24.7	10.1	5.6	13.0	26.6
1976–77	9.6	9.7	6.2	11.8	20.8	9.2	5.6	12.0	26.4
1979–80	9.8	9.7	6.4	11.8	23.5	10.1	6.0	12.7	29.6
1980–81	10.6	10.6	6.2	12.3	22.9	10.6	6.5	13.4	28.9
1981–82	10.8	10.8	6.4	12.5	23.0	10.7	6.6	13.3	29.7
1982–83*	10.7	10.7	6.3	12.7	23.6	10.6	7.0	12.6	32.9
Associate Professors									
1972–73	16.3	15.8	12.3	17.4	24.3	17.2	12.9	19.1	34.3
1974–75	16.9	16.1	13.3	17.0	24.7	18.6	13.5	20.8	26.6
1976–77	17.6	17.3	13.8	17.7	26.6	18.3	14.4	20.0	28.5
1979–80	19.4	19.1	16.2	18.9	29.4	20.3	16.6	21.6	42.7
1980–81	20.6	20.4	16.7	20.3	29.8	21.1	17.6	22.4	42.3
1981–82	21.5	21.3	17.6	21.0	31.7	21.9	18.8	23.0	40.7
1982–83*	22.0	21.9	17.9	22.0	33.0	22.3	19.4	23.3	35.8

Assistant Professors

1972–73	23.8	23.7	20.0	24.7	31.3	24.1	19.0	25.7	41.3
1974–75	27.1	27.0	24.4	27.6	33.8	27.3	22.4	28.7	43.2
1976–77	30.3	30.4	27.6	30.7	35.8	30.1	26.2	31.4	46.0
1979–80	33.9	33.8	31.1	34.5	38.6	34.2	30.0	35.4	52.9
1980–81	35.3	35.2	31.3	35.9	40.3	35.4	30.7	37.2	51.2
1981–82	35.9	35.8	31.8	36.8	40.9	36.1	30.9	40.0	51.3
1982–83*	36.1	35.9	30.7	37.7	41.6	36.5	32.2	37.9	49.8

Instructors

1972–73	39.9	39.2	44.4	44.0	35.1	42.5	41.0	41.5	53.8
1974–75	40.6	39.4	49.6	47.7	34.2	46.5	44.8	46.2	51.0
1976–77	50.6	61.1	53.8	51.5	48.1	49.5	48.6	49.0	59.4
1979–80	51.8	52.1	55.7	52.7	47.7	51.0	48.6	51.0	57.4
1980–81	52.8	58.3	56.0	53.7	50.7	51.5	49.6	51.6	56.3
1981–82	53.3	54.3	56.6	54.7	52.1	51.2	47.2	51.5	59.1
1982–83*	51.7	52.2	54.6	52.1	50.8	50.6	50.6	50.1	56.9

Lecturers

1972–73	34.9	35.1	30.3	40.2	51.2	34.2	29.1	38.1	52.9
1974–75	39.8	39.5	36.3	43.8	50.0	40.5	35.9	46.2	91.7
1976–77	40.8	41.1	40.9	39.7	54.6	39.6	36.3	43.6	87.5
1979–80	44.7	45.3	44.4	46.4	46.1	45.2	42.1	49.9	—
1980–81	46.5	46.2	45.8	45.2	54.8	47.3	46.1	46.9	90.0
1981–82	47.1	47.4	47.3	46.2	55.9	45.7	47.3	43.3	70.0
1982–83*	47.5	47.4	46.1	47.2	57.7	47.7	48.5	46.4	55.6

No Academic Rank

1972–73	32.8	32.3	23.4	38.8	32.4	34.7	10.0	30.1	40.6
1974–75	34.3	34.0	39.1	39.9	33.7	35.5	10.0	30.8	44.5
1976–77	34.8	34.5	53.1	46.5	34.2	37.6	42.7	35.1	40.2
1979–80	34.3	33.8	38.6	33.3	33.8	42.4	40.8	36.9	48.8
1980–81	36.1	35.7	40.3	36.0	35.7	40.4	40.1	33.3	46.7
1981–82	36.4	36.1	43.2	39.8	36.0	39.8	42.2	33.4	46.2
1982–83*	36.5	36.2	37.3	36.3	36.2	38.7	45.5	31.4	44.6

Source: Betty M. Vetter and Eleanor L. Babco, *Professional Women and Minorities* (Washington, DC: Commission on Professionals in Science and Technology, 1986), p. 123.

*Includes both 9- and 12-month contracts.

Table 11.4   Trends in Percentage of Faculty Tenured: 1975–1976 to 1985–1986

	1975–1976	1977–1978	1979–1980	1981–1982	1985–1986
Men	64%	66%	71%	70%	69%
Women	46	45	53	48	47

Sources: National Center for Education Statistics; "Annual Report on the Economic Status of the Profession 1985–86," *Academe,* Bulletin of the AAUP, March-April 1986.

Table 11.5   Academic Salaries: 1972–1973 to 1986–1987

	Assistant Professor		Percentage of Men's Salary	Full Professor		Percentage of Men's Salary
Year	Men	Women		Men	Women	
1972–73	$12,190	$11,510	94%	$19,405	$17,122	88%
1975–76	$14,154	$13,506	95	$22,866	$20,257	88
1979–80	$17,712	$16,971	96	$28,653	$25,910	90
1982–83	$22,586	$21,130	94	$35,956	$32,221	90
1986–87	$28,910	$26,180	90	$46,070	$40,630	88

Sources: National Center for Education Statistics, *Digest of Education Statistics, 1987* (Washington, DC: NCES, 1987), p. 159; and *Chronicle of Higher Education,* July 15, 1987.

tials are widest in the natural sciences as a group compared with the social sciences, arts, and humanities.

According to a survey conducted by Minter and Associates and reported in the *Chronicle of Higher Education,* the salary differentials by broad fields in 1982–1983 were:

Field	Men	Women	Percentage of Men's Salary
Arts	$24,456	$22,657	93%
Humanities	$25,494	$22,184	87
Social Sciences	$26,896	$25,177	94
Natural Sciences	$27,850	$22,601	81

In the sections that follow we examine more closely the specific factors that have affected the progress of women and the extent to which discrimination is a factor. Minority representations on faculties, both male and female, have improved only slightly since the mid 1970s.

Factors Affecting the Progress of Faculty Women

What explains the degree of progress of academic women during the 1970s? What factors have facilitated and what factors have hindered their advancement? In order to provide some answers to these questions, we draw on detailed information collected from academic personnel at 92 institutions in both 1972 and 1980. This sample includes 22 universities, 58 four-year colleges, and 12 two-year colleges. The 1972 survey was conducted by the American Council on Education and the 1980 survey was conducted by the Higher Education Research Institute at UCLA. The sample size for 1972 was 13,487 and for 1980 it was 9,039.

Hiring Patterns

During the 1970s there was significant progress in the representation of women among new hires and among all academic personnel in these 92 institutions. In 1972 women accounted for 14.4 percent of the academic personnel and by 1980 their representation had increased to 18.1 percent, an increase of about one fourth. While women constituted only 16.7 percent of all new hires between 1967 and 1972, the proportion rose to 24.5 percent between 1975 and 1980, an increase of nearly one half. Furthermore, by 1980 women were faring better with respect to hiring at universities and highly selective institutions, although the overall representation by type of institution still favors men.

Teaching and Research

If we look at the research versus teaching activities of women at academic institutions in 1980, we find that women still lagged behind men, although the difference had narrowed somewhat since 1972. In 1972, 14.5 percent of women compared with 7.7 percent of men spent more than 17 hours in the classroom. The 1980 cohort of women continued to teach more hours than men, but only 10.9 percent of women compared with 7.5 percent of men spent more than 17 hours in the classroom. Past research has demonstrated the fact that women faculty spend a disproportionate amount of time on teaching compared with men, who devote more time to research. This disadvantages women in terms of their scholarly productivity. However, despite the disproportionate time spent on teaching, there was indeed a rise between 1972 and 1980 in the proportion of women faculty who received some type of support for research. For example, in 1972, 38 percent of women and 62 percent of men reported having funds for research. By 1982 these percentages increased to 53 percent and 69 percent, respectively.

Academic Rewards: Salary and Rank

To what extent has progress been made in academe in reducing inequities in regard to rank and salary? Studies prior to 1972 indicate a great disparity between men and women faculty members with respect to the distribution of rewards. In particular, studies based on 1969 and 1972 national surveys of colleges and university faculty conducted by Helen Astin and Alan Bayer examined sex differentials in rank, tenure, and salary, controlling for relevant variables.[2] These studies found that women faculty members of similar background, achievement, and work settings as men held positions approximately one fifth of a step below their counterparts. To achieve equity in rank would require an average compensatory increase from slightly below to slightly above the assistant professor level. To award women faculty the same salary as men of similar rank and other variables would require an average raise of $1,000. This is the amount of actual salary discrimination identified as not attributable to discrimination in rank. Based on analyses of the cohort in 1980, women were still receiving disproportionately low rewards in terms of rank and salary.[3] In 1980 overall median salaries were higher for both men and women, but women still earned only 77 percent of men's salaries. This discrepancy varies greatly by type of institution. At universities, particularly at the full professor level, the differential has narrowed somewhat. By 1980 women full professors at universities earned 90 percent of men's salaries compared with 83 percent in 1972.

Salary differentials in 1980 were also explored by comparing predicted and actual salaries for single and married women faculty, using the weights derived from a regression analysis that predicted the salaries for men faculty. The predicted mean salary is based on a regression equation that takes into account the factors that are significant predictors of men's salaries, such as highest degree obtained, publication record, field, and type of employer institution. The regression analysis for the 1980 data, based on teaching faculty only, indicated that salary inequities are declining. The actual salary for married women was $1,622 less than predicted salary, while the actual salary for single women was $1,895 less. In 1980 the differences were lower. The actual salary for single women was $1,080 less than the predicted salary and for married women it was $421 less than predicted.

With regard to tenure, evidence from the 1972 and 1980 sample data indicates that once in the system, women are not advancing as fast as men. The proportion of tenured men increased by 17.7 percentage points, from 68.5 percent in 1972 to 86.2 percent in 1980. Over the same years the proportion of women faculty with tenure increased by only 13.4 percentage points, from 54.6 percent to 68.0 percent. In 1982–1983, as shown in Table 11.3, women in higher education institutions overall constituted 52 percent of instructors and 36 percent of assistant professors but only 22 percent of associate professors and 11 percent of full professors.

In two other areas related to the tangible reward structure in academe, outside consulting and number of job offers, women have made significant advances. In 1980, compared with 1972, higher proportions of both men and women reported outside paid consulting, 51 and 40 percent, respectively. This represents an increase of 9 percent for men and 12 percent for women. Fewer faculty members, both men and women, reported receiving job offers in 1980 than in 1972, but the decline was greater for men than for women. In 1972 38 percent of men versus 39 percent of women reported having "an outside firm offer," whereas the proportions in 1980 were 27 percent for men and 30 percent for women. The higher proportion for women in both years clearly reflects affirmative action efforts.

Research Productivity

Generally, rewards such as rank and salary are based largely on productivity, and women's lower status in academe has often been attributed to the lower scholarly productivity of women. Thus, it is important to identify the factors that can act to inhibit or facilitate the research productivity of women compared with men and to determine whether the same inhibitors and facilitators existed in 1980 as in 1972.

An analysis of research productivity for women faculty in 1972 indicates that indeed there is a difference in productivity rates in favor of men. In this connection it is interesting to note that there is no difference in the productivity of single and married women. Single and married women published about the same number of books and articles for all fields combined; in some fields married women published somewhat more than single women. Further evidence that rank as such directly influences productivity is provided in a 1980 study of highly productive social science academics conducted by Helen Astin and Diane Davis.[4] They found that the number of articles and books published by single and married women as well as by men increased as rank increased. Thus, the relationship between rank and productivity holds regardless of sex or marital status. However, in general, the number of articles published by men was slightly greater than by married and single women at all ranks, while the number of articles published by married women was greater than that of single women at all ranks. These findings lead us to look more closely at what determines productivity patterns, particularly for women. Being married generally has been identified as a major inhibitor to productivity; yet the data for a 1980 sample of faculty across all disciplines and within a subsample of highly productive social scientists indicate otherwise. In fact, for women, being single was negatively correlated with productivity for both the full sample and the highly productive subsample. Hence, we are forced to look at other factors besides marital status that may influence productivity.

Facilitators and Barriers to Productivity

In order to identify the factors that acted as facilitators or barriers to productivity, a regression analysis was carried out on the 1980 sample of over 9,000 faculty members at 92 institutions. It was found that the factors associated with increased productivity for both men and women were being young; having higher rank; having one's highest degree in the health sciences; coming to the university with previous employment in nonacademic research, nonacademic administration, university teaching, or having been at a postdoctoral position; spending more time on research and writing than does the typical academic; having substantial funds or outside resources for research; subscribing to more journals than does the average academic; and spending more days off campus. At the same time, there were some factors that differentiated women from men. For example, while being at a selective university was a facilitator for men, it was not for women. Also, while spending time advising students or consulting outside the university was positively associated with men's productivity, it was not the case with women.

We get further information about the different influences affecting the productivity of men and women by looking at the factors that emerged as barriers. The most striking difference is that being single was a barrier to women's productivity, but not to men's. Furthermore, for women, coming to university directly from a student status was a barrier to productivity, but it was not so for men.

How can the barrier of being single be interpreted? A possible interpretation is that women without a male partner are more likely to be excluded from the "boys" network, important connections and critical information, to a greater extent than are married women. A second possibility is that a subtle discrimination operates against single women.

That is, a perception exists that single women are different from the model academic who is a married man. Thus, singlehood, particularly for women, may be feared and misinterpreted, and that may further isolate and keep women out of the circles of male scholars.

To examine these issues further, we examined the data collected from the subsample of highly productive academics. Members of this subsample were asked to identify in their own words what made it possible for them to be productive or what impeded their research productivity. The open-ended responses by the survey participants were coded into 16 categories reflecting facilitators and 12 categories of inhibitors—obstacles to productivity.

An examination of facilitators listed by this sample identifies two items that differentiate the sexes significantly; motivation and support from spouse and/or family are both listed as important facilitators significantly more often by women. Another variable, having graduate students as assistants, was endorsed significantly more often by men. In order to assess differences based on major categories, we organized the 15 facilitators in two clusters: personal characteristics and organizational characteristics. An examination of sex differences under these two major clusters indicates that women are more likely to attribute their research productivity to "personal" variables such as hard work, being motivated, being interested in their research topic, and possessing the necessary skills to do the work. Men, on the other hand, tend to attribute their success to organizational factors and to having institutional resources such as time, student assistants, funds, and general resources.

Comparing men and women with regard to personal and organizational factors, we observe further differences. Under personal variables, men attribute success in research productivity to curiosity, valuing scholarship, and greater ambitions. Under organizational variables, women emphasize the importance of personal relationships such as having good colleagues, a supportive institutional environment, and a spouse or family that provides a facilitative structure.

The most significant conclusion from the analysis of facilitators is that women are less likely than men to endorse the importance of organizational and/or structural variables in enhancing their research or scholarly productivity. In view of the fact that most studies of research productivity have identified the organizational variables as critical, the question that arises is whether underutilization of institutional resources lowers the research productivity and visibility of women and, further, whether this underutilization is more the result of institutional barriers than lack of knowledge or personal choice on the part of the women.

To explore these possibilities, we turn to an examination of *inhibitors* in research productivity. Women differ significantly from men in their identification of limited availability of time because of family responsibilities, teaching loads, and administrative duties. Men attribute most of their problems to lack of funds, institutional support, or student assistance. So whereas men see limited resources as the primary inhibitors, women identify limitations that are the result of their participation in time-consuming activities that are expected of them, such as family, teaching, and committee work. What is interesting here is that men identify inhibitors which they have less personal control over, whereas women indicate situations and conditions where they could exercise greater control.

These findings highlight the importance of making women aware of how the organization and social structure influence research performance and how to take advantage of available institutional resources. Personal characteristics, however important, are not sufficient to ensure equity in the achievement of academic rewards.

Patterns of Productivity Over the Life Cycle

A critical question that has been raised in the literature on research productivity is the extent to which there are age differences in productivity and variations in productivity over the career cycle. Are there factors related to either the personal life cycle or professional career cycle of academics that are gender-specific and that have an impact in productivity? Among the sample of highly productive academics studied in 1980, it was found that although women's yearly productivity rate prior to achieving tenure was found to be significantly lower than that of men's, their rate after tenure was higher. Both men and women remained productive after tenure. Women's lower pretenure rate seems to be explained as much by the difference between single and married women as by their general status as women.

An examination of the productivity of 735 social scientists in the group as they progressed from assistant to associate to full professor sheds further light on these findings. Subgroup differences were examined for single and married women and for men[5] as they varied by numbers of published articles and books over time, as well as by the number of publications during the previous two years of the survey. The patterns of productivity observed were the same as those found in the 1972–1973 study by Astin and Bayer.[6] At the full professor level, married women are more productive than single women. Moreover, married women's productivity patterns are closer to those of married men than to those of single women; that is, married women's cumulative article publication rate is higher than that of single women and almost identical to that of married men.

These results support the hypothesis that marriage does not necessarily prevent women from publishing. In fact, the study indicates that married women may learn early on what they need in terms of commitment to maintain their research and publishing activities. It was observed that a smaller proportion of married women at the assistant professor level spend large amounts of their total time in teaching preparation compared with single women or married men. Further, married women at the assistant professor level tend to spend an amount of time on research and writing similar to that of married men.

While single women were found to have the lowest rates of article publication, they have the highest rates of book publication over their career span. This finding is particularly important because it signifies that single women are in fact publishing at high rates, but that the types of research or scholarly publication are different from those of men and married women.

There could be a number of reasons for this, some of which have important implications for understanding the "barriers" to productivity for women in academia. First, it may be that single women, who do not have family obligations and hence perceive themselves as having more time, may choose to devote their energies to large-scale efforts such as writing books rather than research articles which may be produced in a shorter time period. The fact that married men are also more likely than married women to publish books supports this notion, since having a spouse who usually takes care of household responsibilities might permit men to devote larger amounts of time and energy to the production of books.

Another interpretation may be that lack of access to funding sources leads single women to write books rather than reports and articles based on funded research. If we look at those with general research funds, it is indeed the case that the proportion of single women who have such funds is lower than that for married men and women. This may be a result of single women's limited access to important networks.

Single women at the assistant professor level are also more likely than married men or women at that stage to become involved in extra-departmental activities such as research and teaching in minority and women's studies programs and centers. Of course, one would expect women to become more involved than men in these activities, in part because of their desire to find structures or vehicles for advancement that are not dominated by men. Yet in the first and critical stage of the professional career, single women are twice as likely as married women to take on that kind of responsibility. Married women do become involved in those activities, but not until the later stages of their professional life when they are generally more established. In conclusion, then, it appears that the key to understanding differences in productivity patterns between men and women comes through taking a closer look at the academic activities and motivations of single women and married women separately. Although much research in the past has focused on the career difficulties of married women in academia, we have seen that married women follow the career patterns of men more closely than do single women.[7] Furthermore, the findings about differences in article and book publication of married and single women and men indicate that gender differences in productivity patterns are more complex than they may initially appear. These complex relationships can be understood only by looking at variations in the types of publications produced as well as different stages in the academic career. With this new information about gender differences in productivity patterns, it is important to look more closely at the reward structure in order to determine whether men and women indeed receive equal rewards, both monetary and nonmonetary, for productivity.

Research Productivity and Reputation

One of the critical academic rewards to publication achievements is reputational standing. In order to analyze the relationship between productivity and reputations, a study was conducted of a subsample of 52 highly productive social scientists who were surveyed in 1980.[8] Reputational standing was measured in several ways, some of which were objective (other persons' perceptions) and some subjective (self-assessment). The reputational indices included citation information, self-reported visibility scores, and externally granted honors. Citation information (the number of pieces cited, the total number of citations, and the number of citations of a self-reported most important published piece) was collected from the 1982 *Citation Index*. Self-reported visibility scores were obtained through a survey questionnaire administered in the summer of 1982 which asked respondents to place themselves on a scale of one to five, with five being the most highly visible. Externally granted honors were a composite measure of information about honors and awards received, as listed in *Who's Who of American Men and Women in Science* (1980). Analysis of the relationship between types of productivity and reputation revealed that the total number of book chapters published is the form of productivity most strongly correlated with the reputation measures used.

The finding seems entirely plausible when we take account of the process and significance of chapter publication in academia. Unlike articles, the primary way that chapters are published is through solicitation by the editor of a book. Thus, inherent in the idea of a published chapter is the notion of reputation or visibility, since the author must be known to the person compiling the book. Second, chapters are often reprints of particularly well-received or notable articles. In other words, they are the "cream" of published articles. It is noteworthy that the number of pieces cited was the only measure of reputation that could be predicted by the quality of the institution where employed, a factor which much research has contended is a general contributor to the reputation. One would have expected that honors and other external rewards might have been so related.

Previous research has shown gender to be an important variable in explaining differentials in productivity and reputational standing. In his study of women scientists, Jonathan Cole reports a negative relationship between female gender and reputational standing. Moreover, he finds that the greatest negative effect of gender relates to men and women who have been most prolific in their research activities.[9] Davis and Astin, on the other hand, did not find that gender was a significant factor in any of the indices of reputation analyzed, even among the most productive. There are two possible explanations for the difference in research results. One is the difference in the historical and social context of the two studies. The Cole study applies to women scientists and their careers between 1957 and 1975, whereas the Davis and Astin study applies to social scientists surveyed in 1980. All indications are that there was a reduction in gender discrimination between the two periods, which would certainly affect the observed relationship between productivity and reputation. Davis and Astin also note that the development of the "new" scholarship about women during the 1970s expanded research and publication opportunities for women. A sizable proportion of the women in their sample, fully 59 percent, have done at least some research on women's issues. New scholarly journals and heightened interest on the part of publishers have provided outlets for such work, thus increasing citations and visibility. This factor then further contributes to the cohort differences between the two samples.

Conclusions

The findings reported in this chapter suggest that academic women are making progress, albeit slowly. Their representation on faculties has increased, their research is gaining recognition, and they are generally becoming more visible. There is, however, a continuing salary gap, and overall there is much unfinished business.

Although women have been hired in greater numbers, in compliance with affirmative action requirements, they have by and large not been welcomed by the male faculty. Women faculty members, and single women in particular, are clearly outside the male network. They do not have the same access to information about institutional research resources and opportunities. They bear a disproportionate share of departmental teaching loads, for which there is little credit under the existing academic reward structure, notwithstanding the lip service that is paid to good teaching. Those who have contributed to the development of the new scholarship on women have tended to be penalized rather than rewarded when it comes to tenure decisions.

The analysis in this chapter suggests that we need to know more about the life styles and careers of single versus married academic women and how both compare with those of men. Institutions would then be in a better position to determine what constitutes a hospitable climate not only for women but for all of their faculty.

Notes

1. Howard R. Bowen and Jack H. Schuster, *American Professors* (New York: Oxford University Press, 1986), pp. 103–104.
2. Helen S. Astin and Alan E. Bayer, "Sex Discrimination in Academe," *Educational Record* (May 1972):101–118; and "Pervasive Sex Differences in the Academic Reward System: Scholarship, Marriage, and What Else?" in D. R. Lewis and W. E. Becker, Jr., eds., *Academic Rewards in Higher Education* (Cambridge, MA: Ballinger, 1979).
3. Helen S. Astin and Mary Beth Snyder, "Affirmative Action 1972–82: A Decade of Response," *Change*, July-August 1982, pp. 26ff.
4. Helen S. Astin and Diane Davis, "Research Productivity Across the Life and Career Cycles: Facilitators and Barriers for Women," in M. F. Fox, ed. *Scholarly Writing and Publishing: Issues, Problems and Solutions*, (Boulder, CO: Westview Press, 1985).
5. The productivity patterns for single men are not presented. We concentrate on a comparison of married men to single and married women for the following reasons. First, the total number of single men in the social sciences was much too low (2.5 percent) to be able to make generalizations from it. Moreover, we are interested here mainly in how women's productivity patterns compare with those of the dominant academic prototype: married men.
6. See also Helen S. Astin, "Factors Affecting Women's Scholarly Productivity," in Helen S. Astin and W. L. Hirsch, eds., *The Higher Education of Women: Essays in the Honor of Rosemary Park* (New York: Praeger, 1978).

7. Other studies have also shown that married women in academia have a higher rate of productivity than single women. One example is reported in Jonathan R. Cole, *Fair Science: Women in the Scientific Community* (New York: Free Press, 1979). Another is a study by Rita Simm, Shirley M. Clark, and K. Galway, "The Woman Ph.D.: A Recent Profile," *Social Problems* 15 (Fall 1967): 221–236. The former is concerned with men and women in the sciences and the latter with faculty members in the social sciences, humanities, and education.

8. Diane Davis and Helen S. Astin, "Reputational Standing in Academe," *Journal of Higher Education* 58 (May-June 1987):261–275.

9. Cole, *Fair Science*, p. 103.

12

Women's Groups
in Professional Associations

To an extent not generally appreciated, women's groups in professional associations have played a strategic role in the advancement of women in higher education. They have functioned as pressure groups on behalf of academic women, with two primary goals—to improve the professional status of women and to encourage scholarly research on women. The origin and development of these groups beginning in the late 1960s was first chronicled by Kay Klotzberger in her essay in *Academic Women on the Move*. There were at that time some 50 such groups which had been formed between 1968 and 1971. Today, there are well over 100, ranging across the academic disciplines and professional fields.[1] The purpose of this chapter is to describe the nature of these groups, to examine their activities, and to assess their achievements.

Functions and Structural Characteristics

Women's groups in professional associations include caucuses, committees, and commissions. In addition, some disciplines have independent associations of women. Although these groups have many objectives in common, they differ in structural characteristics and methods of operation. Caucuses are organized by women in the profession, whereas committees and commissions are officially established by the associations. Caucuses may be informal or formal in structure and may operate inside or outside the association, but the important point is that they are independently governed and supported rather than dependent on the parent association.[2]

Historically, caucuses preceded association committees, although this was not always the case. Typically, women in the association formed a caucus to press for change, and the caucus was then followed or superseded by a committee on the status of women formally constituted by the association. In some associations, however, these committees were established without the prior formation of a caucus, and this pattern became more common once the need for such committees became more widely accepted. The pathbreaking caucus groups were those in the sociology, history, political science, psychology, and modern language associations. During the 1970s most associations established committees or commissions on the status of women, and this is now the most prevalent form among professional women's groups. At the same time, there are independent women's groups within professional fields that function separately from the central association: for example, the Association for Women in Psychology, the Coordinating Committee on Women in the Historical Profession, the Association for Women in Science, and Sociologists for Women in Society. These groups are more activist in orientation than are the commissions on the status of women, although the two groups usually work in collaboration. In some fields there are also special groups for minority women—for example, the Association of Black Women Historians.

The main function of the committees of the associations initially was to achieve equity for women in the association and in the profession at large, but they have not limited their activities to this end. They have devoted efforts also to issues of sex bias in research and the curriculum. The objectives of the independent women's groups include other concerns as well, those involving issues of social responsibility and political action on behalf of women. Women's groups have played a critical role in the evolution of women's studies. In the political arena, professional women's groups supported the activities of the larger women's movement, particularly in the drive for passage of the Equal Rights Amendment (ERA). For example, during the 1970s professional associations, under pressure from their caucuses and committees, voted to hold meetings only in states that had ratified the ERA.

Influencing Professional Associations

The initial activity of professional women's groups was, of course, the formation of the caucus itself, however informal. The caucus provided essential mutual support and a channel of communication among concerned women. Following the example of the women's caucus of the American Sociological Association, led by Alice Rossi, the first order of business was to carry out a study of the status of women in the profession or to recommend to the association that a committee on the status of women be established. During the brief period from 1969 to 1972, approximately 30 studies on women in academic disciplines were conducted or sponsored by women's caucuses, committees, or independent associations.[3] Most such studies were carried out during the early 1970s and clearly documented pervasive patterns of discrimination and the need for remedial action.

Nearly all academic disciplines now have standing committees on the status of women. Similar groups or offices exist in educational associations such as the American Association of University Professors (AAUP) and the American Association for Higher Education. The AAUP Committee W on the Status of Women was first established in 1918, retired after ten years, and reactivated in 1970.[4] In addition to Committee W at the national level, local AAUP chapters across the country organized Committee Ws, which then proceeded to press universities to conduct campus-wide surveys on the status of women on their faculty and in their research institutes.[5] Institutional surveys were carried out at major research universities such as Chicago, Berkeley, Harvard, Illinois, Indiana, Columbia, and Stanford. Associations other than the AAUP also maintain local or regional committees on women.

Although academic women first organized in the social sciences and humanities, they were soon followed by women in the natural sciences. One of the earliest of the scientific women's activist organizations was the Association for Women in Science (AWIS). It was formally organized in 1971 as an independent caucus of biomedical scientists and then expanded to include all scientific disciplines.[6] AWIS now has 4,000 members and a number of local chapters. There are now also numerous committees within scientific associations—for example, the Committee on the Status of Women in Physics of the American Physical Society, founded in 1973, and the Committee on the Status of Women of the American Astronomical Society, founded in 1978.

In addition to initiating university surveys, these women's groups have sought better representation among the officers of the association, greater participation in the annual meeting program, and a more significant role in the editorial policies of the association journals. In these efforts they have been largely successful. In some cases it was sufficient simply to raise the awareness of officials of the need to include women on a slate of candidates. More often the groups produced the names of eligible women. Occasionally, they have nominated by petition. For example, women in the 26,000-member Modern Language Association found that it took only 50 signatures for a petition candidate to be accepted. Women in the American Psychological Association were successful in increasing their representation on the 12-member Board of Directors from zero in 1975 to four in 1986, and they made similar gains in standing committees and the governance structure in general.[7]

With regard to journal publication policies, women in associations have worked to institute anonymous review of articles, citing evidence based on research that women have a better chance of having their paper accepted when referees do not know the identity of the author.[8] Some disciplines had a blind review procedure before the 1970s; others have responded to pressure from women's groups and changed their practices. Blind refereeing is now common procedure in most disciplines, with exceptions mainly in the natural sciences. Caucuses and committees have also conducted studies of the participation of women in the manuscript review process. The Committee on Women in Psychology organized a workshop on the subject for the annual convention of the association in 1982.

At annual meetings, women have perceptibly increased their appearance on programs. Women's groups have also argued for provision of childcare facilities at their meeting, and by the mid-1980s about two thirds of the associations provided this service.

Effecting Change

The activities described thus far relate to efforts to influence professional associations. These are part of the broader effort of academic women's groups to effect change in the discipline at large, a considerably more difficult task. The effort covers a wide range of activities focusing on two main concerns—equity in employment and sex bias in research and curriculum content; or, to put it another way, affirmative action, on the one hand, and women's studies, on the other. Of the two areas, the women's studies efforts have clearly been more successful.

Although the gains in affirmative action have not been large, it is doubtful that they could have been achieved at all without the activities of the women's caucuses and committees. What are some of these activities? Almost all of the groups have conducted surveys of departments in their fields to determine the number and proportion of women at various faculty and administrative ranks. (The Committee on the Status of Women in Physics referred to the resulting tabulation as "the Zeros

Table.") These surveys have been used not only to raise the awareness of the underrepresentation of women, but to monitor subsequent progress toward equity. The Committee on the Status of Women of the American Sociological Association, as part of its report in 1983, included an assessment of the progress of women in departmental positions during the 1970s. The data presented showed a slight improvement between 1970 and 1981 in both faculty and administrative positions. Nevertheless, the basic structure of gender inequality remained, and women continued to be underrepresented relative to their number and proportion in the available pool of sociologists.[9] Women were shown not only to be underrepresented as faculty members, but also underrepresented as department chairs relative to their numbers on the faculty. This was particularly true with graduate faculties, and even more so in the larger and more prestigious departments. In graduate departments women in 1981 still represented a small minority in administrative positions overall, including directors of graduate study.

Based on these results, the Committee on the Status of Women in Sociology drew up a set of guidelines to assist departments in improving the representation of women on their faculties. The guidelines were approved by the Council of the American Sociological Association and issued in 1984. The guidelines also set departmental hiring goals for 1990 in the following terms:

> Given the current availability of Ph.D. sociologists, women could reasonably comprise at least 23% of the tenured faculty in sociology departments by 1990. This figure therefore should serve as a target for departments as they hire and promote during the next six years. Moreover, since nearly half of the new Ph.D.s granted annually are now received by women, who are thus available for recruitment and appointment, departments should anticipate that half of their assistant professor appointments between now and 1990 would go to women.[10]

Other associations, such as the American Historical Association, also issue guidelines for hiring women faculty based on the reports and recommendations of their women's committees. In its 1983 report on women faculty, the association identified departments that were shown to take affirmative action seriously. A somewhat different approach was used in anthropology. The Committee on the Status of Women in Anthropology (COSWA) of the American Anthropological Association proposed a resolution that was passed by the association in 1972 calling on all departments of anthropology to initiate or continue fair practices of hiring and promotion to bring the number of women in all ranks to a level that reflects the proportion of women to men in the profession. At the end of a five-year period, 1972–1977, departments that failed to comply with the resolution were subject to censure by the association. COSWA was charged with monitoring compliance with the resolution. The report of the committee in 1977 resulted in a controversy and delay within the administration of the association, but eventually five departments were censured, and a new resolution was passed in 1981 continuing the assessment procedure for another five years beginning in 1982–1983.[11] In the four years following their censure, three of the five departments named hired women, although it is not clear whether public censure was a factor in the change.

Another way in which professional women sought to promote the implementation of affirmative action policies was through the creation of rosters of scholars in their discipline. The rosters were perceived as an instrument for achieving equal employment opportunity and as aids in identifying women as candidates for appointments to advisory committees or review boards. Many women's groups established such rosters, as did minority groups. Rosters are usually lists of individuals containing information about their qualifications, including degrees, position, field of specialization, and other pertinent information. Although there are few examples in which job placements were made directly from rosters, the rosters did serve as a starting point from which further inquiries could be made. They are also useful to show the size of the availability pool.[12]

In order to assist women in their profession, caucuses and committees have also sponsored career advancement, workshops coaching women on résumé writing, interviewing techniques, getting papers published, and strategies for achieving tenure. Some have prepared survival handbooks for graduate students and new faculty members, covering such things as mentoring relationships, dealing with sexual harassment, or funding research. Committee W of the AAUP drafted policy statements on nepotism rules, parental leave, affirmative action, and other matters, statements that were adopted by the association and promulgated as operating policy.

While pursuing vigorous affirmative action efforts, the caucuses and committees of professional associations have also been concerned with the discipline as such and the treatment of women in research, teaching, and practice. They played an important role in the evolution of women's studies, particularly in the early stages when they provided a support structure and a network through which academic women could be kept informed and their efforts coordinated. They have encouraged scholarly research on women and have pushed for sessions on women at annual meetings. Such sessions, once rare, are now quite widespread throughout the associations. The Modern Language Association Commission on the Status of Women was instrumental in the publication and dissemination of a series of women's studies guides in the early 1970s when the field was in its infancy. These guides provided valuable information about course titles, syllabi, program descriptions, and bibliographies.[13] The Committee on Women Historians of the American Historical Association sponsored two summer institutes in women's history for high school teachers, funded by the National Endowment for the Humanities. One was held at Sarah Lawrence in 1977 and the other at Stanford University in 1978. The Committee on the Status of Women of the American Political Science Association designed and produced a series of instructional units called "Women and American Government: Correcting and Improving Students' Knowledge about the Political Contributions, Skills and Interests of Women." The units, which are intended for general class use, were written by a special task force, financed by the Fund for the Improvement of Post-Secondary Education.

In some professional associations, women's groups have lobbied successfully for the establishment of women's studies as a new area of specialization. Among the foremost examples are the Division of the Psychology of Women (Division 35), which was formed in the American Psychological Association in 1973; the Special Interest Group/Research on Women and Education of the American Educational Research Association; and the Division on Women's Studies in Language and Literature, which was organized in the Modern Language Association in 1975.[14]

Substantial contributions to the development of women's studies were also made by separate groups of professional women, operating independently or in coordination with the parent association. History is a case in point. The Berkshire Conference of Women Historians has held a series of conferences since 1973 for presentations of research on women's history. The meetings have been held on women's college campuses and have drawn upwards of 2,000 scholars, not only historians but also scholars from other disciplines. The Coordinating Committee on Women in the Historical Profession (CCWHP), which was formed at the 1969 meeting of the American Historical Association, included among its goals the development of women's history as a branch of historical study. CCWHP sponsors conferences and other major projects relating to women's history. For example, the Metropolitan New York chapter of CCWHP launched the Institute for Research in History in 1975 as an independent community of scholars engaged in historical research and writing. The institute has a special commitment to the promotion of scholarship among women historians and to the support of research in women's history. Its publication program includes a series of monographs on women and history.

In addition to matters of career advancement, scholarly research, and the curriculum, professional women's groups have been concerned with issues of sexism in the application of their discipline to public policy and practice. Two cases are illustrative of activities in these areas. Beginning with the 1980 census, the Census Bureau no longer uses the designation "head of household" in its data collection. Instead, the census questionnaire asks for the identity of the person "in whose name the dwelling unit is owned or rented." The change was made in response to several years of agitation by a group of feminist sociologists, economists, demographers, and psychologists organized as Social Scientists for Population Research. In the past, married women (and children under age 16) were considered ineligible to be considered head of household. The social scientists who argued for the change were concerned that the term "head of household" perpetuated the notion of a male authority figure in households where a husband was present. It was also pointed out that the term was imprecise and did not conform to the changing public perception of a family head.[15] In another arena, the Committee on Women in Psychology has been actively concerned with sexism in mental health diagnosis and practice. In 1985 the committee directed a public education campaign that prevented the addition of new misogynistic diagnoses to the Diagnostic and Statistical Manual of the American Psychiatric Association.[16] The proposed additions would have included premenstrual syndrome and self-defeating personalities as psychiatric disorders. Feminists objected to the former on the ground that it would stigmatize women with menstrual problems as psychiatrically disturbed when their problems might be more biological. They objected to the latter on the ground that it might wrongly ascribe a self-defeating personality disorder to individuals who are trapped through no fault of their own in situations in which they can be mistreated or fail.[17]

The Concerns of Minority Women

Professional women's groups have been sensitive to the need to include minority women in their efforts, but few at first had special programs to address their particular concerns. At least part of the difficulty had to do with lack of data. Studies of the status of women in the various disciplines relied heavily on information in the Doctorate Records File of the National Research Council. Data on women have been part of the file since its starting point in 1920, but information on minorities has been collected only since 1973.[18] Information on minority doctorate recipients in 1973 and 1974 is incomplete, and reliable data are not available until 1975. That is considerably later than the time when most caucuses and commissions initiated surveys on the status of women.

While minority women in the professions have the same problems as do other women, their needs are more acute. Because of their small numbers in most disciplines, they face conditions of greater isolation and lack of influence. In order to increase their status in the profession, minority groups place a higher priority than do women's groups in general on increasing their numbers. They support efforts to recruit minority scholars in high school, produce promotional films and brochures, provide information on job opportunities, create job rosters for minority students, and establish student-mentor relationships.

Minority women do, of course, participate in the minority caucuses, but as in the women's caucuses they perceive themselves as lacking in influence. They view minority caucuses as dominated by men. Usually there are separate groups representing women's interests and minority interests, but one case in which the concerns of women and minorities are combined in a single committee is the Committee on the Status of Women and Minorities of the American Philological Association. The situation of minority women is further complicated by the fact that they represent different ethnic and racial groups, mainly black, Hispanic, Native American, and Asian. Their needs do not always coincide, and mutual support systems among them are difficult to organize. Special efforts to establish networks of minority women have been made by the Office of Opportunities in Science at the American Association for the Advancement of Science. This office, established in 1973, has from the outset been concerned with women and minorities jointly, first under the direction of Janet Welsh Brown and later under Shirley Mahaley Malcom. In 1975 the office sponsored a conference of minority women in science which provided an opportunity to share experiences and articulate their needs.[19] On the recommendation of the conference participants, the office subsequently established the National Network of Minority Women in Science, a group consisting of 320 members at latest count (1984). The principal other discipline-oriented minority women's group is the Association of Black Women Historians, founded in 1978, which was originally an outgrowth of the Association for the Study of Afro-American Life and History; it now has a membership of 50, drawn from several associations of historians. This figure is indicative of the problem of small numbers, of which minority women are so keenly aware.

Most associations do not have separate committees for minority women's concerns. They may be covered, however, by special programs and projects of the overall women's groups. For example, the Committee on Women in Psychology has made one of its priorities to increase the visibility and participation of ethnic minority women. Toward this end it has published a *Directory of Hispanic Women in Psychology* (1983) and a *Directory of Black Women in Psychology* (1984). Other such efforts can be expected in the future as minority women increase in number and influence.

Lesbian Groups

Women's groups in professional associations include some that are lesbian in orientation. Until the civil rights movement was extended to cover discrimination on the basis of sexual preference, lesbian women were seldom visible as such. They have been active, however, along with other women in the work of the caucuses and commissions whether or not they have made their sexual preferences known. Academic women's groups have made a point of protecting the rights of all women, regardless of race or sexual preference. Nevertheless, as with minority women, lesbians have felt the need to form their own networks or organizations for mutual support. These networks and organizations are, for the most part, informal.

Formal committees and independent organizations for homosexual members have been established within about a dozen disciplines, primarily in social science and the humanities. The Gay and Lesbian Caucus of the Modern Language Association and the Committee on Gay and Lesbian Concerns of the American Psychological Association are two examples. However, these organizations tend to be dominated by men. Women are less active than men in mixed homosexual groups in part because they are greatly outnumbered there and in part because their concerns do not overlap sufficiently. Lesbians are interested not only in equity in employment but also in the inclusion of lesbian issues in women's studies.

Women's studies has created a climate hospitable to lesbian scholars and provided the conditions under which networks could be formed. At its founding meeting in 1977, the National Women's Studies Association established a lesbian caucus which is now one of the major constituencies of the organization. This caucus is interdisciplinary and serves as a network of lesbian scholars of diverse professional interests.[20] Through their own efforts and the support of women's groups in a number of other associations, lesbian issues have been able to make gains on the elimination of overt discrimination in employment and in the recognition, understanding, and acceptance of their concerns on the research agendas of the women's studies disciplines. Subtle discrimination continues, however, and many lesbians are still reluctant to "come out" in the professional environment. As a consequence, much of the mutual support among lesbians in academic life remains behind the scenes.

Educational Associations

In addition to the women's groups related to the scholarly associations, there are a number of women's organizations that represent other constituencies in higher education or women in higher education generally. These include:

American Association of University Women

American Association of Women in Junior and Community Colleges

Association of Black Women in Higher Education

National Association of Women Deans, Administrators, and Counselors

National Coalition for Women and Girls in Education

American Association for Higher Education: Women's Caucus

These are membership organizations that serve as mutual support networks, advocacy groups, and vehicles for career advancement.

The most common activity among these groups has been career advancement. For example, the National Association of Women Deans, Administrators, and Counselors has had sessions at its national meetings and articles in its quarterly journal on topics such as interpreting college budgets, acquiring computer literacy, and developing mentoring relationships as well as nuts-and-bolts topics such as preparing a résumé. The American Association of Women in Junior and Community Colleges has offered similar guidance. The Association of Black Women in Higher Education has run a job bank and has kept members informed on scholarship, fellowship, and internship opportunities. To further career advancement, some of the groups have offered training programs. The American Association for Women in Junior and Community Colleges has conducted a survey of women who have been unsuccessful candidates for positions as presidents or provosts to identify the skills that they are purported to lack. Based on this information, it has held programs for women to help build these skills.

In their capacity as advocacy groups, women's educational organizations have engaged in a variety of activities to increase the visibility of women in academic life and to raise public awareness of issues affecting women in higher education. The Women's Caucus within the American Association for Higher Education runs a program on women's concerns at the annual meeting of the association. The American Association of University Women (AAUW) holds conferences and conducts studies on subjects of concern to women in higher education, such as the representation of women on boards of trustees. In addition, AAUW provides extensive financial support to women for research at the doctoral and postdoctoral levels. The National Coalition for Women and Girls in Education, a Washington-based organization of 50 members, lobbies for educational equity in the public policy arena.

Coalition Building

The National Coalition for Women and Girls in Education, founded in 1975, provides an effective mechanism for close collaboration and joint efforts by advocacy groups. There is no similar mechanism for coordinated efforts among the discipline-oriented scholarly groups, although there is some exchange of information through informal channels. Two attempts were made during the 1970s to organize a coalition of such groups. The first was a Roster Coordination Project carried out in 1973–1974 under the auspices of the Office of Opportunities in Science of the AAAS. The purpose of the project was to coordinate the efforts of professional associations in the design and use of rosters of women and minorities. A survey and analysis of rosters was conducted, and the results were presented in a workshop of representatives from organizations maintaining rosters. The primary objective of the project was to develop an integrated system and common format for the collection of data. A further objective was to develop plans for continued coordination of activities through a national center or clearinghouse.

The importance of this project in assessing both the benefits and limitations of rosters is discussed in chapter 14. The national center, however, never materialized, owing in large part to lack of funding.

The second attempt was an effort in 1978 to establish a formal Coalition for Women in the Humanities and Social Sciences. The project came about as the follow-up to a conference of women's committees and caucuses that was sponsored by the Organization of American Historians, with financial support from the National Endowment for the Humanities. Over 125 delegates attended the three-day conference, including representatives from 46 professional groups. The purpose of the proposed coalition was to strengthen ties, facilitate exchange of information, and coordinate activities of women's groups. The director of the project was D'Ann Campbell, then chair of the OAH Committee on the Status of Women in the Historical Profession. As a first step it was proposed to develop a uniform questionnaire for a survey of the status of women, for use in monitoring progress toward equity in the various disciplines. Notwithstanding the support of the constituent groups for the uniform questionnaire survey, this project also failed to materialize when efforts to raise the necessary funding were not successful.

Future Goals

What is the current role of women's groups in professional associations and what are their goals for the 1980s? We have seen that most caucuses and committees came into being in the late 1960s and early 1970s and started their activities with basic studies of the status of women in their respective disciplines. They also pressed for and won greater representation in official positions of the associations, greater visibility in annual meeting programs, and greater influence in editorial policies. During the 1970s they monitored the progress of affirmative action efforts and publicized the results. Some committees issued guidelines for departments, providing hiring goals and information about resources and methods to aid in the recruitment of women faculty members. Throughout the 1970s women's caucuses and committees gave strategic support to the development of women's studies. During the latter part of the 1970s they began to give particular attention to the special needs of minority women and lesbians. All of this was accomplished with minimal budgets, seldom more than a few thousand dollars a year, provided either through the associations or from membership dues. On occasion, funding for specific projects was forthcoming from foundations or government agencies, but the amounts were usually small.

As they moved into the 1980s, women's groups and some associations began to take stock of progress in their profession, to assess the effectiveness of the strategies that had been employed to promote the advancement of women, and to identify new or continuing needs. The Committee on the Status of Women in the Economics Profession has commissioned a study to investigate why women have not progressed in the field as rapidly as men during the period between 1975 and 1985.[21] The Committee on Women in Psychology has undertaken a survey on what faculty members in the profession are working on women's studies. Committee W of the AAUP has undertaken a study of the extent to which faculty members who specialize in women's studies face discrimination in the tenure process.[22] These are all in-depth second-generation studies that build on the earlier work of the committees.

It seems clear that much would be gained by sharing information and coordinating activities across the disciplines. Earlier efforts at coalition building may well have been premature and a new effort in the 1980s might well succeed. The tasks of the committees and caucuses are by no means complete and they will not be easy. There is need for continued vigilance over hiring practices at a time when government enforcement of affirmative action has been weakened. It is also important to ensure that women are not left out of new faculty hiring in the 1990s, when an upturn is anticipated to meet replacement needs and the needs of an expanded college-age population. History tells us that increasing the number of qualified women is not sufficient to promote their advancement in the professions.[23]

Notes

1. Kay Klotzberger, "Political Action by Academic Women," in Alice Rossi and Ann Calderwood, eds., *Academic Women on the Move* (New York: Russell Sage Foundation, 1973); American Association of University Women, *Professional Women's Groups Providing Employment Assistance to Women* (Washington, DC: AAUP, 1983); and Michelle Aldrich and Alicia Leach, *Associations and Committees of or for Women in Science, Engineering, Mathematics and Medicine* (Washington, DC: Office of Opportunities in Science, American Association for the Advancement of Science, 1984).

2. There is some overlap in nomenclature among the various groups. Occasionally, caucuses called themselves committees.

3. Laura Morelock, "Discipline Variations in the Status of Academic Women," in Rossi and Calderwood, *Academic Women on the Move.*

4. A number of academic women's groups appear to have been formed in the immediate post–World War I period in part, at least, derived from the suffrage movement.

5. "Report of Committee W, 1970–1971," *AAUP Bulletin* (Summer 1971): 215–216.

6. Anne M. Briscoe, "Phenomenon of the Seventies: The Women's Caucuses," *Signs* 4, no. 1 (Autumn 1978):152–153.

7. Committee on Women in Psychology, *Women in the American Psychological Association 1986* (Washington, DC: American Psychological Association, 1986).

8. Committee on the Status of Women in the Economics Profession, *Newsletter*, May 1986.

9. Bonnie Thornton Dill, Evelyn Nakano Glenn, and Bettina J. Huber, "Women in Departmental Administrative Positions," *ASA Footnotes* 2 (August 1983):10–11.

10. Committee on the Status of Women in Sociology, American Sociological Association, *Guidelines for Incorporating Women Faculty into Departments of Sociology During the Eighties* (Washington, DC: ASA, 1984), p. 7.

11. For an account of the controversy over the COSWA report and the delays encountered in implementing it, see Roger Sanjek, "The American Anthropological Association Resolution on the Employment of Women: Genesis, Implementation, Disavowal, and Resurrection," *Signs* 7 (1982):845–868; and Naomi Quinn and Carol A. Smith, "A New Resolution of Fair Employment Practices for Women Anthropologists: Fresh Troops Arrive," *Signs* 7 (1982):869–877.

12. A further discussion of rosters and their use appears in chapter 14 on women in higher education administration.

13. The guides started with *Female Studies I,* edited by Sheila Tobias (Pittsburgh: KNOW, INC., 1970), and extended to *Female Studies X,* edited by Deborah Silverton Rosenfelt (Old Westbury, NY: Feminist Press 1975). The MLA Commission sponsored the earlier volumes in the series.

14. The activities of women's groups in the MLA and other associations with respect to women's studies are described in Florence Howe and Paul Lauter, *The Impact of Women's Studies on the Campus and the Disciplines* (Washington, DC: National Institute of Education, U.S. Department of Health, Education, and Welfare, 1980).

15. Committee on the Status of Women in the Economics Profession, *Newsletter,* Winter 1983.

16. Committee on Women in Psychology, *Women in the American Psychological Association,* p. 4.

17. *New York Times,* July 2, 1986.

18. National Research Council, *Summary Report 1985: Doctorate Recipients from United States Universities* (Washington, DC: National Academy Press, 1985), p. 12.

19. For a report of the conference proceedings, see Shirley Mahaley Malcom, Paula Quick Hall, and Janet Welsh Brown, *The Double Bind: The Price of Being a Minority Woman in Science* (Washington, DC: American Association for the Advancement of Science, 1976).

20. Margaret Cruikshank, *Lesbian Studies* (New York: Feminist Press, 1982), p. ix.

21. "Report of the Committee on the Status of Women in the Economics Profession," *American Economic Review* 76 (May 1986):452–457.

22. *Higher Education Daily* (Alexandria, VA), October 23, 1986, pp. 1–2.

23. This point is amply illustrated by Mary Roth Walsh, in "Academic Professional Women Organizing for Change: The Struggle in Psychology," *Journal of Social Issues* 41 (Winter 1985):17–27.

13

Research Centers

The emergence and development of women's studies as an area of teaching and research during the 1970s represents probably the most powerful force affecting women in higher education. In this period the isolated efforts of individual scholars were galvanized under the impetus of the women's movement to form organized curricula and research programs. The evolution of the "new scholarship about women," as it is also sometimes known, is nothing less than phenomenal, particularly when viewed against a background in which higher education generally was in a period of retrenchment. Notwithstanding the prevailing conditions of financial stringency, women's studies activities encompassing research, teaching, and publication have continued to flourish. Chapter 7 dealt with the teaching and curriculum aspects of women's studies and the impact of women's studies on the mainstream liberal arts courses. Here we are concerned with research, its growth and institutionalization, and its applications beyond the curriculum.

The Evolution of Research About Women

Research about women is not in itself new; the study of women and sex roles can be traced back to the nineteenth century.[1] Historical work on the condition of women and their contributions to society first appeared in the 1830s, according to Gerda Lerner in *Teaching Women's History*.[2] This period coincided with the rise of the women's rights movement in the United States, which provided the inspiration for efforts to illumi-nate and document women's lives. The social sciences were not yet developed at that time, and social science research about women came later, dating from the late nineteenth century, when the new research universities were formed. In *Beyond Separate Spheres*, Rosalind Rosenberg describes the work of the female social scientists in those universities who pioneered the study of sex differences.[3] While none of these women are well known today, their ideas were carried forward by lead-ing women scholars such as Margaret Mead in a succeeding generation.

In the early decades of the twentieth century there was a resurgence of scholarly research concerning women, corresponding with the sec-ond wave of the women's rights movement and the drive for women's suffrage. Other contributing factors were the participation of women in World War I and their expanding role in the labor force. Attention was focused during this period on women's wages and working conditions, their education, and their role in the family, as well as their role in reform movements, settlement houses, and various philanthropic en-deavors. In addition to the efforts of individual scholars, studies were conducted by public agencies such as the Women's Bureau of the De-partment of Labor, which was founded in 1920. Studies about working women were also carried out by the Russell Sage Foundation, which was founded in 1907 as a private organization for social science research. Between 1910 and 1917 the Committee on Women's Work, functioning as an integral part of the foundation, conducted a series of major studies under the direction of Mary Van Kleeck on the conditions of employ-ment of women and girls in New York City.[4]

After 1920, when women won the right to vote, concern for women's issues dropped from public view until the 1960s when the new feminist movement emerged and took up the drive for full equality. During that period of four decades scholarly research about women maintained a low profile. Margaret Mead's work on sex roles was an exception. Nota-ble contributions were also made by Charles and Mary Beard to the study of women's role in history. Outside academic life, important theo-retical analysis was done by Simone de Beauvoir. Virginia Woolf's work was also a major influence on subsequent feminist thinking. The publi-cation of Betty Friedan's *The Feminine Mystique* in 1963 touched off a new wave of feminism that by 1970 was in full swing.

On-campus women's studies courses were established and scholarly research about women came to the fore, beginning a period of unprece-dented growth. This growth was made possible by the fact that there was in existence a larger cadre of women scholars in the humanities and social sciences than had ever before been available. Institutional facilities for research about women were scarce, however, and for the most part modest. Chief among them were the Schlesinger Library on the History of Women in America, which was established in 1943 at Radcliffe College, and the Bunting Institute, also at Radcliffe, which was established in 1960 as a center of independent scholarship by women. Elsewhere there were women's history archives, such as the Sophia Smith Collection at Smith College and the Gerritson Collection of Women's History at the Spencer Research Library of the University of Kansas.

Working with the resources available and with limited financial support, feminist scholars committed to the movement undertook studies documenting the widespread discrimination against women in public and private life. Published books and articles dealt extensively with discrimination in wages and employment practices, in education, in opportunities for professional advancement, in access to credit, and in political participation. They dealt also with the absence of women in decision-making positions, their absence or neglect in the study of history and other disciplines, and stereotypic treatment of women in the social sciences. As they delved further into the subject, they began to challenge traditional assumptions about women in their respective disciplines, notably in history, literature, sociology, psychology, and economics.

Among the pioneers in history was Joan Kelly, who questioned the traditional periodization of history and its applicability to women's experience. She pointed out, for example, that there was no renaissance for women during the Renaissance.[5] In sociology, Alice Rossi, in a landmark essay on equality between the sexes, challenged traditional concepts of women's roles in contemporary society and paved the way for the extensive research that followed.[6] In economics, pathbreaking work was done in the early 1970s by Carolyn Shaw Bell, who exposed the fallacy of the assumption of the conventional family as consisting of a single breadwinner, a nonworking spouse, and an average of two children.[7] Her work had widespread implications for economic policy and theories of labor market participation rates.

Feminist scholarship, while espoused enthusiastically by its adherents across the disciplines, was slow to gain acceptance by the academic community at large. That this was so is not surprising given the fact that there were so few women in positions of power and that established theories were being threatened. The new research tended to be ignored or minimized as polemic, and women scholars aspiring to tenure pursued their work at the risk of their careers. The same disadvantage did not seem to apply to male faculty members who were also doing feminist research.

An important factor in the development of feminist research during the 1970s was the formation of women's caucuses or committees within professional associations. The activities of these groups are described at greater length in chapter 12. Suffice it to say here that they not only provided mutual support networks and pressed for greater recognition of women scholars, but they also directed attention to women as a legitimate subject of research in the academic disciplines.

The research efforts of women scholars were further advanced during this period by financial support from foundations and government agencies. In 1972 the Ford Foundation established a national fellowship program for research on the role of women in society. Awards were made at both the faculty and doctoral dissertation levels and were open to men as well as women. Apart from the financial support involved, this pioneer program (the first of its kind) served to give visibility and legitimacy to studies concerning women. Other foundations that provided substantial support for women scholars were the Carnegie Corporation, the Lilly Endowment, and the Mellon and Rockefeller foundations. The Carnegie fellowships were designed to provide research opportunities to nontenured women faculty members to promote their career advancement. Although this was a program for research by women rather than about women, a significant proportion of the recipients did, in fact, pursue projects relating to women. The Bunting Institute and the American Association of University Women also made fellowship grants to women for research projects that were frequently though not necessarily about women.

Federal funding sources for research about women included the Fund for the Improvement of Postsecondary Education, the National Institute of Education, the Women's Educational Equity Program, the National Endowment for the Humanities, and the National Science Foundation. Federal funding for research primarily took the form of project support rather than fellowship awards. After the mid 1970s, government funding surpassed that of private foundations in total volume.[8] Federal funding was primarily, through not exclusively, devoted to empirical research relating to policy issues and was particularly valuable for providing the means for large-scale data collections and longitudinal surveys such as those on the labor force participation of women and the panel studies of family income dynamics.

The Emergence of Research Centers

As the women's movement gathered momentum, it generated a growing need for research to contribute to the formation of public policy and to public understanding of the legal, economic, and social inequities faced by women. At the same time, there was a demand for material to sustain the growth of women's studies programs. To supplement the efforts of individual scholars and to make possible large-scale and interdisciplinary research programs, organized centers for research on women were established. There are today nearly 60 such centers throughout the United States, most of them founded after 1970.[9] About three quarters of these centers are campus-based and tend to be oriented toward women's studies. A few are affiliated with other nonprofit organizations, such as the American Council on Education or the Urban Institute. The rest are independent organizations, and these include the main policy-oriented centers located in Washington, D.C. General or core support was provided by private foundations, and additional support for targeted projects was provided by government agencies and other sources.

Among the earliest of the centers to emerge in the 1970s was the Center for the American Woman and Politics, a unit of the Eagleton Institute of Politics at Rutgers University. The center was founded in 1971 to conduct research, develop educational programs, and provide information services relating to women's participation in the political process. Another of the early entries into the field was the Center for Women Policy Studies organized in 1972 in Washington, D.C. This is a free-standing nonprofit organization with a staff of professionals in the fields of economics, law, sociology, and social work. Its research program has focused on legal and economic policy issues such as discrimination in employment and credit, women in the criminal justice and social service systems, and the economic status of older women. By the middle of the decade three major new centers came into being—the Center for Research on Women at Wellesley College, the Center for Research on Women at Stanford University, and the Research Program on Women and Family Policy at the Urban Institute in Washington, D.C.

These centers provided models for the rapid expansion of research centers that followed. The Wellesley Center, under its founding director, Carolyn Elliott, was the prototype for many of the subsequent campus-based centers. The original charge of the Wellesley Center was to generate research and disseminate information about women in higher education and the professions. Over time the scope of the program was broadened to include employment and family issues. The center gave particular attention to the dissemination of research results through conferences, workshops, and contacts with women's groups and corporations.

The Stanford Center was established with an enabling grant from the

Ford Foundation, the first of a series of grants that were specifically designed to strengthen the academic base of women's studies by providing on-campus institutional resources. Between 1974 and 1981 twelve new centers were established and three existing centers received supplementary support as part of the series. Three of the centers were established to provide regional resources in women's studies. The first of these was the Southwest Institute for Research on Women (SIROW) at the University of Arizona, which was founded in 1979. SIROW is a research and resource center servicing scholars primarily in Arizona, Colorado, New Mexico, and Utah. It promotes collaborative, interdisciplinary research focused on southwestern problems or populations, identifies and disseminates research on women in the Southwest, maintains a clearinghouse of the work of scholars in the region, and links researchers with community organizations and policymakers. A similar regional center for the Northwest region was established—the Northwest Center for Research on Women, at the University of Washington, Seattle. In the southern region, the joint Duke University and University of North Carolina Women's Studies Research Center was established in 1982 to carry out and promote research in women's studies in North Carolina, South Carolina, and Virginia. Its primary research concern is the intersection of gender, race, and class in the lives of southern and Third World women. A second center for the southern region, established at the same time, is the Center for Research on Women at Memphis State University. These two centers work collaboratively with a third center in the South, established at Spelman College in Atlanta in 1981 with a grant from the Charles Stewart Mott Foundation.

In addition to the regional centers, other campus-based centers were established to advance research and teaching in specified broad subject areas. Examples are (1) the Women's Studies Research Center at the University of Wisconsin–Madison, which undertook a major research program on motherhood, its functions in society and its influence on women's lives, and (2) the Pembroke Center for Teaching and Research on Women at Brown University, which began with a three-year project to investigate cultural constructions of the female.

In some cases, centers that were established for other educational or professional objectives relating to women included or added a research component. The Center for Continuing Education of Women at the University of Michigan is an example. Created in 1964 to provide counseling and other services for re-entry students, the center has developed a research program on women's issues in higher education with an emphasis on the transition from education to employment and the factors affecting career development across the life course.

As of 1987 we have identified 57 centers for research both on- and off-campus. They are listed in Appendix 13.1 according to the year in which they were established. On a decade-by-decade basis, the number of centers formed is as follows: 1940–1949, 1; 1950–1959, 1; 1960–1969, 4; 1970–1979, 31; and 1980–1987, 20.

Some centers have maintained formal programs of research concerning women as a component of rather than their sole or even their main activity. Three of these phased out such formal programs under budgetary pressures during the early 1980s and moved to integrate their work on women-related issues within their other research interests. Thus, the program on Sex Roles and Social Change at the Center for the Social Sciences at Columbia, the Program of Policy Research on Women and Families at the Urban Institute, and the Center for Human Resource Research at Ohio State University are no longer in existence as separate units. On the other hand, new centers continue to be formed, and it is clear that there will be a further increase in the aggregate number by the end of the 1980s.

Building a Network

As the number of research centers grew during the 1970s, it became increasingly apparent that there was much to be gained by closer communication among them regarding definition of research priorities and other matters of mutual concern. Toward that end a meeting of center directors was held in New York in 1979, which provided an opportunity for exchange of information about research programs, educational and public service activities, means of communication among them, and the dissemination of research results. This meeting led to the establishment of an informal network among the centers and a regular exchange of information through newsletters, working papers, and other publications.

A second meeting of program directors was held in the spring of 1981 in Washington, under the auspices of the Women's Research and Education Institute (WREI) of the Congressional Caucus on Women's Issues. WREI had been established in 1977 as the research and training arm of the caucus and was charged, among other things, with maintaining liaison with the research community in areas of concern to women. The purpose of the Washington meeting was to bring together researchers and policymakers to discuss research and information needs. The meeting was the first step in a program undertaken by WREI to develop regular channels of communication between the research centers and caucus members and their staffs. The program has proved to be an effective vehicle for cooperative efforts to provide policymakers with the most recent research on women's issues, on the one hand, and to keep research centers updated on legislative, regulatory, and other policy-related activities, on the other.

Federal budget cuts during 1981 and the prospect of more to come posed problems for the centers, nearly all of which have received substantial project support from government sources. In order to share information on ways of dealing with these problems and to explore the possibilities of sharing resources, the directors of the centers met again toward the end of the year, this time under the auspices of the Institute for Research in History in New York. Participants in the meeting examined common research interests; methods of creating more efficient storage and retrieval systems for data needs; and means of sharing skills in management, finance, and long-range planning. As a result of the meeting a working alliance was formed, and plans were made to establish a continuing organization to coordinate activities and facilitate joint research. In 1983 the organization was legally incorporated as the National Council for Research on Women.

At the time that it was founded, the council consisted of 28 chartering member institutions. By the end of 1987 there were 57 members, representing virtually all of the research centers then in existence. In 1984–1985 the council conducted a questionnaire survey of member centers designed to provide basic information about their organizational characteristics, research directions, and other programmatic activities. The survey, updated to include new centers formed after 1985, is the main source of information presented here and in the following two sections of this chapter.

Organizational Characteristics of Research Centers

The survey provides information about the organizational characteristics of the research centers in terms of their structure or affiliation, size, and sources of financial support. Structurally, the centers may be classified as either independent entities or units affiliated with universities or other organizations. Of the 57 centers, 9 are incorporated as independent entities. Six of them are located in Washington and 3 in New York. Forty-four of the centers are affiliated with universities and 5 with other organizations. Of the campus-based centers, 10 are located at women's colleges (Barnard, two at Wellesley, Smith, Spelman, three at Radcliffe, Hartford College for Women, and Douglass). Appendix 13.2 lists the research centers classified by type of affiliation.

Among the campus-based centers there is considerable variation in the degree of autonomy with which they operate and the nature of their affiliation. The preponderant number are related in some way to academic departments or teaching programs, and by and large they rely on faculty members for research staff. The others are more or less autonomous and recruit research staff outside normal departmental channels. These include, for example, the Center for the American Woman and Politics at Rutgers, the Center of Research on Women at Wellesley, and the Center for Women in Government at the State University of New York at Albany. Since campus-based centers are for the most part interdisciplinary, they are not ordinarily tied to a single department. In general they report to an academic dean, vice president, or provost, except at Radcliffe, where the Bunting Institute, the Murray Center, and the Schlesinger Library report to the president.

The size of the centers may be measured in terms of the amount of the annual operating budget or the number of individuals involved as research, clerical, or administrative staff members. Size can also be measured in terms of physical facilities. Based on the initial survey questionnaires, the annual operating budgets of the research centers during the 1982–1985 period ranged from a low of $10,000 to a high of $1.2 million. The low figure is misleading, however, since it does not include faculty salaries and other expenses provided by the university which do not appear on the center budget. For independent centers, the budgets ranged from $240,000 to $600,000. The median budget for all of the centers is on the order of $350,000.

In measuring size on the basis of the number of individuals involved, it is necessary to distinguish between core and permanent staff, those holding fellowships or other short-term appointments, and affiliated scholars who may or may not be paid and who may or may not be working in-house. For example, the Bunting Institute has 6 full-time staff members and approximately 40 scholars annually who are engaged in research on postdoctoral fellowships. Another example is the Center for the Study of Women in Society at the University of Oregon, which has a central staff of approximately 10, but which funds 12 other scholars not located at the center. In terms of in-house staff, Wellesley is by far the largest of the centers. It has a research staff of about 30 scholars and approximately 20 additional project and administrative staff members for a total of nearly 50. The center also has a substantial number of visiting scholars on hand each year. The Stanford Center also has a research cadre of approximately 30, but they are for the most part faculty members affiliated with the center rather than research staff members who are independently recruited as such, as at Wellesley. Except for Wellesley, few, if any, centers maintain a regular staff of more than 15, although they may have affiliated scholars ranging in number up to 200 within their regions. The total number of research staff members and affiliated scholars for all centers combined is in excess of 1,000. In terms of the size of physical facilities, the Schlesinger Library, the Bunting Institute, and the Murray Center at Radcliffe are the foremost centers, and their combined resources for research about women are unmatched anywhere in the United States if not in the world.

With regard to sources of funding, the survey covered federal, state, foundation, university, and other sources including dues, endowment income, earned income for services, and gifts and contributions from individual or corporate sources. The main sources of funding for the centers during the 1982–1985 period were foundations and the federal government. While there was wide variation among the centers reporting, on the average centers received 33 percent of their income from foundations and 20 percent from the federal government. The third main source of funding for the campus-based centers was the home institution, or, in the case of state universities, state sources. On the average, university/state sources represented 36 percent of the income of these centers. For independent centers, the third main source of income was corporate contributions and gifts: 23 percent. Only four centers relied substantially or primarily on endowment income—one at the University of Oregon and three at Radcliffe. Income from dues and fees was negligible, but several of the centers reported earned income of 15 percent or more from sale of publications and other products or services.

Program Activities

While all of the centers are engaged in research, there are substantial differences among them in the role of research in their overall program. Most of the centers have multiple program activities encompassing various combinations of research, education, training, technical assistance, advocacy, and community outreach. The relationship of research to other activities and the degree of emphasis on research varies considerably among the centers. Very few of the centers are engaged in research to the exclusion of other activities. The foremost examples are the Higher Education Research Institute at UCLA and the Murray Center at Radcliffe. Most centers combine research with curriculum development, training, or technical assistance programs. Some carry out research as a subsidiary to other program activities, rather than their primary activity.

Most of the campus-based research centers conduct related educational activities such as seminars and colloquia, course development, and summer institutes. These include, among others, the research centers at Arizona, Brown, Duke, Memphis, Stanford, Wellesley, and Wisconsin. SIROW at Arizona, Duke, and Wellesley have major ongoing curriculum development programs in women's studies combined with their research programs. Three of the centers combine research with education, training, and advocacy in their respective areas of specialization. They are the Center for the American Woman and Politics at the Eagleton Institute, the Center for Women in Government at the State University of New York (SUNY), Albany, and the Institute for Women and Work of the New York State School of Industrial and Labor Relations at Cornell. Two other centers combine a research emphasis on women in developing countries with technical assistance and policy analysis in that area. They are the Equity Policy Center and the International Center for Research on Women, both in Washington, DC. Finally, there are the centers for which research plays a role that is more or less subsidiary to an action or service program. An example of this type is the Center for Continuing Education of Women at Michigan, which conducts research on career development and related issues in connection with its counseling and other services for returning women in higher education. Another example is the Indiana-based National Resource Center of the Girls Clubs of America, which conducts research and collects statistical data relating to the development of programs for girls.

Research Directions

What are the principal areas of research in which the centers are engaged? To what extent do they specialize? How do they set priorities? The bulk of the centers surveyed reported their research emphasis as "women studies," and that was by far the most frequent response of the campus-based centers. Next in order of frequency was the broad area of education, and this group included several off-campus centers, such as the Project on the Status and Education of Women of the Association of American Colleges, the Project on Equal Education Rights of the NOW Legal Defense and Education Fund, and the Office of Women in Higher Education of the American Council on Education. Several centers cite employment and family issues as their principal area of research, including most recently the Women and Work Research and Resource Center at the University of Texas at Arlington. Also high on the research agendas of the centers are issues at the intersections of race, class, and sex, and ethnic issues. Seven centers are concerned with these issues as a primary or collateral field of activity.

Four of the centers emphasize research of particular interest to their region of the country. Five centers have international interests focusing on women in development, two of them operating exclusively in that area. Although public policy issues are on the agenda of a good many of the centers, only five identify public policy as such as their primary concern and all but one are located in Washington, D.C. The exception is the Center on Women and Public Policy at the Humphrey Institute for Public Affairs, University of Minnesota. Two centers, both outside Washington, concentrate on women in public life, one in elective office and one in public administration. Other areas of specialization represented among the centers are the following: women in the arts (Women's Interart Center, New York), rural women (Center for Rural Women, Pennsylvania State University), women in business (Center for the Study of Women in Business, Baruch College, City University of New York), and women and health (Institute for Women's Health, School of Medicine, Indiana University).

The full array of research interests is as follows: The total number adds up to more than 57 since most centers are active in more than one area.

Women's Studies	20
Education	14
Employment and Family Issues	10
Race, Class, and Sex, Ethnic Issues	7
Public Policy	5
Women in Developing Countries	5
Regional Studies	4
Women in Public Life	2
Adolescent Girls	2
Adult Development	2
Mental Health	2
Trade Union Women	1
Women and Health	1
Rural Women	1
Women in the Arts	1
Women in Business	1
Male Roles	1

Although women's studies research centers are now the most numerous group, they were unknown prior to the mid 1970s. The earliest of the research centers were formed for a specific mission, most frequently the professional advancement of women—in higher education, in politics, in trade unions, and in the arts. These were followed by centers for the study of public policy issues—discrimination in credit, employment, social security, and family welfare. During this period women's studies, which had emerged as an academic discipline at the beginning of the 1970s, was growing rapidly and gaining increasing acceptance. Women's studies research centers came to the fore with the formation of the Stanford Center for Research on Women in 1974.

From then on, women's studies research centers became the fastest-growing segment among the centers. As of 1987, new women's studies research centers continued to be formed on campus, albeit with minimal funding for the most part. In any event, the growth of these centers implies more emphasis in the 1980s on basic conceptual and long-range issues than was previously the case.

There are few areas relating to women and their roles in which there is no ongoing research, but some areas are much farther along than others. As indicated in the listing above, education, employment, and family issues are receiving a good deal of attention, with race, class, and sex issues close behind. Women's studies, of course, embraces a broad range of research including, in addition to those just noted, extensive work on women in history, images of women in literature, the psychology of women, and women and the law. Research areas that developed slowly during the 1970s and became more salient in the 1980s are women in science and technology, women in developing countries, and health issues, including mental health.

How do the centers set research priorities? Within the overall guidelines indicated by the general mission of the center, the initiative for new research projects usually comes from the research staff or the director. Although most centers have research advisory committees, such committees do not ordinarily set the research agenda. They may be consulted by the director and their formal approval of the research program may be required, but they seldom exercise the controlling influence. Where centers rely on outside funding for project support, which is generally the case, the priorities of the funding source, of course, play a significant role. Thus, the research program of the centers is the end result of an interactive process involving the staff, the director, the advisory committee, and the funding source. The relative influence of each varies from center to center depending on the type of affiliation, the scope of the research program, and the funding situation. In the case of the campus-based centers, with a broad mandate covering women's studies across the disciplines and a research staff composed of teaching faculty members, the interests of the staff, indirectly or collaboratively, are likely to be the driving force. Where the mission is more specific, the director has a stronger role to play whether the center is university-affiliated or independent.

Educational Programs and Other Related Activities

As already noted, few of the centers restrict their activities solely to the pursuit of research. Nearly all conduct ancillary programs of various kinds, and in some cases research is itself the ancillary rather than the main activity of the organization. Research-related activities may include curriculum development; training programs; sponsorship of summer institutes, seminars, and lecture series; fellowship and visiting scholar programs; presentation of exhibitions; advocacy for women on campus or in public arenas; and outreach programs.

In general, of course, it is the campus-based centers that are engaged in various aspects of curriculum development, and most but not all of them do so. They may develop new courses or course material for women's studies and other programs, carry out projects to foster the integration of women's studies into the general curriculum, and conduct summer institutes for faculty development. For example, the Stanford Center was instrumental in developing a course on the Victorian Heritage for the Department of Modern Thought and Literature and subsequently the formation of a feminist studies program at the university. SIROW has a university-wide faculty development project designed to integrate scholarship on women in traditional courses, and also a region-wide curriculum integration project involving colleges and universities in 16 western states. The Memphis Center has made a significant contribution to curriculum integration through its Summer Institute on Teaching, Research, and Writing About Women. The Wellesley Center has a comprehensive national program encompassing faculty development and the integration of new material about women into the liberal arts curriculum, and Duke and Spelman have coordinated programs of curriculum development for the southern region.

In addition to their work with mainstream liberal arts courses, campus-based research centers also give noncredit courses or training programs for nontraditional students under their own auspices. The Center for Women in Government at SUNY/Albany develops curriculum material for noncredit courses for women in the public sector as well as for a graduate seminar on women and public policy. Similarly, the Center for the American Woman and Politics at Rutgers has been active in the development of credit and noncredit courses at ten women's colleges across the country on women's participation in the political process. The Institute for Women and Work at Cornell conducts educational programs for trade union women on both a college credit and noncredit basis. Several of the centers have instituted programs relating to women in science, including research awards for women scientists (Bunting Institute) and recruitment and career planning programs (Michigan, SIROW). The three HERS organizations carry out research and action programs to improve the status of academic women in administrative positions.

Many campus-based centers and some of those off campus have programs for affiliated or visiting scholars. Affiliated scholars are usually active researchers in the region who have no other university affiliation and who may be appointed for a year or more on a renewable basis. Typically, such scholars do not receive stipends, other than those under project grants they may generate, but they receive office and library privileges, and possibly some access to secretarial assistance. Visiting scholars may be national or international and usually, though not always, receive a stipend. Wisconsin, SIROW, and Stanford are among those centers that have affiliated scholar programs, while Brown, Oregon, Wellesley, and Radcliffe are the chief centers offering support for visiting scholars. Nearly all centers, both campus-based and other, employ students in some way, whether as research assistants, as interns, or in some other capacity, under work-study programs. They generally also offer resources for dissertation students.

All centers report outreach programs of some kind. For campus-based centers, these may take the form of lectures, colloquia, or seminars open to the academic community at large or to the general public. They may also take the form of in-service training programs for public school or college teachers in the region, or participation in community educational events. Off-campus centers may also sponsor or participate in conferences open to policymakers, women's groups, and the general community.

The majority of campus-based research centers do not perceive their function to be to serve as advocates for women students, faculty, or staff, although a few have indicated that they serve that role in an indirect way by virtue of their presence. The chief responsibility for advocacy on behalf of women usually lies elsewhere on campus—in the office of a dean, an affirmative action officer, or a committee on the status of women.

The Washington-based centers inform public officials, testify on policy issues concerning women, provide technical assistance for field projects, and carry out public information programs. Centers outside Washington, such as the Women's Interart Center, also function as advocates for women.

Conclusions

What have been the main contributions of the research centers to women in higher education and to higher education generally? First, as intended, they have provided institutional resources for women's studies and women's studies scholars. Such resources include library facilities, access to clerical and research assistance, aid in preparing grant proposals, contact with scholars having related research interests, and a generally supportive environment. Mutual support was particularly essential in the early days of the research centers when the academic community was hostile to women's studies, but the need is a continuing one for any group of scholars with shared interests and limited means. Second, they have provided research opportunities, employment, and access to academic careers to a substantial number of scholars at a time when openings in higher education were limited, particularly in the humanities. Third, they have provided a mechanism to increase the flow of funding for research about women by attracting grants, contracts, corporate support, and contributions beyond the capacity of individual scholars. Fourth, by virtue of their presence on campus, they have increased the visibility and strengthened the position of women's studies on campus and the faculty members involved. More specifically, they have provided course material, developed new courses, and conducted programs for integrating the new scholarship into the liberal arts curriculum.

What can be said about the contributions of the centers to the nature and extent of research about women? How, if at all, have they influenced research priorities? In what ways have they carried out large-scale and interdisciplinary research or otherwise influenced the research process? Clearly, the centers have served to increase the volume of research about women, but it is less clear how they have affected research priorities, the scale of research undertaken, or the research process. As we have noted, some centers have specific missions, such as women in politics, trade union women, or women in development, while others have a broad mandate covering women's studies in general. There are also centers that are intermediate in range of topics covered; that is to say, they may have a particular focus, but one that is rather broadly defined, such as rural women, women of color, or women in a particular region of the country. In this way, individual centers have influenced research directions and priorities.

Overall, the centers, while encompassing theoretical research, have tended to emphasize policy- or practitioner-oriented research and have been a force in expanding such research as it relates to women. Partly this results from the interests and concerns of the centers themselves, which include action programs as well as research. Partly also it results from the interaction among the centers. Through the National Council, campus-based centers are brought into direct contact with Washington-based centers as well as with each other, inevitably affecting subjects and modes of analysis. In the process, interdisciplinary perspectives have been brought to bear on issues of social policy, even though this may not be evident in the form of large-scale multidisciplinary projects. In a recent article on social science as public philosophy, sociologist Robert Bellah argues for an approach to the study of society that transcends the boundaries between the social sciences and humanities and takes account of historical, philosophical, and cross-cultural insights.[10] The research centers by virtue of their nature and interrelationships contribute to such an approach.

In the universe of research centers in the social sciences and the humanities, the centers for research on women do not bulk large.[11] While they are numerous, they are for the most part quite small in size. None approach the size of the Brookings Institution or the Newberry Library, for example. Many of the centers, particularly those formed in the 1980s, have been campus-based units organized with university resources that are often minimal. External funding from government agencies and private foundations has declined sharply, raising concern for the future of existing centers, particularly the independents. Thus far, most have managed to compensate for the decline at least partially from other sources such as state and local organizations, corporate contributions, revenues from sales of publications, fund-raising events, and capital drives. These take a lot of effort and a high level of entrepreneurial ability and drive. Meanwhile, campus-based research centers are beginning to make their appearance abroad, in both Europe and developing countries.

All things considered, there is reason to expect further growth rather than a decline in research centers at least through the 1980s. In the longer run, it is possible that some will encounter declining support and survive in name only. Others may be integrated into their parent organization and lose their identity as a separate program. For most of the campus-based centers, however, their continued existence is not in question. A few have endowments, and others have achieved a place on the regular university budget. Comparable centers were established during the 1950s and 1960s in foreign area studies, urban studies, and ethnic studies. While not all of them have survived, the strongest of them are settled in and continue to play an important role in their respective fields. There is no reason to expect any less from women's studies research centers.

Appendix 13.1
Chronological Growth of Research Centers

1943 Schlesinger Library on the History of Women in America, Radcliffe College
1957 Business and Professional Women's Foundation, Washington, DC
1960 Bunting Institute, Radcliffe College
1964 Center for Continuing Education of Women, University of Michigan
1966 Center for Human Resource Research, Ohio State University
1969 Women's Interart Center, New York
1970 Feminist Press, City University of New York (originally Baltimore)
1971 Center for the American Woman and Politics, Eagleton Institute of Politics, Rutgers University
      Women's Center, Barnard College
      Project on the Status and Education of Women, Association of American Colleges
1972 Institute for Women and Work, Cornell University
      Center for the Study, Advancement and Education of Women, Berkeley
      Center for the Study of Women and Society, University of Oregon
      Center for Women Policy Studies, Washington, DC
      Higher Education Resource Services, HERS/New England, Wellesley College
1973 Office of Women in Higher Education, American Council on Education
1974 Center for Research on Women, Stanford University
      Higher Education Resource Institute, UCLA

Center for Research on Women, Wellesley College
HERS/Mid-America, University of Denver
Women's Resources and Research Center, University of California, Davis
Project on Equal Education Rights, Washington, DC
1975 Institute for Research in History, New York
Program for the Study of Women and Men in Society, University of Southern California
Program of Policy Research on Women and Families, Urban Institute
1976 Henry A. Murray Research Center, Radcliffe College
International Center for Research on Women, Washington, DC
1977 Women's Studies Research Center, University of Wisconsin—Madison
Women's Research and Education Institute, Congressional Caucus on Women's Issues, Washington, DC
Center for the Study of Women and Society, Graduate Center, City University of New York
Women's Studies Program and Policy Center, George Washington University
1978 Center for Women in Government, State University of New York, Albany
Equity Policy Center, Washington, DC
Project on Women and Social Change, Smith College
1979 Southwest Institute for Research on Women, University of Arizona
Program on Sex Roles and Social Change, Center for the Social Sciences, Columbia University
HERS/West, University of Utah
1981 National Resource Center, Girls Clubs of America
Pembroke Center for Teaching and Research on Women, Brown University
Women's Research and Resource Center, Spelman College
Northwest Center for Research on Women, University of Washington
Stone Center, Wellesley College
1982 Women's Studies Research Center, Duke–University of North Carolina
Institute for Research on Women, Douglass College, Rutgers University
Center for Research on Women, Memphis State University

1982   Research and Resources Unit, Center for Women's Studies, University of Cincinnati

Center for Rural Women, Pennsylvania State University

1983   Center for Advanced Feminist Research, University of Minnesota

Alice Paul Center for the Study of Women, University of Pennsylvania

Women's Research Institute, Hartford College of Women

1984   Center for the Study of Women, University of California, Los Angeles

1985   Center on Women and Public Policy, Humphrey Institute for Public Affairs, University of Minnesota

Women and Work Research and Resource Center, University of Texas, Arlington

Institute for Women and Gender Research, Utah State University

1986   Center for the Study of Women in Business, Baruch College, City University of New York

Institute for Research on Women and Gender, Columbia University

1987   Institute of Women's Health, School of Medicine, Indiana University

Institute for Women's Policy Research, Washington, DC

Institute for Research on Women, State University of New York, Albany

Appendix 13.2
Classification of Research Centers by Type of Affiliation

University-Affiliated

Southwest Institute for Research on Women, University of Arizona

Women's Center, Barnard College

Center for the Study of Women in Business, Baruch College, City University of New York

Pembroke Center for Teaching and Research on Women, Brown University

Center for the Study, Education, and Advancement of Women, University of California, Berkeley

Women's Resources and Research Center, University of California, Davis

Center for the Study of Women, University of California, Los Angeles

Higher Education Research Institute, University of California, Los Angeles

Research and Resources Unit, Center for Women's Studies, University of Cincinnati

Institute for Research on Women and Gender, Columbia University

Center for the Study of Women and Society, Graduate Center, City University of New York

Institute for Women and Work, Cornell University

Women's Studies Research Center, Duke–University of North Carolina

Women's Studies Program and Policy Center, George Washington University

Women's Research Institute, Hartford College for Women

HERS/Mid-America, University of Denver

HERS/New England, Wellesley College

HERS/West, University of Utah

Institute of Women's Health, School of Medicine, Indiana University

Center for Research on Women, Memphis State University

Center for Continuing Education of Women, University of Michigan

Center for Advanced Feminist Research, University of Minnesota

Center on Women and Public Policy, Humphrey Institute for Public Affairs, University of Minnesota

Center for Women in Government, State University of New York, Albany

Institute for Research on Women, State University of New York, Albany

Center for Human Resource Research, Ohio State University

Center for the Study of Women in Society, University of Oregon

Center for Rural Women, Pennsylvania State University

Alice Paul Center for the Study of Women, University of Pennsylvania

Bunting Institute, Radcliffe College

Henry A. Murray Research Center, Radcliffe College

Schlesinger Library on the History of Women in America, Radcliffe College

Center for the American Woman and Politics, Eagleton Institute of Politics, Rutgers University

Institute for Research on Women, Douglass College, Rutgers University

Project on Women and Social Change, Smith College

Program for the Study of Women and Men in Society, University of Southern California

Women's Resource and Research Center, Spelman College

Center for Research on Women, Stanford University

Women and Work Research and Resource Center, University of Texas, Arlington

Institute for Women and Gender Research, Utah State University
Northwest Center for Research on Women, University of Washington
Center for Research on Women, Wellesley College
Stone Center, Wellesley College
Women's Studies Program and Research Center, University of Wisconsin–Madison

Other Affiliation

Office of Women in Higher Education, American Council on Education
Project on the Status and Education of Women, Association of American Colleges
National Resource Center, Girls Clubs of America
Program of Policy Research on Women and Families, Urban Institute
Project on Equal Education Rights, NOW Legal Defense and Education Fund

Independent

Business and Professional Women's Foundation, Washington, DC
Center for Women Policy Studies, Washington, DC
Equity Policy Center, Washington, DC
Feminist Press, City University of New York
Institute for Research in History, New York
Institute for Women's Policy Research, Washington, DC
International Center for Research on Women, Washington, DC
Women's Interart Center, New York
Women's Research and Education Institute, Congressional Caucus on Women's Issues, Washington, DC

Notes

1. For an excellent anthology of feminist writings beginning in the late eighteenth century and extending to the mid-twentieth century, see Alice S. Rossi, ed., *The Feminist Papers* (New York: Columbia University Press, 1973). The anthology includes selections from Mary Wollstonecraft, Elizabeth Cady Stanton, John Stuart Mill, Virginia Woolf, and Simone de Beauvoir, among others. Here we are concerned, of course, not with essays or literature per se, but rather with research-based writing.

2. Gerda Lerner, *Teaching Women's History* (Washington, DC: American Historical Association, 1981).

3. Rosalind Rosenberg, *Beyond Separate Spheres: Intellectual Roots of Modern Feminism* (New Haven: Yale University Press, 1982).

4. John M. Glenn, Lilian Brandt, and F. Emerson Andrews, *Russell Sage Foundation: 1907–1946*, 2 vols. (New York: Russell Sage Foundation, 1947).

5. Joan Kelly-Gadol, "Did Women Have a Renaissance?" in Renate Bridenthal and Claudia Koonz, eds., *Becoming Visible: Women in European History* (Boston: Houghton Mifflin, 1977).

6. Alice S. Rossi, "Equality Between the Sexes: An Immodest Proposal," in Robert J. Lifton, ed., *The Woman in America* (Boston: Beacon Press, 1967).

7. Carolyn Shaw Bell, "Should Every Job Support a Family?" *Public Interest*, no. 40 (Summer 1975):109–118.

8. Although private foundations preceded the government in activating programs for research on women, government support grew rapidly during the 1970s, surpassing foundation support about 1975. Government funding reached a peak in 1980–1981 and since then has declined precipitously. While private foundations have maintained and even increased slightly their overall support of women's programs, there is some evidence of a shift in emphasis toward social service rather than research programs. For further information about sources, volume, and type of support, see *Financial Support of Women's Programs in the 1970's: A Review of Private and Government Funding in the United States and Abroad*, a Report to the Ford Foundation, New York, 1979. Also National Council for Research on Women, *A Declining Federal Commitment to Research about Women, 1980–84*, a Report from the Commission on New Funding Priorities (New York: National Council for Research on Women, 1985).

9. For an earlier account of the emergence and growth of research centers in the 1970s, see Mariam Chamberlain, "A Period of Remarkable Growth—Women's Studies Research Centers," *Change*, April 1982, pp. 24–29.

10. Robert N. Bellah, "Creating a New Framework for New Realities: Social Science as Public Philosophy," *Change*, March-April 1985, pp. 35–39.

11. The literature on research centers in the social sciences and humanities is sparse, in part because they are comparatively recent in origin and in part because of their limited size and number relative to those in science and engineering. Useful source material is provided in Hannah Wartenberg, "Social Science Research Institutes," a paper presented at the annual meeting of the American Sociological Association, 1983. While noting the origins of empirical social research in Europe, particularly in German universities, she traces the modern social science research institute back to the 1920s when the first university-based centers were funded by private foundations such as Russell Sage, Carnegie, and Rockefeller. Another useful source is "A Guide to Humanities Centers in the United States," prepared by Lydia Bronte as an internal working paper of the Rockefeller Foundation. A good general work on the subject is Harold Orlans, *The Nonprofit Institute: Its Origins, Operations, Problems and Prospects*, a study for the Carnegie Commission (New York: McGraw-Hill, 1972).

Photo courtesy of the Office of University Relations, George Washington University

Following World War II, campuses were crowded with returning veterans who were supported by the "G.I. Bill." This is a class in European Civilization at George Washington University in 1946.

Photo courtesy of the American Association of Community and Junior Col

Under the impetus of the women's movement beginning in the 1960s, women entered higher education in unprecedented numbers. For many, particularly minority and returning women, the point of entry was the community college. This photograph of a community college commencement reflects a student body that includes a high proportion of women, minorities, and older students.

Photo by Richard Chase

During this period women also substantially increased their representation in prestigious professional schools, as illustrated here in a classroom at the Harvard Business School.

Title IX of the Education Amendments of 1972 prohibiting sex discrimination in any educational program or activity opened up new opportunities for women in athletics. Here Marcia Greenberger, Co-Director of the National Women's Law Center (*left*) and Patricia Reuss, Legislative Director of the Women's Equity Action League, brief athletes on the application of Title IX to women in sports.

Photo courtesy of WEAL

The University of Pennsylvnia Women's Ice Hockey Team.

© 1988 JEB (Joan E. Biren)

Photo courtesy of the Center for Continuing Education, University of Michigan

Beginning in the 1960s women returned to college in large numbers after having interrupted their education to marry and have children. The students pictured here were among the re-entry women at the University of Michigan who received guidance and other services of the Center for Continuing Education on campus to assist their transition to higher education. The student at the left completed a graduate degree in music education and went on to teach in Mississippi. The student second from the left was a farm wife with ten children whose lifelong ambition had been to be a doctor. She is now a physician in a Detroit hospital (also pictured with microscope). The students third and fourth from the left completed PhDs in population planning and human genetics, respectively, and are now university faculty members.

Seven College Presidents, 1945

...erbert J. Davis	Katherine E. MacBride	Virginia C. Gildersleeve	Wilbur K. Jordan	Mildred McAfee Horton	Henry N. MacCracken	Roswell G. Ham
SMITH	BRYN MAWR	BARNARD	RADCLIFFE	WELLESLEY	VASSAR	MOUNT HOLYOKE

Photo courtesy of Schlesinger Library

In 1978, for the first time the presidents of all the women's colleges known as the Seven Sisters were women. Pictured are the presidents in 1945 and in 1978.

Seven College Presidents, 1978

Jill Conway	Elizabeth Kennan	Mary McPherson	Matina Horner	Jacquelyn Mattfeld	Barbara Newell	Virginia Smith
SMITH	MOUNT HOLYOKE	BRYN MAWR	RADCLIFFE	BARNARD	WELLESLEY	VASSAR

Photo courtesy of Schlesinger Library

Photo courtesy of Spelman College

Although Spelman College is the foremost black liberal arts college for women in the country, it did not have a black woman president until 1987 when Dr. Johnetta B. Cole, pictured here, was appointed to the position. Previous presidents in the 107-year history of the college were black men or white women.

Pioneers of Women's Studies

Above left, Sheila Tobias, who originated the Cornell Conference on Women in 1969 and the subsequent program on women's studies which led the way to similar programs on other campuses. Tobias later advanced women's studies by disseminating course syllabi and in numerous other ways. She is also known for her work in addressing "mathematics anxiety," particularly as it concerns women and minorities.

Above right, Florence Howe, founder and director of the Feminist Press, which came into being in 1970. Howe was also instrumental in the formation of the National Women's Studies Association and has been at the forefront of the development of women's studies not only in the United States but also worldwide.

Right, Catharine Stimpson, founding editor of *Signs: Journal of Women in Culture and Society*, the premier vehicle for the new scholarship on women. Stimpson has played a leading role as a women's studies scholar and advocate.

All photos © JEB (Joan E. Biren)

The growth of women's studies is depicted in these three scenes from the 1983 annual meeting of the National Women's Studies Association, held at Ohio State University: a large welcome sign to greet arriving participants, a plenary session, and the book exhibits.

Photo Researchers, Inc. 1984 © Barbara Pios

Women's studies literature reached beyond the campus and became widely available through special women's bookstores as well as through standard commercial channels. Womanbooks in New York and the Women's Bookstore in Toronto shown here are two of many such outlets throughout the world.

Photo © 1982 JEB (Joan E. Biren)

The Barnard College Women's Center was one of the most prominent and active of the campus-based centers that emerged during the 1970s. Its annual "Scholar and Feminist" conference, highlighted in the banner shown here, drew participants from across the country and from abroad. The conferences provided a forum for joint discussion of issues of concern to feminist scholarship and the women's movement.

Photo courtesy of Barnard College

Radcliffe College has provided unparalleled resources for the study of women. Shown here are the Arthur and Elizabeth Schlesinger Library on the History of Women in America (*left*) and the Henry A. Murray Research Center (*right*). The Murray Center is a national repository for social science data on the changing life experiences of American women. Also at Radcliffe, but not shown here, is the Mary Ingraham Bunting Institute, a research center for independent study by women scholars in all academic fields.

Photo by John D. Loch

The leading figure in the campaign against sex discrimination in higher education during the 1970s was Bernice R. Sandler, shown at left. She initiated the historic class action complaint filed under Executive Order 11375 by WEAL in 1970, charging a widespread pattern of discrimination against women in the academic community. Sandler went on to head the Project on the Status and Education of Women at the Association of American Colleges, providing information on policies and practices affecting women in higher education.

Photo courtesy of the Project
on the Status and Education of Women

As Assistant Secretary for Education during the 1970s and as a member of the U.S. Commission on Civil Rights during the 1980s, Mary Frances Berry, Professor of History and Law at Howard University, has been a forceful advocate of affirmative action.

Photo courtesy of the Feminist Press

The prestigious ACE Fellows program provides internships and opportunities for upward mobility for promising higher education administrators. Over the years most of the fellows have gone on to leadership positions in higher education administration. The growth in the representation of women and minorities in the group over the last two decades is reflected in these photographs of the ACE Fellows Class of 1965–1966 (above) and Class of 1984–1985 (below).

Photographs courtesy of the American Council on Education

Women in Administration and Governance

14

Women in Educational Administration

In November 1971 Alan Pifer, then president of the Carnegie Corporation, chose as his topic for a speech to the Southern Association of Colleges and Schools, "Women in Higher Education." Addressing a largely male audience, he documented inequalities in the participation of women at all levels. With regard to women in educational administration, he noted:

> In the top ranks of college and university administration, if one excepts the Catholic women's colleges, one has to look far and wide to find a woman. There are currently virtually no four-year coeducational institutions headed by a woman. Even among the nonsectarian women's colleges female presidents number just eight. There are only a few women deans, as opposed to deans of women. Of the 50 largest academic libraries not one is headed by a woman. Schools of social work, which a few decades ago had many women deans, are now headed almost exclusively by men. Truly women are the marginal people of higher education, essential to its existence but often invisible.[1]

The overwhelming majority of women who were college presidents at that time were also nuns. Of 1,500 persons who were presidents of four-year colleges, 95 were women and of these 84 were nuns and 2 were ex-nuns. Of the remaining 9, 5 were presidents at private women's colleges or former women's colleges, 2 at teacher's colleges, 1 at a business college, and 1 at a music institute. While 60 men were presidents of women's colleges, no woman was the president of a men's college.[2] The only other administrative position of consequence that women held was

317

that of dean of women, a position then in the process of being phased out at many coeducational institutions, to be replaced by a dean of students, usually a man.[3]

The 1972 annual meeting of the American Council on Education was devoted to the subject of women in higher education, reflecting the growing pressure for equality of women. The principal paper on college and university administration was given by Jacquelyn Mattfeld, then associate provost and dean of academic affairs at Brown University. In it she identified three categories of administrators: (1) persons who are employed to maintain and develop the physical plant and to manage the business operations, alumni and other public relations, and development; (2) those who work in admissions, financial aid, student affairs, counseling, placement, and the registrar's office; and (3) the academic leaders of the university—the president, chancellors, provosts, and deans. Although it was well known that women were underrepresented in all categories,[4] it was Mattfeld's view, based on her analysis of the qualifications specified for the positions in each group, that there was no shortage of qualified women for the first two categories.[5] Traditionally, openings in these areas—business and student services—were filled by men who were recent recipients of the bachelor's or master's degree. It was not the practice, as it is now, to advertise such positions, and prior training or work experience was not seen as a prerequisite. Mattfeld included in category 2, or student services, a subset of academic positions such as assistant or associate deans of students or student affairs, tutors, house deans, and counselors. These positions tend to be filled from the ranks of junior faculty members, such as lecturers, instructors, or assistant professors, ranks in which women are not hard to find. The situation for women in academic leadership positions was quite different, however. Here the pool of candidates was quite small as there were few women in the types of senior faculty positions or levels of administration from which appointments are usually made. The prospect at the start of the 1970s was that affirmative action programs and changes in institutional attitudes and practices could increase the representation of women in the lower echelons of academic administration, but that other remedies over a longer period of time would be needed to advance women into top administration.

The Measurement of Change

In the mid-1970s the total number of those employed full time in executive, administrative, and managerial positions in higher education institutions was 102,465. Of this total 23.1 percent were women, including 2.8 percent minority women. By 1981 the total had increased to 116,557, of which 30.2 percent were women, including 3.4 percent minority women. This represents an increase of 13.8 percent in administrative positions during the period, an increase considerably higher than the increase in faculty positions during that time. Faculty positions increased by only 4.6 percent.[6] The increase in the number of administrative positions is due in part to external requirements for financial accountability and affirmative action and internal needs for new services of various kinds. These forces have led to the introduction of positions such as affirmative action officers, minority student program specialists, institutional research officers, and government relations officers. Positions of this kind are regarded as middle management positions and are usually held by nonacademic professionals.[7]

The first national survey directed toward employment patterns and salary levels of women and minorities in higher education administration was carried out in 1975–1976 by Carol Frances for the College and University Personnel Association (CUPA). The survey covered 1,037 institutions including universities, liberal arts colleges, and two-year institutions. The study analyzed 52 primary administrative positions classified according to the type of responsibility—chief executive officers, administrative affairs, and external affairs. Overall questionnaire responses reported data on 18,035 administrative employees in first-line or primary positions. Thus, deans were included, but not associate or assistant deans; registrars, but not associate or assistant registrars; budget directors, and so on. The results conclusively showed that the large majority of people holding the 52 administrative positions examined were men. At all institutions men dominated the chief executive positions, holding 96 percent of those posts. Women held 16 percent of all the administrative positions at the survey institutions, including minority women who held 2 percent of the positions. Women and minorities were generally best represented in positions relating to student affairs and external affairs. With regard to salaries, women—both nonminority and minority—were paid about 80 percent as much as men with the same job title when employed by the same type of institution.[8]

In 1978–1979 Frances and her associates carried out an in-depth follow-up survey for CUPA to determine what progress was being made in employment of women and minorities. The number of administrative positions covered was expanded from 52 to 81, representing 26,104 administrators in 1,222 institutions. The results show some progress, albeit slow. Men continued to dominate the top positions in all categories of administrative work. They held at least 94 percent of the chief executive positions, approximately 80 percent of the administrative affairs and academic affairs positions, and 74 percent of the external affairs positions. Overall, women held 20 percent of all administrative positions, including 2 percent minority women, compared with 16 percent in 1975–1976. Of the 81 positions covered by the study, the only administrative job in which the proportion of women and minorities exceeded that of nonminority men was Director of Affirmative Action and Equal Employment. With regard to salary levels, women continued to earn less than men in virtually all administrative positions.[9]

CUPA has not carried out any further special studies of employment patterns and salary comparisons of women and minorities. It has, however, conducted annual surveys of salary levels of college and university administrators which provide data on sex and race differentials. The number of positions covered has continued to grow as new jobs are created.[10] The *1985–1986 Administrative Compensation Survey* covers 99 primary positions. In addition, data are provided for 69 secondary positions (for example, assistant to the president, associate budget director). Positions are grouped in five categories: academic affairs, administrative affairs (business, finance, general counsel, facilities), external affairs (development officer, alumni affairs, news bureau), student services, and executive affairs (chief executive officers and vice presidents). Sex and race breakdowns are given only for the primary positions. Of a total of 38,085 primary positions reported, 28 percent were women.[11] The breakdown by categories is as follows:

	Total Number	Number of Women	Percentage Women
Academic Affairs	11,336	3,149	28%
Administrative Affairs	10,969	2,363	22
External Affairs	4,242	1,650	39
Student Services	9,857	3,521	36
Executive Affairs	1,681	153	9

Although the highest proportion of women are in external affairs positions, the largest number of women are in student services. The lowest proportion is, of course, executive affairs at 9 percent, but even that represents an increase from 4 percent in 1975–1976 and 6 percent in 1978–1979.

There were six positions in which the number of women exceeded that of men. They were:

director, affirmative action/equal employment
director, news bureau
director, alumni affairs
director, information office
director, publications
director of student health services (nurse administrator)

The largest numbers of women were in the following positions (in descending order):

director, student financial aid
registrar
director, student health services (nurse administrator)
director, library services
director, bookstore
director, student placement
director, student affairs

Overall, then, women have shown a steady gain in administrative positions, including upper-level positions, over the 1975–1985 period. They remain underrepresented, however, not only as chief executives but also in other positions of influence such as deans and financial and planning officers.

Salary levels present a different picture. Salary differentials between men and women have been widening instead of narrowing. In the 1985–1986 CUPA survey, women's salaries were on the average 43 percent lower than those of men in similar positions compared with 20 percent lower ten years earlier. Titles with the widest salary differentials were director of international studies education, director of information systems, and director of athletics. Titles with the narrowest differentials were dean of music, director of student health services/nurse administrator (where there were 6 men and 489 women), dean of special programs, and general counsel. Women's salaries exceeded those of men in two positions: director of athletics/women and dean of home economics.

There are several possible explanations for the widening gap in mean salaries during this period. One is the high proportion of women newly entering the administrative ranks, with the result that they may be expected to have less experience than their male counterparts. The average years of service of women in their position at the time of the 1985–1986 survey was 33 percent lower than those of male incumbents. This factor was tested statistically by Frances as part of the 1978–1979 follow-up survey for CUPA. She found that no relationship could be identified between the comparative length of time women and men had held their jobs and the ratio of women's salaries to men's salaries for the same job. Indeed, some of the biggest gaps in salary were for positions in which women had held their jobs longer than men.[12] Clearly, men were being brought in from outside at salaries higher than those being paid to women already in the job. Another possible explanation of the salary gap is that women are more likely to hold senior-level administrative positions in lower-ranking and lower-paying institutions than men. Frances found that that was in fact the case. Institutions employing the largest proportion of men paid higher salaries than those employing the largest proportion of women.

Strategies for the Advancement of Women in Administration

How did the increase in the representation of women in higher education administration come about? To what extent is it due to affirmative action programs and changes in institutional attitudes and practices and to what extent to other factors? As we have seen in chapter 8, affirmative action programs, while only partially effective, have been instrumental in promoting institutional practices and search procedures that are more open to the employment of women. There is also some evidence of a reduction in prejudice against women on the part of academic administrators.[13]

Although affirmative action programs and changes in attitude reduced barriers to women in academic administration, efforts by women themselves were needed to benefit from the new opportunities. Without these it is unlikely that we would have seen as much progress as we have. A number of special programs were launched during the 1970s to help identify women with a potential for and an interest in higher education administration, to facilitate their entry into administrative careers, and to promote their advancement to leadership positions.

Establishing Rosters

One of the first steps to be taken was to establish rosters of professional women to provide information about the talent pool available for faculty and administrative positions. Rosters were developed by the women's caucuses and committees of professional associations such as the American Historical Association and the American Psychological Association and by other organizations concerned with the advancement of women. Something of a clearinghouse for such rosters was maintained by the Office of Opportunities in Science of the American Association for the Advancement of Science.

In 1973 the Office of Opportunities in Science undertook a study of the uses of rosters and their effectiveness as tools to advance equality of opportunity for women and minority professionals. Information was collected on over 70 rosters then in existence, and in 1974 a workshop was conducted bringing together roster directors, users, and equal opportunity specialists for exchange of information and coordination of efforts. Three types of rosters were identified: those that were simply directories, those that gave additional information on the qualifications of the individuals listed, and those that were registries, providing complete dossiers on each individual. Very few were of the third type. A report based on the workshop results and subsequent analysis indicated both the benefits and limitations of the various kinds of rosters.[14] It was found that for purposes of hiring women or minorities for faculty or administrative positions, rosters that were not registries were useful but not sufficient in and of themselves to enable institutions to identify specific qualified candidates. Although rosters served to enlarge the pool of visible candidates, further information and references were usually needed to assure serious consideration. On the other hand, rosters did provide a means of communication among the women and minorities themselves, a mechanism for transmitting information about job opportunities, organizing efforts, and other activities and news of interest. Over time, rosters came to be used more and more in that way, while playing a subsidiary if lesser role in direct recruitment efforts.

The evolution from rosters to other measures to foster the employment of women in higher education administration is demonstrated by the experience of the organization Higher Education Resource Services (HERS), which was founded in 1972. HERS originated as a project of a small group of academic women under the leadership of Sheila Tobias, then associate provost of Wesleyan University.[15] The group called itself the Committee for the Concerns of Women in New England Colleges and Universities. Members of the group, which consisted of high-level administrators, were beginning to receive many requests to nominate women for academic positions as institutions came under the newly issued federal affirmative action regulations. The idea of the Concerns Committee, as it was called, in establishing Project HERS was to set up a central registry or talent bank to which such requests could be referred. From the outset, however, there were associated services with the talent bank—referrals, academic career advising, and consultation with colleges and universities regarding affirmative action programs. At a later stage, HERS expanded its activities further and offered seminars and courses for training in administrative skills to strengthen the qualifications of women candidates. In the process, a growing network of academic women was created, and the support of such networks became an important function of HERS.

Maintaining Networks

The HERS project in New England soon served as a model for similar programs in other regions of the country. HERS/Mid-Atlantic, formed in 1974, was a spin-off from the original group. HERS/New England, based at Wellesley College, and HERS/Mid-Atlantic, based at the University of Pennsylvania, cooperated in various ways and worked within the same general framework, but each has also developed its own programs. Another sister organization, HERS/West, was established in 1979 at the University of Utah. Like its counterparts, it maintains a network of women administrators in higher education and conducts professional development programs. In 1983 HERS/Mid-Atlantic moved to the University of Denver and has since operated from there as HERS/Mid-America.

Another kind of network for the advancement of women in higher education administration is the National Identification Program established by the American Council on Education (ACE) in 1977. This program, which is also known as ACE/NIP, was developed by the Office of Women in Higher Education at ACE under the direction of Emily Taylor, followed by Donna Shavlik. It is designed to identify talented women, to increase their visibility as leaders, and to create networks of women and men in the academic community who share a commitment to the advancement of women and who could recommend and sponsor them. Because ACE's constituency is primarily senior administrators, the program focuses on increasing the number of women as presidents, vice presidents, and deans. In this respect, ACE/NIP differs from the HERS network, which is concerned with women at all levels of administration.

The ACE/NIP structure consists of a series of interlocking networks connecting state-based programs with other activities at the national level.[16] Each state has a coordinator, who holds a high-level administrative post, and a state planning committee composed of 10 to 15 women administrators representing all systems of higher education. In addition, there are state and national panelists who are leaders in higher education or in positions to influence higher education. Panelists include women and men who are college and university presidents, trustees, association heads, public officials, and civic leaders. Panelists participate in the National Identification Program in a variety of ways such as attending state or national forums or other programs.

ACE/NIP forums provide an opportunity to discuss educational issues of regional or national concern. Their main purpose, however, is to promote contacts between participants and panelists that would continue beyond the forum and result in recommendations or nominations for positions or memberships on councils and committees. To complement the efforts of national and state programs, the Washington office of the National Identification Program also works directly with search committees, presidents, and board members to increase the number of women in senior administrative positions.

Developing Training Programs

A further strategy for the advancement of women in higher education administration is one that has already been alluded to—the development of special training programs. It is interesting to note that prior to the 1970s there were few training programs in academic administration either for women or for men. Schools of education offered degrees in educational administration, and some offered degrees in higher education administration. However, those degrees were more likely to lead to positions in public school administration or to government positions in education than to college and university positions, except at less prestigious institutions.

In general, colleges and universities put greater emphasis on scholarly qualifications, and advance preparation in administration was not seen as a prerequisite. Entry into administrative careers was usually through one of three routes. For some kinds of positions, such as financial and technical ones, specialists might be hired from outside the university, often from among alumni of the institution who had an interest in returning to the campus. There are also many examples of presidents being drawn from public life or business. For most academic positions faculty members, usually men, were chosen largely from the ranks of department chairmen where they were presumed to have acquired administrative experience. Or younger men might be chosen after having served an apprenticeship as assistant dean or other junior-level position or as member of a college or university committee of some kind. Further staff training and development was not standard practice.[17] In this respect, institutions of higher education differed from other large organizations in business, government, and the military, which devoted substantial resources to in-house education for administrative staff and regularly sent executives to external training programs. Among the few programs available in higher education were those offered by the American Council on Education for newly appointed deans and presidents. They were short-term, typically two days, but they provided at least some degree of orientation and exposure to such subjects as financial planning, legal issues, and personnel selection and development.

During the 1970s, colleges and universities began to give more attention to the training of academic administrators. Several reasons are usually cited for this change—the growth in size and complexity of higher education institutions after World War II, increasing financial pressure and the need for cost control,[18] and new requirements for accountability to federal, state, and local public funding sources. The most ambitious and prestigious training program was the Institute for Educational Management (IEM) at Harvard University. The institute, established in 1970, offered and continues to offer a six-week summer program for senior-level administrators, usually presidents, vice presidents, chancellors, and provosts. The annual enrollment is approximately 125, and the curriculum covers topics such as budgeting, information systems, fundraising, endowment management, and government relations. Another kind of program that has played an important role in the recruitment and training of academic administrators is the ACE Fellows Program. This program consists of a year-long internship combined with a series of seminars on basic administrative skills, public policy issues, and career planning. Established in 1965, it was one of few training programs available at that time and has continued successfully to the present day.

As might be expected, women were at first little more than a token presence in these programs. In the case of the IEM, this reflected in part the small number of women in senior-level positions. To increase the representation of women the institute found that special efforts were needed to identify and recruit eligible candidates. With the aid of a grant from the Ford Foundation, the institute undertook such an effort to seek out women and was able to recruit 62 women administrators up to 1974.[19] A photograph of the ACE Fellows Program class of 1965–1966 shows only one woman, a nun, in a group of 24 men; a photograph of the class of 1984–1985 shows a noticeable difference. See photographs following page 314.

As a new strategy, training programs specifically designed for women first appeared in 1973 when the University of Michigan established the Institute for Administrative Advancement of Academic Women. This was a six-week summer program, later reduced to four weeks, directed toward women in junior-level faculty and administrative positions. About 30 women participated in the program each year. The curriculum covered topics such as personnel management, collective bargaining, legal problems of universities, and computer simulation in academic decision-making. After two years at the University of Michigan, the institute moved to the University of Wisconsin–Madison, where it was called simply the Institute for Administrative Advancement (IAA) and was opened up to men as well as women. In this form, the program continued for two more years before being phased out.

Notwithstanding its demise, IAA led the way to other training programs geared to the particular needs of women. The most successful of these is the Summer Institute for Women in Higher Education Administration co-sponsored by Bryn Mawr College and HERS/Mid-America, which was established in 1976. The institute is a four-week residential program held on the Bryn Mawr College campus. It is open to women administrators and faculty members from the United States and abroad. In recent years minority participation has reached 20 percent. The curriculum consists of six components: academic governance, administrative uses of the computer, finance and budgeting, management and leadership, human relations skills, and professional development. In the professional development component special attention is given to the needs of women in planning and managing careers. Another distinctive feature of the program is the emphasis on the development of a network of women administrators for mutual support. The institute places a high priority on this aspect of the program and over the years has committed a sizable proportion of its resources to the fostering of a network of peers, sponsors, and mentors who can provide information, resources, and useful contacts to one another.[20] Communication with past participants, faculty, and staff is maintained through a newsletter, directories, and reunions throughout the country. There is also an interlocking relationship with the other networks concerned with women in administration: HERS and ACE/NIP.

Training programs for women administrators are also conducted by the other two HERS offices. They differ in size and format from the summer institute, although they share course material. HERS/New England established a management institute in 1977 consisting of a series of technical skills seminars over five weekends throughout the academic year. The subjects covered are similar to those of the summer institute. HERS/West conducts an institute in the format of a conference each summer in which seminars and workshops in professional development are provided over a period of several days for women administrators in the region.

During the 1970s a number of internship programs were also established to train women for careers in higher education administration. Perhaps the best known among them was the program funded by the Carnegie Corporation and based at Cedar Crest College. Sixteen colleges that primarily enroll women cooperated in the program, which offered a ten-month internship experience in college management to recent women graduates. One graduate under age 30 from each college was assigned, following a 15-day workshop, to work directly with a senior administrator at an affiliated institution. Upon completion of the internship the participants were assisted in finding positions or seeking graduate or professional training.

Evaluation of Progress to Date and Outlook for the Future

To what extent have the strategies and programs we have described been successful in achieving their goals? How effective are rosters, networks, and training programs in increasing the representation of women in college and university administration? We have noted that there has been a slow but steady increase in the number of women administrators. To what extent is it attributable to the particular strategies that have been followed and to what extent to other factors? Can we expect continued progress or is there a slowdown in store? How long will special efforts on behalf of women be needed?

Each of the strategies followed has been subject to evaluation, and the findings are available in published reports. Based on these reports, the general conclusion is that the efforts have been at least partially successful. The report on the effectiveness of rosters has already been noted. With regard to the National Identification Program, the ACE Office of Women in Higher Education reported that of the 20 women who attended the first forum in 1977, 7 were appointed to presidencies within a few years. In the eight years since that time approximately 600 women participated in national forums. Of these, 200 have changed to positions of higher management responsibility and 29 have become college and university presidents.[21] HERS/New England conducted an evaluation of the administrative skills program in 1980 in order to determine the effect of the program on the subsequent career advancement of participants. The study matched the initial group of participants with a comparison group of nonparticipants in a questionnaire survey covering the 1978–1980 period. Although two years is a short period in which to measure advancement, it was found that 30 percent of the participant group compared with 20 percent of the nonparticipant group reported promotions during that time.[22] Both HERS/New England and ACE/NIP are aware that self-selection may influence the results; nevertheless, the evidence seems clearly to support the conclusion that the programs do contribute to career advancement.

It is true that these programs have not in themselves changed institutional procedures and practices, but that has been accomplished through affirmative action regulations, as described in chapter 8. Thus far, then, we have attributed the increase in the number and proportion of women in higher education administration to three factors: (1) affirmative action regulations, (2) career development and support programs, and (3) some increase in gender awareness and receptivity to women in academic life reflecting changes in society at large. However, while there has been progress, much of it has been at the lower levels of administration. The various programs we have described helped to fill the pipelines to the higher administrative ranks, but the pace of upward movement has been slow. The studies that Carol Frances conducted for CUPA clearly showed that neither retrenchment nor low turnover in administrative positions can account for the slow progress. She concluded: "Thus those who say that the differential patterns of employment are not the results of discrimination have less and less of a foundation on which to base that claim."[23]

In terms of equity, women should be represented at all levels of higher education administration in accordance with their representation in the availability pool. In the long run, the pool depends in large part on the flow of new PhDs into academic careers initially as faculty. The proportion of women among the new doctorates reached 34 percent in 1984 compared with 16 percent in 1972. Moreover, throughout that period a higher proportion of men than women doctorate recipients entered careers in business and industry rather than academia. We have seen that the proportion of women holding administrative positions in academic affairs is 28 percent, a figure which leaves room for improvement.

Equity is not the only reason for seeking to increase the number of women in higher education administration. There are other benefits as well. A larger pool of qualified candidates available to institutions is conducive to more effective administration. In this connection, it is interesting to note that as of 1986 there was still no training program for men comparable to that for women interested in careers in administration. Even more important than efficiency, a larger pool is equated with higher quality and better leadership. A larger number of women is essential to ordering the priorities of higher education institutions in such a way as to permit all students, women as well as men, to achieve their potential. Also, women in leadership positions in more visible numbers serve as much needed role models or mentors to women students aspiring to academic careers. It is also important that men should be accustomed to seeing and working with women in such roles. We are as yet short of that goal.

Notes

1. Alan Pifer, "Women in Higher Education," speech delivered at the Southern Association of Colleges and Schools, Miami, November 29, 1971 (pamphlet, Carnegie Corporation of New York).

2. Margaret Mulvehill Culley, "Sisterhood Was Powerful," *Commonweal*, October 4, 1974, p. 16.

3. Patricia Albjerg Graham, "Women in Academe," *Science*, September 25, 1970, p. 1288.

4. Ruth M. Oltman, *Campus 1970: Where Do Women Stand?* (Washington, DC: American Association of University Women, 1970).

5. Jacquelyn A. Mattfeld, "Many Are Called, but Few Are Chosen," in W. Todd Furniss and Patricia Albjerg Graham, eds., *Women in Higher Education* (Washington, DC: American Council on Education, 1974).

6. These figures are based on data compiled by the Equal Employment Opportunity Commission from over 3,000 colleges and universities in the United States. In general, there is little published data on the number of administrators in higher education institutions. Information on this subject is not regularly collected by the Department of Education. The *Digest of Education Statistics, 1983–1984*, provides information based on a special study, the *Survey of Employees in Institutions of Higher Education, 1976–77*, carried out by the National Center for Education Statistics.

7. For a study of the role of middle managers in the overall functioning of institutions of higher education see Robert A. Scott, *Lords, Squires and Yeomen: Collegiate Middle Managers and Their Organizations*, AAHE-ERIC/Higher Education Research Report no. 7 (Washington, DC: American Association for Higher Education, 1978).

8. Carol Frances, with R. Frank Mensel, Julie S. Withers, and F. Stephen Malott, "Women and Minorities in Administration of Higher Education Institutions," *1975–76 Administrative Compensation Survey*, Special Supplement (Washington, DC: College and University Personnel Association, 1977).

9. Carol Frances and R. Frank Mensel, *Women and Minorities in Administration of Higher Education Institutions: Employment Patterns and Salary Comparisons*, A

Special Report (Washington, DC: College and University Personnel Association, 1981).

10. In a study of college administrators carried out in 1981 by the Center for the Study of Higher Education at Pennsylvania State University, it was found that 18 percent of those surveyed were the first person to hold their position. Further information about the project, with particular reference to career paths of women administrators, is provided by Kathryn M. Moore, "Careers in College and University Administration: How Are Women Affected?" in Adrian Tinsley, Cynthia Secor, and Sheila Kaplan, eds., *Women in Higher Education Administration* (San Francisco: Jossey-Bass, 1983).

11. Carol Frances and R. Frank Mensel, *1985–86 Administrative Compensation Survey* (Washington, DC: College and University Personnel Association, February 1986). The proportion of minorities in primary positions was 9 percent. The gender breakdown for minorities is not given.

12. Frances et al., "Women and Minorities." pp. 36–39.

13. One example of a shift toward more egalitarian ideas is provided in the questionnaire described in chapter 11. The responses of academic administrators in 1980 compared with 1972 indicated a sharp decline in the proportion of those who viewed the competence of women students below that of men.

14. Janet W. Brown, Heather Coleman, and Susan E. Posner, *Rosters of Minority Women Professionals*, (Washington, DC: American Academy for the Advancement of Science, 1975).

15. Lilli S. Hornig, "HERStory," *Grants*, March 1978, pp. 36–42.

16. Donna Shavlik and Judy Touchton, "Toward a New Era of Leadership: The National Identification Program," in Tinsley, Secor, and Kaplan, *Women in Higher Education Administration.*

17. The Training of Future Academic Administrators (Madison: Program in University Administration, University of Wisconsin—Extension, 1972).

18. George Keller, *Academic Strategy: The Management Revolution in Higher Education* (Baltimore and London: Johns Hopkins Press, 1983), p. viii.

19. Alison R. Bernstein, "Foundation Support for Administrative Advancement: A Mixed Record," in Tinsley, Secor, and Kaplan, eds., *Women in Higher Education Administration*, p. 80.

20. Cynthia Secor, "Preparing the Individual for Institutional Leadership: The Summer Institute," in Tinsley, Secor, and Kaplan, eds., *Women in Higher Education Administration*, p. 32.

21. Shavlik and Touchton, "Toward a New Era," p. 53.

22. Jeanne J. Speizer, "The Administrative Skills Program: What Have We Learned," in Tinsley, Secor, and Kaplan, eds., *Women in Higher Education Administration*, p. 42.

23. Frances and Mensel, *Women and Minorities in Administration of Higher Education Institutions: Employment Patterns and Salary Comparisons*, p. i.

15

Women as Trustees

Scholars differ on the origins of lay boards of higher education. Some point to Harvard's first external board of overseers as a uniquely American governance structure.[1] Others cite prototypes of twelfth-century Italian city-states where boards of citizens served as liaisons between students and instructors. Educational policy in the Netherlands and Scotland following the Reformation in fact vested responsibility in lay leaders instead of the clergy.[2]

Whatever the colonists' precedents or innovation, however, Harvard's founding in 1636 eventually resulted in a lay governance structure that, with few challenges, became the model for American higher education. Oxford and Cambridge had been moving toward increasing lay control, but both they and their European counterparts, evolving from models of medieval master guilds, resisted the trend. They were, and with some modification still are, controlled by their senior faculties, at least in principle.[3] Critics of American higher education have been known to praise English and European systems as models of self-regulating control, but although we borrowed many Old World academic traditions, our governance structures *de jure* did not vest control in the hands of the faculty. Although we do have faculty governance systems that exercise power over academic matters, American colleges and universities are for better or for worse governed by lay boards, the ultimate sources of authority for the institutions whose assets they hold "in trust."[4]

Clergymen dominated governing boards of the early American colleges. With few experienced faculty members in the colonies, well-educated clergy provided both needed expertise and essential links between their colleges and the church and community. Experienced clergy also saw themselves as sources of vocational guidance—colonial colleges trained ministers.[5]

As higher education expanded in the late eighteenth and early nineteenth centuries, however, trustee selections diversified. With the rise of liberal arts colleges and professional and graduate schools, and especially with the founding of the land grant universities and state teachers' colleges, trustees began to include among their numbers representatives of the public-at-large, lay community leaders, business executives, and wealthy patrons who were expected to provide their institutions with one or more of the three Ws: "Work, Wealth, and Wisdom." Especially in the private sector, wealth played an increasingly important role, with the private sector trustee expected to "give, get, or get off." The history of universities in the late nineteenth century is fraught with tensions generated by wealthy, powerful donors—the Stanfords, for example—as their faculties struggled for academic freedom.[6]

Responsibilities and styles of boards have in fact varied considerably with the types of institutions governed; but although designated responsibilities have changed over the years, most noticeably reflecting the increasing complexity of higher education since World War II, the primary functions ascribed to boards have remained remarkably similar. In addition to fund-raising and institutional advocacy, a conventional summary includes responsibility for setting institutional policies and priorities; long-range planning; approving and monitoring budgets; and, judged by many to be the single most important role, selecting and evaluating the president.

Trustees are thus vested with considerable power and authority. They constitute the legal "body," the corporate presence of the institution. Reviewing both individual histories of institutions and the conventional body of trustee literature, however, it is apparent that trustee power, especially in the postwar decades, exists mostly as potential, power delegated but seldom exercised. Although critics such as Thorstein Veblen in an earlier day have contended that "boards are of no material use in any connection,"[7] the more common view among scholars and others is that that trustee power "could be a vital factor in strengthening and improving the operations of countless institutions."[8] One community college trustee observed that an effective board can counterbalance the teachers and administrators whom he sees as "notoriously conservative when it comes to change."[9]

This potential for implementing change, for "strengthening and improving," has for over a century sporadically caught the attention of women concerned with issues of women's education, but the attention paid to women on boards—their roles, their routes to and orientation on boards, even their potential for influence—is striking in its absence. There is little mention of women on boards in the scholarly literature— in the history of women's colleges or women's education, for example. Nor is there mention of women on boards in the most recent studies of women in higher education.[10] Even more curious, with several exceptions, little awareness of women's roles or potential as trustees has informed the shared strategies and programs of contemporary women activists in higher education. (See Appendix 15.1 for a summary and assessment of organized activities for women trustees during the last 20 years.)

Still more puzzling, however, is the surprising dearth of information about boards in general, information about board functioning or about those individuals who fill the roles of trustees and how they get to be who they are. One of the first attempts to describe and assess attitudes of a national sample of the trustee population was made in 1968 by Rodney Hartnett. A subsequent study in 1976 by Irene Gomberg and Frank Atelsek included a larger sample but a less comprehensive focus and analysis.[11] As Hartnett pointed out in the introduction to his study, ". . . it is somewhat remarkable that so little is known about who trustees are, what they do in their roles as trustees, and how they feel about current issues in American higher education."[12] The closer we get to describing board dynamics, in fact, the more elusive board functioning seems, and what little we know about the history and dynamics of women on boards offers one of the more depressing chapters in the history of women in higher education.

One noted scholar of boards points out that in colonial days "the collegiate boards had few (if any) members from the distaff side . . . [and] the aversion to women trustees and regents continued for a century."[13] One of the first official records we have of attention paid to women on governing boards of colleges and universities dates from April 1887. The occasion was an annual meeting of the American Association of University Women (AAUW), then known as the Association of Collegiate Alumnae (ACA). According to the official AAUW history, in a paper entitled "The Relation of Women to the Governing Boards and Faculties of Colleges," an ACA leader concluded that "no active effort should be made to urge the appointment of women to professorships, but . . . the appointment of well-trained and qualified women as trustees was a measure worthy of hearty endorsement."[14]

Fortunately, as we have seen elsewhere in this volume, the speaker's suggestions to ignore the absence of women faculty were not heeded; almost a century later, however, her concern for women trustees reads like a progressive agenda for the 1990s. Boards remain bastions of white male privilege. The average trustee is white, male, Protestant, and Republican. In his late fifties, in business or a prestige profession, he personifies the traditional American definitions of success. Collectively, the network of higher education trustees in this country has access to the primary sources of wealth and power in our culture—a predominantly white male system of corporate and political influence. In spite of some attention paid to the need for more diverse representation on boards, the numbers of women and minority trustees have increased insignificantly, even in the last decade, and periodic efforts to raise issues of women in higher education to the board level, including the special concerns of women's own roles on boards, have met with little success.

A Theoretical Framework

Before pursuing in more detail the history and current issues of women on boards, however, it may be useful to describe a theoretical perspective that attempts to account for some of what we do know about board roles and functioning, especially as those roles relate to issues of institutional change and equal opportunity. Broadly sketched, higher education in America can be seen to have several contradictory strands: on the one hand, higher education has evolved as a heritage of the elite, a socialization process for the upper classes. The Ivy League institutions have for generations provided the imprimatur of success for the (male) children of the rich and the powerful. On the other hand, in a uniquely American tradition, colleges and universities have been expected to provide routes to upward mobility for the less privileged. As institutions, they have also been expected to serve as models of pluralism and collegial governance. With the evolution of the land grant universities and normal schools, the City University of New York and the California public college and university systems, for example, there has been an explicit tradition, an essential part of our national heritage and self-image, that colleges and universities provide not only access to the American dream, but themselves function as microcosms of egalitarian culture. And following the turmoil of the 1960s, even boards of elite institutions have been pressured to define as part of their institutional missions the role of fostering diversity and equal opportunity.

There are implicit contradictions here. Boards are by their very nature conservative. As one higher education scholar pointed out, it is a curious paradox that, for a democratic nation, we have evolved "a plan of university control which technically and legally does not show even a trace of democracy."[15] Yet board governance structures are not unique to higher education; and, perhaps more important, they are structures which, at least in broad outline, dominate the life of many social and political institutions, from corporations and government bureaucracies to churches and other community organizations.

A board is the corporate identity of its institution, the legal and symbolic structure which preserves institutional continuity through time. Faculty members, students, administrators, even alumni—all are transient, weaving in and out of the life of the institution. Constituent groups, traditions, buildings, and archives all shape a college's life and history, but only the board—the structural body of the institution— holds the "trust," both financial and symbolic. And as preservers of the trust, they engage in activities that, more often than not, are designed to preserve and extend their institutions in their own image. Among private boards, for example, selecting new trustees is the decision-making process trustees describe they are most directly involved in—an activity more frequently cited than fund-raising, long-range planning, even investment counsel.[16] Functional strategies for "conserving" the institution will obviously differ among boards in different types of institutions—in public institutions, for example, trustees are politically appointed or run for election—but the point is that boards, virtually by definition, are governing bodies which exist to perpetuate the institutions they represent. And few factional views survive this fundamental conserving force on boards. (Even student representatives soon take on both the dress and concerns of the institution "as a whole.")

Besides these structural constraints, however, there are also the inherent tensions generated by elites functioning in a democratic society.[17] Trusteeship offers a powerful reward/status position that marks success and power. While trustees "serve the public good"—in fact empowering and not infrequently financing much of the voluntary sector—board positions provide political rewards and a status system in the public sector, the epitome of club membership in the private sector. A marker of success and affiliation with "one's own kind," trusteeship offers connections and the best educated status money can buy. It is "what one does" in the professional, political, and social circles most private trustees and many public trustees move in.

This is not to deny the generosity of board members, their considerable volunteer support, and their contributions of both time and money. Yet this social perspective of status, privilege, and political and social affiliation is also essential for understanding the basic conserving function of boards.

Boards have little impulse to espouse diversity. Hence the conflict: Many of our institutions share at least the rhetoric of social mobility and an egalitarian society. The idea of the collegium is itself idealized as the model of a self-governing, learning community of scholar-teachers and students. Even elite institutions in the last decade have defined for themselves roles as leaders of diversity and have espoused, with and without government intervention, their roles in diversifying their student bodies, faculties, administrations, and boards. Yet the boards which govern these institutions, both the elite institutions and the colleges and universities of the American dream, are, with few exceptions, inclined to preserve and protect the status quo—both structurally, as the corporate actors of their institutions, and individually, as board members drawn from the ranks of the privileged and powerful. They tolerate diversity to the extent of opening the gates and letting in nonwhites and nonmales, but only if they are "truly qualified," which is to say, "like us," individuals who will fit the expectations of existing social systems and hierarchies. Equal opportunity understood in all its implications is a radical challenge to the economic and governance structures of our institutions. Acknowledging the legitimacy of equal opportunity inevitably involves closer scrutiny of existing hierarchies and their functioning and requires closer scrutiny of the unexamined issues and assumptions affecting latent board functions. "Excellence" and other qualifications or "admissions" criteria are not objective systems of evaluation free of class or cultural bias.

Given these frames of reference and historical contexts, then, let us turn to a more detailed history and current assessment of women on boards—where they were and are and how they function. The objective of this chapter, finally, is to assess women's roles on boards as a microcosm of social change: how their experiences illuminate the bedrock of organizational structures and functioning which we must better understand if we are ever to evolve more equitable institutions capable of genuine diversity and equal opportunities. As Richard Lyman, president of the Rockefeller Foundation and former president of Stanford University, observed in taking on the leadership of Independent Sector, "The rhetoric of pluralism is cheap; learning, not just to tolerate diversity but to glory in it, is what counts."[18]

The History of Women on Boards

Limited data are available about the history of women on boards. A 1917 study of 143 colleges and universities found 75 women trustees, or 3 percent of the total of 2,470 trustees.[19] A 1947 study of 30 universities documents only 3.4 percent women.[20] With few exceptions, the only other sources of data available are archival records or published histories of individual institutions. Reviewing several published histories, it quickly becomes apparent that even those institutions which should have been more alert to the need for women on boards—the elite women's colleges, for example—reveal patterns strikingly similar to most other colleges of their day. Vassar, Smith, and Bryn Mawr, for example, were formed with all-male boards and, in Smith's case at least, they were "all men of superior ability, of sterling Christian character," all but one from Harvard, Yale, Brown, Amherst, or Williams.[21]

Unique among its sister institutions, Barnard was founded with a majority of women on its first board.[22] By 1889, however, attributed in part to the Association of Collegiate Alumnae's "hearty endorsement" cited earlier, "several positions of trust" had been opened to women in other ACA colleges. In 1889, seven ACA members served as trustees, representing four governing boards: Boston University, Smith, Vassar, and Wellesley. Responding to the association's mission to wield influence for women's education, they formed a Committee on Collegiate Administration which considered a range of issues affecting women's education, among them the organization of boards, methods of financial administration, the selection and appointment of teachers, relations of alumnae associations, and the status of special students.

The late 1890s and early 1900s saw a rapid increase in the numbers of students, men and women, attending colleges and universities. This influx, however beneficial for women at first, quickly became the excuse to prompt boards to adopt quotas, and policies of sex segregation in formerly integrated institutions became commonplace. Responding to "the seeming significance of this new movement toward the higher education of women," the ACA trustees committee established themselves as a group "watching and questioning tendencies in the higher education of women."[23] By 1909 the committee numbered 23 members serving on boards of six colleges and one university—Wisconsin; a woman had also been appointed to the Cornell board; and collectively, women trustees more rigorously focused on broader issues of concern to both women and to their institutions. By 1914 the committee had reconstituted itself as the Conference of Women Trustees and, until 1929, held meetings in conjunction with the biennial association conventions.

In 1914, however, they formalized their concerns as part of a national association resolution. Among broader institutional priorities identified—high academic standards and a "uniform and self-explanatory system of college accounting," for example—the resolution passed defined women trustees' responsibilities to include monitoring women faculty salaries "to see that the women teachers . . . receive salaries equal to those of men teachers of the same academic standing, and . . . are not assigned social and other non-academic duties not required of men scholars of equal rank. . . ." The women trustees' conference also owned as their responsibility the need "to take active measures to secure for all women teachers . . . the same opportunities of promotion in position and salary" that were afforded to men of comparable rank and standing. The committee also drafted what is most likely the first instance on record of availability pools. They resolved that women faculty be promoted "to head professorships in proportion to the relative numbers of men and women employed as instructors of higher grade in the colleges or universities which we represent. . . ."[24]

These explicit agendas must have provided some mutual support and resolve while they lasted but, then as now, a major issue confronting women on boards was the more fundamental reality of acceptance. Before women trustees could pursue the concerns they had outlined, they had to become active, functioning trustees. There is some evidence that then, as now, women were seen by at least some of their colleagues as active trustees and indeed took their board work seriously. One scholar commented on a decision the Smith board and others made in the 1920s to reduce life terms for trustees to renewable ten-year terms: "That the board would function better without these part-time members was a conception rapidly grasped by the livelier, especially the feminine, trustees."[25] In spite of commitment and liveliness, however, an earlier episode is probably more characteristic of the subtle and not so subtle barriers women trustees had to overcome. One of the first women trustees at Smith recalls:

> When I first became an alumna trustee, in 1906, it was the unwritten custom for the three women to sit in a demure row on the sofa, and the president, with his characteristic fine courtesy, always placed a footstool before each one of us. When Miss X. came on the board and attended the first meeting, she sat down in one of the chairs, with no perception that she was doing anything out of the ordinary. The president looked at her once or twice with a vague discomfort and finally said, "Miss X. would you not be more comfortable on the sofa with the other ladies?" Miss X. replying, "Oh no, I am quite comfortable here, thank you," he gave it up and thereafter the feminine three sat anywhere it happened to be convenient.[26]

The Current Status of Women on Boards

The Smith trustee who recalled the sofa incident also describes the "stately politeness" which distinguished trustee meetings. It is perhaps this disjuncture between perceived politeness and pervasive, albeit genteel, discrimination that accounts, at least in part, for the few cycles of attention paid to women on boards (see Appendix 15.1)—and accounts, at least in part, for women's own conflicting perceptions and self-images. For in describing the status and roles of women on boards, one is struck by profound contradictions. These are contradictions most likely endemic to any marginal group making a bid for acceptance and self-regard (it is difficult for anyone who is trying to work effectively in a group to acknowledge or confront directly the reality of marginal status), but in the case of women trustees—in most instances women of wealth and class—their energy, their often perceptive analyses of issues, and their self-images are riddled with contradictions. Women on school boards interviewed in 1973, for example, vigorously denied any problems with sex discrimination, yet went on to describe their routes to the board as "rough and narrow," with no room for "a tough broad" or "a frilly female." And in spite of no perceptions of sex discrimination, they point out that a woman board member must have "a strong back, a thick skin, and an indomitable will" if she is successfully to withstand the pressures she will face.[27]

These contradictions run through many women trustees' perceptions. Although over 65 percent of women trustees responding to a 1978 Pennsylvania study disagreed—or strongly disagreed—with the observation that women belonged to less powerful board committees than their male peers, the largest groups of women trustees belong to committees which at least 94 percent of the same respondents did not view as most important. These contradictions notwithstanding, however, most women trustees responding to the Pennsylvania study also felt they were listened to, did not need to present a united front to be taken more seriously, and did not feel hampered by lack of access to informally shared information.[28]

In a series of interviews of New Jersey college and university board members conducted in 1982, the contradictions become more striking.[29] Women trustees often speak encouragingly about their institutions' commitments to affirmative action, for example. In one instance, a woman trustee comments that her president was actively supporting women on campus, yet she later observes that "he won't pull anything because he knows I'm here." These contradictions take their toll. To maintain what is essentially a split vision, women often blame themselves. Rather than criticize their boards for not setting up more effective orientation programs—a problem cited by both women and men trustees—they will protest that they did not know enough or were not able to find the time to catch up. In interview after interview, the women speak knowledgeably about board issues and dynamics—in authoritative tones of voice, in complex syntax—only to revert to stereotypically feminine, breathy responses and disjointed syntax riddled with pauses and hesitant interjections when they describe their own roles on their boards: classic symptoms of people who feel themselves not taken seriously.

In terms of numbers, there have been some gains in the representation of women on trustee boards, but the gains have not been large. The late 1960s saw numerous articles and stories in the popular media heralding "dramatic" institutional changes following in the wake of anti-war demonstrations and student unrest. Hartnett did a followup to his 1968 survey to measure the changes that a *New York Times* October 1969 editorial described as a "healthy tide . . . running toward reform of college boards of trustees to add diversity to their membership."[30] Twelve percent of the 376 boards responding to his followup had added one woman trustee; under 4 percent had added two, and less than 1 percent had added three. In a sense, the data suggest the reality of tokenism. Those institutions with few or no women were those which most often responded with additions or intentions of adding a woman trustee. Those boards with the highest representation of women on their boards in the 1968 study reported the fewest additions.

More recent data is provided by two studies conducted by the Association of Governing Boards of Universities and Colleges. The first was a survey of the composition of trustee boards in 1977, and the second was an update carried out in 1985. The studies concluded that the characteristics of the boards governing colleges and universities have not changed dramatically since 1977. There are estimated to be in all about 48,000 trustees and regents serving on 2,200 governing boards, of which about 200 are multi-campus boards. In 1985 the proportion of board members who were women was 20 percent compared with 15 percent in 1977. Six percent of board members were black in 1985 and that percentage was unchanged from 1977.[31] Table 15.1 provides a summary of the characteristics of governing board members in 1977 and 1985.

Women fare best on boards of women's colleges and in community and junior colleges. The 1976 survey conducted by Suzanne Howard for the American Association of University Women reported that women constituted 45 percent of the boards of women's colleges.[32]

In the 1978 Pennsylvania study, women trustees constituted 33 percent of the boards of women's colleges, and 5 of the 11 women's colleges responding to the study reported majority female boards.[33] The representation of women on community college boards in 1985 was 31 percent, according to a survey conducted under the auspices of the Association of Community College Trustees.[34]

Where women have made gains on trustee boards, the gains seem to

Table 15.1   Characteristics of Governing Boards: 1977 and 1985

	1977	1985
Sex		
Men	84.9%	79.9%
Women	15.1	20.1
Total	100.0	100.0
Race		
White	93.0	90.1
Black	6.0	6.3
Hispanic	*	0.6
Other Minority	1.0	3.0
Total	100.0	100.0
Education		
Less Than High School	0.4	0.0
High School Diploma	6.5	4.4
AA, AS	2.8	2.9
BA, BS	38.8	40.2
MA, MS, MAT	19.4	22.8
MD, JD	21.2	18.9
PhD, EdD	11.0	10.7
Total	100.0	100.0
Age		
Under 30 Years	2.2	2.0
30–39 Years	7.3	6.8
40–49 Years	24.4	20.8
50-59 Years	35.0	38.1
60–69 Years	24.7	24.1
70 Years and Over	6.5	8.2
Total	100.0	100.0

Source: Association of Governing Boards, *Composition of Governing Boards, 1985* (Washington, DC: AGB, 1986), p. 36.

*Not available.

have been a function of external pressures and legal mandates. The 1982 New Jersey data, for example, reflect the results of one of the only laws in the country mandating at least two women on each state and community college board: By 1982, 13.2 percent of state boards and 28.6 percent of community college boards were women. As in the Pennsylvania study, women do better on the boards of women's colleges, and because a relatively high proportion of private colleges in the state are Catholic women's colleges, the private and public sector figures in fact show remarkably similar proportions. Disaggregating the figures, however, it is clear that the gains show only in the public sector—with the impact of the state law—and in women's colleges.

Not only are women generally underrepresented on boards, but once on boards, women trustees are underutilized. The Pennsylvania study describes 75 percent of respondents citing the executive committee as one of the two most important committees of their boards. Only 25 percent, however, in fact served on executive committees, even though 37 percent felt qualified to do so. Over 45 percent also cited the finance or budget committee as one of the most important board committees, yet only 17 percent of women trustees served on finance and budget committees compared with the over 30 percent who reported they felt qualified to serve.[35] Clearly, these data also reveal an issue of women trustees' confidence and self-image: Given the demographic profiles of the trustees in the study, their educational background, their professional and volunteer experience, and their other board service, they underestimate their qualifications. But considering the discrepancies between the competencies they do acknowledge and the opportunities they have for using those skills effectively, a strong case can be made for interpreting even their own assessment of their qualifications as evidence of stereotyping and feedback which the women themselves have internalized.

Women trustees' committee service echoes the conventional stereotypes of women's abilities and ambitions: service-oriented and concerned with the nurture and education of the young. Women "best" serve on those committees—student affairs and academic affairs, for example—that draw on those traditional female skills and experiences. And those are not the skills or the powerful committees which—at least on most boards—set institutional agendas and, in effect, control the "trust." But even where women's experience or self-images go beyond the stereotypes, they are still constrained and not given opportunities to use the skills they see themselves having to offer. Even though fewer women than their male peers in both the Pennsylvania and national samples have business-related professional experience, for example, most of those with business experience were not members of finance or budget committees.[36] And the third most-cited committee women felt qualified to serve on in the Pennsylvania study, for example—development, one of the traditionally more important committees in private institutions—ranks sixth among those on which women actually serve.

In positions of leadership on their boards, the situation is even bleaker for women trustees. Overall, 39 percent of respondents in the Pennsylvania study felt qualified to chair 258 committees. In fact, 18 percent chaired 67 committees. Even among those committees on which women trustees most often served—student affairs and academic affairs—women chaired 5 percent and 4 percent, respectively, compared with 23 percent and 18 percent who felt qualified to chair.[37] Clearly, as women generally in their fifties and more traditionally conservative, women trustees have internalized many of the role expectations and limitations imposed on women in our culture; what is striking, however, is that the data describing even their own expectations and qualifications document such limited opportunites for their abilities.

More implicit discrimination on boards, while harder to measure, is also rampant. A number of the New Jersey women trustees interviewed, for example, report being excluded from informal decision-making exchanges, interrupted or not recognized in group discussions, and generally not drawn into the mainstream of board activity. The standard behavior of dominant numbers of men in groups prevails: Behaviors described ranged from "stately politeness" on one board—with all the women seated around the periphery of the room, none at the main conference table—to elaborate apologies for off-color language and concern for the "ladies" present and, at the worst, sexist jokes.

A content analysis of several major national trustee publications reveals, at best, benign neglect. Not only do most articles ignore concerns of women's issues on campus, women trustees themselves do not figure in the informal culture reflected in the news items and photographs.

Clearly, women have not been integrated into "newsworthy" trustee activities—not even as part of the re-created descriptions of events which so often serve as opportunities to put forth a better public image. They may no longer be relegated to the sofa, but it is little wonder that women trustees manifest a sense of themselves as marginal.

The Contributions of Women on Boards

In spite of considerable odds operating against their effective trusteeship, however, women trustees constitute an important presence on boards—at least to those concerned with boards functioning as more flexible, liberal governance structures. In the one comprehensive survey of trustee attitudes available, women trustees reflect a significantly more liberal presence on boards than do their male peers.

Hartnett found, for example, that women trustees were more supportive than their male peers of free faculty expression of opinions and were more opposed to administrative control of the student newspaper and loyalty oaths for faculty members. Hartnett also documents women trustees' interest in their institutions' taking active roles in solving social problems and being "less enamored with organized fraternities and sororities as a positive influence for undergraduates." As Table 15.2

Table 15.2 Educational Attitudes of Male and Female Trustees at Four-Year Colleges and Universities: 1968

| | Female Trustees | | | | Male Trustees (N = 3,943) | |
| | Women's Institutions (N = 230) | | Other Institutions (N = 289) | | | |
Educational Attitudes	Agree	Disagree	Agree	Disagree	Agree	Disagree
Academic Freedom						
Faculty members have right to free expression of opinions	83%	10%	78%	16%	66%	29%
Administration should control contents of student newspaper	16	77	21	69	42	50
Reasonable to require loyalty oath from faculty members	35	59	43	47	54	37
Who Should Be Served by Higher Education						
Attendance is a privilege, not a right	93	5	91	4	93	4

	Agree	Disagree	Agree	Disagree	Agree	Disagree
Academic aptitude should be the most important admissions criteria	76	19	69	24	74	21
Should be opportunities for higher education for anyone who wants it	91	6	89	6	84	12
Colleges should admit disadvantaged not meeting requirements	62	26	68	18	66	23
Others						
Institution should attempt to solve social problems	65	23	70	17	61	25
Students punished by local authorities for off-campus matters should also be disciplined by the college	33	52	43	45	50	38
A coeducational institution provides a better educational setting	31	54	69	19	67	20
Fraternities/sororities provide positive influence	27	66	36	43	47	34

Source: Rodney T. Hartnett, *The New College Trustee: Some Predictions for the 1970's* (Princeton, NJ: Educational Testing Service, 1970), p. 35.

Notes: Statements in table are abridged and modified.

Percentage "Agree" is a combination of those reponding "Strongly Agree" and "Agree." Percentage "Disagree" is a combination of those responding "Strongly Disagree" and "Disagree." Percentages do not add to 100 because of those responding "unable to say."

shows, women trustees of women's colleges were also somewhat more supportive of academic freedom. Hartnett points out that, overall, the women trustees in his sample more often held positions in "helping" professions (volunteer work, for example, or education)—and were more likely to be Democrats and liberal—but he concludes that using these background characteristics to explain the substantial differences in attitudes between men and women trustees is relatively unimportant: "What is important is that their appointment to trusteeships will probably contribute a more liberal viewpoint to most governing boards."[38]

The New Jersey interviews corroborate these findings. The women trustees interviewed generally tend to be more supportive of student concerns, especially of the needs of women students. Various women trustees (and few men trustees) express concern for and, at the least, awareness of such issues as part-time matriculation and the need to accommodate more flexible "rhythms" for women's education; student housing; role models for women students, especially in the sciences; and the need to foster leadership potential of students, especially women students. Women trustees are alert to issues such as day care and more flexible schedules for students, faculty, and staff. On one community college board interviewed, for example, several of the women trustees pointed to their responsibility for saving a day care program on campus that at least one trustee acknowledged would have been cut had it not been for women trustees' support. It is also the women trustees who pay attention to other "quality of life" issues on campuses which affect women and men students, faculty, and staff— adequate lounge space, food services, student centers, and dormitory accommodations, for example.

In addition to paying attention to these "soft" issues, women trustees are also more inclined to ask the "hard questions," requesting data on numbers of women and minorities on campus, for example, and questioning which numbers got collected and why. On the whole, women trustees are more alert than their male counterparts to their institution's legal mandates and responsibilities for affirmative action compliance.

Still another theme running through the interviews, however, is essentially a concern for more effective board functioning: on the need for consensus and the need to facilitate better group interaction by drawing out new trustees or trustees who do not participate; on the need for putting in place more efficient orientation programs and committee structures. It was a woman trustee on a liberal arts college board, for example, who developed a plan to rotate committee membership, giving all trustees more exposure, training them better in the process, and, as she described, eliminating the perceptual bias working which excluded women from such key committees as finance. Women trustees are also more likely to point to a necessary balance between social "grease" on a board and too much "in-group" socializing. On several boards, it was the women trustees who got the boards together for more structured informal socializing, using in at least one instance home entertainment as a strategy. This trustee was especially intent on drawing out members of the board who had not been participating and opening up other informal channels of communication in addition to the chairman's "touch base" network that had effectively cut out many of the women and men on the board. Time and again, it is also the women on boards who are most critical of elitism, of the narrower perspectives of, as one put it, "the corporation boys." More often than not, it is a woman trustee who describes the need to get more information, more diverse perspectives on issues coming before the board. While as aware as their male peers of the boundaries of governance and management, women trustees seem to assume more responsibility for soliciting information from other sources on campus, for being conduits to the board for information from various constituencies on campus.

Women trustees, generally, express preference for more direct involvement with campus activities. They take the time, in many instances, to get to know their institutions better than do their male counterparts. A number of male trustees in fact define their roles as better served with less involvement on campus—at all costs avoiding tripping over administrative boundaries. At least several of the women trustees, however, unobtrusively introduced themselves on campus and as a consequence seem to have evolved a more informed knowledge of the institutional styles and issues they are responsible for—without interfering with their presidents' prerogatives.

Conclusions

It is important to stress that the trustee activities and perspectives described as "women's contributions" are in fact issues of effective governance. The structural and social constraints defined earlier—the conserving nature of any "corporate actor" and the social pressures of status and power—often seem to operate against effective management. Coupled with the powerful constraints of stereotyping and perceptual bias, which women themselves often internalize, boards exhibit many of the dynamics which hamper opportunities for more vital, better-managed institutions.

Some of the tentative conclusions drawn from analysis of the New

Jersey interviews corroborate these perspectives. Rauh observed in 1959 that trustees with more diverse backgrounds provide broader points of view and make for a more effective board.[39] In fact, the most diverse New Jersey board interviewed—with the broadest mix of age, gender, racial/ethnic heritage, and political affiliation—was the board which most successfully survived several major institutional crises. Of all boards interviewed, this group, operating as a "committee of the whole," paid the most attention to affirmative action at all levels of the institution. (The collective concerns did not evolve without some individual struggles to set the agenda, but concerns gradually were listened to and began to be articulated by most board members, eliminating the need of minorities and women to assume isolated advocacy roles.) Of all boards interviewed, this board also most effectively drew on the various strengths of all its members.

This is a public board, governing a relatively young institution, with change to some extent forced on it through external mandates, through political appointments and affirmative action pressures. At least two of the women on the board, for example, owe their appointments to other women on the board or on the state nominating committee. And it is a board quite different in tone and make-up from the boards that governed the first years of the institution. There are still considerable pressures to preserve the institutional status quo, and the college has barely survived several bitter power struggles, both within the institution itself and on the board. Yet, better than any of the other boards interviewed, they seem to have learned to work together and to listen to each other, and the women on the board have been instrumental, at least in several instances, in facilitating that exchange.

The status quo is all too often unnecessarily restrictive, a function of institutional structures blindly perpetuating themselves, a function of individuals preserving and protecting only partially understood prerogatives of status and class. Fresh energy brings new insights. Higher education needs all the resources it can attract in the coming decades, and drawing on pools of women and minorities with diverse experience and perspectives can offer valuable assets for institutional governance. Women have obviously made both gains and contributions as trustees, but they have yet to take places in numbers comparable to the talent available. And all of us—women and men, students, faculty, staff, and trustees—have paid too high a price for discrimination. As boards diversify to reflect more accurately the populations they serve, as they become more aware of the subtle biases at work countered by proven strategies for more effective governance, higher education may come closer to what we have demanded of it for at least 200 years: models of opportunity and collegial governance, diverse communities of learning.

Appendix 15.1
Organizing Women Trustees

At least three attempts to organize women trustees in the last 20 years have generated conferences, published conference proceedings, and a series of forums and workshops; but unlike the AAUW Conference on Women Trustees in 1887—which evolved over a 25-year period and, once organized, functioned for another 15—each contemporary effort has been short-lived. In 1964 the AAUW Committee on Standards in Higher Education held a conference in Washington which brought together trustees and administrators representing over 80 AAUW colleges and universities and national associations. The proceedings describe three questions addressed:

> How can the woman trustee best support the development plans of her institution in such areas as finance, high education quality, stimulating collegiate atmosphere, and preparation of the student for her life role?
>
> How can the trustee function in the area of women faculty recruitment, development, and promotion?
>
> What would help you to be a more effective trustee and assist you in working in the above-mentioned areas?[40]

In 1976, Cornell University, with funding from the Association of Governing Boards for publication of the proceedings, sponsored a two-day conference—Gateways and Barriers for Women in the University Community—for approximately 50 participants who were women trustees from ten colleges and universities, mostly Ivy League. The conference included presentations on affirmative action in the participating institutions; a panel, "Affirmative Action Today: An Interpretation"; a keynote address, "Role and Contributions of Woman Trustees and Administrators," by Judith Younger, deputy dean of the Cornell Law School; and workshops on women trustees and decision-making; trustee-administrator interaction; alumnae as future leaders; women administrators; and women faculty: recruitment, development, promotion, and remuneration. The published proceedings also included an annotated bibliography on women in higher education.[41]

In 1979 the North Carolina Planning Committee of the American Council on Education's National Identification Program for the Advancement of Women in Higher Education (ACE/NIP) sponsored a workshop for North Carolina women trustees which featured a speech by Anne Scott: "The Feminist Responsibilities of Women Trustees." The following year, the New Jersey ACE/NIP Planning Committee sponsored a forum for New Jersey women trustees, "Increasing the Effectiveness of Governing Boards," which raised a number of board/management issues directly or indirectly affecting women on boards and on campus: trustee selection, essentials of orientation and training, uses and limits of trustee power, the affirmative action advocacy roles of women and minority trustees, and the relationships of boards to constituencies in the Department of Education and Board of Higher Education. A gathering of women trustees in 1981 brought together a representative group of trustees who worked with the planning committee to develop and sponsor a finance workshop, one of several recommended information sessions trustees had identified as a need. Other activities included updated annual listings of all women trustees in the state; mailings to women trustees sharing newsletters, topical issues of concerns, and information about the nominations processes for all state and private colleges and universities; several rounds of active solicitation of trustee candidates; panel presentations and informal outreach to other professional women's networks in the process of soliciting nominations for boards; and the research project described in this chapter which interviewed women and men trustees on five representative college and university boards.

What is striking about all these efforts, however, is the difficulty of sustaining them. Meetings, workshops, and roundtables have been sponsored at national Association of Governing Boards conferences, initially drawing a number of interested participants. Other state ACE/NIP planning committees—Maryland and New York, for example—as well as the New York City metropolitan area have sponsored day-long conferences or forums. Unlike other professional women's networks, however, women trustee networks have not been ongoing or self-sustaining. Although goal-focused state, regional, and national programs seem to draw enthusiastic one-time audiences, other strategies are needed to reach larger numbers. At this juncture, it seems clear that the limited resources available for national and regional projects are best spent on developing resources women trustees can avail themselves of: updated state lists of women trustee names and addresses; information on representation of women on boards; bibliographies and lists of other resources; and strategies for increasing both the numbers of nominations and pools of potential trustees by facilitating more contacts among senior women in education, business, the professions, nonprofits, and government.

Notes

1. Lawrence A. Cremin, *American Education: The Colonial Experience, 1607–1783* (New York: Harper & Row, 1970), pp. 221–222.
2. J. L. Zwingle, "Evolution of Lay Governing Boards," in Richard T. Ingram, ed., *Handbook of College and University Trusteeship* (San Francisco: Jossey-Bass, 1980), p. 16.
3. Although in principle controlled by their faculties, these systems, more informally than are their American counterparts with lay boards, may also be de facto governed by elites, a ". . . small number of leading civil servants, government ministers, university vice-chancellors, and members of the University Grants Commission who shaped the face of the British university system for many years in small committee rooms or around tables at the Athenaeum Club." Martin Trow, *Problems in the Transition from Elite to Mass Higher Education* (Berkeley, CA: Carnegie Commission on Higher Education, 1973), p. 12.
4. See Cremin, *American Education*, p. 222; also Gerald P. Burns, *Trustees in Higher Education: Their Functions and Coordination* (Washington, DC: Independent College Funds of America, 1966), p. 5; Anne Gary Pannell, "Myth and Reality in Trustee-President-Dean Relationships," in *The Woman Trustee: A Report on a Conference for Women Members of Governing Boards, December 1, 1964* (Washington, DC: American Association of University Women, 1965), p. 23.
5. Burns, *Trustees in Higher Education*, p. 6. Trustee guidance continues to be a role defined by trustees, by corporate board members, for example, who offer expertise on the educated "manpower" most needed in coming decades.
6. See, for example, "Academic Freedom and Big Business," in Richard Hofstader and Walter P. Metzger, *The Development of Academic Freedom in the United States* (New York: Columbia University Press, 1955), pp. 413–467.
7. Thorstein Veblen, *The Higher Learning in America: A Memorandum on the Conduct of Universities by Business Men* (New York: Reprints of Economic Classics, Augustus M. Kelley, Bookseller, 1965; orig. ed., 1918).
8. Burns, *Trustees in Higher Education*, p. 15.
9. George E. Potter, "Responsibilities," in Victoria Dziuba and William Meardy, issue eds., *Enhancing Trustee Effectiveness: New Directions for Community Colleges* 15 (Autumn 1976):6.
10. See, for example, Alice S. Rossi and Ann Calderwood, eds., *Academic Women on the Move* (New York: Russell Sage Foundation, 1973); Carnegie Commission on Higher Education, *Opportunities for Women in Higher Education* (New

York: McGraw-Hill, 1973); W. Todd Furniss and Patricia Albjerg Graham, eds., *Women in Higher Education* (Washington, DC: American Council on Education, 1974); and Carnegie Council on Policy Studies in Higher Education, *Making Affirmative Action Work in Higher Education* (San Francisco: Jossey-Bass, 1975).

11. Rodney T. Hartnett, *College and University Trustees: Their Background, Roles and Educational Attitudes* (Princeton, NJ: Educational Testing Service, 1969); Irene L. Gomberg and Frank J. Atelsek, *Composition of College and University Governing Boards*, Higher Education Panel Reports no. 35 (Washington, DC: American Council on Education, August 1977).

12. Hartnett, *College and University Trustees*, p. 12. Although, as noted, there is consensus on a range of legal and "prescriptive" responsibilities trustees *should* hold, there is in fact little data and less agreement in the trustee literature about what, in fact, boards *do*. A comprehensive overview of the literature synthesizes what the authors describe as the "somewhat pedestrian and largely descriptive literature in the field"; Robert E. Engel and Paul P. W. Achola, "Boards of Trustees and Academic Decisionmaking," *Review of Educational Research* 53 (Spring 1983):58. Engel and Achola observe in passing what is in fact a critical point: that, while several studies have attempted to document and analyze the actual trustee decision-making process by using content-analyses of board minutes, some of the most important decisions and issues affecting board decisions never reach the written record. These may be "nondecisions"—which "if brought into open debate, would seriously shred the social fabric," as Engel and Achola observe—or they might be the more implicit, often unexamined issues and assumptions affecting latent board functions—how assumed criteria for selection of new trustees, for example, perpetuate the board in its own image. No comprehensive board research has yet to tackle these more complex or subtle dimensions of trustee power and influence. This dearth of research is also true of research on boards in other sectors. One of the most recent studies of corporate boards, for example, describes as impetus for the study the authors' curiosity: "We were intrigued by this lack of information on director attitudes and behavior . . . ," Thomas J. Whisler, *Rules of the Game: Inside the Corporate Boardroom* (Homewood, IL: Dow Jones-Irwin, 1984).

13. Burns, *Trustees in Higher Education*, p. 7.

14. Marion Talbot and Lois Kimball Matthews Rosenberry, *The History of the American Association of University Women: 1881–1931* (Boston: Houghton Mifflin, 1931), p. 194.

15. Morton A. Rauh, *College and University Trusteeship* (Yellow Springs, OH: Antioch Press, 1959), p. 15.

16. Hartnett, *College and University Trustees*, p. 47.

17. These are also concepts apparently unresolved in the relevant social science literature. One strategy for reconciling the contradictions of democracy and elitism has been the concept of accountability, defining for the elite special

fiduciary responsibilities and calling them accountable to the general population. Other scholars see trustee elites—especially given this concept of public accountability—as balancing the inherent elitism of the faculty (knowledge-based elitism) and the administration (information-controlling elitism); Engel and Achola, "Boards of Trustees," p. 57.

18. Richard W. Lyman, "Comments by the Incoming Chairperson," Independent Sector Annual Membership Meeting and Assembly, October 25, 1983.

19. Scott Nearing, "Who's Who Among College Trustees," *School and Society* 6 (September 1917):298.

20. Hubert Park Beck, *Men Who Control Our Universities* (New York: King's Crown Press, 1947), p. 92.

21. L. Clark Seelye, *The Early History of Smith College: 1871–1910* (Boston: Houghton Mifflin, 1923), p. 18.

22. Alice Duer Miller and Susan Myers, *Barnard College: The First Fifty Years* (New York: Columbia University Press, 1939).

23. Talbot and Rosenberry, *History of the AAUW*, pp. 196–197.

24. Talbot and Rosenberry, *History of the AAUW*, p. 200.

25. Margaret Farrand Thorp, *Neilson of Smith* (New York: Oxford University Press, 1956), p. 299.

26. Harriet Seelye Rhees, *Laurenus Clark Seelye: First President of Smith College* (Boston: Houghton Mifflin, 1929), p. 198.

27. Laura T. Doing, "Women on School Boards: Nine Winners Tell How They Play the Game," *American School Board Journal* 160 (March 1973):34–38.

28. Mona Norman Generett, "The Role of Women Trustees in Private Independent Colleges and Universities of Pennsylvania As Defined by Their Characteristics, Functions and Perceptions," unpublished doctoral dissertation, University of Pittsburgh, 1978, p. 52.

29. Mary Ellen S. Capek, "College and University Trusteeship in New Jersey," *Networking*, newsletter of the New Jersey Planning Committee of the American Council on Education National Identification Program, Spring 1983.

30. Rodney T. Hartnett, *The New College Trustee: Some Predictions for the 1970s* (Princeton, NJ: Educational Testing Service, 1970), p. 66.

31. Association of Governing Boards, *Composition of Governing Boards, 1985* (Washington, DC: AGB, 1986).

32. Suzanne Howard, *But We Will Persist: A Comparative Research Report on the Status of Women in Academe* (Washington, DC: American Association of University Women, 1978), pp. 56–57.

33. Generett, "Role of Women Trustees," p. 26.

34. Sheila Korhammer, "The Increasing Influence of Women on Community College Boards," *Trustee Quarterly*, Fall 1986, p. 22.

35. Generett, "Role of Women Trustees," pp. 52, 54.

36. Generett, "Role of Women Trustees," p. 60.

37. Generett, "Role of Women Trustees," p. 56.
38. Hartnett, *New College Trustee,* pp. 33–36. See also Helen Ruth Godrey, "A Profile of Female Trustees of Four-Year Public Colleges and Universities and a Comparison of Female and Male Trustee Perceptions of Selected Trustee Functions and University Issues," unpublished doctoral dissertation, Michigan State University, 1971.
39. Rauh, *College and University Trusteeship,* p. 37.
40. American Association of University Women, *The Woman Trustee: A Report on a Conference for Women Members of Governing Boards, December 1, 1964* (Washington, DC: AAUW, 1965), p. 5.
41. Cornell University, *Gateways and Barriers for Women in the University Community: Proceedings of the Mary Donlon Alger Conference for Trustees and Administrators,* sponsored by the Board of Trustees of Cornell University, September 10 and 11, 1976 (Ithaca, NY: Office of University Publications, Cornell University, 1977).

PART V

Summary and Conclusions

16

Progress and Prospects

We have seen that the history of higher education for women spans a period of 150 years, a period far shorter than that for men, which in the United States began with the founding of Harvard College in 1636. In Europe at that time there was a well-established tradition of university education for men, but not for women. The onset of the Civil War and the need to maintain university enrollments followed by a growing need for teachers during the latter part of the nineteenth century provided the conditions under which women entered higher education in growing numbers. By the start of the twentieth century the struggle for access as such had been won, and women represented a third of the student body in higher education.

During the early part of the twentieth century, women gained increasing acceptance in colleges and universities, although many doors remained closed including the most prestigious men's colleges and professional schools of law, medicine, and business. For example, Harvard did not admit women to its medical school until 1945, its law school until 1950, and its business school until 1963. Yale and Princeton did not admit women undergraduates until 1969. Most institutions in the United States are now coeducational, but there are wide disparities in the educational experiences of men and women within those institutions. There have been, and continue to be, persistent differences in patterns of career choice and field of college major. Disparities also persist in patterns of financial aid, opportunities in athletics, and treatment in the classroom.

In overall terms, women made steady progress in higher education until World War II, although some institutions introduced quotas in the late nineteenth century as a reaction to what they felt to be too many women in the student population. The aftermath of World War II, however, proved to be a period of severe setback for women. Returning veterans, funded by the G.I. Bill, swelled enrollments and overwhelmed classrooms and other campus facilities. The proportion of women among degree recipients dropped below prewar levels and remained below throughout the 1960s. Priority was given to full-time students, and nontraditional students—those wishing to enroll part time or older women—were given a cold shoulder. Minority women were all but invisible except in the predominantly black institutions.

The cohort of men who received doctorates during this period moved into faculty ranks in the 1960s and 1970s, filling tenure slots as higher education expanded. The proportion of women doctorate recipients began to increase during the 1960s and continued through the 1970s and 1980s, but they have found the number of faculty possibilities limited by the large body of newly tenured faculty combined with the slowdown in the rate of growth of higher education.

These forces will not play themselves out until the 1990s when the bulk of faculty members reach retirement age. Student demographics also point to a more favorable situation for faculty hiring at that time. The decline in birth rates recorded between 1961 and 1975 has bottomed out and higher births since 1975 will mean an upturn in the number of potential college-going 18-year-olds in the early 1990s. Under those conditions women will have a better opportunity to increase their representation on college and university faculties. How good the opportunities are and what the competition for available positions will be will depend on the financial situation of higher education at that time and the extent to which there are more lucrative career opportunities outside academic life. Whatever the situation, women will need to be vigilant to assure an equitable share of new faculty appointments. History suggests that one cannot assume continuous progress without setbacks. Since the early 1970s, women have steadily increased their representation in the pool of available candidates for faculty positions. In 1986 they accounted for 35 percent of the PhDs awarded, and the proportion was rising annually. Under the circumstances, 35 percent would seem to be a minimum target figure for the representation of women in higher education faculties in the 1990s.

Achievements Since 1970

In summarizing the advances that women have made in higher education since 1970, it is important to emphasize that these advances have not come about without a struggle. Reference was made in chapter 2 to the efforts of women's rights groups, mainly in Washington, DC, to press for legislation prohibiting sex discrimination in educational institutions and to monitor the enforcement of that legislation. Chapter 8, on affirmative action, describes the obstacles and resistances that women had to contend with in seeking legal redress. A recent study of academic discrimination lawsuits found that faculty plaintiffs have only a one-in-five chance of winning. Moreover, it was reported that an almost certain consequence of litigation, regardless of outcome, is scarred careers and anguish for everyone involved.[1] Chapter 12 chronicles the activities of women's caucuses and commissions of professional associations and their contributions to the advancement of women in higher education. They helped to achieve greater recognition of women in the scholarly disciplines and played a strategic role in the evolution of women's studies. The struggle is not yet over, but it is time to take stock, to see how far we have come, and to determine what steps are needed to ensure further progress toward full equity.

The Application of Law

Until the late 1960s there were no legal remedies for sex discrimination in higher education. The Fourteenth Amendment to the Constitution, which assures all persons equal protection of the laws, was applied to race, but not sex, discrimination. Title VII of the Civil Rights Act of 1964 prohibited discrimination in employment, but did not apply to educational institutions. Executive Order 11246 prohibited discrimination by all federal contractors, including colleges and universities, on the basis of race, color, religion, and national origin, but not sex. In 1968 the Executive Order was amended to include discrimination based on sex, and that provided the opening wedge for the use of legal remedies in the campaign against sex discrimination in higher education.

A battery of legislation mandating equal educational opportunity for women is now on the statute books. Title VII, as amended in 1972, prohibits sex discrimination in employment in educational institutions. Title IX of the Education Amendments of 1972 prohibits sex discrimination in all educational programs receiving financial support from the federal government, including discrimination against students as well as discrimination in employment. While enforcement of this legislation leaves something to be desired, particularly as applied to employment, it has been found to be indispensable in overcoming overt discrimination in the general rules and procedures of colleges and universities. Official policies no longer sanction restrictive practices against women in college admissions, financial aid, student services, and parietal rules. In athletics, gross discrimination has been mitigated although equity is not yet at hand. During the 1980s issues of sexual harassment began to be addressed.

Notwithstanding these achievements, subtle forms of discrimination remain and they will be hard to eradicate. Attitudes and behaviors that devalue women's achievements, while less blatant than before, continue to be manifested inside the classroom and more widely on the campus. To a large extent they are inadvertent, but their combined effect is to dampen the self-confidence and aspirations of women students. For example, after ten years of experience with coeducation, at Princeton it was found that although women students achieved essentially identical results as men in terms of academic performance, they were appreciably less confident about their academic abilities than men.[2] A similar pattern of behavior has been reported at other institutions.[3]

Studies have shown that women as well as men tend to perceive the work of women as less important than that of men, in society at large as well as in academic institutions. While attitudes and behaviors are changing, there is still a need for sensitivity on the part of faculty and administration to residual differences in the treatment of men and women students in classroom and other campus settings.

Affirmative Action Methods

A second major advance for women in higher education over the last two decades is the introduction of affirmative action programs and procedures in employment under the impetus of government regulations. Under Executive Order 11375, colleges and universities receiving federal contracts are required to have affirmative action plans in place. Such plans cover not only faculty and administrative positions but also employment generally throughout the campus, and they apply to hiring, promotion, salaries, and training opportunities. Affirmative action programs could also be required by court order upon a finding of discrimination under Title VII. In addition, regulations issued in 1975 under Title IX required colleges and universities to conduct self-evaluations of institutional policies and procedures for possible discriminatory effects and to take remedial measures to ensure compliance with the law.

There has been much controversy over affirmative action, as graphically described in chapter 8, and its effectiveness as a remedy for employment discrimination has been limited by the lack of vigorous enforcement. Nevertheless, affirmative action laws and regulations have helped to break down old patterns of faculty hiring that relied on the informal word-of-mouth network of professional colleagues and were clearly discriminatory. Faculty recruitment procedures today typically include public announcement of the opening, specific efforts to reach women and minority candidates, and administrative review of the selection process and outcome by the academic and affirmative action officers of the institution.[4]

Affirmative action as applied to academic employment of women came into play at a time of financial stringency in higher education and a period in which there was a tapering off in the rate of growth in number of faculty members. In part for that reason affirmative action policies have not resulted in an increase in the representation of women in faculty and administrative positions commensurate with their representation in the pool of available candidates, except at entry-level positions. Nevertheless, employment practices and procedures have been permanently changed to a more open system, and in that sense affirmative action must be considered a major achievement in the drive toward equity for women, as it was earlier for minorities.

Changes in Degree Attainment

Another major achievement by women over the period since 1970 is the spectacular gains that have been made in degree attainment. Women now earn a majority of all bachelor's and master's degrees, and they have increased their share of doctorates from 13 percent in 1970 to 35 percent in 1986. At the same time there has been a large-scale movement of women into the traditionally male-dominated fields and a narrowing in the disparity in fields of concentration between men and women. Particularly striking is the massive entry of women into the professional fields of law, business administration, medicine, and theology. Women have also made significant advances in the social sciences, where in some fields—psychology, sociology, and anthropology—they now surpass men in number of doctorates earned. On the other hand, women have continued to enter the traditional "women's fields" in large numbers and have increased their concentration in the humanities and in the professional fields of teaching, social work, library science, and nursing.

Although women may predominate in some fields in terms of degree attainment, there is no field other than nursing that is female-dominated in terms of control of the profession. In the humanities, education, social work, and library science as well as the scientific fields and more prestigious professions, men hold the preponderance of senior faculty and administrative positions. They also hold the leading positions in the professional associations. To some extent, the discrepancy between doctoral degree attainment and control of the discipline or profession may be reduced over time as larger cohorts of women make their presence felt. But the discrepancy is also a result of the fact that within fields men are concentrated in the more prestigious and upwardly mobile specialties. Future studies of degree attainment will need to take a closer look at relative changes in the subspecialties.

The Development of Women's Studies

At least as important as the other advances that women have made in higher education since 1970 is the introduction and growth of women's studies as a formal area of teaching and research. Virtually unknown prior to 1970, women's studies began as a marginal enterprise on a few campuses, more often than not conducted on a voluntary basis by committed feminist scholars. Women's studies courses are now available on most campuses, whether as courses within existing disciplines or as an interdisciplinary field of concentration. Although the exact number is not known, it is estimated that more than 30,000 women's studies courses are now being offered by colleges and universities throughout the country. Formal degree programs in women's studies have become widespread, and their numbers are still growing. Increasingly, women's studies courses and programs are making their appearance abroad, not only in Europe but also in developing countries.

Women's studies is still perceived by many as separate from the mainstream liberal arts curriculum, but this view is not shared by its proponents. The new knowledge and perspectives that have emerged from women's studies scholarship have implications for the assumptions, methods, and content of the traditional academic disciplines. Studies of the impact of women's studies on the mainstream curriculum began in the mid-1970s. At that time the influence of women's studies on the general liberal arts curriculum was just beginning to be felt. Since then an extensive effort has been under way to incorporate women's studies into the core disciplines. The effort consists of a variety of activities including faculty development programs, summer training institutes, and organized curriculum revision projects. New studies are needed to determine the extent to which, through these efforts and in other ways, women's studies scholarship has been integrated into the general liberal arts curriculum.

Women's studies today encompasses not only teaching programs but also a network of research centers or institutes, professional journals for the publication of the new scholarship, and specialized library resources. Women's studies research has had a direct influence on public policy as well as on the academic curriculum, and women's studies literary work is widely available to the general public through commercial publishers. Indeed, publishers have found the market for such work—whether literary criticism, biography, or fiction—highly lucrative.

In short, women's studies has made extraordinary progress since it appeared on the academic scene in 1970. There are no signs of slow-down in the rate of progress, and the prospects are for continued expansion over the coming years. The potential influence of women's studies on the traditional liberal arts curriculum is vast and has only just begun to be felt. It appears inevitable that the new and developing scholarship on women will be an important factor in the advancement of women and the education of men throughout the 1980s and 1990s.

Women's Centers and Other Support Services

In addition to campus-based research centers, which are designed to provide institutional resources for women's studies programs and scholars, women's centers of another kind were established during the 1970s, and in some cases before, to meet the needs of other constituencies of women on campus, particularly students. These centers provided a meeting place and a variety of programs and services of special interest to women. Their activities and services include conferences, lecture series, noncredit courses, library resources and documentary material on women's issues, and contacts with women's rights groups off campus.

These centers have played an important role in building a mutual support network among women on campus and in serving as advocates for women. There are estimated to be approximately 600 such centers, most of them budgeted at extremely modest levels from institutional sources such as student activity fees. Many of the functions that women's centers carried out in the past have now been absorbed by off-campus community groups. After a period of growth during the 1970s, the number of centers appears to have stabilized. In recent years, however, their role on campus has changed somewhat. Their activities are oriented much more than before toward student concerns and less toward outside activism, and they work more closely with college officials responsible for career planning and other student services. In the campus environment of the 1980s, it is important that they continue as a voice for women students.

During the past two decades re-entry women have constituted a large and growing segment of the enrollment of higher education institutions. To meet the special needs of this population of students, continuing education programs for women were established during the 1960s. They offer counseling, training in study skills, refresher courses, financial aid, and other support services. Although a majority of colleges and universities now offer some types of services or programs for returning women, there are relatively few with fully developed programs. Except for two-year institutions and women's colleges, re-entry women have not been welcomed into mainstream academic programs. Overall, institutional policies have not kept up with the diverse needs of these students.

As a supportive environment for women in higher education, women's colleges have an illustrious history. Unfortunately, they have not fared well since the 1970s in the competition with coeducational institutions and the future does not look promising as their numbers continue to dwindle. From the viewpoint of higher education as a whole, they have not played a leadership role for women in the developments of the last two decades. They may, however, have a growing role to play as a resource for women in higher education.

Partial Achievements

While there has been much progress for women in higher education on the whole, there are two critical areas in which progress over the last 15 years has been slow or halting. One is the representation of women in faculty and administrative positions at the policymaking level. The other is the rate of enrollment of minority women and their rate of advance as faculty members and administrators.

The percentage of women as full-time faculty members of institutions of higher education increased from 22 percent in the early 1970s to 27 percent in the early 1980s, but most of the gain was in untenured positions and in two-year institutions rather than four-year colleges and universities. Over the same period, the increase in the percentage of women full professors was all but imperceptible. The progress of women in administrative positions is somewhat better, having increased from 23 percent in the mid-1970s to 30 percent in the early 1980s. On the negative side, salary differentials between men and women faculty members and administrators have widened rather than narrowed during this period. As far as trustee positions are concerned, women increased their representations on boards from 15 percent in 1977 to 20 percent in 1985. During the same period the proportion of minorities remained the same.

Education has been viewed by minorities and other disadvantaged groups as an important means of upward mobility. That is so much so that, holding socioeconomic status constant, the educational aspirations of minority youth are higher than those of whites. However, because of economic and other barriers, minority women still fall behind white males in terms of educational achievement and, for the most part, have not achieved parity with white women. In spite of their unique needs, minority women are usually seen as either women or minorities rather than a constituency in their own right. Separate studies are rare and separate data are seldom available. From the little information that is available, it is possible to trace a rapid increase in college enrollment of minorities during the late 1970s, but the growth tapered off during the 1980s and the number and proportion of blacks actually declined. The enrollment of Hispanic students has continued to rise slightly, but lags far behind their overall representation in the population. Asian Americans are the only minority group to show substantial gains in the 1980s.[5] Minority representation in faculty and administrative positions remains low.

The Tasks Ahead

Given our progress to date, what further steps are needed in the years ahead for women to reach full equality in higher education? What can women's groups do, what can educational institutions do, and what can the federal government and other agencies do?

Solving the Problem of Subtle Discrimination

Women students in the 1980s appear to take equality for granted and do not appear to be aware of the many forms of subtle discrimination that are still ongoing in the classroom, in departmental practices, and in the campus at large. The tendency to undervalue the work of women is pervasive, among women as well as men. Some institutions are beginning to address this issue and are taking steps to sensitize faculty members to differential treatment of men and women and the cumulative effects of such treatment on the self-esteem and aspirations of women students. More needs to be done along that line. One of the most active organizations in the field is the Project on the Status and Education of Women of the Association of American Colleges. In recent years it has devoted a good deal of attention to the classroom climate for women, and its papers are being widely distributed and discussed in the academic community. In a number of institutions, such as MIT, Michigan State, and Harvard, women's groups on campus have conducted sur-

veys of the environment for women on campus which have served to
raise the awareness of students and faculty alike.[6]

The campus environment for women is not, of course, a static phenomenon. Nor is it the same across all types of institutions. In-depth
studies of the dynamics of change in campus life in the 1980s should be
on the research agenda for higher education. Such studies are not readily quantifiable, but they are nonetheless important. In this context, it is
relevant to note the extent to which women's concerns on campus have
been institutionalized. There are now women's centers, women's studies programs, women's research institutes, affirmative action offices,
rape crisis centers, and other structures to attend to the needs of women
students, faculty, and staff.

Providing for the Needs of Nontraditional Students

Institutions of higher education have not thus far been fully responsive
to the diverse needs of the nontraditional student body. Special courses
and services have been offered to some extent, but by and large these
students have not been brought into the mainstream of campus life.
Part-time and older students, a majority of them women, constitute a
large and growing segment of the student population. Equal educational
opportunity without regard to age or sex requires more institutional
flexibility than is the norm today.

Programs for re-entry women that were developed during the 1960s
and 1970s suggest some of the educational policies and support services
that would be conducive to greater equity and efficiency in higher education. To go further, we need to know more about the total population
of nontraditional students and its composition, men as well as women.
How do the women in this population differ from the men in terms of
their life stages and educational needs? What is the low-income and
minority component? How well is the issue of financial aid for part-time
students being addressed?

Federal aid programs are currently available to students who are enrolled at least half time. In addition, institutions receiving federal funds
for student-supported programs are permitted to allocate up to 10 percent for part-time students, and some states also offer such aid. Reports
indicate, however, that funds available for part-time students are not
being fully utilized.[7] It is important to determine whether this is due to
lack of knowledge on the part of those who are eligible, to the structure
and conditions of the financial aid offered, or to the exercise of institutional preference for full-time students.

Accelerating Affirmative Action Efforts

A major piece of unfinished business for women in higher education in the coming decade is further progress in faculty and administrative positions. The gains that have been made so far, disappointing as they may be, could not have been achieved without the concerted efforts of women's groups and the assistance of federal laws and regulations against discrimination. The force of federal support was considerably weakened with the change in political climate brought about by the Reagan administration during the first half of the 1980s, but women's advocacy groups have not been deterred. As we have seen, they succeeded through persistent efforts in obtaining passage of the Civil Rights Restoration Act in 1988, reversing the restrictive effects of the 1984 Supreme Court decision in *Grove City College* v. *Bell*.[8]

The next ten years will be a critical period for women from the viewpoint of faculty hiring and tenuring. Demographic trends indicate a high rate of faculty retirement and an upturn in the college-going age group of the population, a combination of factors which should make for an increase in the number of faculty openings unless offset by adverse economic or other external conditions. It is estimated that institutions of higher education will have to hire about 500,000 new faculty members by the end of the century.[9] It will be incumbent on caucuses and commissions of professional associations and other academic and women's rights groups to monitor hiring and promotion practices and outcomes closely. The proportion of qualified women candidates is large and growing, but without vigorous affirmative action efforts they may never take their rightful place on college and university faculties. In the past, labor unions, with the exception of Committee W of the American Association of University Professors, have not been particularly salient in the efforts on behalf of academic women, but they, too, have a growing role to play in the future as women make their presence felt in union ranks.

Increasing Data Collection

Research on women in higher education is seriously hampered by the availability of relevant statistics at the federal level. Although statistics on enrollments and earned degrees are reported annually, current information about the number and composition of faculty members and administrators is woefully inadequate. Data published by the Department of Education are often two years out of date, and sometimes longer. The *Digest of Education Statistics, 1987* provides limited data on instructional faculty in institutions of higher education, showing classification by sex for 1985–1986, but not by discipline. For faculty classified by racial/ethnic groups the latest figures shown are for 1983. In view of the growing minority population of the United States, classification by racial groups as well as by sex should be standard procedure for educational statistics. In view of the large and growing component of nontraditional students in higher education, classification by age is also important. The 1987 *Digest* provides no information at all on administrators in higher education institutions, and there have been no systematic studies of women and minorities in administrative positions since the special report in 1978–1979 by Carol Frances and her associates for the College and University Personnel Association. Information on academic administrators and other noninstructional staff members of higher education institutions is not regularly collected by the Department of Education.

The data resources of the Department of Education have long suffered in comparison with the standards set by other federal agencies such as the Bureau of Labor Statistics and the Census Bureau. Moreover, the staffing and funding of the National Center for Education Statistics declined significantly between 1980 and 1986 under the budget policies of the Reagan administration. Reflecting concern with the condition of educational statistics at the public policy level, the National Academy of Sciences in 1984 was asked by the Department of Education to undertake an evaluation of the data collection programs of the center. To carry out the study a panel was established under the Committee on National Statistics of the National Research Council. The report of the panel, entitled *Creating a Center for Education Statistics: A Time for Action*, issued in 1986, cites lack of timeliness as one of the foremost problems of the center and recommends that the center establish, publish, and adhere to a set of fixed release dates for selected key education statistics.[10] The report also recommends changes in the content and direction of data collection programs which provide the basis for future improvements in statistics on higher education issues, including issues of particular concern to women and minorities.

Conclusion

In the concluding statement of *Academic Women on the Move*, Alice Rossi found reason to view the future for women in higher education "with at least a moderate degree of optimism." In this volume, 15 years later, we echo that statement. Significant gains have been made, but much remains to be done. With continued vigilance and sustained efforts on the part of women's groups, we remain moderately optimistic.

Notes

1. George N. LaNoue and Barbara A. Lee, *Academics in Court: The Consequences of Faculty Discrimination Litigation* (Ann Arbor: University of Michigan Press, 1987).

2. Princeton University, *Report of the President*, April 1980, p. 19.

3. Brown Project, *Men and Women Learning Together: A Study of College Students in the Late 70's*, Report of the Brown Project, Brown University, April 1980. The Brown Project was based on a survey of over 3,000 undergraduates at six institutions.

4. For a case study in the application of the new procedures, see Neil Smelzer and Robin Content, *The Changing Academic Market: General Trends and a Berkeley Case Study* (Berkeley: University of California Press, 1980).

5. Office of Minority Concerns, American Council on Education, *Minorities in Higher Education: Fifth Annual Status Report* (Washington, DC: ACE, 1986), p. 5.

6. Roberta M. Hall and Bernice R. Sandler, *Out of the Classroom: A Chilly Campus Climate for Women* (Washington, DC: Project on the Status and Education of Women, Association of American Colleges, 1984), p. 3.

7. Mary Moran, *Student Financial Aid and Women: Equity Dilemma?* AAHE-ERIC/Higher Education Report no. 5 (Washington, DC: American Association for Higher Education, 1986); also New York State Higher Education Services Corporation, *The New York State Aid for Part-Time Study Program, 1985–86*, Albany, 1986.

8. The Grove City decision weakened not only Title IX but potentially other civil rights laws as well.

9. *Chronicle of Higher Education*, June 24, 1987.

10. Daniel B. Levine, ed., *Creating a Center for Education Statistics: A Time for Action* (Washington, DC: National Academy Press, 1986).

Bibliography

Abrams, Morris B. "Affirmative Action: Fair Shakers and Social Engineers." *Harvard Law Review* 99 (April 1986):1312.

Acosta, R. Vivian, and Linda Jean Carpenter. "Women in Athletics—A Status Report." *Journal of Physical Education, Recreation and Dance*, no. 6 (August 1985):30–34.

Ahern, Nancy C., and Elizabeth L. Scott. *Career Outcomes in a Matched Sample of Men and Women Ph.D's*. Washington, DC: Committee on the Education and Employment of Women in Science and Engineering, National Academy Press, 1981.

Aldrich, Michelle, and Alicia Leach. *Associations and Committees of or for Women in Science, Engineering, Mathematics, and Medicine*. Washington, DC: Office of Opportunities in Science, American Association for the Advancement of Science, 1984.

American Association of University Women. *Professional Women's Groups Providing Employment Assistance to Women*. Washington, DC: AAUW, 1983.

———. *The Woman Trustee: A Report on a Conference for Women Members of Governing Boards, December 1, 1964*. Washington, DC: AAUW, 1965.

———. *Women and Student Financial Aid: A Policy Brief*. Washington, DC: AAUW, 1985.

American Council on Education. *Report of the National Commission on Student Financial Assistance*. Washington, DC: Division of Policy Analysis and Research, American Council on Education, 1984.

———, Office of Minority Concerns. *Minorities in Higher Education: Fifth Annual Status Report*. Washington, DC: ACE, 1986.

American Economic Association, Committee on the Status of Women in the Economics Profession. "Annual Report, 1985." *Newsletter*, February 1986, pp. 2–3.

American Psychological Association, Committee on Women in Psychology. *Women in the American Psychological Association 1986*. Washington, DC: American Psychological Association, 1986.

American Sociological Association, Committee on the Status of Women in Sociology. *Guidelines for Incorporating Women into Departments of Sociology in the Eighties*. Washington, DC: American Sociological Association, 1984.

Andrews, Patricia Hayes. "Upward Directed Persuasive Communication—Attribution of Success and Failure toward an Understanding of the Role of Gender." Paper presented at the Communication, Language and Gender Conference, Oxford, Ohio, October 14–15, 1985.

Antler, Joyce. "After College, What?: New Graduates and the Family Claim." *American Quarterly* 32, no. 4 (Fall 1980):409–435.

———. "Culture, Service, and Work: Changing Ideals of Higher Education for Women." In Pamela J. Perun, ed., *The Undergraduate Woman: Issues in Educational Equity*. Lexington, MA: Lexington Books, 1982.

Association of American Colleges, Project on the Status and Education of Women. *Nontraditional Careers* (selected articles from *On Campus with Women*), 1981–1983.

———. *Re-entry Women: Packets I–III*. Washington, DC: AAC, 1980.

Association of Governing Boards. *Composition of Governing Boards, 1985*. Washington, DC: Association of Governing Boards, 1986.

Astin, Alexander W. *Four Critical Years*. San Francisco: Jossey-Bass, 1977.

Astin, Alexander W., et al. *The American Freshman: National Norms Annual Series*. Los Angeles: Higher Education Research Institute, Graduate School of Education, University of California, 1971–1988.

Astin, Alexander W.; Margo R. King; and Gerald T. Richardson. *The American Freshman: National Norms for Fall 1975*. Los Angeles: Higher Education Research Institute, Graduate School of Education, University of California, 1975.

Astin, Alexander W.; Robert J. Panos; and John A. Creager. *National Norms for Entering College Freshman: Fall 1966*. Washington, DC: American Council on Education, 1967.

Astin, Helen S. "Factors Affecting Women's Scholarly Productivity." In Helen S. Astin and W. L. Hirsh, eds. *The Higher Education of Women: Essays in the Honor of Rosemary Park*. New York: Praeger, 1978.

———, ed. *Some Action of Her Own: The Adult Woman and Higher Education*. Lexington, MA: Heath, 1976.

Astin, Helen S., and Alan E. Bayer. "Pervasive Sex Differences in the Academic Reward System: Scholarship, Marriage, and What Else?" In D. R. Lewis and W. E. Becker, Jr., eds. *Academic Rewards in Higher Education*. Cambridge, MA: Ballinger, 1979.

———. "Sex Discrimination in Academe." *Educational Record* (May 1972):101–118.

Astin, Helen S., and Diane Davis. "Research Productivity across the Life and Career Cycles: Facilitators and Barriers for Women." In M. F. Fox, ed. *Scholarly Writing and Publishing: Issues, Problems and Solutions*. Boulder, CO: Westview Press, 1985.

Astin, Helen S., and Mary Beth Snyder. "Affirmative Action 1972–82: A Decade of Response." *Change*, July-August 1982, pp. 26ff.

Bales, Susan Nall, and Marcia Sharp. "Women's Colleges—Weathering a Difficult Era with Success and Stamina." *Change* 13 (October 1981):53–56.

Baum, Charlotte; Paula Hyman; and Sonya Michel. *The Jewish Woman in America*. New York: New American Library, 1977.

Beck, Hubert Park. *Men Who Control Our Universities.* New York: King's Crown Press, 1947.

Bein, Natalie. *Daughters of Rachel.* New York: Penguin, 1980.

Bell, Carolyn Shaw. "Should Every Job Support a Family?" *Public Interest,* no. 40 (Summer 1975):109–118.

Bellah, Robert N. "Creating a New Framework for New Realities: Social Science as Public Philosophy." *Change,* March-April 1985, pp. 35–39.

Bell-Scott, Patricia. "Black Women's Higher Education: Our Legacy." *Sage* 1 (Spring 1984):8–11.

———. "Schooling Respectable Ladies of Color: Issues in the History of Black Women's Higher Education." *Journal of the National Association of Women Deans, Administrators, and Counselors* 42, no. 2 (Winter 1979):22–28.

Berkowitz, Tamar; Jean Mangi; and Jane Williamson, eds. *Who's Who and Where in Women's Studies.* Old Westbury, NY: Feminist Press, 1974.

Bernard, Jessie. *Academic Women.* University Park: Pennsylvania State University, 1964.

———. *Women and the Public Interest.* Chicago: Aldine and Atherton, 1971.

Bernstein, Alison R. "Foundation Support for Administrative Advancement: A Mixed Record." In Adrian Tinsley, Cynthia Secor, and Sheila Kaplan, eds. *Women in Higher Educational Administration.* San Francisco: Jossey-Bass, 1983.

Bertelson, Judy. "Women's Center Survey." In *Two Studies of Women in Higher Education,* unpublished, Ford Foundation, May 1974.

Borus, Michael E., ed. *Tomorrow's Workers.* Lexington, MA: Heath, 1983.

Boserup, Ester. *Women's Role in Economic Development.* New York: St. Martin's Press, 1970.

Bowen, Howard R., and Jack H. Schuster. *American Professors.* New York: Oxford University Press, 1986.

Bowler, Sister Mary Mariella. "A History of Catholic Colleges for Women in the United States of America." Doctoral dissertation, Catholic University of America, Washington DC, 1933.

Bowles, Gloria, and Renate Duelli Klein, eds. *Theories of Women's Studies.* London: Routledge & Kegan Paul, 1983.

Briscoe, Anne M. "Phenomenon of the Seventies: The Women's Caucuses." *Signs* 4, no. 1 (Autumn 1978):152–153.

Bronte, Lydia. "A Guide to Humanities Centers in the United States." Rockefeller Foundation working paper, 1980.

Brown, Janet W.; Heather Coleman; and Susan E. Posner. *Rosters of Minority Women Professionals.* Washington, DC: American Academy for the Advancement of Science, 1975.

Brown Project. *Men and Women Learning Together: A Study of College Students in the Late 70's.* Providence: Brown University, April 1980.

Burns, Gerald P. *Trustees in Higher Education: Their Functions and Coordination.* Washington, DC: Independent College Funds of America, 1966.

Campbell, Jean. "The Integration of Service, Advocacy and Research in a University Women's Center." Paper presented at the International Interdisciplinary Congress on Women, Haifa, Israel, December 1981.

———. "Women Drop Back In: Educational Innovations in the Sixties." In Alice Rossi and Ann Calderwood, eds. *Academic Women on the Move*. New York: Russell Sage Foundation, 1973.

Capek, Mary Ellen S. "College and University Trusteeship in New Jersey." *Networking*, newsletter of the New Jersey Planning Committee of the American Council on Educational National Identification Program, Spring 1983.

Caplow, Theodore, and Reece McGee. *The Academic Marketplace*. New York: Basic Books, 1958.

Carnegie Commission on Higher Education. *Opportunities for Women in Higher Education*. New York: McGraw-Hill, 1973.

Carnegie Council on Policy Studies in Higher Education. *Making Affirmative Action Work in Higher Education*. San Francisco: Jossey-Bass, 1975.

Carroll, Constance M. "Three's a Crowd: The Dilemma of the Black Women in Higher Education." In Alice Rossi and Ann Calderwood, eds. *Academic Women on the Move*. New York: Russell Sage Foundation, 1973.

Chamberlain, Mariam. "A Period of Remarkable Growth—Women's Studies Research Centers." *Change*, April 1982, pp. 24–29.

Chayes, Abram. "The Role of the Judge in Public Law Litigation." *Harvard Law Review* 89 (May 1970):1281.

Childers, Karen; Phyllis Racklin; Cynthia Secor; and Carolyn Tracy. "A Network of One's Own." In Gloria De Sole and Lenore Hoffman, eds. *Rocking the Boat*. New York: Modern Language Association, 1981.

Clayton, Obie, Jr., et al. "Subjective Decision Making in Medical School Admissions: Potentials for Discrimination." *Sex Roles* 10 (1984):527–532.

Cless, Elizabeth. "The Birth of an Idea: An Account of the Genesis of Women's Continuing Education." In Helen S. Astin, ed. *Some Action of Her Own: The Adult Woman and Higher Education*. Lexington, MA: Heath, 1976.

Clinchy, Blythe, and Claire Zimmerman. "Epistemology and Agency in the Development of Undergraduate Women." In Pamela J. Perun, ed. *The Undergraduate Woman: Issues in Educational Equity*. Lexington, MA: Lexington Books, 1982.

Cogle, Susan L. *Summary Report 1985: Doctorate Recipients from United States Universities*. Washington, DC: National Academy Press, 1986.

Cole, Jonathan R. *Fair Science: Women in the Scientific Community*. New York: Free Press, 1979.

College and University Personnel Association. *1985–1986 Administrative Compensation Survey*. Washington, DC: CUPA, 1986.

Committee on the Education and Employment of Women in Science and Engineering. *Climbing the Academic Ladder: Doctoral Women Scientists in Academe*. Washington, DC: National Academy Press, 1979.

———. *Climbing the Ladder: An Update on the Status of Doctoral Women Scientists and Engineers*. Washington, DC: National Academy Press, 1983.

Committee on Employment and Human Resources. "The Changing Face of American Psychology." *American Psychologist* 41, no. 12 (December 1986): 1311–1327.

Committee on Women in Psychology. *Women in the American Psychological Association 1986*. Washington, DC: American Psychological Association, 1986.

Committee to Study the Status of Women in Graduate Education and Later Careers. *The Higher the Fewer: Report and Recommendations.* Ann Arbor: University of Michigan Graduate School, March 1974.

Conable, Charlotte Williams. *Women at Cornell: The Myth of Equal Education.* Ithaca, NY: Cornell University Press, 1977.

Conway, Jill K. "Perspectives on the History of Women's Education in the United States." *History of Education Quarterly* 14 (1974):6.

Cornell University. *Gateways and Barriers for Women in the University Community: Proceedings of the Mary Donlon Alger Conference for Trustees and Administrators.* Ithaca, NY: Office of University Publications, Cornell University, 1977.

Crane, J. L. *Salary Comparisons of 1979–80 College Graduates by Sex in 1981: Analytic Report.* Washington, DC: U.S. Government Printing Office, 1984.

Cremin, Lawrence A. *American Education: The Colonial Experience, 1607–1783.* New York: Harper & Row, 1970.

Cruikshank, Margaret. *Lesbian Studies.* New York: Feminist Press, 1982.

Culley, Margaret Mulvehill. "Sisterhood Was Powerful." *Commonweal,* October 4, 1974, p. 16.

Daniels, Jane Z., and William K. LeBold. "Women in Engineering: A Dynamic Approach." In Sheila M. Humphreys, ed. *Woman and Minorities in Science: Strategies for Increasing Participation.* AAAS Selected Symposium no. 66. Washington, DC: American Association for the Advancement of Science, 1982.

Davis, Diane, and Helen S. Astin. "Reputational Standing in Academe." *Journal of Higher Education* 58 (May–June 1987):261–275.

Dill, Bonnie Thornton; Evelyn Nakano Glenn; and Bettina J. Huber. "Women in Departmental Administrative Positions." *ASA Footnotes* 2 (August 1983):10–11.

Dinnerstein, Myra; Sheryl R. O'Donnell; and Patricia MacCorquodale. *How to Integrate Women's Studies into the Traditional Curriculum,* paper no. 9. Tucson: Southwest Institute for Research on Women, University of Arizona, 1981.

Doing, Laura T. "Women on School Boards: Nine Winners Tell How They Play the Game." *American School Board Journal* 160 (March 1973):34–38.

Dziech, Billie Wright, and Linda Weiner. *The Lecherous Professor: Harassment on Campus.* Boston: Beacon Press, 1984.

Eccles, Jacqueline. "Sex Differences in Achievement Patterns." Paper presented at the Nebraska Symposium on Motivation, Lincoln, October 1983.

Eckstrom, Ruth; Marjory Marvel; and Jean Swenson. "Educational Programs for Adult Women." In Susan Klein, ed. *Handbook for Achieving Sex Equity through Education.* Baltimore: Johns Hopkins University Press, 1984.

Edwards, Harry T., and Virginia Davis Nordin. *Higher Education and the Law.* Cambridge, MA: Institute for Educational Management, 1979.

Eliason, Carol. *Women in Community and Junior Colleges: Report of a Study in Access to Occupational Education.* Washington, DC: American Association of Community and Junior Colleges, 1977.

El-Khawas, Elaine. *Campus Trends, 1984.* Higher Education Panel Report no. 65. Washington, DC: American Council on Education, February 1985.

Engel, Robert E., and Paul P. W. Achola. "Boards of Trustees and Academic Decisionmaking." *Review of Educational Research* 53 (Spring 1983):58.

Farley, J. "Co-Education and College Women." *Cornell Journal of Social Relations* 9 (1974):87–97.

Feldman, Saul D. *Escape from the Doll's House*. New York: McGraw-Hill, 1974.

Fidell, L. S. "Empirical Verification of Sex Discrimination in Hiring Practices in Psychology." *American Psychologist* 25, no. 12 (1970):1094–1098.

Fishel, A., and J. Pottker. *National Politics of Sex Discrimination in Education*. Lexington, MA: Lexington Books, 1977.

Fleming, Jacqueline. "Sex Differences in the Impact of the College Environment on Black Students." In Pamela J. Perun, ed. *The Undergraduate Woman: Issues in Educational Equity*. Lexington, MA: Lexington Books, 1982.

Frances, Carol, and R. Frank Mensel. *1985–86 Administrative Compensation Survey*. Washington, DC: College and University Personnel Association, 1986.

Frances, Carol; with R. Frank Mensel, Julie S. Withers, and F. Stephen Malott. "Women and Minorities in Administration of Higher Education Institutions." *1975–76 Administrative Compensation Survey*, Special Supplement. Washington, DC: College and University Personnel Association, 1977.

Freeman, Richard. *The Overeducated American*. New York: Academic Press, 1976.

Friedman, Joel M. "Congress, the Courts and Sex-Based Employment Discrimination in Higher Education: A Tale of Two Titles." *Vanderbilt Law Review* 34 (1981):37.

Frieze, Irene. "Women's Attributions for and Casual Attributions of Success and Failure." In Martha T. Mednick, Sandra S. Tangri, and Lois W. Hoffman, eds. *Women and Achievement: Social and Motivational Analysis*. Washington, DC: Hemisphere, 1975.

Furniss, W. Todd, and Patricia Albjerg Graham, eds. *Women in Higher Education*. Washington, DC: American Council on Education, 1974.

Geis, F. L.; M. R. Carter; and D. J. Butler. *Seeing and Evaluating People*. Newark: Office of Women's Affairs, University of Delaware, 1982.

Generett, Mona Norman. "The Role of Women Trustees in Private Independent Colleges and Universities of Pennsylvania as Defined by Their Characteristics, Functions and Perceptions." Unpublished doctoral dissertation, University of Pittsburgh, 1978.

Giraud, Kathryn L.; Patricia A. Sorce; and Joan L. Sweeney. "Increasing the Effectiveness of Women's Programs on College Campuses: A Summary of the Activities and Accomplishments of the National Women's Training Project." National Women's Center Training Project, Everywoman's Center, University of Massachusetts at Amherst, and the U.S. Department of Health, Education, and Welfare (unpublished, no date).

Glenn, John M.; Lilian Brandt; and F. Emerson Andrews. *Russell Sage Foundation, 1907–1946*. 2 volumes. New York: Russell Sage Foundation, 1947.

Godfrey, Helen Ruth. "A Profile of Female Trustees of Four-Year Public Colleges and Universities and a Comparison of Female and Male Trustee Perceptions of Selected Trustee Functions and University Issues." Unpublished doctoral dissertation, Michigan State University, 1971.

Goldberg, Phillip. "Are Women Prejudiced Against Women?" *Trans-Action* 5 (1968):28–30.

Gomberg, Irene L., and Frank J. Atelsek. *Composition of College and University Governing Boards.* Higher Education Panel Report no. 35. Washington, DC: American Council on Education, August 1977.

––––––. *Full Time Humanities Faculty, Fall 1982.* Higher Education Panel Report no. 61. Washington, DC: American Council on Education, August 1984.

Goodson, William Dale. "A Career Class Does Have an Impact: A Ten Year Follow-up." Paper presented at the Convention of the American Personnel and Guidance Association, Detroit, March 17–20, 198?.

Gould, Jane S. "Personal Reflections on Building a Women's Center in a Women's College." *Women's Studies Quarterly* 12 (Spring 1984):4–11.

Graham, Patricia Albjerg. "Expansion and Evaluation: A History of Women in American Higher Education." *Signs* 3 (1978):766.

––––––. "Women in Academe." *Science,* September 25, 1970.

Grant, W. Vance, and Thomas D. Snyder. *Digest of Education Statistics, 1983–84.* Washington, DC: National Center for Education Statistics, 1983.

Green, Elizabeth. *Mary Lyon and Mount Holyoke: Opening Its Gates.* Hanover, NH: University Press of New England, 1979.

Green, Kenneth C., et al. *The American College Student, 1982: National Norms for the 1978 and 1980 College Freshman Two and Four Years After Entering College.* Washington, DC: American Council on Education, 1983.

Grimm, James W. "Women in Female-Dominated Professions." In Ann H. Stromberg and Shirley Harkess, eds. *Women Working.* Palo Alto, CA: Mayfield, 1978.

Groneman, Carol, and Robert N. Lear. *Corporate Ph.D.* New York: Facts on File Publications, 1985.

Guy-Sheftall, Beverly. "Black Women and Higher Education: Spelman and Bennett Colleges Revisited." *Journal of Negro Education* 51 (Summer 1982):278–281.

Hall, Paula Quick. "Minority Women in Science—A Statistical View." *Newsletter of the National Network of Minority Women in Science* (undated).

––––––. *Problems and Solutions in the Education, Employment, and Personal Choices of Minority Women in Science.* Washington, DC: American Association for the Advancement of Science, August 1981.

Hall, Roberta M., and Bernice R. Sandler. *The Classroom Climate: A Chilly One for Women?* Washington, DC: Project on the Status and Education of Women, Association of American Colleges, 1982.

––––––. *Out of the Classroom: A Chilly Campus Climate for Women.* Washington, DC: Project on the Status and Education of Women, Association of American Colleges, 1984.

Haring, Marilyn, et al. "Sex Biased Attitudes of Counselors: The Special Case of Non-Traditional Careers." *Counseling and Values* 27 (1983):242–247.

Harmon, Lindsey R. *High School Ability Patterns—A Backward Look from the Doctorate.* Scientific Manpower Report no. 6. Washington, DC: National Academy of Sciences, 1965.

Hartnett, Rodney T. *College and University Trustees: Their Background, Roles and Educational Attitudes.* Princeton, NJ: Educational Testing Service, 1969.

————. *The New College Trustee: Some Predictions for the 1970s.* Princeton, NJ: Educational Testing Service, 1970.

Hearn, James C., and Susan Olzak. "The Role of College Major Departments in the Reproduction of Sexual Inequality." *Sociology of Education* 54 (1981):195–205.

Heller, Jack F.; C. Richard Puff; and Carol Mills. "Assessment of the Chilly Climate for Women." *Journal of Higher Education* 56 (1985):445–461.

Hofstader, Richard, and Walker P. Metzger. *The Development of Academic Freedom in the United States.* New York: Columbia University Press, 1955.

Holahan, Carole Kovalic. "Stress Experienced by Women Doctoral Students, Need for Support and Occupational Sex Typing: An Interactional View." *Sex Roles* 5 (1979):425–436.

Hornig, Lilli S. "HERStory." *Grants,* March 1978, pp. 36–42.

————, and Ruth B. Ekstrom. *The Status of Women in the Humanities.* Forthcoming.

Horowitz, Helen. *Alma Mater: Design and Experience in the Woman's Colleges from Their Nineteenth Century Beginnings to the 1930's.* New York: Knopf, 1984.

Howard, Suzanne. *But We Will Persist: A Comparative Research Report on the Status of Women in Academe.* Washington, DC: American Association of University Women, 1978.

Howe, Florence. "Feminist Scholarship: The Extent of the Revolution." *Change,* April 1982, pp. 14–15.

————. *Myth of Co-Education: Selected Essays, 1964–1983.* Bloomington: Indiana University Press, 1984.

————. "A Report on Women and the Professions." *College English* 32 (May 1971):847–854.

————. *Seven Years Later: Women's Studies Programs in 1976.* Report of the National Advisory Council on Women's Educational Programs, 1977.

————. "Women's Studies and Social Change." In Alice Rossi and Ann Calderwood, eds. *Academic Women on the Move.* New York: Russell Sage Foundation, 1973.

————; Suzanne Howard; and Mary Jo Boehm Strauss, eds. *Everywoman's Guide to Colleges and Universities.* Old Westbury, NY: Feminist Press, 1982.

Howe, Florence, and Paul Lauter. *The Impact of Women's Studies on the Campus and the Disciplines.* Washington, DC: National Institute of Education, 1980.

Huber, Bettina J. *Employment Patterns in Sociology: Recent Trends and Future Prospects.* Washington, DC: American Sociological Association, 1985.

Institute for Research in History. *Outside Academe: New Ways of Working in the Humanities.* New York: Institute for Research in History and the Haworth Press, 1981.

Iowa State University, Committee on Women. *Sexual Harassment of Students at Iowa State University, Subcommittee Report Approved by the University Committee on Women.* Ames, Iowa: Committee on Women, 1982.

Irvine, Betty Joe. "Differences by Sex: Academic Library Administrators." *Library Trends* 34, no. 2 (Fall 1985):235–257.

———. "Women in Librarianship." *ALA Yearbook of Library and Information Services '86*, vol. 2. Chicago: American Library Association, 1986.

Jencks, Christopher, and David Riesman. *The Academic Revolution*, rev. ed. Chicago: University of Chicago Press, 1977.

Johnson, Michael P., and Suzan Shuman. *Sexual Harassment of Students at the Pennsylvania State University*. University Park: Pennsylvania State University, 1983.

Johnston, John D., Jr., and Charles L. Knapp. "Sex Discrimination by Law: A Study in Judicial Perspective." *New York University Law Review* 46 (1971):675.

Journal of Negro Education 51 (Summer 1982). Special Issue on the Impact of Black Women in Education.

Karp, David A., and William C. Yoels. "The College Classroom: Some Observations on the Meaning of Student Participation." *Sociology and Social Research* 60 (July 1976):421–439.

Keller, Evelyn Fox. *Reflections on Gender and Science*. New Haven: Yale University Press, 1985.

Keller, George. *Academic Strategy: The Management Revolution in Higher Education*. Baltimore and London: Johns Hopkins Press, 1983.

Kelly-Gadol, Joan. "Did Women Have a Renaissance?" In Renata Bridenthal and Claudia Koonz, eds. *Becoming Visible: Women in European History*. Boston: Houghton Mifflin, 1977.

Kennedy, Randall. "Persuasion and Distrust: A Comment on the Affirmative Action Debate." *Harvard Law Review* 99 (April 1986):1327.

Klotzberger, Kay. "Political Action by Academic Women." In Alice Rossi and Ann Calderwood, eds. *Academic Women on the Move*. New York: Russell Sage Foundation, 1973.

Koltum, Elizabeth. *Jewish Women: An Anthology*. Waltham, MA: Schocken Books, 1973.

Komarovsky, Mirra. *Women in College*. New York: Basic Books, 1985.

———. *Women in the Modern World*. Boston: Little, Brown, 1953.

Korhammer, Sheila. "The Increasing Influence of Women on Community College Boards." *Trustee Quarterly*, Fall 1986.

Langland, Elizabeth, and Walter Gove, eds. *A Feminist Perspective in the Academy*. Chicago: University of Chicago Press, 1981.

LaNoue, George N., and Barbara A. Lee. *Academics in Court: The Consequences of Faculty Discrimination Litigation*. Ann Arbor: University of Michigan Press, 1987.

Leland, Carole. "The Case-Study Programs: Academic Misfits Which Lasted." In Helen S. Astin, ed. *Some Action of Her Own: The Adult Woman and Higher Education*. Lexington, MA: Heath, 1976.

Lentz, Linda P. "The College Choice of Career-Salient Women: Coed or Women's?" *Journal of Educational Equity and Leadership* 1 (1980):28–35.

———. "College Selectivity, Not College Type, Is Related to Graduate Women's Career Aspirations." Paper presented at the annual meeting of the American Educational Research Association, New York, March 1982.

Lerner, Gerda. *Teaching Women's History*. Washington, DC: American Historical Association, 1981.

Levine, Daniel B., ed. *Creating a Center for Education Statistics: A Time for Action*. Washington, DC: National Academy Press, 1986.

Lipman-Blumen, Jean. *Gender Roles and Power*. Englewood Cliffs, NJ: Prentice-Hall, 1984.

Lott, Bernice. "The Devaluation of Women's Competence." *Journal of Social Issues* 4 (1985):43–60.

Lowe, Gary R. "The Graduate Only Debate and Social Work Education, 1931–59, and Its Consequences for the Profession." *Journal of Social Work* 21, no. 3 (Fall 1985):52–62.

Lyman, Richard W. "Comments by the Incoming Chairperson." Independent Sector Annual Membership Meeting and Assembly, October 25, 1983.

Maack, Mary Niles. "Women in Library Education: Down the Up Staircase." *Library Trends* 34, no. 3 (Winter 1986):421.

Macauley, Stewart, and Elaine Walster. "Legal Structures and Restoring Equity." In June Tapp and Felice Levine, eds. *Law, Justice, and the Individual in Society: Psychological and Legal Issues*. New York: Holt, Rinehart and Winston, 1977.

Maitland, Fredric. *Equity*. 2nd ed. London: Cambridge University Press, 1936.

Malcom, Shirley Mahaley; Paula Quick Hall; and Janet Welsh Brown. *The Double Bind: The Price of Being a Minority Woman in Science*. Washington, DC: American Association for the Advancement of Science, 1976.

Manis, Jean D. "Combining Professional Careers with Marriage and Parenthood: Preliminary Findings from a Survey of Recent Recipients of Graduate or Professional Degrees." Ann Arbor: University of Michigan, 1983. CEW Research Report no. 12.

———. "Professional Women Today: Interrelationships Among Career Satisfaction, Marital Satisfaction, and Division of Household Labor." Ann Arbor, University of Michigan, 1983. CEW Research Report no. 13.

———. "Relationships Among Career Orientation: Employment Status, Self-Esteem, and Life Satisfaction of Women: An Analysis of Age Differences." Paper presented at the annual meeting of the American Educational Research Association, New York, March 22, 1982. CEW Research Report no. 10.

———. "Some Correlates of Self-Esteem, Personal Control, and Occupational Attainment: An Overview of Findings from CEW Surveys of Educated Women." Paper presented at the Center for the Study of Higher Education and the Program in Adult and Continuing Education, University of Michigan, April 11, 1984. CEW Research Report no. 18.

———, and Hazel Markus. "Combining Families and Careers: Views from Different Points in the Life Cycle." In *Changing Family, Changing Workplace*. Ann Arbor: Center for Continuing Education of Women, University of Michigan, 1980.

Markowitz, Judith. "The Impact of the Sexist Language Controversy and Regulation on Language in University Documents." *Psychology of Women Quarterly* 8 (1984):337–347.

Marteena, Constance H. "A College for Girls—Bennett College." *Opportunity* 16 (October 1938):306–307.

Mattfield, Jacquelyn A. "A Decade of Continuing Education: Dead End or Open Door?" Unpublished manuscript, Sarah Lawrence College, 1971.

———. "Many Are Called, but Few Are Chosen." In W. Todd Furniss and Patricia Albjerg Graham, eds. *Women in Higher Education.* Washington, DC: American Council on Education, 1974.

Maxfield, Betty D., and Mary Beslisle, *Science, Engineering, and Humanities Doctorates in the United States: 1983 Profile.* Washington, DC: National Academy Press, 1985.

Miller, Alice. "Wooing College Women in a Post-Feminist Era: The Challenge Facing Women's Centers." Paper presented at the first annual convention of the National Association of Women's Centers, San Antonio, May 29–June 1, 1986.

Miller, Alice Duer, and Susan Myers. *Barnard College: The First Fifty Years.* New York: Columbia University Press, 1939.

Moore, Kathyrn M. "Careers in College and University Administration: How Are Women Affected?" In Adrian Tinsley, Cynthia Secor, and Sheila Kaplan, eds. *Women in Higher Education Administration.* San Francisco: Jossey-Bass, 1983.

Moran, Mary. *Student Financial Aid and Women: Equity Dilemma?* AAHE-ERIC/ Higher Education Report no. 5. Washington, DC: American Association for Higher Education, 1986.

Morelock, Laura. "Discipline Variations in the Status of Academic Women." In Alice Rossi and Ann Calderwood, eds. *Academic Women on the Move.* New York: Russell Sage Foundation, 1973.

Morris, Lorenzo, with Floyd Hayes and Doris James. *Equal Employment Opportunity Scoreboard: The Status of Black Americans in Higher Education, 1970–79.* Washington, DC: Institute for the Study of Educational Policy, 1981.

Murray, Alexander. *Reason and Society in the Middle Ages.* Oxford: Clarendon Press, 1978.

Myrdal, Alva, and Viola Klein. *Women's Two Roles: Home and Work.* London: Routledge & Kegan Paul, 1956; 2nd ed., 1968.

Nash, Peter G. "Affirmative Action Under Executive Order 11246." *New York University Law Review* 46 (1971):225, 229.

National Advisory Committee on Black Higher Education and Black Colleges and Universities. *Admission and Retention Problems of Black Students at Seven Predominantly White Universities.* Washington, DC: U.S. Office of Education, October 1980.

———. *A Losing Battle: The Decline in Black Participation in Graduate and Professional Education.* Washington, DC: U.S. Office of Education, October 1980.

National Center for Educational Statistics. *Fall Enrollment in Higher Education.* Washington, DC: U.S. Government Printing Office, various years.

———. *Survey of Employees in Institutions of Higher Education, 1976–77.*

National Commission on Student Financial Assistance. *Signs of Trouble and Erosion: A Report on Graduate Education in America.* New York: NCSFA, 1983.

National Council for Research on Women. *A Declining Federal Commitment to Research About Women, 1980–84*. Report from the Commission on New Funding Priorities. New York: National Council for Research on Women, 1985.

National Council on Social Work Education. *Statistics on Social Work Education in the United States: 1985*. Washington, DC: National Council on Social Work Education, 1986.

National Institute of Education. *Conference on the Educational and Occupational Needs of American Indian Women; Conference on the Educational and Occupational Needs of Asian and Pacific American Women; Conference on the Educational and Occupational Needs of Black Women; Conference on the Educational and Occupational Needs of Hispanic Women*. Washington, DC: National Institute of Education, 1978–1980.

National Research Council. *Humanities Doctorates in the United States, 1985 Profile*. Washington, DC: National Academy Press, 1986.

———. *Minority Groups Among United States Doctorate-Level Scientists, Engineers and Scholars, 1973*. Washington, DC: National Academy of Sciences, 1974.

———. *Summary Report: Doctorate Recipients from United States Universities*. Washington, DC: National Academy Press, various years.

Nearing, Scott. "Who's Who Among College Trustees." *School and Society* 6 (September 1917):298.

Newcomer, Mabel. *A Century of Higher Education for American Women*. New York: Harper & Row, 1959.

Nieva, Veronica F., and Barbara Gutek. "Sex Effects of Evaluation." *Academy of Management Review* 5, no. 2 (1980):267–276.

Noble, Jeanne L. *The Negro Woman's College Education*. New York: Columbia University Press, 1956.

Norman, Elaine. "A New Look at Salary Equity for Male and Female Faculty in Schools of Social Work." *Affilia: Journal of Women and Social Work* 1, no. 4 (Winter 1986):42.

Oltman, Ruth M. *Campus 1970: Where Do Women Stand?* Washington, DC: American Association of University Women, 1970.

Orlans, Harold. *The Nonprofit Institute: Its Origins, Operations, Problems and Prospects*. New York: McGraw-Hill, 1972.

Palmieri, Patricia A. "Here Was Fellowship: A Social Portrait of Academic Women at Wellesley College, 1895–1920." *History of Education* 23, no. 2 (Summer 1983):195–214.

———. "In Adamless Eden: A Social Portrait of the Academic Community at Wellesley College, 1875–1920." Doctoral dissertation, Harvard Graduate School of Education, 1981.

———. "The Matter of Difference: The Women's College Tradition in Higher Education." Paper presented at the Mount Holyoke Sesquicentennial, Fall 1984.

Paludi, Michele A., and William D. Bauer. "Goldberg Revisited: What's in an Author's Name?" *Sex Roles* 9, no. 3 (1983):387–390.

Paludi, Michele A., and Lisa A. Strayer. "What's in an Author's Name? Differential Evaluations of Performance as a Function of Author's Name." *Sex Roles* 12, nos. 3–4 (1985):353–361.

Pannell, Anne Gary. "Myth and Reality in Trustee-President-Dean Relationships." In *The Woman Trustee: A Report on a Conference for Women Members of Governing Boards, December 1, 1984.* Washington, DC: American Association of University Women, 1965.

Perkins, Linda. "Black Feminism and 'Race Uplift': 1890–1900." Radcliffe Institute working paper, 1981.

———. "The Education of Black Women: A Historical Perspective." Paper presented at the annual meeting of the Organization of American Historians, April 4–7, 1984.

Pifer, Alan. "Women in Higher Education." Speech delivered at the Southern Association of Colleges and Schools, Miami, November 29, 1971.

Pion, Georgine M.; Paul Bramblett, Jr.; and Marlene Wicherski. *Graduate Departments of Psychology, 1985–1986: Report of the Annual APA/COG DOP Departmental Survey.* Washington, DC: American Psychological Association, 1986.

Potter, George E. "Responsibilities." In Victoria Dziuba and William Meardy, issue eds. *Enhancing Trustee Effectiveness: New Directions for Community Colleges* 15 (Autumn 1976):6.

Powers-Alexander, Susan, et al. "Attribution of Success in College to Women: Effort or Luck?" Paper presented at the annual meeting of the American Education Research Association, Montreal, April 11–15, 1983.

Powicke, F. M., and A. M. Emden, eds. *Rashdall's Medieval Universities,* vol. 1. Oxford: Oxford University Press, 1936.

Quinn, Naomi, and Carol A. Smith. "A New Resolution of Fair Employment Practices for Women Anthropologists: Fresh Troops Arrive." *Signs* 7 (1982): 869–977.

Ramist, Leonard, and Solomon Arbeiter, *Profiles, College-Bound Seniors, 1982.* New York: College Entrance Examination Board, 1984.

Rauh, Morton A. *College and University Trusteeship.* Yellow Springs, OH: Antioch Press, 1959.

Read, Florence. *The Story of Spelman College.* Princeton, NJ: Princeton University Press, 1961.

———. "The Place of the Women's College in the Pattern of Negro Education." *Opportunity* 15 (September 1937):267–270.

Reiter, Rayna R., ed. *Toward an Anthropology of Women.* New York: Monthly Review Press, 1975.

Reuben, Elaine, and Mary Jo Boehm Strauss. *Women's Studies Graduates.* Washington, DC: National Institute of Education, 1980.

Rhees, Harriet Seelye. *Laurence Clark Seelye: First President of Smith College.* Boston: Houghton Mifflin, 1929.

Rice, Joy K. "Operation and Chance." *Journal of the National Association of Women Deans, Administrators, and Counselors* 46, no. 4 (Summer 1983):3–10.

Roby, Pamela. "Institutional Barriers to Women Students in Higher Education." In Alice Rossi and Ann Calderwood, eds. *Academic Women on the Move.* New York: Russell Sage Foundation, 1973.

Rosaldo, Michele, and Louise Lamphere, eds. *Women, Culture and Society.* Stanford: Stanford University Press, 1974.

Rosenberg, Rosalind. *Beyond Separate Spheres: Intellectual Roots of Modern Feminism.* New Haven: Yale University Press, 1982.

Rosenfelt, Deborah Silverton, ed. *Female Studies X.* Old Westbury, NY: Feminist Press, 1975.

Rossi, Alice S. "Equity between the Sexes: An Immodest Proposal." In Robert J. Lifton, ed. *The Woman in America.* Boston: Beacon Press, 1967.

———, ed. *The Feminist Papers.* New York: Columbia University Press, 1973.

Rossi, Alice, and Ann Calderwood. "Women's Colleges Make a Comeback." *McCall's,* April 1980, pp. 56–57.

———, eds. *Academic Women on the Move.* New York: Russell Sage Foundation, 1973.

Rossiter, Margaret W. *Women Scientists in America: Struggles and Strategies to 1940.* Baltimore: Johns Hopkins University Press, 1982.

Rowe, Mary R. "Building Mentorship Frameworks as Part of Our Equal Opportunity Ecology." In Jennie Farley, ed. *Sex Discrimination in Higher Education: Strategies for Equality.* Ithaca: New York State School of Labor Relations, Cornell University, 1981.

Safilios-Rothschild, Constantina. *Sex Role Socialization and Sex Discrimination: A Synthesis and Overview of the Literature.* Washington, DC: National Institute of Education, 1979.

Sanjek, Roger. "The American Anthropological Association Resolution on the Employment of Women: Genesis, Implementation, Disavowal, and Resurrection." *Signs* 7 (1982):845–868.

Scott, Ann Firor. *The Southern Lady: From Pedestal to Politics, 1830–1930.* Chicago: University of Chicago Press, 1970.

Scott, Robert A. *Lords, Squires and Yeomen: Collegiate Middle Managers and Their Organizations.* AAHE-ERIC/Higher Education Research Report no. 7. Washington, DC: American Association for Higher Education, 1978.

Secor, Cynthia. "Preparing the Individual for Institutional Leadership: The Summer Institute." In Adrian Tinsley, Cynthia Secor, and Sheila Kaplan, eds. *Women in Higher Education Administration.* San Francisco: Jossey-Bass, 1983.

Seelye, L. Clark. *The Early History of Smith College: 1871–1910.* Boston: Houghton Mifflin, 1923.

Shakeshaft, Carol. "Strategies for Overcoming the Barriers to Women in Educational Administration." In Susan S. Klein, ed. *Handbook for Achieving Sex Equality through Education.* Baltimore: Johns Hopkins University Press, 1985.

Shavlik, Donna, and Judy Touchton. "Toward a New Era of Leadership: The National Identification Program." In Adrian Tinsley, Cynthia Secor, and Sheila Kaplan, eds. *Women in Higher Education Administration.* San Francisco: Jossey-Bass, 1983.

Shea, John R. *Years for Discrimination: A Longitudinal Study of the Educational and Labor Market Experience of Young Women,* vol. 1. Columbus: Center of Human Resource Research, Ohio State University, 1971.

Sherman, Julia A., and Evelyn Torton Beck, eds. *The Prism of Sex.* Madison: University of Wisconsin Press, 1981.

Shils, Edward. *Tradition.* Chicago: University of Chicago Press, 1980.

Showalter, Elaine. *These Modern Women: Autobiographical Essay from the Twenties.* Old Westbury, NY: Feminist Press, 1978.

Simm, Rita; Shirley M. Clark; and K. Galway. "The Woman Ph.D.: A Recent Profile." *Social Problems* 15 (Fall 1967):221–236.

Smelzer, Neil, and Robin Content. *The Changing Academic Market: General Trends and a Berkeley Case Study.* Berkeley: University of California Press, 1980.

Smith, Elizabeth P., et al. "Role Appropriateness of Educational Fields: Bias in Selection." Paper presented at the annual meeting of the American Education Research Association, Montreal, April 11–15, 1983.

Smith, Michael R. "Protecting Confidentiality of Faculty Peer Review Records: Department of Labor v. University of California." *Journal of College and University Law* 8 (1981–82):20–53.

Solomon, Barbara Miller. *In the Company of Educated Women: A History of Women in Higher Education in America.* New Haven: Yale University Press, 1985.

Spanier, Bonnie; Alexander Bloom; and Darlene Boroviak, eds. *Towards a Balanced Curriculum: A Sourcebook for Initiating Gender Integrating Projects,* based on the Wheaton College Conference. Cambridge, MA: Schenkman, 1983.

Speizer, Jeanne J. "The Administrative Skills Program: What Have We Learned." In Adrian Tinsley, Cynthia Secor, and Sheila Kaplan, eds. *Women in Higher Education Administration.* San Francisco: Jossey-Bass, 1983.

Spelman College. *Women's Research and Resource Center Newsletter,* vol. 1, no. 1, March 1982.

Spender, Dale, ed. *Men's Studies Modified.* New York: Pergamon Press, 1981.

Stalke, Jayne E.; Elaine F. Walker; and Mary V. Speno. "The Relationship of Sex and Academic Performance to the Quality of Recommendation for Graduate School." *Psychology of Women Quarterly* 5 (1981):512–522.

Sternglanz, Sarah, and Shirley Liberger-Ficek. "Sex Differences in Student-Teacher Interactions in the College Classroom." *Sex Roles* 2 (1979):321–343.

Stimpson, Catharine R. "Women at Bryn Mawr." In Editors of Changes, *Women on Campus: The Unfinished Liberation.* New Rochelle, NY: *Change,* 1975.

———, with Nina Kressner Cobb. *Women's Studies in the United States.* New York: Ford Foundation, 1986.

Stone, Elizabeth. "What Can an All-Women's College Do for Women?" *Ms.,* May 1979, pp. 61–63.

Story, Joseph. *Equity Jurisprudence.* Boston: Little, Brown, 1939.

Stroebel, Marian Elizabeth. "Back Home for Keeps?: Women in Higher Education in the 1950s." *Furman Studies* 19 (December 1983):1–21.

Syverson, Peter D. *Summary Report 1981: Doctorate Recipients from United States Universities.* Washington, DC: National Academy Press, 1982.

Talbot, Marion, and Lois Kimball Matthews Rosenberry. *The History of the American Association of University Women: 1881–1931.* Boston: Houghton Mifflin, 1931.

Theodore, Athena. *The Campus Troublemakers: Academic Women in Protest*. Houston: Cap and Gown Press, 1986.

Thorne, Barrie, and Nancy Henley, eds. *Language and Sex: Difference and Dominance*. Rowley, MA: Newbury, 1975.

Thorp, Margaret Farrand. *Neilson of Smith*. New York: Oxford University Press, 1956.

Tidball, M. Elizabeth. "Perspective on Academic Women and Affirmative Action." *Educational Record* 54 (Spring 1973):130–135.

———. "The Search for Talented Women." *Change* 6 (May 1974):51–52.

———, and Vera Kistiakowsky. "Baccalaureate Origins of American Scientists and Scholars." *Science*, August 20, 1976, pp. 646–652.

Tittle, Carol, and Elenor Denker. *Returning Women Students in Higher Education*. New York: Praeger, 1980.

Tobias, Sheila, ed. *Female Studies I*. Pittsburgh: KNOW, Inc., 1970.

Tolpin, Martha. *Directory of Programs: Integrating Women into Higher Education Curricula*. Wellesley, MA: Center for Research on Women, 1981.

Trow, Martin. *Problems in the Transition from Elite to Mass Higher Education*. Berkeley, CA: Carnegie Commission on Higher Education, 1973.

UNESCO. *Final Report and Recommendations*. Document SS-80/Con. 626/9, Research and Teaching Related to Women: Evaluation and Prospects Meeting, Paris, May 20, 1980.

U.S. Bureau of the Census. *Historical Statistics of the United States: Colonial Times to 1970*. Bicentennial Edition. Washington, DC: U.S. Government Printing Office, 1975.

———. *Statistical Abstract of the United States, 1984*. Washington, DC: U.S. Government Printing Office, 1984.

———. *Statistical Abstract of the United States, 1986*. Washington, DC: U.S. Government Printing Office, 1986.

U.S. Bureau of Labor Statistics. *Employment and Earnings, 1985*. Washington, DC: U.S. Government Printing Office, 1986.

U.S. Congress, House of Representatives. *Discrimination Against Women*. Hearings before the Special Subcommittee on Education of the Committee on Education and Labor, 91st Congress, 2nd sess., section 805 of H.R. 16098, June and July 1970.

U.S. Department of Labor, Women's Bureau. *Continuing Education Programs and Services for Women*. Employment Standards Administration Pamphlet no. 10, 1971.

University Microfilms International. *Women's Studies: A Catalogue of Selected Doctoral Dissertation Research*. Ann Arbor: University Microfilms International, 1986.

Veblen, Thorstein. *The Higher Learning in America: A Memorandum on the Conduct of Universities by Business Men*. New York: Reprints of Economic Classics, Augustus M. Kelley, Bookseller, 1965. Orig. ed., 1918.

Vetter, Betty M., and Eleanor L. Babco. *Professional Women and Minorities*. Washington, DC: Commission on Professionals in Science and Technology, 1981, 1984, 1986, and 1987.

Walsh, Mary Roth. "Academic Professional Women Organizing for Change: The Struggle in Psychology." *Journal of Social Issues* 41 (Winter 1985):17–27.

Walzer, Judith B. "New Knowledge or a New Field Discipline?" *Change,* April 1982.

Wartenberg, Hannah. "Social Science Research Institutes." Paper presented at the annual meeting of the American Sociological Association, 1983.

Weathersby, Rita, and Jill Tarule. *Adult Development: Implications for Higher Education.* AAHE-ERIC/Higher Education Research Report no. 4. Washington, DC: American Association for Higher Education, 1980.

Weis, Lois. "Progress But No Parity." *Academe* 71, no. 6 (November-December 1985):29–33.

Whisler, Thomas J. *Rules of the Game: Inside the Corporate Boardroom.* Homewood, IL: Dow Jones-Irwin, 1984.

Whitmore, Robert L. *Sexual Harassment at UC Davis.* Davis: University of California, 1983.

Women on Words and Images. *Dick and Jane as Victims: Sex Stereotyping in Children's Readers.* Princeton, NJ: Women on Words and Images, 1972.

Women's College Coalition. *A Profile of Women's College Presidents.* Washington, DC: Women's College Coalition, 1982.

———. *A Profile of Women's Colleges.* Washington, DC: Women's College Coalition, 1980.

———. *A Profile of Women's Colleges—Analysis of the Data.* Washington, DC: Women's College Coalition, 1980.

———. *Profile II: A Second Profile of Women's Colleges.* Washington, DC: Women's College Coalition, 1981.

———. *Profile II: A Second Profile of Women's Colleges—Analysis of the Data.* Washington, DC: Women's College Coalition, 1981.

———. *A Study of the Learning Environment at Women's Colleges.* Washington, DC: Women's College Coalition, 1981.

Woody, Thomas. *A History of Women's Education in the United States.* New York: Octagon Books, 1966. Orig. ed., 1929.

Zwingle, J. L. "Evolution of Lay Governing Boards." In Richard T. Ingram, ed. *Handbook of College and University Trusteeship.* San Francisco: Jossey-Bass, 1980.

Index

life sciences, 201, **205**, 258; doctoral degrees, **258**; financial support, **211**
Light, Donald, 156
Lilly Endowment, 294
Lipman-Blumen, Jean, 131*n*
literature, 142, 157, 225, 231, 232; courses, 151; employment, 233, **234–235**. *See also* publications
litigation, 181–182. *See also* cases; lawsuits
loans, 7, 210
Local 28, Sheetmetal Workers' International Association v. *U.S.*, 188*n*, 190*n*
Lott, Bernice, 32*n*
Louisiana v. *U.S.*, 169–170, 189*n*
Lowe, Gary R., 252*n*
Lyman, Richard W., 338, 355*n*
Lynn v. *University of California–Irvine*, 182

Mc

McDonald Douglas-Burdine standard, 182
McGee, Reece, 167, 189*n*
McGuigan, Dorothy Geis, 189*n*, 222*n*
McIntosh, Peggy, 160*n*

M

Maack, Mary Niles, 252*n*
Macauley, Jacqueline, 191*n*
Macauley, Stewart, 167, 188*n*
MacCorquodale, Patricia, 161*n*
mainstreaming, 142, 147, 157
Maitland, Frederic, 169, 189*n*
majors, 25
Malcom, Shirley Mahaley, 283, 289*n*
male: faculty, 272; doctorates, 210, 229; participation, 201. *See also* men; students
male–female comparisons, 28, 269, 362; in academic employment, 214–217, 229; in curriculum, 153; for degree attainment, 77, 194–195, 197–202, 207–208, 231; for doctorates, 226, 231–232, 256–258; in education, 239–241, 367; for enrollment rates, 40–43, 46; for financial sup-

port, 210; in the humanities, **237**; in library science, **246**; in productivity, 265–270; in salaries, 259, **262**, 264, 319–322, 366; in social work, 241–245; in teaching and research, 263–264, 363–364; in tenure, **262**, 265; in test outcomes, 208; as trustees, 345–349
Malott, F. Stephen, 330*n*
management degrees, 193–194, 196, 198
Mangi, Jean, 160*n*
Manis, Jean D., 80*n*, 81*n*
Markowitz, Judith, 30*n*
Markus, Hazel, 80*n*
marriage rates, 110
married: couples, 70; men, 268–269, 272*n*; women, 70, 264–266, 268–270, 272, 273*n*, 282
Marteena, Constance H., 129*n*
Marvel, Marjory, 80*n*
Mary Baldwin College, 109
Marygrove College, 113
Marymount Manhattan College, 109, 127
Mary Sharp College, 111
The Masters (C. P. Snow), 179
master's degrees, 7, 45, 46–48, 77, 197–199; in the arts, 231; earned by women, 194, 196, **197**, 199, 231, 363; in education, 239–241; in library science, 245, **246**; in nursing, 249, **250**; in social work, 242, **243**; in women's colleges, 117; in women's studies, 136, 137, 141
mathematics, 25, **26**, 52, 125, 198, 210, 220; disparities in, 202, 212; faculty positions in, 233; parity indices, 201, **205**, 207
Math/Science Network, 125
Mattfeld, Jacquelyn A., 64, 65, 79*n*, 318, 330*n*
Maxfield, Betty D., 221*n*
MBA degrees for women, 198, **199**
Mead, Margaret, 292
medical schools, 18, 194, 206
medicine, 4, 8, 146, 193, 363; degrees, 50, **51**; parity indices, 202, **203**, **204**, 206. *See also* veterinary medicine